# Lenyalo

## Marriage Cultures and Processes in Botswana

## Past and Present

alubdev

**Lenyalo: Marriage Cultures and Processes in Botswana: Past and Present**

First Published in 2022 by

Lightbooks, an imprint of Lentswe La Lesedi (Pty) Ltd.
publisher@lightbooks.co.bw
PO Box 2365, Gaborone, Botswana

*on behalf of the*

Alumni of the University of Botswana Development Trust (ALUBDEV)
PO Box 53355, Broadhurst, Gaborone, Botswana
elizabeth@spaceandplace.co.bw

ISBN: 978-99912-71-63-7



Cover Design: Charles Bewlay

Typesetting, Design and Layout: Lentswe La Lesedi (Pty) Ltd

# Dedication

*This book is dedicated to*

*all married partners, husbands and wives.*

*participants in, promoters of, and aspirants to,*

*the institution of marriage.*

# Contents

# Acknowledgement of Contributors

The originator and sponsor of this work, the Alumni of the University of Botswana Development Trust (ALUBDEV) wishes to express profound gratitude to the following contributors for their original research, documentation and chapter presentation:

Prof. Tonic Maruatona;

Mr. Jabulani Dick Makwanda;

John Christian Makgala;

Montle Siya;

Mr. Allan Manyeneng;

Prof. Mabel Magowe;

Prof. Brankie Nlhekisana;

Dr. Pearl Seloma;

Dr. Eagilwe Segosebe;

Prof. G.T. Tsayang;

Ms. Siphiwe Mguni;

Dr. Ndana Ndana;

Kandondi Kapweke;

Mr. Tshisimogo Leepang;

Mr. Isaac Saul;

Mrs. Esther Kanaimba-Senai; and

Lydia Nyati-Saleshando.

# Preface

Given the societal importance of the marriage *'lenyalo'* institution in Botswana, the Alumni of the University of Botswana Development (ALUBDEV) Trust deemed it well within the scope of its mandate to commission and fund nation-wide research on past and current marriage practices and processes in Botswana.

This research sought to find out the commonalities and variations in *lenyalo* marriage culture and practices in past and present Botswana. It was hoped that the research would culminate in an elaborate account of the series of stages, events as well as processes, which would be a reference point for Botswana's evolving society, and perhaps a rallying point for convergences and the finding resolutions to some of the problems that are seen as being associated with marriage in today's society.

This book attempts to cover the formal *lenyalo* processes as can be recounted, though perhaps not always as comprehensively as desired, on the issues that follow: courtship stages (*go kokota/go itshupa*)*;* bride-seeking (*patlo*); lobola (*bogadi*); bride and groom counselling (*go laya*); the wedding ceremony (*kemo/mokete wa lenyalo*); the transfer of a bride to her in-laws; (*go isa monyadiwa*); and the bride being taken back to her natal home (*go gatisiwa*). In the course of recounting these events, these marriage rites, the significance of metaphorical language and symbolic actions are discussed. The rights, privileges and benefits associated with traditional marriage practices are brought into focus. Roles of maternal, as opposed to paternal, uncles and aunts are discussed. Problems and challenges that are prevalent in Botswana marriages, as well as possible remedies and standardization of the practices. are also discussed. The book also highlights significant factors of change as well as their impact on traditional marriage rites and processes.

Regarding factors of change, the book captures, among others, the onset of *bogadi* expectations, noting, for example, that Balete used not to expect or require *bogadi* traditionally; and that among Bangwato, expectation or a request for *bogadi* is a relatively recent development, only coming to the fore in the past two decades or so. In fact, according to K. Mogapi, originally there was no *bogadi* among Batswana: *"Wa tlholegong ya Setswana, go ne go se na bogadi mo nyalong … ngwana wa maitibolo o nnela botsetsi kwa ga gabomogolo, bo beilwe ke motsala mmaagwe mosetsana. Go ne gatla gore ba bogwe ba ntshe kgomo –ka bobona –ba e romela kwa bogwagadi, gore e gamelwe motsetsi, ngwana le ene atle a bone mašwi"* (A primipara would be confined at her mother's place for the birth of the first child. The [bride's] in-laws would voluntarily offer a milk-cow for the new mother and the newborn, to feed on its milk).

He continues, *"Ka batho ba rata go gaisana, yo mongwe a ba a ntsha dikgomo di le pedi, a di romela kwa bogwagadi. Tsa nna tsa oketsega jalo, go ya ka go kgona ga batho. Selo se sa fetoga tlwaelo, mme morago sa fetoga mokgwa. Kgabagare ya nna konokono ya thulaganyo ka ga lenyalo"*. In summary, people are naturally competitive, the cows kept increasing in number, and changing to heifers, not just any cows. This practice turned into a cultural value. It became the quintessence of marriage. Some cultures like those of Bangwaketsi and Barolong have put a maximum cap on the number of *bogadi* cows and their cash equivalent.

It is possible for wedding rites to take place, with *bogadi* deferred until the male is ready to produce it. But before he does so, he may not receive *bogadi* for any of his daughters. The deferment of *bogadi* has not been without frustration to couples, resulting in 'shacking up' or informal conjugation. This has resulted in a number of interventions to regularise such informal arrangements to formal marriage. An example of such interventions is the 'Re a Nyalana' project.

Another significant factor of change also discussed in the book is the advent of Christianity. As a patriarchal society, Batswana practiced polygamous marriages (and polygamy is still legal), and the number of wives taken varied, depending on the size of the male's estate. An example is drawn from *Kgosi* Sechele of Bakwena, who was forced to relinquish his harem, except the first wife, in order for him to be baptised as a Christian. This was not without resistance, as the *kgosi* cited King Solomon (in the Old Testament), who had a number of wives. Another marriage- associated traditional practice that was impacted negatively by Christianity was that of initiation of mature boys and girls into manhood and womanhood, respectively. The initiation schools typically taught history and moral and family values and as such served as a foundation for marriage education and counselling. These practices were taken to be out of line with Christian teachings, and were thus discouraged and campaigned against by the Christianity expansion effort. Names of events, places, and communities used in this book appear as supplied by interviewees and other participants, even where these may vary from official names and orthography.

As regards research methodology adopted towards data gathering, different tools were utilised, including desk studies, administration of structured questionnaires, and open-ended interviews with community focus groups. These research activities were made possible through funding provided by the Alumni of the University of Botswana Development Trust (ALUBDEV).

# Foreword

## *Chairman of Ntlo Ya Dikgosi, Kgosi Puso Gaborone*

The Botswana traditional *kgotla* system of consultation has been acclaimed as the crucible of our modern democratic society. The system provided a forum for free and wide consultation by members of any community, without fear of reprisals or favour. It is a forum for consensus building and conflict resolution that is anchored in our traditional culture. By logical extension, this forum emanated from stable family settings of married couples. It is therefore imperative that in order to understand family origins and to maintain them, we should interrogate the history of Botswana marriage processes and practices, as they obtain throughout the country, so as to clearly understand and articulate beneficial practices for the family unit; for it is this unit out of which our nation is formed, forged and nurtured.

This book is a logical sequel that synergises with the work done by the Joint Advisory Committee of Ntlo Ya Dikgosi, and the Botswana Council of Churches on Social Values, which was concluded in October 2008. Notable among observations and recommendations, which dovetail, as well as articulate, well with this book on *lenyalo* include, among others, commercialization of bogadi, cohabitation, gender-based violence, rape, the role of the institution of *bogosi*, churches and other religious institutions, as well as the media.

It is therefore with great pride and privilege that I pen the foreword to this magnificent and timeous product of incisive country-wide research into marriage practices and processes. This book should provide marriage guidance and counselling practitioners and lawmakers a basis for understanding the changes that continually buffet, as well as challenge, the family unit through different marriage practices and processes, so as to better inform appropriate remedies.

Our society has seen gradual shifts from polygamous, and often arranged, marriages, through to nuclear families, as well as single-parent headed households. Such changes merit constant attention and a robust vigil if we are to preserve our core national character, of *mmualebe o bua la gagwe* (freedom of speech, without fear or favour).

In my capacity as Chairman of Ntlo Ya Dikgosi, the primary custodians of our culture and sustainable preservation, I extend hearty appreciation to the conceivers and researchers, and the magnanimity of the funders, of this all-important project. I can only encourage them in their pursuits, as well as their taking up of the baton.

---

*Kgosi Puso Gaborone wa Batlokwa (Modulasetilo wa Ntlo Ya Dikgosi)*

# 1

# Babirwa

*Prof. Tonic Maruatona*

## Introduction

### Information sources and data collection

The data for this paper were premised on qualitative design. The sources of the data were primarily 11 elderly married individuals or couples, six men and five women in the Bobirwa villages of Bobonong, Molalatau and Gobajango. They were senior citizens whose ages ranged from 75 to 95. Interviews with them were supplemented by background material gleaned from published material, as acknowledged.

### Historical background

Available data suggests that the Babirwa originate from a legendary place called Nareng, presumed to be an area to the east of present day Phalaborwa in the former Transvaal. Molosiwa (2016) points to a section of Babirwa who had adopted *nare*, the buffalo, as their totem, and were well established in the area as far back as between 1510 and 1590. Some of them, led by Chief Tshukudu, left Nareng and migrated to the Blauwberg area, also in the Transvaal. From there they did not cross the Mogalakwena River and Limpopo to the west directly into Botswana, but went to Rhodesia (Zimbabwe) (Westphal, 1975; Mmapetla, 2012; Molosiwa, 2016). Mmapetla (2012) corroborates this assertion by noting that the Babirwa are historically a breakaway group of the Pedi kingdom that existed in the Northern Transvaal until the 18th century. The kingdom collapsed under the leadership of King Sekhukhune during the Mfecane wars, when people fled to the mountain cliff-tops to hide from Shaka Zulu's marauding impis and amaNdebele.

The history of the present day Babirwa occupying the villages of Bobonong, Molalatau, Semolale, Gobajango, Mathathane, Mabolwe, Tsetsejwe and Mothabaneng can be traced to a period before about 1710, or when the Babirwa who had migrated to Zimbabwe sought to escape Mambo overlordship (Westphal, 1975). One group retraced their steps and travelled southwards back to the Transvaal. Another group remained in Zimbabwe for some time, but in 1837, when they were attacked by the amaNdebele of Mzilikazi they left Zimbabwe altogether and moved to Botswana. They settled in the area around the confluence of the Shashe and Limpopo rivers among the Ngwato, the Kalanga and the Ndebele.

The genealogies and many references in Birwa history indicate that the Babirwa were not a highly centralised and homogenous group like other mainstream Tswana communities. They constituted many small sections, closely associated with each other, but strongly independent nevertheless (Molosiwa, 2016). For this reason, the histories of each section appear to be totally independent of any other, but according to earlier research they can be "tied up to an overall Birwa history reaching very far back into our South African histories and into the histories of southern Africa in general" (Westphal, 1975: 192). Consistent with this, Mmapetla (2012) observed that there were two sections fighting over the Babirwa Chieftainship, the Malema and Sekoba houses. In his submission he concurs with earlier historical accounts that the Sekoba clan was the first to settle in Bobonong, and the Malema clan was forcefully removed from their ancestral lands in the Tuli Block area.

## Understanding Marriage among the Babirwa

Notwithstanding the rather chequered political history outlined above, the present study seeks to establish how the Babirwa organise marriages as socio-cultural events, with focus on various stages of arranging a marriage ceremony, beginning with courtship all the way to the final ritual, namely that of taking the bride back to her natal home. It stresses the role of key players in arranging a marriage among the Babirwa and the rights and privileges associated with it. It also compares the organization of traditional marriages in the past with the way they are organised at present. The study further looks at factors influencing change in traditional marriages, and in the institution of marriage itself, in order to explore what can be done to help stabilise the modern marriage institution in Botswana. The chapter also assesses the changes the practices associated with *lenyalo* have undergone as a result of the Babirwa's interaction with other cultures, in the context of the changing socio-economic environment. The intention is to contribute towards an improved mutual understanding and respect of each other's traditions among various communities in the country as they are increasingly drawn into interaction with each other.

Babirwa are one of several ethnic groups in Botswana that speak mutually intelligible dialects of Setswana. They traditionally live in the Tuli block on the confluence of the Shashe and Limpopo rivers in the north-east of the country. However, in recent times, especially after independence in 1966, ethnicity in Botswana has become fluid, and Babirwa, like members of other ethnic groups, are widely dispersed, especially in the nation's urban areas, and have developed multiple ways of interacting with both the changing socio-economic landscape as well as with other ethnic groups (Molosiwa 2016). Babirwa too, experience the tension between the government-led aspiration to forge a unified national identity on the one hand and their own desire to preserve the authenticity of their traditions on the other. One area of culture in which this tension is especially salient is the institution of marriage and the traditional practices associated with it, known collectively as *lenyalo*. The surface appearances of the marriage practices may appear mere formalities that can be easily standardised. In reality, however, the practices are highly symbolic and contain meanings and lessons that each ethnic group is careful to preserve as it enters into the unity in diversity compact that a common Botswana nationhood implies.

As Molosiwa points out, marriage in traditional Babirwa culture is crucial to the biological and social reproduction of the community, as it leads to the reproduction of children, the accumulation of household wealth, and increases family social capital. Marrying off daughters and the labour of sons increases wealth, but also, because Babirwa are a spiritual people, it renews ties with the divinity and the spiritual world. Like other ethnic groups in the country Babirwa also view marriage as the means of constituting the family, which is the basic unit of society and the main organ through which the values of a society are inculcated and practised. Hence the surface appearances of the marriage process may appear to be mere formalities that can be easily standardised or discarded, as noted above, but in reality they are highly symbolic and contain meanings and lessons that each ethnic group regards as crucial to its identity and is careful to preserve these meanings and lessons. So, when they express anxieties about the dangers of a reified single homogenised national identity, as indeed other groups also do, it is not because they want to return to the past, but because each community seeks to preserve its identity, within the spirit of unity in diversity.

## THE MARRIAGE PROCESS

The marriage process in Sebirwa, traditionally consisted of ritual stages that were followed scrupulously, to ensure the authentic solemnization of the union between two people as husband and wife. It began with the procedures for identifying or choosing prospective future marriage partners, roughly equivalent to courtship, then making the marital intentions known, and ending with the ritual installation of the newly-weds in their marital home. The procedures were as outlined below.

### IDENTIFYING PROSPECTIVE MARRIAGE PARTNERS

Among the Babirwa, identification of future marriage partners and informing the families of the marital intentions is traditionally done in various ways. Some of the most common approaches were as follows.

#### (a) *Go bona lelwapa* (Parents identifying the bride)

This was a tradition whereby parents identified a suitable future wife for their son from among the other families in the community. The criteria that they used included the social standing and reputation of the bride's family. Hard-working families, unsullied by suspicions of antisocial or devious behaviours such as witchcraft, were prized. Distant relatives were preferred. When the parents had identified such a family and made the initial approach, one informant noted, "The young man would be asked to acquaint himself with the family and identify any one of the young women there and make a choice". In some cases, however, the parents only pointed out to their son a suitable household and after some encouragement left it up to him to identify and woo a possible wife from there. In this instance, the young man, having done so, would report back to his parents and ask them to initiate the marriage process.

### (b) *Mokombo* (Young people eloping)

Another means through which young people identified their future marriage partners involved the young couple starting a love affair and eloping. The young man would quietly take the woman to his place overnight. This was called *mokombo* or *tshabiso*. The expectation was that he would leave a coin or a safety pin under her bedding to symbolise that she had been taken by a suitor. The young man's parents would then send a message to the woman's parents to indicate that she was with them. In this way, both families were made aware of the couple's marital intentions and were, in practice, engaged to be married. The woman would after this be allowed to pay frequent visits to her future in-laws' place till arrangements were made to seek her hand in marriage.

### (c) *Peeletso* (Betrothal)

In this tradition of identifying future marital partners, parents of the young man selected a very young underage girl from a suitable family as a possible future wife for their son. With the consent of the girl's family, they would support her in return for the pledge that she would marry their son in future, when she reached womanhood, and was ready for marriage when the formalities of the marriage process were started.

### (d) *Tshenyo* (Enforced marriage)

This type of identifying future marital partners was adopted in situations in which a man and a woman fell in love with each other, and in the course of their relationship the woman fell pregnant – before marriage. The woman's parents generally informed the man's parents about the pregnancy as soon as it was known. In most cases, the man's parents took this as the cue to initiate the marriage process. According to the informants, "In some cases, the couple would either have met and started the relationship independent of the influence of their respective families, or would have carried on the relationship with the knowledge of only the girl's family". However, the man or his parents had to pay a fine for the infringement of impregnating a girl before marriage in order for marriage negotiation to be launched or resumed, as the case may be.

In all these instances, the parents of the future groom, or the young man himself, initiated the marriage proposal process by visiting the girl's parents, and formally informed them of his intentions. Then the girl's parents informed their daughter of the intention of the man to marry. From the informants' accounts, in all cases, "there was very limited room for objection". Even in cases of *peeletso* where the parents arranged the match, when the young man was informed that 'his parents had identified a decent woman for him to marry, he could not refuse'. After informing the girl's parents about his relationship with their daughter and his intention to marry her, the young man was required to also inform his own family of his plans and the outcome of his discussions with the girl's parents. He generally reported to his family either through his father's eldest brother, but more often, youngest brother, or his mother's brother (his maternal uncle) about his intention to seek a wife. Then all would be set for the next stage in the process, namely 'bride-seeking'.

## PRELIMINARY VISITS AND BRIDE-SEEKING (*PATLO*)

Regardless of how the identification of the future marital partners was done, and how the parents on both sides acknowledged the plans for the future marriage, bride-seeking began with a preliminary visit (or visits) paid by the family of the man to the home of the future bride. In some cases, the purpose of these preliminary visits was to enable the man's father to sound out the girl's parent's feelings about his son's intention to look for a wife in his household. The intention was also to enable the man's parents to familiarise themselves with a family that was so distinguished that it was identified as a suitable family from which to seek a prospective bride. The future groom was encouraged to also visit and familiarise himself with his intended wife, although at this point, as one participant observed, "…it was not expected that he could turn down his father's choice of a wife for fear of embarrassing both families or seeming to be insubordinate".

The process of bride-seeking, in this context, was led by the paternal uncle, who was the youngest or eldest brother of the man's father. Traditionally he was considered 'the '*father* of the young man'. The parents formally entrusted to the paternal uncle the task to 'lead the search for a wife for his brother's son'. The paternal uncle or *rrangwane* was the protagonist in this marriage drama, and was given all authority to find a wife for his brother's son. The maternal uncles did not have any role in seeking a wife for their sister's son, as is the case nowadays. One of the paternal uncle's first tasks was to collaborate with the groom's parents to identify a 'mediator or go-between', called *sebanga* or *mmaditselena.* As one participant puts it, *sebanga* was not a relative but a "reasonable person, often a man or woman whom the family trusted to serve as a loyal mediator between them and the parents of the future wife". Such a man or woman was trusted as a "skilful negotiator, [with] decorum and deep understanding of the intricate procedures of Sebirwa marriage culture".

*Sebanga* was tasked to look for a wife for the young man on behalf of the parents. His or her task was to convey messages from the man's family to the future in-laws, and vice versa. *Sebanga* carried messages between the two families till the woman's parents agreed to give her away as a wife. The *sebanga*'s main duty was to convince future in-laws that the proposing family was serious and sincere. One participant observed that "the future groom stayed away because in all these processes, he was not expected to see or even talk to his parents-in-law or wives of his brothers-in-law". *Sebanga* visited the future bride's house to see the potential bride at night, and left under the cover of darkness. Normally, it was not expected that the future daughters-in-law would turn down a proposal of marriage. The woman was, however, required to offer token or ritual resistance at the beginning of the negotiations. The parents easily prevailed over her because, as one participant puts it, "...those days children were loyal to parents". At the conclusion of the bride-seeking ritual, the woman's parents demanded that in-laws bring some presents to seal the negotiations before the girl could be formally handed over as a wife.

There was one rule which the *sebanga* and others were to observe during these preliminary visits: the *sebanga*'s trip to the in-laws was undertaken only during a full moon. Visits while it was dark were not allowed. The *sebanga* and his or her team thus always had to wait till the next full moon to make their visits. The waiting afforded each family the chance to consult relatives before communicating their response to the future in-laws. An elderly gentleman observed that "it was taboo to seek a woman's hand in marriage in the dark. It was believed that the light from a full moon symbolised transparency and trustworthiness". The young man was also forbidden to visit the woman during the bride-seeking period; as one lady informant put it, "to avoid accidentally impregnating her before she is officially given to him".

## HANDING OVER THE BRIDE (*KATHOLO*)

The process of handing over the woman to her in-laws was called *katlholo* or 'handing over of the wife". This is the stage during which the bride's paternal uncle informed the *sebanga* that they were ready to release the wife to her future husband. The *sebanga* then informed the man's family of the presents the bride's family demanded in order to complete this phase of bride-seeking, and trigger the ritual of handing over of the bride.

The future in-laws of the groom were required to purchase: (i) a jacket for the father-in-law, (ii) a shawl or blanket for the mother-in-law, and (iii) dresses, blankets and other clothes for the bride, (iv) the material used for wrapping the clothes, which was given to the aunt of the bride to be used during future ceremonies such as taking her to the in-laws, and (v) the proposing family was to bring a cow called a *sobola* to be killed during the handing-over ceremony. One participant noted that "this was for the bride-seeking team and their future in-laws to 'clean their teeth after the exhaustions of the protracted bride-seeking months'". The cow was slaughtered and shared out during the ceremony at the same time as the required clothes were delivered to the in-laws. The woman's mother was given the chest (*sehuba*) and the hip (*setlhana*) of the slaughtered cow. This was to recognise her for bearing and raising the bride. *Sebanga* was given a hind quarter of the cow, to thank her or him for successfully undertaking bride-seeking. The bride's maternal uncle was given the head and neck of the cow to share with whoever he deemed deserving. The rest was shared by relatives and the public during the ceremony. In addition, the bride's aunts (*rakgadi*) had to send snuff jars with the bride to her new home.

As part of the giving away the bride ceremony, there was also an exchange of presents, called *ditoisi/disholwane* or snuff jars. According to the informants, as part of the exchange the aunts of the bride were required to grind snuff and pack it into two jars, a big one representing a cow and a small one representing a calf. These were called *disholwane*. The in-laws were expected to receive these and distribute them to the whole family. In return, it was expected that the groom's family would pay a cow and calf to the bride's family. The jars were dispatched to the in-laws along with the bride when she was handed over to her in-laws. Once the husband's uncles received the snuff and used it, they were conceding that they would pay a cow and a calf to the bride's family to be passed to her uncles. (Nowadays, aunts and uncles exchange sugar and a packet of tea because of the health challenges associated with snuff.) After this process, the bride was considered given away to the groom and was handed over to her in-laws to be transported to her new home. The marriage process at this stage was practically completed and she was considered married. The informants all point out that the ceremony was key to the marriage process and was followed scrupulously. However, in the case of a bride who was getting married for the second time, for whatever reason, her parents were not allowed to demand any presents. The clothes and cattle needed for marriage were only demanded when a bride was married for the very first time. This was to avoid tempting parents to have their daughters married several times.

Several things have now changed in terms of preliminary visits and bride-seeking. First, men are the ones who identify the woman and initiate everything, including marriage proposals, and are allowed to familiarise themselves with the future in-laws. Men set the criteria for the selection of a future wife without the participation of parents. Second, the maternal uncles are now the ones charged with seeking the wives for their nephews. Third, *rangwane* is no longer the main actor in the arrangements of the marriage. Fourth, *sebanga* can be approached and dispatched by the man's biological father or mother as most parents make marriage arrangements for their children. Following bride-seeking and 'awarding' of a wife, the next stage was paying bride-wealth. *lobola*.

## PAYING OF BRIDE-WEALTH (LOBOLA OR BOGADI)

Following bride-seeking, which ends with the ritual giving away of the bride, the next stage was paying bride-wealth or *bogadi*. Among the Babirwa, bride-wealth constituted an unspecified number of cattle that were given to the parents of the woman to thank them for raising her properly and 'preparing her to be someone who is eligible to be married'. As one participant noted, "It was never treated as buying, such as in the market, but was an act of appreciating her family for giving away their child to come to bear children for the husband's family". He went further to state that "the bride-wealth was viewed as a thank you token by the family of the groom to that of the bride".

In most cases, the bride-wealth was paid by the parents and not the groom. Each person rewarded the in-laws according to their economic status. Some participants mentioned that it was acceptable to pay anywhere between two and four head of cattle, but there was no consensus on the actual number. The bride-wealth was for the bride's parents. For example, the mother of the bride was entitled to one cow called *kgomo ya sebeko* or a cow for *sebeko*. It was exclusively given to her as a way of thanking her for raising the daughter. Note that other relatives were not entitled to any cattle from the bride-wealth, and were not expected to contribute much. Nowadays, by contrast, aunts and uncles are entitled to a cow called *mosebe* among the *bogadi* cattle. This is because the uncle's family is required to buy expensive changes of clothes for the bride.

Traditionally there were several ways of paying bride-wealth depending on the socio-economic status of the family. These were as below.

(a) **Immediate payment of lobola**. Parents of the groom who were rich paid bride-wealth as soon as they had been 'granted' the wife, while those who were poor could not pay immediately.

(b) **Taking the bride on loan.** In some cases, when the family was poor, the husband took the wife, raised a family with her and bore children, even if he had not paid any *bogadi*. The husband was allowed to work and find some cattle, and could pay later.

(c) **Using the daughter's bride-wealth.** The other alternative was that if the husband did not have cattle to pay the *bogadi*, his daughter's *bogadi*, when she got married, was passed on to her mother's parents to pay the mother's *bogadi*. Though it was not compulsory to pay *bogadi*, there were measures to ensure that it was paid. For example, children born into such a family could not use the 'defaulting' husband's surname or his totem. It was only after the payment of *bogadi* that they were allowed to acquire his surname and totem. As one participant puts it, "Once he paid the bride-wealth, a ceremony was organised to give children the name and totem of their father".

One very important aspect associated with paying *bogadi* was that the wife was expected to bear children for her husband. In a case where there were no children, whether *bogadi* was paid or not, the man's family demanded them. In some cases, the women would be 'compelled' to allow the husband to marry another wife to bear children for them. The wife fully participated in the selection of the second wife and her consent was necessary. Note that participants all agreed that it was never considered that in childless marriages, the man could be infertile.

Participants did not recall a fixed number of cattle required for bride-wealth. As one participant puts it, "It was not a form of payment for some commodity". By contrast, nowadays, all participants agreed that there are dramatic changes in the requirements for payment of the bride-wealth because the issue now, as one of them succinctly put it, "is on the value of the bride in terms of her educational background, work experience and/or salary". The higher each of these items, the higher the bride-wealth demanded by her parents. It also has to be paid before the bride is formally handed to the in-laws. One woman noted that, "This is in contrast to the traditional practice where we were granted our husbands even before they paid bride-wealth".

Another stage in the marriage process was the wedding ceremony, which often followed the successful payment of the bride-wealth or the reception of the wife by the husband in the traditional system.

## WEDDING CEREMONY (*MOKETE* OR *KEMO*)

Traditionally, the wedding ceremony, *popeletso,* took place following successful completion of bride-seeking and, where possible, the payment of bride-wealth. The ceremony took place even if there was no bride-wealth. The bride was escorted to the in-laws very early in the morning, accompanied by the aunts and paternal uncles, and was received by the man's paternal uncles and aunts. The aunts carried firewood, sorghum meal on their heads, and other household belongings, especially her marriage blankets. All these were received with ululations and song by the man's aunts, who escorted the bride's aunts into the homestead. This process was again led by *sebanga,* who was to officially deliver the bride to her in-laws.

The groom sat alone in the hut and the bride was escorted to him after a short ceremony. Participants indicated that the bride was handed to the groom after payment of all that was needed for her to be handed over, *go atlholwa.* The bride was handed over to her husband's family as a wife. Most Sebirwa marriage rituals ended at this point, and there was no major pomp or ceremony that accompanied this process. The bride was quietly sent to her in-laws through a small ceremony involving key family members such as aunts and uncles. She was considered ready to perform all her functions as a wife. Some had a small ceremony to welcome her, and a few Christians performed their ceremonies.

The ceremony of transferring the bride to the in-laws in the traditional context was presided over by *borrangwane,* the paternal uncles on both sides. The uncle of the bride delivered her to that of the groom at this ceremony. The *sebanga* was given the bride to present to the in-laws. It should be noted that maternal uncles were invited by paternal uncles, and did not have any prominent roles as is currently the case. Members of the general public were not expected to give any gifts, but only did so out of goodwill to help kick-start the newly-weds' married life. During the ceremony, there was no strict dress code, but certainly the bride's parents were expected to put on the clothes they had demanded from the groom as pre-conditions to giving him his wife. The transferring of the bride to the in-laws ceremony included the following two important aspects as below.

### (a) Presenting blankets (*Go supa dikobo/kgoroso*)

For the ceremony a goat and a few chickens were slaughtered to welcome the bride, and the main activity was for the wife to come and show the man's family the blankets and clothes he bought for her.

The bride was accompanied by a young maiden from her home, who could be a younger sister or a cousin called a *teejane.* She was to help the bride with domestic chores for a few weeks as she settled down in her new home. The maiden was primarily responsible for warming water very early in the morning, for in–laws and all relatives, and to to wash their hands; and she served them tea. She also helped the bride to fetch water, firewood and to sweep the yard and cook food for the in-laws. After presenting the blankets, the bride would stay for a couple of weeks and later go back to her natal home. The in-laws would send *sebanga* to borrow her from her parents, now that she was their wife. Her parents would release her to join her husband. This was the end of the marriage ceremony because she would not go back home after that, unless on occasional visits, until they made preparations for paying *bogadi*.

### (b) *Singing and dancing*

Singing and dancing were always the most significant activities at the welcome ceremony. Days before the actual ceremony, choirs prepared a relevant song for the event. Songs were used to caution the parents-in-law, while the newly-weds were advised and counselled through singing and dancing. For example, the mother-in-law was asked to kindly give way for the bride to take care of cooking in the household. The daughter-in-law was cautioned to be patient, tolerant and appreciative of all and sundry among her in-laws. Among the Babirwa the marriage process was conducted in the home as opposed to the church or any other public space, and did not involve a major public fanfare.

## THE COUNSELLING SESSION (*GO LAYA*)

Following the wedding ceremony, in the evening, parents of both couples gathered together in an open space to counsel their children. This was restricted to only people who were or had once been married. Traditionally, each family counselled its own child. The parents informed the newly-wed bride that she was now a member of the new family, and that they were her parents henceforth; and the groom was given the same message in front of the bride's parents. As one participant noted, "The parents exchanged children on that day … each of them knew that he or she belonged to the new parents, going forward". The bride was warned that she should take care of all her in-laws and all the elderly people in her husband's clan. She should cook for and take care of her in-laws". At the core of counselling was the need for the bride to behave well, take care of the in-laws, and to serve her husband at all times. Both were informed of the paths to follow when there were challenges in the marriage. The woman was to inform the paternal uncle of her husband, and he too was told to consult her paternal uncle (*rangwane*) in case she misbehaved. According to one old woman, "The two were advised to love and care for each other and not allow third parties from either side to interfere and, more importantly, they were advised not to listen to gossip".

This contrasts with the cost of weddings now, where both the bride and groom go through prohibitively high expenses to organise a wedding. In the past, wedding expenses were footed by parents and not the groom. Other things have also changed. For example, in the past when a cow was killed for a wedding, aunts on the male's side were not given any specific portions. However, now they are entitled to cut small pieces of meat from various portions such as hind and forequarters of a cow: these are called *dipolwapolwane*. They cook these small pieces of meat in a separate pot and eat them just as a group of aunts. According to participants there are conflicting accounts around this practice. Some believe it is borrowed or adopted, because in the past Babirwa did not have the practice. The rest of the meat was cooked for everybody who attended the wedding, though there was no formal invitation for them, as is the case now.

The last stage in marriage was taking the bride to her natal home.

### TAKING THE BRIDE TO HER NATAL HOME

According to participants it was anathema for the bride who had been brought to the in-laws to be taken back to her natal home. They revealed that once the bride had been handed over to the in-laws she was part of the family and there was very limited opportunity for her to be taken back. However, some indicated that she could visit for a few days if she came from another village, or could visit her home during the day like any other person if she resided in the same village. When at her natal home, she was treated with respect because she was someone's wife and no longer just their child. She was expected to behave like an adult and participate in key decision-making meetings, accessible only to adults who were married. This was more so because, most of the time, she visited her parents with her husband. The long-term visits were often arranged with the husband with the consent of her in-laws. A few participants pointed to certain extraordinary instances where the bride was taken to her natal home when she was accused of some act of misconduct such as being very lazy, constantly fighting with the husband, or being associated with antisocial behaviour such as witchcraft, though this was very rare. In cases of incessant conflict, she could be released to go back home to be counselled, only after several interventions to reconcile the couple had failed.

Most of the time she was sent back to be counselled by her parents if the in-laws felt she was not listening to their counsel. A few of them recalled a situation where the man became mentally unstable, and the woman was sent home because it was feared that he could harm her. Others contradicted this account and gave examples of people who lived with their mentally sick wives and husbands till they died.

In rare cases, where a woman was sent back home, *sebanga* was called and asked to facilitate the process of sending word to her parents that the in-laws intended to return her home. The reasons for returning her had to be convincing. There was no formal ceremony. She was accompanied by a few people with her belongings, quietly returned and was quietly received. The bride was returned with a cow called *lekopolo,* which was given to her parents because she had failed to perform her duties, or for other reasons. The groom's parents paid the in-laws for breaking the promise to keep her for life as a wife. Participants observed that if a husband decided to divorce his wife, he left her in the family and did not take any property such as cattle or land, though he took his clothes and a few other things. He was to start afresh with the new partner of his choice, who the parents might not recognise. When the woman was the one who decided to divorce, she left without property. Whoever decided to divorce lost the right to family property, as it was bequeathed to the remaining spouse. This is in contrast to current cases of divorce, which are handled by the High Court, at times without the consent of families.

Traditional Sebirwa marriage was built on certain rites and metaphors.

## MARRIAGE RITES AND METAPHORS

The institution of marriage has certain rites, privileges and metaphors associated with it among the Babirwa people. For example, the woman was referred to as *sego sa metsi,* a 'water gourd', because she was brought into the family to come and serve the parents of the groom by way of fetching water and firewood for the household. As one female participant put it, "She cooked food for in-laws and her husband ... Serving food to the father-in-law was the only thing she was restricted from doing during the early days of her arrival. The mother-in-law had to teach her to serve her father-in-law". Porridge was served in layers, one on top of each other to make various heaps called *magákgo*, which was only served to the father, and her husband was served like other family members. She only served *magákgo* for him after they had left the parents' household, when one of his siblings marry, and a new bride had arrived. She lived with her in-laws as long as she was the only bride in the family. She inherited the homestead. One participant indicated, "They lived with parents to ensure that they lived in peace and were taught traditional mores and how to behave as a married couple".

The other common metaphor was that of '*mogwe morula o a monwa*' or 'a man is like the fruit of a Morula tree, he is to be sucked'. According to the accounts of most participants, traditional men were supposed to work for their in-laws. He was expected to remove stumps from their fields, plough for them for a couple of seasons, look after cattle, build a hut for them, and look after their general welfare at times, as part of reducing the bride-wealth. Hence, the idea of a man being compared to a nutritious Morula fruit – always there every season without fail. One participant indicated that men did all of these in appreciation of the in-laws raising his wife.

Marriage among Babirwa was a rite of passage to adulthood, symbolised by the fact that the bride moved from her people to go and live permanently among the in-laws, learn new ways of cooking, and undertaking all types of adult household chores. For example, the bride was given the privilege of cooking for, and later being taught how to serve, *magákgo* for her father in-law, something they might not have been done in their natal household because it was the preserve of the elders. Being a married woman therefore, regardless of age, ushered her into the realm of the elders. As an elder she was called upon to participate in all sorts of ceremonies, from which she had initially been restricted at her natal home. She engaged in meetings where they discussed marriage arrangements for her brothers and sisters-in-law, even if they were older than her.

The man also became an active member of his wife's and his own clan with the privilege of participating in all ceremonies and discussions reserved for men in both families. He was now supposed to perform certain tasks at his in-laws, and was entitled to gifts or presents such as a cow from the father in-law to help his family, if he was poor. These were in the form of *mafisa* (loaned cattle). Both men and women were entitled to such privileges as conjugal rights from their partners. The woman had to be provided for by the husband and be shielded from abject poverty, and was afforded the social status of a married woman.

The mother and father-in-law enjoyed certain privileges, for example, the bride's parents were entitled to all the cattle paid for bride-wealth. They could dispose of them as they wished and were not obliged to return them even if the marriage did not work. The groom's parents paid *bogadi* for the bride and were entitled to her services such as fetching water, cooking, and washing clothes. They were her lifelong educators who taught her the mores and values of their culture to prepare her for her adult roles.

Metaphors such as *sego sa metsi* reflected a reality that contrasts with what occurs today where a wife is married solely to take care of her husband, and has no obligations to the in-laws and his extended family members. While efforts are made to encourage the cultural practice of getting women to assist their in-laws, it is no longer mandatory, and much is left to the kindness of the wife. Also, men work to take care of their wives and have little time to spare to serve their in-laws. As one old man indicated, "Nowadays, at times the bride's parents use the fact that the man is poor as an excuse to get rid of him and find a wealthier man for her, instead of supporting him as was the case in the past". This is probably the main reason why men now pay bride-wealth beforehand to ensure that they do not owe the in-laws anything. One old lady observed that "this new fashion has broken a much-needed bond between families, and as a result the family structure is weak and not coherent". However, these metaphors are still appropriate for sentimental reasons, because it helps to remind women and men of their roles in their new families. The man was made to appreciate that he is to take care of his in-laws because their daughter would have been taking care of them in their old age. However, in practice, the current lifestyle works against this because people live in nuclear and not traditional or extended families.

## Changes in Babirwa Traditional Marriage

As in other communities, the institution of marriage among the Babirwa has undergone several changes over time. Participants observed that it is no longer comparable to what they had in the distant past. There is a consensus that over time marriage practices have changed significantly in the ways that follow.

(a) **Changed courtship and marriage processes.** The courtship and marriage decisions are no longer under the influence of parents. Couples select each other outside the community and receive marriage lessons from churches and counsellors. The decision as to who to marry is predominantly the choice of the groom and bride. As one participant put it, "Parents now are just distant spectators who have nothing to contribute to the decision of who marries their son or daughter". The participants agreed that this was because men now pay their own *lobala* and decide where their wives will stay, and in-laws do not contribute to these key decisions. The bride and groom are no longer married to take care of the in-laws, but to take care of each other. The groom is no longer expected to help the in-laws with their household chores and 'this denies them the chance to bond with them as his new parents'.

(b) **Use of maternal uncles in bride-seeking.** The participants cited the use of maternal and not paternal uncles to seek wives for their nephews as a challenge. They also attributed this to the predominance of inter-cultural marriages, which at times compels parents not to use their culture in processing marriages. One old man noted that "paternal uncles are now invited by the maternal uncles to their 'son's' marriages. In the past, it would be an abomination to have such an arrangement because the paternal uncle was considered the father of the groom. He was tasked with seeking a wife for him and he invited the maternal uncle at the appropriate time and not vice versa". Also, some key features of Sebirwa marriage such as the role of the *sebanga* have now been diminished, and sidelined; and given to the uncles and aunts on the mother's side.

(c) **Failure to keep family secrets.** In the past, family secrets were securely kept. If a woman made a mistake and had a child with another man while the husband was working somewhere, he was to take responsibility for the child. He could not easily divorce the wife on those grounds. Failure to take responsibility for the child led to potential loss of his property because the parents might decide to keep the wife and ask him to leave the house. The man who fathered the child was not punished. By contrast, in current marriages, the man can sue the father of the child in the public courts, and even divorce the wife. One old lady complained that "in the past, men just had children outside the family and left them there without taking care of such children and there was nothing wrong. Nowadays, they are compelled to take care of them, which is a good thing".

(d) **Polygamy.** The other issue was that a man was allowed to have more than one wife under traditional or customary law. The first wife participated, or did not participate, in the selection of the second or third wife. The man had authority over who he married as a second wife. Nowadays, a man is legally bound to marry one wife under common law, and there is no legitimate place for a second wife unless married traditionally, and such a marriage is not recognised under common law. One woman blamed the one-woman policy for "the infidelities that are a common occurrence nowadays … a man is a bull and should not be restricted to one kraal. In the past, arrangements for a second marriage were negotiated with the wife".

(e) **Marriage nowadays is too expensive.** There is a consensus among participants that marriages nowadays are so expensive that the bride-wealth is treated as a commercial or business transaction. It is clearly not a token of appreciation as was the case in the past. One elderly man decried the fact that "in-laws emphasise that their daughter is educated and the higher her education or occupation (e.g., a doctor), the more expensive her bride-wealth." The other aspect is that there are too many expensive ceremonies, yet in the past there was just one ceremony for the bride to be welcomed to her new home. A woman was sought from her parents and immediately brought home to start a family without incurring a lot of expenses celebrating the marriage. This allowed the newly-weds to use whatever they had, with the support of their families, to start their own lives and sustain themselves without being impoverished by these very expensive marriage ceremonies. One old woman observed that "this is one of the sources of instability and increased divorce rates among modern marriages".

## SUGGESTIONS FOR STABILISING THE MARRIAGES OF YOUNG COUPLES

Participants were asked to suggest what could be done to help stabilise marriages, and make couples more tolerant of each other and their in-laws, and to help them endure the challenges of marriage. While participants acknowledged that current marriages are different from what they went through, they felt that some things can be done to help stabilise and increase tolerance in marriages. They suggested the below.

(a) **Involving parents in a more effective way in some key stages of marriage.** A feature of present marriages is that parents no longer have much control over who their sons or daughters marry. There is only a limited level of consultation with them, and the parents' input is not highly valued. Participants felt that, given their vast experiences in marriage and life generally, they would have helped to assess the families to which they would refer their son, and hopefully help him find a person whose cultural background is reconcilable with theirs, and they would hopefully make a more compatible couple who better understood each other. Participants suggested that parents should not place too many expectations on their married children; instead, they should allow them to work and support each other without any unnecessary interference in the affairs of the new families from both sides.

Parents nowadays do not have the means to pay expensive bride-wealth, and most decisions about the key aspects of the marriage are made by the couples. One participant noted that, "The effect of seeking a bride alone is that the couples end up with partners who do not share any values with them. Most couples end up not being able to reconcile their differences. Women no longer view themselves as subservient to husbands but as social, and at times economic, equal and life partners". This makes it difficult for husbands to exert any type of control in the house and if they try to do that, both of them beccome stressed. One old man said, "We have given up; on the one hand, they are both working and the wife cannot be expected to do all the household chores, but some men do not assist in the house; this becomes a source of tension.... On the other hand, some parents seem not to appreciate this fact about the new couples, and do not encourage their sons to help in family chores. Some actually discourage him from working in the house, claiming that helping shows that the wife bewitched him". Parents therefore need not influence their sons against helping their wives to help them live longer together.

(b) **Married couples need to minimise receiving advice from friends.** Participants felt strongly that present-day marriages are run by the couples and their friends, some of whom are either not genuine or inexperienced in the institution of marriage. The couples need to make sure that they minimise external influences from relatives and friends in their marriage. Even in the past, marriage was for the two. Parents only intervened when it was necessary, but nowadays, couples cry foul and run to their families and are not told to 'go back and endure the difficulties of marriage'. Parents do not hold necessary reconciliatory meetings with distressed couples to discuss issues affecting their marriages with the aim of reconciling them. Instead, some parents are looking at the fact that they will share property equally and are ready to 'encourage their child to leave the marriage even if he/she is the one who is wrong'. In the past, it used to be that whoever was wrong faced a punishment from the parents and the community. For example, 'the guilty party' was made to leave the house and not take anything, so that everyone tried to do the right thing for fear of losing support from both families. Parents and relatives came together to determine the problem and tried to address it. They genuinely wanted to help the couple to stay married because they viewed marriage as a revered and socially valuable institution, which made both parents proud of their status as in-laws.

(c) **Review the legal framework to discourage instability in families.** The current national legal framework requires divorcing couples to go to the High Court to resolve broken marriages. This is at times done without giving parents any opportunity to discuss the issues that could be distressing the couple. Participants were of the view that parents should be part of the divorce process. They observed that the High Court should not complete divorce proceedings without seeking documented input from both parents. As one of them indicated, "The court needs to know that couples have a circle of parents and relatives who helped them to get married. It should somehow establish their input in the divorce proceedings before judgment is passed, or before dissolving the marriage". The courts could ask couples to consult their in-laws, as was done in the past. The customary court could be asked to intervene and render a local-level decision before the final judgment, which should consider failed efforts to reconcile the divorcing couple at the lower courts. One of them felt that the laws did not only ignore parents, but seem not to be "our law because those who crafted it should have known better about how a traditional marriage is run and how conflicts are traditionally resolved and would have factored that into the law of the land". While there are limitations in the way decisions were made in the past, it would seem sensible to ask the divorcing couples what the efforts of their parents and other structures, such as churches, were in helping them to resolve their differences before the courts dissolve their estates. One participant noted that, "Some of the dissolved marriages could have been salvaged through such a consultative process". These efforts would have helped to stabilise some families and encouraged couples to endure and reconcile their differences in a harmonious way, and keep their marriages.

## REFERENCES

Krathwohl, D.R. (1998). Methods of educational and social science research: An integrated approach (2nd ed). New York: Longman.

Mmapetla, M. (2012). The Bobirwa chieftanship: the broken mirror image. https://www.sundaystandard.info/the-bobirwa-chieftanship-the-broken-mirror-image/. Last accessed 6 June 2022.

Molosiwa P. (2016). Bakgomong: The Babirwa's transboundary pastoralist identity and social change in late 19th century Botswana. https://repository.nwu.ac.za/handle/10394/19405. Last accessed 6 June 2022.

Westphal, E.O.J. (1975). Notes on the Babirwa *Botswana Notes and Records*, Vol. 7 pp. 191-194 https://www.jstor.org/stable/40979440 Accessed: 16-02-2019 09:06 UTC.

# 2

# BAKALANGA

*Jabulani Dick Makwanda*

## INTRODUCTION

This chapter outlines the ingredients of what, in Ikalanga traditional culture, would be considered a properly conducted marriage process. It delineates the stages, processes and actors that are involved. As in other cultures in the country, marriage among the Bakalanga is considered a rite of passage whose procedures must be adhered to strictly. This is because they enact and reinforce values and beliefs that are regarded as crucial to their identity and integrity as a people.

The data for this chapter were obtained principally from personal observations and intuitions by the author as an adult native of Ikalanga culture, who participates in various cultural activities of the people, including marriage rituals. In addition, the author arranged qualitative in-depth interviews with carefully selected informants whose special knowledge and experience in matters of traditional Ikalanga culture were generally acknowledged. These sources were complemented by data from online and archival resources, which yielded oral traditions, archaeological findings and writings of early Portuguese and other European travellers to the area. Recent academic research and court records have also been gleaned for the light they shed on the ways in which Ikalanga society and its traditions are evolving and adapting to the changing socio-economic environment in Botswana. The perspective adopted in this chapter is that the Kalanga are a dynamic people, justly keen to guard the integrity of their cultural traditions, but at the same time aware that identity and traditions are flexible and negotiable. They have demonstrated great aptitude at asserting their distinct identity, while projecting the national ideal of unity in diversity that modern Botswana seeks to inculcate.

## HISTORICAL BACKGROUND

The Bakalanga are not a single homogenous group, but a historically constituted affiliation of peoples linked by a common history that can be traced back over more than a thousand years of continuous settlement in the region (Huffman, 1974; Rusare, 2015). Archaeological evidence even links them to the Leopard's Kopje people thought to be the earliest inhabitants of the area, who were settled in the area between 450 AD and 1050 AD. They are also linked to the great empires that arose subsequent to that period, namely the Mapungubwe Kingdom c.1075-1220, the Great Zimbabwe Empire c.1000-1500, and finally the Rozwi Kingdom c.1684-1850 that was overrun by marauding *impis* in the course of the havoc caused by the *difaqane*.

Today, however, the term is generally used to refer specifically to the Kalanga-speaking peoples who traditionally occupied the area bestriding the border between north-eastern Botswana and south-eastern Zimbabwe, in which countries, according to some estimates, they number approximately 700,000 and 150,000, respectively (Rusare, 2015). Apart from this common history and language, Kalanga identity coalesces around the Mwali (Ngwali) religion. The Mwali religion is central to Ikalanga culture and it is obvious that the ritual practices of their marriage process reflect a world view and value system informed by the religion. Consequently, marriage is regarded as a rite of passage which confers to the initiates the rights and privileges of adulthood as well as access to the sacred (secret) knowledge of the culture. Marriage is, hence, not just a social institution bringing together a man and woman to start a family, but also crucially a religious ritual through which the culture reaffirms its values and its relationship with the 'Supreme Being', Mwali, and the ancestors (Rodewald, 2010).

## THE SIGNIFICANCE OF MARRIAGE IN IKALANGA CULTURE

Ikalanga culture, like that of other Botswana ethnic groups, is dynamic and has evolved over the years, as have its marriage practices and customs. One of the major factors in the evolution of Ikalanga marriage traditions and practices has been colonialism, which introduced Christian and Western style marriage practices into the culture. It is also through colonialism that Bakalanga people were brought into close contact with other ethnic groups such as the Ndebele in Zimbabwe and the Tswana-speaking communities in Botswana with whom they did not necessarily share the same traditions originally. Furthermore, Ikalanga culture has been affected by the introduction of money. As to the results of changes caused by all these factors, there is no consensus on both the traditions that are retained from the past and those that have been newly acquired. The 'dowry' (*malobolo*), for instance, is one area on which no consensus exists, and is guided largely by what prevails as good practice from time to time and place to place. In fact, according to some sources, the payment of *malobolo* is not an essential ingredient of a valid marriage because it can be delayed, paid in instalments or waived altogether (BLR, 2008). Today, Ikalanga marriage practices have borrowed heavily from the traditions of Setswana-speaking communities as well as from Western culture. The dilemma that Bakalanga, face, as do other ethnic groups in the country, is that of how to safeguard their identity and cultural traditions while at the same time being part of a diverse but unified national and distinctly modern Botswana culture. Many fear that there may be an erosion of Ikalanga culture and traditions over the years in favour of a monolithic state-sponsored Setswana identity. Strenuous effort needs to be exerted to allay such anxieties.

As pointed out above, in Ikalanga culture marriage is a rite of passage and marks a man's entry into the status of male adulthood; it defines a man and confers upon him the privileges and responsibilities of a man before Mwali and the community (Rodewald, 2010). One of such privileges is to own a piece of land for dwelling and ploughing. A bachelor is *not* permitted to be granted such rights.That is, it separates the men from the boys. Furthermore, in addition to the size of his herd of cattle and his wealth, especially in the form of agricultural produce, a man's position in society is determined by his marital status and the size of his family. An unmarried man is defined as *swimbolume*, a derogatory name meaning someone who is not answerable to anyone but himself. His words at a *khuta/kgotla* meeting are insignificant. He is not allowed to sit in marriage preparatory meetings, and he cannot play any role in marriage matters, no matter how old he may be. Hence the Ikalanga idiom that says '*swimbolume ino budziwa nti wa wha*', a figure of speech that means that an unmarried man does not attend important meetings, and is only told of the outcome when the meeting is over and done with. The literal meaning is that an unmarried man only knows about the cutting of a tree after it has been felled. He is an outcast.

Similarly, an unmarried woman was also treated with derision and given the derogatory label *gwimba*, meaning a woman who sleeps with anyone at will. Children born of such a woman did not have totems and assumed the totem of their mother, which was regarded as a shameful thing to have and to do. They occupied a lowly status as extra children of their maternal uncles.

It was society's expectation that all men and women would get married. No parents would want their sons and daughters to remain unmarried and be given the derogatory names *swimbolume* and *gwimba*. It was considered a curse to have such a child in the family. Such people were looked down upon in society and were denied the rights and privileges given to married people. However, in traditional Ikalanga society unmarried people who had attained maturity were very rare. Polygamy was part of the culture and it helped to balance or manage the ratio between males and females.

## TYPES OF MARRIAGE

All three types of marriage found in Botswana, namely customary, civil and Christian are practised in Ikalanga culture today. Although one is enough to solemnise a union into a marriage, there are cases when two or all three have been combined in one marriage. Regardless of which type of marriage is adopted, there are stages that are expected to be concluded in order to mark a properly conducted marriage. The first of the stages, as described below, includes the identification of marital partners and the initiation of the marriage process.

## Identification of Prospective Marriage Partners

Traditionally Ikalanga culture had four methods through which prospective marriage partners were identified and marriage proceedings initiated. The identification of future marital partners and initiation of the marriage process was known as *bambiwa kwe n'ndobolo*. The four methods were as below.

(a) Arranged/forced marriage (*Piwa kene bigidzigwa nkadzi*)

(b) Personal choice proposal (*Pala*)

(c) Stealing the bride during the night (*Nkumbo*)

(d) Bride presented as a form of payment in-lieu of healing (*N'galu/Ganu*).

These methods will be discussed in detail in this section. It should be noted that while the methods do differ in terms of their set-up, the end product in three of them is the wedding ceremony known as *bukwe*. This is not necessarily the conclusion in the fourth method where the bride may be handed over to the husband without ceremony as a form of payment for medical treatment or healing (*n'galu/ganu*).

### Arranged/forced marriage

In this method of marriage partner identification occurred without courtship. The boy's father identified a suitable future daughter-in-law from among his friends' daughters and proposed the match to his friend. If the girl's father accepted the proposal the deal would be sealed, and from that day onward both families would regard the two children as pledged to be married to each other when they reached the age of maturity. This was how betrothals were made, from time immemorial, and this was the most common method of marriage partner identification among the Bakalanga people. This was what was deemed culturally correct. In modern times the practice has declined but is occasionally practiced in pockets of rural Bukalanga.

Mothers of both the boy and the girl were seldom consulted. They were only informed of the agreement after the matter had been concluded between the two men. On rare occasions, the mother of the boy child would also identify a future wife for her son. Once she had thus identified the girl, however, she asked her husband or her own father to approach the girl's father to make the proposal. Once the betrothal was agreed, throughout their teenage years the boy and the girl would be recognised as future husband and wife. When the girl reached the age of maturity, a necklace known as *mmamani* would be placed around her neck as a sign that she was taken or had already been identified to be married to someone. The necklace was made from beads, *ndalama*, and was a sign of engagement. The necklace was meant to give the girl dignity and respect among her peers and the community at large. A girl who wore *mmamani* was then known as *phandala*, while those not yet assigned future husbands, but mature enough to get married, were known as *phokosha*.

Identification of marital partners under this method normally happened when the girl was still an infant and the boy at least one year old. When both of them reached the age of maturity their union was formalised and they were introduced to each other as prospective husband and wife. The formalization meant that the process of negotiating and paying *malobolo* could start. Sometimes such arranged marriages were done even before the birth of the girl through a 'booking system' known as *bigidzigwa*, under which future girl children could be pledged in marriage to males from a family that would have made the 'booking'. In the event of the death of the boy before the actual marriage took place, the girl was passed on to any of the boy's brothers who was willing to take her as a wife. In the event of the girl's death her family replaced her with another girl.

The choice of a family to marry from was based on many factors including friendship between respective parents, social standing, a good name in the community, and a reputation for hard work (especially in agriculture). Families suspected of practicing witchcraft (*boloyi*) were avoided.

### Personal choice proposal

In this method of marital partner identification there was some courtship because the boy made a proposal to a girl of his own choice or as instructed by his father. Once the proposal was accepted, it was followed by a period of dating during which intimacy was forbidden. The couple was expected to respect and treat each other as mere friends. The friendship would escalate to marriage only after the families on both sides had been consulted and given their approval.

When a boy came of age and felt ready to marry, he would first inform his paternal uncle (*batatenini/rangwane*) of his intentions to get married. The uncle would inform the boy's parents and then convene a meeting of elders made up of married relatives and inform them of the boy's intention to marry. The purpose of the meeting would be to consider and approve the boy's choice on the basis of such criteria as her family's standing in the community, economic status, reputation, and so forth. Marrying from a family of lazy and ill-mannered people was highly discouraged; the family would reject such a proposal outright and instead offer assistance in identifying a more suitable partner. Marrying from a related family was considered taboo. Relatives included all people who shared a similar totem (*ntupo*). A totem symbolises the same clan and no matter how far the families lived from each other, as long as they shared the same totem they were considered to be related.

The meeting of the elders to consider the boy's choice was normally preceded by a visit by one of the elders, the boy's uncle, who was required to undertake going to the girl's home to scout. The person who performed this duty was known as *dombo*, literally meaning a hill, probably a reference to a hilltop from which it would be possible for a person to spy on a homestead from afar. His duties were to spy on the girl's family and produce a report to the elders. *Dombo* was expected to find his way into the girl's homestead during the day. He would not reveal the real purpose of his visit but would give some other reason for it. He would probably enter the yard on the pretext of being thirsty, and ask for some water to drink from the girl's parents. He would talk of many things like the weather, the harvest, the livestock and other topics to disguise his mission. In Ikalanga culture when there is a visitor to the home, all the children are called in to greet the visitor (*butjila*). This would also happen in the case of the *dombo's* visit. As the children took their turns to greet him, the *dombo* would carry out a light-hearted conversation with each child, intended to enable him to gauge their intelligence and general temperament. When it was the earmarked child's turn to greet him, the scout would pay particular attention to the child's physical appearance, behaviour and manners. Boys perform *butjila* by putting their hands together in a clapping position and extending them to *dombo,* who would grab and kiss them. The girls would do the same but would also curtsy by bending both knees simultaneously. *Dombo* might seize the opportunity to observe the girl closely by asking her to fetch him some water to drink. At this stage he would pay attention to the girl's gait and the manner in which she carried herself as she went about getting the water ready for him. He would note, especially, if in handing the water to him she knelt before him on both knees as good manners required.

When the children are called in to greet visitors in Ikalanga homes, both parents are generally present to observe how their children perform, and occasionally to encourage the shy ones to greet with confidence and respect. *Dombo* would observe them too and note the upkeep of their yard/homestead. Elderly people in Bukalanga are very particular about how they receive visitors. They know the importance of taking care of a visitor and that a mere visit may lead to greater things, including the marriage of a daughter and other life favours.

When *dombo* was satisfied he would leave; he was not expected to stay too long. After this expedition, *dombo* would return home to convene the meeting of elders and give his report. Once there was consensus on the suitability of the girl to be married, the process of marriage consultations would begin. The process shall be detailed under the subheading 'Bride-seeking'.

## THE STEALING OF THE BRIDE/GIRL

This method of marital partner identification is known as *tola nkumbo*: taking a wife by abduction at night. When arranged marriages as described above declined from the 1960s to the 1980s this became the most popular method of identifying marital partners and declaring intentions to marry among the Bakalanga. *Tola nkumbo* was different from an arranged marriage because it was not initiated through consultations between families in a process commonly known as *pala*. The method was a 'grab and capture' ritual staged at the instigation of the prospective bride and groom. On many occasions, however, it led to fights between the boy's and girl's families during which, sometimes, even deaths occurred when one side of the family was hostile to the proposed union.

This method of courtship normally occurred when a boy and a girl, who would have been seeing each other secretly, agreed that they were ready to marry and wished to make their intentions known to their families. In some cases it was initiated by the boy's father who, having identified a suitable future partner for his son, would instruct his son to approach the girl and ask for her hand in marriage. If the girl accepted his proposal, they would date secretly for some time. When they were both ready, the boy would inform his paternal uncle of his intention to marry. The uncle would give his approval after consulting the boy's father and mother. No other meetings within the family were held, nor were there advance meetings with the girl's family. The girl on the other side would also inform an aunt (*manini/bammaadzi*). *Manini* could be the younger sister of her mother's or her uncle's wife, known as *mma-rrangwane* in Setswana. *Bammaadzi* was any of the father's sisters. They too would keep the couple's relationship and plan secret.

The actual abduction of the girl was a smooth and swift operation. On the day agreed between the few relatives on either side privy to the plan, the boy would go on his own to fetch his bride from her parents' home. Alternatively, he sent an uncle or an aunt to do the job on his behalf. Careful planning and stealth were necessary because the abduction was supposed to be undetected by anyone in the girl's family. The abductor(s) would have to find their way to the girl's hut and enter undetected. The girl would have obviously been forewarned of the plan and would be expecting them so that she would not scream in fear and alert her parents or other people at home. She would have bags ready for her escape. Before departure a white cloth or a small amount of money (two Pula, say) was placed underneath her blanket or sleeping mat. At the main entrance of her parents' yard, she would perform a ritual feigned reluctance to leave her home and refuse to proceed with the journey, and the 'abductors' would have to encourage her with a gift of some money. This ritual feigned resistance would be repeated at several major points on the journey, such as at road junctions and before river crossings, and each time she would have to be given more money to persuade her to continue. When they finally arrived at her future husband's home she would stop again at the gate, put her belongings down and refuse to go any further. The boy would then go in alone to inform his parents that he had managed to bring the bride home but she would not enter the yard. His parents would now make the necessary payment to encourage her to cross the threshold and enter their yard. When she reached the entrance of the groom's hut/house she would stop again, until more money was given to her. The feigned resistance ritual only ended when she was given the final payment to overcome her reluctance to sit on her nuptial bed (*pinda tilale*). This process of ritual feigned reluctance, overcome by gifts of money to the bride-to-be was known as *fupa nlongo*. Normally the money was a few coins only and was really a mere formality to enable the ritual to continue. She could use this money to buy herself personal effects such as domestic utensils.

The following morning when the girl's parents awoke, they would discover that the girl and all her belongings had disappeared. Underneath the mat they would find a white cloth or the two Pula, an indicator that their daughter had been abducted for marriage purposes. The father would be furious and call his brothers and his wife to discuss a family response. Meantime the boy's homestead would be a hive of activity with the beginning of a new phase of life. The mother-in-law would wake up very early in order to introduce the bride to her new home. The bride was also expected to get up very early to meet her mother-in-law for the occasion. The mother-in-law would show her the yard, open all the huts and explain to her what each hut was used for and who slept where in it. She gave the bride instructions about how the yard and all its huts were to be swept every day without fail at break of dawn. A girl in the family would be assigned the role of her assistant to make her feel at home around the homestead. The girl would point out to her such things as where to fetch water, which of the cooking utensils were available for her use, and the fireplace. This process was known as *luba*.

Two days later, *dombo* would be sent to the girl's parents to inform them of their daughter's whereabouts, a process known as *shakilani ngeno*. As the girl's parents might be furious for various reasons, such as not liking the boy and/or his family, it was not safe for *dombo* to approach them directly. He would, instead, report the *shakilani ngeno* to either a neighbour or one of the girl's uncles first, who would be less likely to harm him. The neighbour or uncle would then escort the *dombo* to the girl's parents' homestead to report the *shakilani ngeno* to the assembled uncles on the girl's side. In his report the *dombo* would make it clear that he was merely the messenger and plead not to be harmed, hence the popular Ikalanga adage *Ntomwa ha ana mbonje*, meaning 'Don't harm or kill the messenger'.

When the message of the girl's whereabouts was received, there would normally be mixed reactions. If the father and the uncles were not happy with the proposed union, or disliked the boy and his family, they might send a person or a group of men to raid the boy's family home and retrieve their daughter. The raiders would be armed with knobkerries and would be in no mood to negotiate. They would enter the groom's homestead by force and take the girl back to her home. However, if she was determined to go ahead with the proposed marriage, the girl would, out of her own volition, escape from home again and go back to her intended husband's home. This would be finally accepted by her parents as evidence enough that the boy and girl were committed to getting married, and negotiations to formalise the union could commence in earnest. Sometimes, however, the girl failed to make the second escape on her own. The groom in such a case would approach her parents and plead with them to release her, in a process called *nkwasha eno bomba*. If his appeal succeeded the girl would be released to return to her prospective husband's home and, in this case too, negotiations to formalise the union would then begin.

After two to three weeks, the boy's family were expected to return the girl to her parents' home but they would take with them a present in the form of a cow known as *phelesi*, meaning the 'one that accompanies the bride'. The cow was both a formal indication of the boy's intention to marry the girl and an apology for the abduction. The girl's parents, by accepting the cow, in turn signalled their approval of the proposed marriage. The girl would remain with her parents for a period of about two weeks for purposes of marriage counselling known as *layiwa*.

At the end of the two weeks' period of counselling by her aunts, the girl was taken back to her husband's home. She would be accompanied by her uncle's wife or any other senior female relative from her family and her younger sister, known in Ikalanga as *nkadzana*, meaning 'little wife". The particular aunt who performed this function was known as *ndwana,* meaning a female who leads marriage discussions and processions. *Ndwana* would carry finely-ground sorghum grains known as *shogwana*. The finely ground sorghum flour was contained in a traditional woven basket (*seme* or *tlatlana*) that the bride would carry on her head. The fine sorghum flour was the epitome of marriage celebrations in Ikalanga culture: it was a symbol of purity.

*Ndwana* and *nkadzana* would stay overnight, and on the evening of their visit a goat would have been killed in their honour. When they left the following day, they would be given half the goat's chest and its leg (*ifuba ne bhandabuko latjo*) to take home with them.

After their visit the process of demanding *malobolo* from the boy's family and preparations for a marriage ceremony or *bukwe* would start.

The girl's family would call a meeting of the elders and decide on the date to go to the boy's family to demand lobola, *malobolo.* Once they had agreed on a date, an emissary, also called *dombo,* from the girl's family, was sent to inform the boy's relatives of the proposed date for the formal demand of *malobolo.* This was also the day of the marriage ceremony known as *pitsha bukwe.*

The father and the mother of the bride did not form part of the entourage that went to demand *malobolo* but remained behind with a few relatives. The team that went to make the demand was led by the uncles and their wives, and included a few other close relatives and *nkadzana.*

On arrival at the boy's home, of all the emissaries, *ndwana* was the only one who entered the boy's yard, leaving the entourage behind. She would be received by a counterpart *ndwana* from the boy's side. It was through their respective *ndwana* that the two sides would communicate. Once the boy's family had shown all *malobolo* to her, the *ndwana* on the girl's side would return to her entourage outside to relay the message. When her entourage was satisfied with her report of the *malobolo* offered, she and her entourage would enter the yard where they would be taken into a special hut (*ngumba ye bezi*). *Malobolo* in this instance was just one cow known as *thukila,* literally meaning a charge for trespassing, a reference to the way the girl had been abducted. After being shown this cow, which must be a young female with small horns or a castrated young ox with horns, they would be shown another cow which was to be slaughtered, known as *phitsha bukwe.* The horns signified purity and meant that the girl was a virgin who had been initiated. A hornless cow and an uncastrated ox were regarded as an insult. If, when they were shown the cow, there were no *mpululu* (ululations) from the emissaries and their *ndwana,* then they were not happy with the cow. The boy's relatives would immediately point to another one until there were *mpululu.* The girl's relatives would now go back to their hut and remain there until they were called out to the kraal again, after the cow had been slaughtered, to authorise the skinning of the cow. Once skinned, half of the cow's chest and its leg (*bhandabuko*) were set aside as reserved portions for the girl's parents. After this there would be celebration, highlighted by feasting and traditional dances known as *wozo* and *ndazula.* When the celebration was over, the party would ask for permission to leave, whereupon they would be given a container full of traditional beer (*nkabo we busukwa*) and the reserved portions of meat to take with them as presents to the girl's parents back home.

With the introduction of writing and the advent of bicycles, the practice of sending *dombo* as described above was replaced by communication via letters. When a girl is abducted as an indication of marriage intentions, a letter would be written to her parents addressed by their clan name and directed to the paternal uncle. Upon receiving the letter informing them of the girl's whereabouts, the girl's uncle and other relatives would convene a meeting and lay charges of *malobolo* in writing. They would list all the items they wanted and the due date thereof. On that date, the groom's family would bring all the required items, which were a cow only or a cow, a goat and a sheep, driven by small boys. They would camp outside the boy's homestead and *ndwana* would be sent to inform the girl's family that visitors had arrived to pay the bride-wealth. A team would be sent to see whether the items were adequate. After inspection the team would inform the elders and seek their approval. The visitors would then be taken into a special hut, *ng'umba ye bakwasha,* where they would spend the day and be served with food. In the evening they would return to their own home, leaving the girl with her parents for counselling.

The girl's relatives would then return her in two to three weeks, after a series of counselling sessions. On that day the wedding celebrations, *ku pitshiwa bukwe* would take place. The procession would be made up of women walking in a single file *baka bopelela,* led by men. The women would carry containers of sorghum grain and bundles of firewood on their heads.

### BRIDE PRESENTED AS OFFER OR PAYMENT IN LIEU OF HEALING

This is probably the most unusual method of identifying marital partners and initiating marriage proceedings in Ikalanga. It only benefitted traditional healers. Surprisingly a lot of girls got married to traditional healers (*n'ganga*) through this method known in Bukalanga as *ganu* or *n'galu.* If the traditional healer was female, which was rare, she would take a girl offered as payment and give her to any of her brothers.

In this type of marriage there was no courtship, nor *malobolo* paid. The traditional healer, after treating an elderly person, whether male or female, simply demanded the hand of their daughter in marriage. Sometimes the healed persons themselves would offer their daughter to the healer in marriage in gratitude. This was a very common practice which led to traditional doctors being married to many wives. After many years of staying with the girl as his wife, and her having borne him children, the traditional healer would decide, of his own volition, to pay the parents with a cow.

## MARRIAGE PROCESSES

### COURTSHIP

In all the four methods of identifying future marriage partners there was very little courtship in the Western sense of individuals developing a romantic relationship with the intention of getting married in the future. In traditional Ikalanga culture, marriages were arranged or forced upon a couple with extremely limited scope for personal choice. One was given a life partner and accepted him/her as they were; beautiful or ugly, tall or short, light skinned or dark skinned. No consent was sought from the couple. Parents, especially the father of the boy, were the sole deciders of who the son would marry. They were usually influenced in their preferences by factors such as friendship with the bride's father, the family's status in society, the girl's reputation for hard work, and their economic standing, among other things. The hallmarks of a prized family to marry into were: reputation for respect towards other people (*buthu*); and a strong work ethic (*shinga*).

The discussion of the Ikalanga marriage processes that follows below will unavoidably repeat some of the material already alluded to in the above discussion of the methods of identifying marital partners and initiating marriage. The reason for this overlap is simply that with respect to Ikalanga the separation between the various stages of the marriage process is made only for the sake of narrative convenience. In practice the processes seamlessly merged into each other. They do not form distinct stages as in some cultures. A case in point is the marriage by abduction in which the rituals of bride-seeking, bride movement between natal and marital homes, *malobolo* negotiations, and settling scores for trespass and abduction, take place at the same time or in quick succession. In the account below these stages are presented as distinct stages only for ease of comparison with the marriage processes of other cultures discussed in this book.

## Initiating the marriage process

Strictly speaking, the methods of identifying future marital partners described above are triggers that set in motion the processes that must be completed in order to constitute a proper Ikalanga marriage. Identifying a future bride, through any of the methods serves as a signal to the family and the community that a marriage is in the offing and that the ritual processes of a marriage should begin. It must be noted at this point that in Ikalanga culture the most important role in the processes of marriage is performed by the paternal uncle. So, in its own way each of these methods is a signal for him to step up and assume his responsibility because the process of starting any marriage proposal, from time immemorial till today, is led by the uncle (*batatenini*). It is the uncle that the boy informs of his intention to marry, in the first instance. It is the uncle who in turn informs the rest of the family of the boy's intentions. It is he who is responsible for conducting the *malobol*o negotiations with the bride's family. On the wedding day, he and his wife must lead the procession, while his wife also acts as the messenger (*ndwana*). On the bride's side it is similarly the wife of the uncle who must be an emissary or *ndwana*. In traditional Ikalanga, the uncles from the maternal side (*bo-basekulu/ malume*) do not play any ritual role in the marriage process. Neither do they participate in marriage meetings. In modern times it is increasingly common to have maternal uncles involved in marriage discussions, but this is as the result of adopting some practices from Setswana ethnic groups, especially in cross-cultural intermarriages where the programmes may include roles for a maternal uncle.

Asked to explain why maternal uncles did not play a role in Ikalanga marriage processes, the Bakalanga elderly informants in this study suggested two explanations. The first one was that since marriages were arranged and forced, it was probably to avert the possible resentment of uncles whom it was assumed were not always pleased with the decisions made by their sister's husbands, especially with regard to the choice of families into which to marry, and the age of the girl at marriage, who would be a very young virgin, more often than not. The second reason they gave was that the maternal uncles were generally not available anyway, since in the olden days they often lived far away from the villages where their sisters were married, and that transport was not available.

## PRELIMINARY VISITS

The first stage of the marriage process following the identification of the marital partners described above is known as the preliminary visits stage. It is the term used for the corresponding stage in the rest of this book for other cultures. It is the stage that marks the fact that marriage preparations are truly underway. In Ikalanga culture, this stage kicks off with a practice known as 'scouting'. This was conducted by the paternal uncle alone. It was performed when the boy had chosen a girl to marry, and the family wished to know more about the girl and the status of her family. After the visit, the uncle would report his findings to the elders on the boy's side. If his report was favourable and there was consensus to marry into the family, *pala* (*patlo* in Setswana) would be arranged. The uncle would then assume the role of *dombo* and return for a second visit to the girl's parents to make the initial marriage proposal known as *koka moto,* which is the equivalent of *go kokota* in Setswana. In Ikalanga *koka moto* was the practice of presenting a marriage proposal to the girl's family and then formally identifying the chosen prospective bride before her family. It involved gathering together all the girls in the homestead in a form of identity parade so that the *dombo* could point out the prospective bride from among them. The uncle must identify the girl and then leave. After a day or two the girl's father would call a meeting of his brothers and elderly relatives and inform them of the proposal that had been received. During this meeting the girl's family, if they approved of the proposed marriage, would also set a date on which to approach the boy's family to demand *malobolo.*

In modern day Bukalanga there have been changes to the process. Preliminary visits are still conducted by the uncle but he is accompanied by his wife. He does not go on his own anymore. Sometimes the maternal uncle and his wife also become part of the entourage; this means the number of people involved has increased from a one-man affair to at least four people.

Another recent modification in the process is that after the preliminary visits of *koka moto*, the boy's family is now expected to write a follow up letter formally announcing their son's intention to marry into their family. On receipt of this letter, the girl's family responds by inviting the boy's family to their home to present the proposal in person. Normally the paternal uncle and his wife are charged with the responsibility of responding to this invitation. The purpose of this meeting is to make introductions and share family histories and genealogies of origin. This has the additional purpose of ensuring that the soon-to-wed couple do not belong to the same clan and therefore are not relatives. Following the meeting, the girl's family charge *malobolo,* communicated in the form of a formal letter to the boy's family. Traditionally this was done through a delegation of the girl's relatives going to the boy's home. This delegation would be instructed to camp outside the groom's home and remain there until all their demands had been met. They would camp for days outside, and only accept the invitation into the yard when everything they had requested was shown to *ndwana.*

## Bride-seeking (*Pala Nkadzi*)

The next stage in the marriage process after the preliminary visits is 'bride-seeking'. In traditional Ikalanga weddings it does not occur as separate from the preliminary visits described above. However, there are activities within it which correspond to what is distinctly the bride-seeking stage in other cultures. These activities are defined as *koka moto* and *pala nkadzi*. *Koka moto* means 'asking for a fire lighter' and *pala nkadzi* refers to 'scratching the ground to seek a bride'. They are led by the paternal uncle. Traditionally, once the uncle had completed the preliminary visits and both families had agreed to the proposed marriage, the bride's family would decide on the date and the members of a delegation to the groom's place to present their demand for *malobolo*. It is this delegation's role that has aspects of bride-seeking.

The delegation traditionally included a young man carrying a load of cow hides. At the entrance of the groom's yard or *nzi we bakwasha* the young man would not proceed into the yard, but would instead turn back and run away in mock unwillingness to surrender his load of hides to the groom's family. The groom's family would then stage a chase by a group of the young man's peers who were expected to outrun him and take the cow hides from him. This mock chase ritual was a symbolic way of signifying to the visitors that they were welcome guests and should harbour no anxieties, as exhibited by the boy's flight, about entering the homestead. The hides were to be softened and turned into a hide blanket or *debgwe,* whuch was meant to be given to the bride's grandmother.

When the bride's family entered the groom's yard, they were assigned a hut and a caretaker, *ndwana*, who would stay for the duration of their visit to make the entourage feel comfortable. They were served food and beverages in that hut while the host *ndwana* sat by the entrance to ensure that they were safe and secure from intruders. The bride's delegation was known as *bakalabgwa,* while the groom's relatives were known as *bakwasha.* A goat would be killed in their honour. This goat was termed *mbudzi ye tjilala pabi*, and signified that the groom's family had agreed to the *malobolo* as demanded by the bride's family. They were then taken to the kraal to inspect the *malobolo,* being one cow, one goat and one sheep. After the inspection, their mission ended, the visitors would leave, taking their daughter with them, but with the undertaking to return with her after two weeks for the marriage ceremony, *bukwe*. During the two weeks that the bride would spend with her family, she would be given counselling on marriage to ensure that she understood her future responsibilities and duties. One of the most important counsels was offered (*walila nlume*) by the aunt (*bammaadzi*), the bride-to-be's father's sister. It included advice on bedroom conduct, how to behave towards her husband, and what was expected of her by the groom's family, chores like cooking for everyone in the homestead, cleaning, and respect towards every relative, including children. The groom's family should be treated like kings by preparing water for them to bathe, and kneeling before them when receiving or handing over items. Also impressed upon her would be such expectations as her building her own dwelling hut, and diligently working on her fields, and so forth.

The groom would undergo similar counselling conducted by his uncles, during which he would be reminded of the essentials of Ikalanga manhood. A man in Ikalanga was defined by having a wife and children and his own homestead, *nzi'*. The homestead must have cattle and goats and the man must plough his field to feed his family. A rich man was defined by the number of cattle he owned. Rich men could marry as many wives as they wished because they could afford to feed them and their children.

Aspects of the bride-seeking practice described above have in recent years changed as the result of the adoption of Setswana culture and Western norms. In modern times, for example, Bakalanga still practice *patlo,* but it is done on the morning before the couple goes to the District Commissioner's offices to exchange vows and register the marriage. The addition of registration at the District Commissioner's office to the process is a modification of traditional practice.

## The 'dowry'/*Malobolo* (*Mangaba e n'ndobolo*)

Although the demanding and paying of *malobolo is* undertaken as part of bride-seeking, as described above, it is such a central issue in the process of marriage that it merits a separate discussion here. In traditional Bukalanga *malobolo* was just one cow. The cow was given to the girl's father. It was offered as a token of appreciation by the man's family to the girl's family for giving their daughter's hand to them in marriage. It was never regarded as the exchange of a woman for a cow. As time went on *malobolo* was increased to one cow, one goat and a sheep. These were presented to the girl's family in a ceremony called *bukwe,* together with traditional tobacco known as *dekwe*, and a cow hide blanket, *debgwe*, made from the hides previously brought by the bride's family during the visit that had demanded *malobolo.* A goat (*tjilala pabi/tjinyadza milomo*) would be slaughtered for the ceremony.

The bride-wealth or *malobolo* is known as *mangaba e n'ndobolo*. The distribution of the bride-wealth was as below.

(a) The cow for the bride's father (*ngombe ye danga/ya tate*).

(b) The goat for the paternal uncle (*batatenini*).

(c) The sheep for the aunt (*phwizi ya mmaadzi*).

(d) The hide blanket (*debgwe*) for the great grandmother.

(e) Traditional tobacco *dekwe* (*tjiyamwa tje fojo*) was brought for old men to smoke. These were dried tobacco leaves glued together into a bar.

It should be noted that all the beneficiaries here would be siblings, and were awarded a share of the *malobolo* in order of seniority by birth. As there would often not be enough items to go round, some of the younger siblings did not benefit. After the father, the next biggest beneficiary from *malobolo* would be the uncle who immediately followed the father by birth order, and would have performed the role of *dombo* in the marriage process. As *dombo* he would have been the chief negotiator or 'bearer of words' during marriage negotiations. If there was none, the role was played by a cousin of the father, i.e., the son of his uncle (*mwana wa batatenini*). Next to benefit after the uncle would be the aunt who was the eldest of the father's sisters. As with the uncle, the aunt benefited as a reward for the role she would have played in the marriage preparations. She would have provided counselling, *laya*, to the bride on her departure from her natal home, and when she arrived in her new family and helped her settle in. She would also have the customary role of providing counselling to the girls in the family when they got married. It was the aunt who knew the history of the family and its deep secrets. The sheep (*phwizi*) was considered the most humble domestic animal because even when slaughtered it didn't scream like a goat: it died silently. Like the sheep given to the aunt, the bride was expected to be humble and mute, to handle pain and suffering without making noise. It should be noted that girls were married as virgins, and as such it was the aunt, *mmaadzi* who would teach the bride sexual issues.

Men from poor families who could not afford a cow for *malobolo* had the option of giving a piece of land or a field for ploughing to their in-laws. The groom would de-bush such land for his in-laws, and plough it.

Over the years bride-wealth has significantly changed. When money was first introduced, what was called two and six (two shillings and six pence, 30 pence) was enough to pay *malobolo*. This amount was later increased to *pontho*, one pound, the equivalent of two Pula in those days. As years passed, the bride-wealth, *mangaba e n'ndobolo* in Ikalanga, has risen to almost unaffordable levels for poor families. The current practice is generally as follows:

**Cattle:** Nine head of cattle. The cattle can be replaced with money at current market prices. Currently this translates to P 2,500.00 per head. Brides' families who are not cattle farmers, and those who live in urban areas, prefer money rather than cattle as *malobolo*.

The cattle are distributed as follows:

(a) one cow for the bride's father;

(b) one cow for the bride's mother;

(c) three cows for the kraal;

(d) one cow for the uncle;

(e) one for the bride, known as *mamwa tshobgwi kene mamenyelo/mamusa*: this is a cow given to the bride on the day she finishes her bridal duties, known as *bulongo*;

(f) one for the eldest brother-in-law known as *nsebe*; and

(g) one to be slaughtered for the wedding celebration known as *phitsha bukwe*.

**Goats:** Eight goats. The goats are to be distributed as follows:

(a) three goats for the kraal;

(b) one goat for the uncle who negotiates marriage (*dombo*) known as *wotsha matsha*, literally meaning 'the one that fattens the bride seeker';

(c) one goat for the maternal uncle (*ye busekugwi*);

(d) one for the bride's great grandmother (*gulugulu*);

(e) one for the bride's grandfather; and

(f) one to be slaughtered on the wedding day known as *nsholo kene phaladza bakalabgwa.*

**Sheep:** One sheep. The sheep is reserved for the eldest paternal aunt (*bammaadzi/ mmaadzi*), who is rewarded for being a marriage counsellor.

**Tobacco:** Traditional tobacco bar (*dekwe*).

**Hides' blanket (*debgwe*):** One. The blanket is for the grandmother.

**Clothes for the bride's father**: These include a hat, jacket, suit, belt, tie, shoes and a walking stick (*lidozo*).

**Clothes for the bride's mother:** This is normally a full dress or a German print skirt including shoes, shawl and *doek.*

**Jacket:** for the elder brother-in-law.

**Clothes:** for the bride.

**Dress:** for the sister-in-law (*nkadzana*).

**Shawls and headgear:** (*doek*) for the two women who lead the wedding procession (*badwana*).

There is no doubt, from the bride-wealth presented above, that the marriage institution has become too expensive for many people. In addition to *malobolo*, there are wedding expenses, including rings, tent or venue hire, sound system, food, accommodation, transport, and more. These expenses incurred during weddings have become very considerable and often makes the whole exercise very stressful for the couple and their relatives. Those interviewed indicated that, in some cases, although not many, some couples abandon the exercise and do not proceed to be married. This suggests that it may be high time *malobolo* rates were regulated.

## WEDDING CEREMONY (*BUKWE*)

The determination of *malobolo* in Ikalanga marriage processes is followed by the wedding ceremony itself, known as *bukwe.* The payment of bride-wealth was not an essential ingredient of the validity of marriage as it could be delayed, paid in instalments or waived altogether. Traditionally, in Ikalanga, the wedding celebration happened a few weeks after the payment of the bride-wealth. It marked the day that the bride would be taken to her in-laws for ever, never to return to her parents except as a visitor. The celebration was held at the groom's place. A cow and a goat were slaughtered for this ceremony. There would be traditional beer, singing and dancing. There was no festive dress code or musical instruments played for the occasion, except the drum, or *dumba*.

The ceremony was attended by all close relatives and ordinary villagers who would bring gifts of sorghum and maize grains in woven baskets. These gifts were to ensure that the newly-weds had enough food before they started ploughing their own field.

The bride's family would bring with them much firewood and finely ground sorghum flour known as *shogwana*, symbolising that their daughter was pure. Firewood was in bundles called *sunga le wuni* carried by all women in the entourage, walking in a single file. The quantities of the firewood were measured by the space they took in a special storage built with poles for this purpose, known as *dala*.

The cow and goat that were slaughtered for the wedding ceremony were known as *phitsha bukwe,* and *phaladza bakalabgwa/nsholo,* respectively, and prepared especially for the in-laws before their departure after the wedding. Handling of meat portions from this slaughtered cow was known as *miteho ye nyama ye ngombe ye bukwe*. The meat was handled and divided as follows:

(a) *omasum* (*tjamphutu*), an organ that filters the food and water, was cooked and eaten by the aunts who lead the wedding procession (*badwana*) for their role;

(b) the right front leg (*bhandaboko le leji*) was given to the in-laws;

(c) the left front leg (*bhandabuko le lemeshwe*) was reserved for the bride;

(d) the tripe (*gulu*) was divided in half and given to the respective mothers of the bride and groom, symbolising that mothers carried the couple in their womb for nine months; and

(e) the rump (*kamba*) was halved and given to the mothers as well rewarding them for having carried the couple on their backs at infancy stage.

The bride's relatives would be given a sledge (*tjileyi*) to transport the meat to their village. This would be formally presented before the bride's parents.

The practice has changed in recent times. In modern times, after the bride-wealth has been paid, the couple officially seal their wedding at the District Commissioner's office where the notice to get married is advertised or gazetted for 21 days. The District Commissioner (or the appointed officer) presides over all weddings and does some counselling. Where the couple belongs to a religious denomination, a priest presides over the marriage and issues a marriage certificate. After this process, a wedding celebration is held the following weekend.

The wedding ceremony is termed 'a white wedding', symbolised by the bride's wedding dress which is normally white. The wedding is held in two sessions; the first leg is at the bride's home and the second and final leg is at the groom's home the day the bride is taken to her in-laws. The celebrations are preceded by traditional rites such as bringing of firewood and sorghum grains (*shogwana*). The dress code here is normally traditional 'German print'. Once the traditional rites are over, the wedding procession will change the dress code to Western-style suits for the groom and his party. This party consists of the best man and a team of five friends. The bride also will have her team consisting of a matron of honour and five friends who would also be dressed in Western-style gowns. The procession is led by a matron of honour and two children, a girl and a boy. The bride and groom lead the party in singing and dancing. Usually, the dance steps of various songs would have been rehearsed for three to five months before the big day. The matron of honour leads the procession into a very big tent that accommodates hundreds of people. After everybody has taken their seats speeches follow, starting with the introductions of the two families and words of encouragement to the couple. After the speeches there is lunch for everyone, followed by a photo session at nearby places of interest. The celebrations continue till late in the evening. In some instances, there is a reception party for friends only which continues until the following morning.

Various dishes are served during the wedding day. Pounded meat (*iswayi/seswaa*) from the slaughtered cow and goat are served with traditional foods such as *thopi, tjimoni,* and *shadza.* Rice and samp also form part of the dishes served.

Today's weddings are glamorous events. A budget of up to P100,000 or more is required to put together all the logistics needed. If we add up the bride-wealth and the wedding day ceremony the budget could easily come close to P200,000. Some weddings actually exceed this budget by hiring expensive venues like five-star hotels, limousines as transport for the day, and renowned bands or artists to perform during the celebration.

## MARRIAGE COUNSELLING (*LAYA*)

In former times, the counselling of the bride and the bridegroom was done by their respective families. The counselling role was the responsibility of the uncles of the groom and the aunts of the bride. This was critical because both the boy and the girl would be meeting for the first time as husband and wife, and would never have been intimate. The aunts were required to take the bride through lessons in sex and sexuality. They also ensured that she was made aware of what chores would be expected of her in her new home. These would include fetching firewood, waking up early to clean the yard, drawing water and cooking various dishes. She would be taught how to behave before the elders, how to serve them food and what clothing would be appropriate for her to wear. This counselling was critical because once the wedding ceremony was over and the girl was handed over to her in-laws, there would be no second chance to get these lessons – she would not return to her own family except as a visitor. She would find herself amongst total strangers. To ease the stress of the experience it was also critical that the bride was accompanied by her sister, *nkadzana*, to help her acclimatise. *Nkadzana* would stay with her for at least two months, helping her to settle into her new home. Acclimatising to an environment of total strangers, who included her husband himself, was the most challenging issue with arranged/forced marriages. It was like torture for the young woman. It is this process that led to the *nkadzanas* ending up being married to their sister's husbands as second wives. Sometimes it was the bride who would decide that her sister stayed with her for good, especially where the in-laws were very hostile and unapproachable.

There have been a few changes to this process. In a modern marriage counselling is done initially by the District Commissioner of the district where the marriage is registered, and often done in group sessions, for many couples at a time, up to the day of the registration of the marriages. Further counselling is provided on the evening of the wedding ceremony by the uncles and aunts from both families. Counselling by relatives has significantly declined as it is increasingly left up to public officers. While Bakalanga elders are not happy about this, they have little control over the process. Among their complaints is that brides no longer perform *bulongo* or bridal duties as was culturally expected. There have been a lot of disappointments from today's married couples according to the elderly people, especially in the way they conduct themselves. The law allows anyone to marry any person of their choice, even if parents do not approve, as long as the two are consenting adults. In some instances, parents are not even aware of the marriages because the couple can get the required witnesses from among their friends, especially in cities.

### Transfer of bride to her in-laws

In the traditional set-up an Ikalanga bride was transferred to her in-laws on the day of the wedding ceremony itself. As discussed elsewhere in this chapter, her transfer took place after the bride-wealth had been paid in full. Adequate counselling was provided during the process of bride-seeking, so that when the day of celebration and of her transfer finally arrived, the girl would be ready for married life. The final transfer event was conducted by relatives who accompanied the bride to her new home. On their departure, after handing over the bride, they left behind her uncle's wife, *ndwana* and her little sister, *nkadzana,* to remain with her for some time. This was done to help the young bride settle down during the first few days of her stay at her new home. *Ndwana* would also take her leave after a few days, leaving only *nkadzana* behind to support the bride. *Nkadzana* would return only when it was felt her sister had settled in comfortably after a few months.

This practice of transferring the bride to her new home is no longer observed in the manner described above. Instead, what happens nowadays is that after the wedding celebrations, the matron of honour or an aunt and the bride's little sister remain to help her clean the yard the morning after and then leave. The traditional one month that the *ndwana* and *nkadzana* spent with the bride at her new home, and carried out related support activities, is no longer observed.

### Bride taken to her natal home

This practice used to be performed only under *nkumbo,* or marriage through abduction/stealing during the night. Under this practice the bride was taken back to her parental home for counselling purposes. She was accompanied by the groom's aunt and other relatives who took with them a live cow to be presented to the in-laws. This cow, known as *phelesi,* was a token of the boy's commitment to the proposed marriage on the part of his family. The entourage would all return on the same day and leave the girl with her parents. There was no ceremony on this occasion. The girl would be given thorough counselling for at least two weeks after which she would return to her in-laws with the delegation of her family when they went to demand *malobolo*.

In traditional Ikalanga culture it was only rarely that, once handed over to her in-laws, a Kalanga bride would return to visit her natal home. It was only in events of death or a wedding ceremony among her siblings that exceptions were made. Generally, frequent visits were not permitted.

### Bridal chores (*Bulongo*)

This was a special period in Ikalanga traditional marriages during which a new bride was given a chance to prove herself before her in-laws. It lasted for a month. It follows the old Ikalanga adage that says '*nkadzi maboko*', meaning that the beauty of a woman is in her hands. This is the reason why fathers would want their sons to marry from hard working families, whose work ethic was unquestionable. During the month of performing prescribed bridal chores the bride was expected to demonstrate, without question, that she is a hard worker. During this month the new bride was referred to as *nlongo*, and the month/period referred to as *bulongo*. During this period, she was bestowed with a special cloth to wear across her body known as *mpakatilo*. The wearing of this cloth was known as *pakatila* and it was worn so that she could be distinguished from the other women in the compound and in the village as a new bride. Villagers would greet her with dignity and respect, and some would give her presents.

Her chores were many and included the following: waking up in the early morning (*kuli mawumwe*) to sweep the yard, fetching water and firewood, preparing bathing water for everyone in the yard, cooking and pounding sorghum in order to grind it into flour or to separate the grain from the chaff.

## The Impact of Change on Traditional Ikalanga Marriage Rites and Activities

Traditional Ikalanga marriage customs and practices have changed significantly over the years. Many of the original traditions of the culture have long been buried and replaced by new ones adopted from other cultures, often against the wishes of traditional leaders and the elders who are the custodians of the culture.

The elderly Bakalanga populace is unhappy about these new developments. They dislike the fact that they find themselves with no say or role to play in choosing their daughters-in-law, neither are they happy that the practices of bridal and groom chores are no longer observed. Similarly regretted is the fact that the discipline expected from married people, such as special greetings to the in-laws, dress code, cooking etc., is no longer observed. They rue the fact that in-laws no longer enjoy the benefits that come with having a daughter/son-in-law. Other sources of disgruntlement with changes in modern marriages include the fact that marriage counselling is nowadays done by public officers and the church, leaving relatives traditionally responsible for this duty, with no role to play except as mere spectators. Moreover, modern counselling is regarded as irrelevant and culturally unsuitable for Ikalanga people since it does not focus on matters that are important to traditional family values. Public officer, and modern counselling in general, tend to encourage, among others, gender equality, believed by Bakalanga to be the source of marriage instability and break-ups today. A daughter-in-law used to belong to the family, and when the husband passed on she wed his brother. Nowadays this would be unacceptable, because going against the whims and wishes of a woman is contrary to human rights. The traditionalists still have to accept that no longer should anyone be married against their will.

The elders see these changes as unwarranted government interference in private family issues. They feel that government has taken over their roles by involving itself in the marriages of their children. This interference, they argue, has led to many divorce cases and lack of discipline in today's marriages in general. They blame the decline in successful marriages on this interference. In former times there was a high premium on people remaining virgins until they got married, which helped prevent extra-marital relationships and promiscuity. The emphasis on virginity before marriage was also beneficial, it is argued, inasmuch as it meant that the newly-weds negotiated the learning curve of married life from scratch together. They grew up together, learning parenthood and other aspects of being a family from their parents like doves in a nest. Their union was true to the vow 'until death do us part'.

It is argued further that today wedding ceremonies have become too expensive for many people to afford. The huge budgets involved in the ceremonies have led to much-stress among the newly-weds right from the beginning of wedding ceremony preparations. This also means that after the wedding celebrations couples start their life in debt. Some fail to recover from the debt and this has led to breakdowns and collapse of marriages within a short span. Current marriages and relationships seem to thrive on economic status, and once the financials are in jeopardy the couple's relationship also breaks down irreparably. Marriage is no longer the life-long relationship that it used to be.

Another aspect of modern marriages, observed with a sense of dismay among the traditionalists, is that in their view men have become weak and are controlled by their wives. The traditional roles of men and women in marriage have been reversed. Men now cook and babysit, which in traditional Ikalanga culture was taboo. Education, gender equality and urbanization are blamed for weakening the marriage institution.

Overall, the adoption of new marriage customs and practices from other cultures has had a negative impact on attempts to observe traditional Ikalanga marriage rites and rituals, as well as on efforts to uphold Ikalanga traditional family values and marital expectations. The traditional leaders have put across the view that if they had the power they would demand a reduced government role in marriages, and a regulation to standardise the financial cost of *malobolo* throughout the country. The government is blamed for bringing marriage into disrepute by turning it into a 'big business' institution with the result that it is plagued by instability. The charge for the bride-wealth is now unlimited. It is even worse when a bride is a graduate: her parents can charge more money or cattle, above what is considered 'normal'. They go further and ask for a glamorous and luxurious white wedding ceremony.

As this chapter demonstrates, the changes in traditional Ikalanga marriage customs and practices have had profound economic and social implications.

# 3

# BAKGATLA

*From Wedding Bells to Marital Death Knell?*
*Evolution and Survival of Marriage among Bakgatla*

*Christian John Makgala & Montle Siya*
(University of Botswana)

*Sedibelo-mollo sea fsa sea tshologa,*
*Sere se fsa metse ya falala,*
*Metse e bile ya tshaba diputlela;*
*Morula o kutu-kgolo, Bakgatla,*
*Bana ba sefatana sa Moruleng,*
*Barwa-mpya e jele mpyanyana ya yona,*
*Dithata tsa ga Molefe a Masilo,*
*Tse di jeleng Mokgoro di o lala.*

## INTRODUCTION

This chapter discusses the evolution of marriage and marital beliefs and rituals or rites among Bakgatla-ba-Kgafela in Botswana, whose totem is the monkey (*kgabo*) also accompanied by flame (*kgabo ya mollo*), from the pre-colonial and pre-Christian era through the colonial period, post-independence era to the new millennium and the twenty-first century. The major observation is that as part of the culture of the Bakgatla, as is the case among Batswana, Africans and humanity in general, marriage has undergone evolutionary and lately radical change owing to fusion resulting from interaction with other peoples, Christianity, colonialism and the forces of globalization. This radical change can best be headlined, 'From Wedding Bells to Marital Death Knell? Evolution and Survival of Marriage among Bakgatla'.

It should be noted that Bakgatla are not a homogenous entity, but have always consisted of other groups, incorporated over generations as a result of conquest, arriving refugees, and inter-ethnic marriage. These new additions brought with them their own marriage practices, rituals, ceremonies and terminology. Therefore, while there is broad similarity in most of these aspects, there were some local variations between different Bakgatla communities, however minor or inconsequential. It is also necessary to indicate that before moving into what became Botswana from the Boer Republic of the Transvaal (in present day South Africa) in the early 1870s, the *dikgoro/dikgotla* (wards) of Bakgatla were distinct villages physically separate from one another. However, in Botswana these were right next to one another, mostly without clear separation, possibly for security reasons.

In the past 20 years or so, as the country's capital and commercial hub, Gaborone, grew rapidly, more and more people who could not find accommodation and residential plots in Gaborone, migrated to the city's peri-urban areas, among which were villages in the Kgatleng District. In this way they were able to infuse their different cultural practices regarding rituals of marriage into the mainstream Sekgatla practices. Nevertheless, these were minor and almost insignificant in most cases. Furthermore, some Bakgatla also travelled or worked in other parts of the country and elsewhere, married into different groups, and learned, as well as adopted, those groups' marital rites or nuptials, which were appealing, if not deemed more practical. It should be noted that whereas there are standard and elaborate Sekgatla marital rites, like other people's cultural practices, these were not static but dynamic, with some aspects ignored or altered if they were found cumbersome or out of sync with modern times.

This chapter starts with a discussion of traditional or pre-colonial and pre-Christian marriage rites among Bakgatla, specifically looking at the processes of *go-kokota* (preliminary visits), *patlo* (bride-seeking), the significance of *bogadi* (bride-gift) and the wedding festivities. This is followed by detailed discussion of the revolutionary changes brought about by Christianity. Contact with Christianity, British colonial rule, general European material culture and Western education in the second half of the nineteenth century significantly altered the marriage rites and rituals of the Bakgatla.

They first had contact with Christianity via the Dutch Reformed Church in the 1860s, while still in Moruleng, in South Africa. However, early contact with Christianity does not seem to have had much impact on Sekgatla rituals, among which was marriage, until 1892 when Kgosi Linchwe I of Bakgatla-ba-Kgafela adopted Christianity at his capital, Mochudi (Makgala, 2009). In a way marriage among Bakgatla became 'modernised'. For instance, the Dutch Reformed Church convinced Linchwe to discard robust *bogwera* and *bojale* initiation rites for boys and girls respectively, leaving a significantly watered-down version. This also saw parental stewardship of the marriage process largely weakened. Polygamy also faced ruthless vilification from the church, forcing even Linchwe himself to relinquish some of his wives, remaining with only one.

The focus then shifts to innovation brought about by an increasingly consumeristic society following Botswana's attainment of independence in 1966 and subsequent economic transformation of the country, largely as a result of diamond wealth. It is demonstrated here how the innovations, which brings witht hem many socio-economic challenges, are a result of greater forces of globalization and aggressive marketing by the wedding industry. These challenges, which include the controversial claim of alleged over-commercialization of *bogadi*, have given rise to the phenomenon of cohabitation and its related challenges. Some concerned and enterprising Bakgatla responded to the challenges by coming up with the Re A Nyalana ('We Are Marrying') initiative that helped marry couples without the usual needed resources. The Re A Nyalana initiative has even been embraced by the government of Botswana through involvement of the relevant ministry, local tribal or village authorities and the district council, and has since spread throughout the country (e.g., see Letshoo, 13 April 2015).

## Methodology

Information for the chapter was obtained from secondary sources, and oral interviews with elders, including *dikgosi* (traditional leaders), in Kgatleng District. The Covid-19 pandemic, however, severely compromised the field research in the second quarter of 2020. Following the easing of movement from the Covid-19 lockdown, we were able to attend a few *patlo* meetings in the village of Morwa in Kgatleng. Sometimes there were differing views on how to proceed in terms of protocol or practice. In some instances, much younger attendants at the meetings reminded elders of the proper sequence of events. This was something observed even in meetings held a few years earlier. The cause of the confusion seems to be the fact that there was no written manual to follow, something one elder once raised. Moreover, in few instances it looked as if some people were prepared to resort to short cuts in order to cut costs and save time. However, generally, where proper procedure was pointed out, it was duly agreed upon to be followed.

Perhaps it should be noted that in Sekgatla the term *lenyalo* is used both for the wedding ceremony and marriage. However, sometimes *mokete-wa-lenyalo* (wedding ceremony) may be used to refer to a wedding ceremony, but this is rare. We do not provide a separate section on Bakgatla marriage rituals and metaphors, but point these out in the processes discussed below. The title 'From Wedding Bells to Marital Death Knell' signifies the undertaking of marriage among the Bakgatla as a desirable institution, whose sanctity was upheld over the generations, followed by its perceived existential threats in the twenty-first century.

## Evolution of Marriage Processes among Bakgatla

Marriage was important to Bakgatla and other groups for purposes of procreation, household labour, social networking, as well as population growth of a tribal polity. Marriage was so important that the responsibilities of a married man were taught to young men during *bogwera* (initiation ceremonies or schools). Girls were taught how to care for their families and husbands, at their own version of initiation school, *bojale*. It was only after one had graduated from these institutions that they could be allowed to marry. Marriage brought respect and honour to a married union.

A married man had legal claim to his children, whereas the woman's people exercised claim on the children if she was not married. An adult person who remained unmarried was called *lefetwa* (one who has been passed-by), which has derogatory connotations. Marriage also brought together families into social networks, critical for economic production in agrarian communities. Just as with most other socio-economic undertakings, marriage was also linked to Sekgatla religious beliefs, which included worship of ancestral spirits. Belief in witchcraft and its perceived evil particularly shaped how people or families related, and marriage was no exception.

Generally, from ancient times young men stayed for prolonged periods at *meraka*, cattle posts, with very limited access to females. A boy did not choose his own partner to marry. It was a duty undertaken by his parents without even consulting him or seeking his consent. It was also uncommon for a male to reject a wife identified for him by his parents. In case of rejection of a girl so identified, the parents could get the support of a *kgosi* (chief). Polygamy was a common practice among Bakgatla, before most of them embraced Christianity. Whereas other Batswana groups called the practice *lefufa,* Bakgatla called it *go nyala mosadi wa bobedi, boraro,* etc. ('marrying a second, third wife, etc'). A man could have two or more wives, depending on his economic status, and ability to support them.

However, the practice of having one's wife imposed on him by his parents was limited to the first wife, as he was free to choose subsequent ones himself. In most cases the first wife had to be consulted and her consent attained. In former times the societal expectation was that the first wife would agree to her husband's request, even if she did not like it. This could be the reason why in some Batswana communities polygamy is called *lefufa* (jealousy) because in most cases the next wife would be younger, and became the husband's favourite. It was not uncommon for girls to be betrothed when they were still toddlers or earmarked for marriage partners, even before birth. Bakgatla called betrothal *peeletso,* and this left the girl so pledged with no choice. Mutual love or affection was not a factor in ancient marriage. In rare instances where a boy and girl fell in love by themselves and insisted on it, they had no choice but to flee (elope) into exile. Penalties for such 'unbecoming' behaviour were severe, if they got caught.

After identifying a girl, the parents of a boy first discussed the possibility of marriage amongst themselves. Having reached an agreement, they would then consult the boy's *malome* (maternal uncle), together with his wife *mmamalome.* The *malome's* involvement was critical, and his advice decisive in most instances, hence being *malome* was a position of immense power, as well as influence. It was only after the uncle and his wife had endorsed the proposal that other relatives would be consulted to rubber stamp it. This consultation was called *morero wa lenyalo.* The girl's background was taken into account.including her attitude, work ethic and humility – being desired attributes. Traditionally, those attributes alone amounted to beauty, which generations later, particularly in the twentieth century, translated into good looks or attractive physical appearance. The social standing of the girl's parents also mattered greatly, and alleged association with witchcraft on their part was a ruinous disadvantage. In most cases, the girl's family also looked for a family that commanded some wealth, and a respectable status in the community.

A preferred wife was a daughter of a close relative or someone in the neighbourhood, with whom the boy's parents were already familiar, in terms of required attributes. Marriage between *motswalo* or *motswalaka* (cross-cousins) was desired. The justification for this was a belief that such marriage would stand the test of time, because of the family connections, and familiarity with each of the people involved. It also had an economic aspect in that the cattle given for *bogadi* would rotate among close relatives instead of getting into the hands of non-relatives. This scenario even gave rise to a popular saying and song '*Ngwana wa malome nnyale dikgomo di boele sakeng*' ('My uncle's son marry me for the cattle to return to our kraal/possession'). Child betrothals were common with these kinds of close-kin arranged marriages. Cousin marriages ranked quite high in polygamous arrangements. Isaac Schapera (1940:42) writes that, "If a man, who already had several wives subsequently married his maternal uncle's daughter, she would rank higher than the others in status, and her eldest son would become his principal heir". Nevertheless, it was common for men to marry non-relatives, mostly in the same village. Senior royals were the ones who sometimes married outside their villages into a different *morafe* (tribe or ethnic group) to create and cultivate strategic socio-political ties. Generally, the cardinal objective of arranged marriage among Bakgatla was to achieve affability and stability. There was no freedom of choice for those immediately concerned, namely the boy and girl or husband and wife to be.

Since boys spent a great deal of their time at *moraka* they had fewer chances of meeting with girls. However, there were occasions whereby girls could also go to *moraka* or they could meet boys in the village or *masimo* (ploughing fields). If a girl fell pregnant, the boy responsible was punished harshly. The boy was forced to marry her or make payment of cattle, called *marebana*, for infringing on her virginity (*go mo diga lebele*). They were subjected to humiliating ridicule and the boy was treated especially badly during the initiation into a *mophato* (initiation regiment).

Once a suitable girl had been identified, there would follow a formal process of *go kokota* (preliminary or exploratory visits). Intermediaries of close relatives were the ones who would undertake the process of *go kokota* and the boy was never part of the process. Usually, these would be *malome* (uncles) from the mother's side, accompanied by a close relative who would act as a witness. These were sent by the boy's parents to the identified girl's father's home to seek and plead for *sego-sa-metsi* ('water gourd', her hand in marriage). The metaphor *sego-sa-metsi* implies the role the girl being sought would play in the boy's household after getting married. Although she would specifically provide her mother and father-in-law with drinking water, there were many other domestic chores she undertook. The *malome* leading the process has to be a married man, and in his absence a close relative was assigned the responsibility. The meeting was mostly held in the family *kgotla* (courtyard), where men discussed issues or held court, outside the *lapa* (compound), which was a sphere for women. A customary response from a girl's father was a non-committal one, based on the need for him to engage other relatives. Upon the departure of the party the father consulted his wife, after which her *bomalome* (girl's maternal uncles) would be involved.

Whereas it may take much longer to involve the boy, sometimes until after the *go kokota* process was complete, the girl's parents may enquire from her if she knew the boy in question, and whether she would be predisposed to having him as her husband. If the girl did not show interest in the boy, the boy's party was informed of the 'unfortunate news' during their next meeting at the girl's home. Nonetheless, this did not necessarily mean that the boy's parents would throw in the towel. The boy's father could still push his luck by asking the party to make another attempt, usually punctuated by prolonged intervals – spanning several months, as customary decorum required. In the meantime, the girl's parents also 'researched' the boy and his family as potential in-laws, if they were not already familiar with them. However, in most cases, since the villages were fairly small during ancient times, chances were that they already had an idea about the boy's family. Patience was one attribute or virtue the families, particularly the boy's, had in abundance during those days, and it mostly paid dividends. At any rate, there was no guarantee for success, and once it dawned on the boy's people that they were only wasting their time, the father would look elsewhere for a wife for his son.

Freedom of choice and courtship would become quite common as the twentieth century wore on, particularly by the second quarter of the century. It became common for a son to participate quite actively in the initial discussions among family elders, and his personal choice of a wife could not be downplayed or ignored. In most cases the girl being considered would have been approached by the boy himself, after which he would seek his parent's facilitation of negotiations for marriage. Increasingly, the girl's parents also involved her, and her feelings for the boy were ascertained. If she was not interested in marrying the boy, that had to be taken into account, and negotiations could be ended.

Another aspect of Sekgatla marriage, which fell by the wayside as time went by, was the betrothal process, *peeletso*. Western moral standards and prejudice played a devastating role in some of these changes. In addition to marriage practices according to Sekgatla tribal law, couples could also get married through European civil law.

The emergence of brick and mortar schools also led to boys and girls meeting and mixing freely, which gave them freedom to choose their mates. Another factor was migrant labour to South Africa, which enabled young Bakgatla to break away from tribal and parental control, and marry those they loved and had chosen for themselves. The desire and pursuit of freedom of choice was entrenched in the saying '*Pelo e ja serati sebatlelwa ga e se batle*' ('The heart eats what it desires, but rejects what is sought for it'. Generally, doing things the European way was a matter of social prestige and admiration, which also aroused envy.

Perceived physical beauty and mutual attraction were some of the determining factors in a boy loving and choosing a girl or courting for marriage. Schapera, writing in 1940 observes that "...physical charm is, however, in itself not always sufficient. The Kgatla youth prefer sexually attractive girls for his mistresses, but demands additional qualities in his future wife. Like his parents in the old days, he pays considerable attention to a girl's behaviour and character. He notes if she is cleanly in her person and keeps her hut neat and tidy; if she is industrious or lazy, quiet or garrulous, good-tempered or quarrelsome" (Schapera, 1940:48). In the past, having a child before marriage was quite rare, and in case it happened it significantly reduced the chances of the girl getting married. It was a disadvantage as the potential suitor suspected that the girl could still carry on with the father of the child clandestinely. At any rate, there were other instances whereby girls with children still got married. For their part, prospective wives also looked for clean, urbane, hardworking boys, and usually from a wealthy background or a prominent family. A 'village celebrity' of sorts also brought an element of pride on the part of a girl. In most cases a boy with some education preferred a girl with similar or a respectable level of education. In most cases even parents endorsed such an approach for their son or daughter. The belief was that it was difficult to sustain a 'sophisticated' conversation with a wife or husband who did not go far with education, let alone one who was illiterate.

The freedom of choice for a wife saw some overzealous boys resorting to improvization called *moratiso*. This was love potion made from ingredients such as parts of birds and plant leaves mixed together, and secretly smeared on the desired girl to make her pliant. It was also not uncommon, but rare, for girls to make the first move – sometimes. If she was interested in a boy, who seemed not to notice her, she would try ways of making him pay attention to her. Sometimes, the girl would suggestively laugh before the boy in a bid to attract his attention. This tell-tale or suggestive laughter was called '*ke kwano*' ('here I am') and usually a girl could be stigmatised for it as being too upfront. Boys were the ones expected to approach girls, and not the other way round. In more serious scenarios, a girl could resort to her own version of *moratiso* if she desired a boy to marry her. However, for 'reliability' *moratiso* could also be obtained from a *ngaka* (traditional doctor), either by a boy or a girl, including church-goers, sometimes with the help or insistence of their parents.

Despite this 'newfound' freedom enjoyed by the youth, parents could still disapprove of a boy's or girl's choice if they felt he or she was undesirable for one reason or the other. In most cases, this was common regarding strangers from outside the *morafe*. Nevertheless, with more and more people travelling to other *merafe* within Botswana and South Africa for employment as well as studies, marriages involving outsiders also increased in number. The result was that in most cases, parents had no choice but to accept marriages between their sons or daughters' choice of a *motswakwa* (foreigner). The church also introduced a rule that children of church-going parents marry fellow church-goers, which parents naturally endorsed. However, by the mid-twentieth century the church was reported to have relaxed the rule of marriage within the church system.

Despite the changes brought about by the church and education, which led to personal choice becoming a key factor towards marriage, cases still existed of arranged or even forced marriages. For instance, if a boy impregnated a girl, the parents could insist that he married her or pay *marebana* and sometimes he could also be flogged for this serious transgression. Sometimes when a boy tells his parents of his intention or desire to marry, but they feel that he is not ready or not fit to marry, they deride him saying, '*ga o utlwa bothitho ba dikobo o setse o re wa nyala*' ('the allure of sex make you think of marrying'). However, modern parents do not appreciate cross-cousin marriages out of fear of the consequences of inbreeding, such as physical and cognitive defects, among other reasons.

## *PATLO* (BRIDE-SEEKING ) AND INNOVATION

If there were indications that something positive was afoot, the intermediaries would keep coming until they were assigned a day on which they had to come for a response. All along, the exploratory party would have been meeting the girl's father on his own, but upon arrival of a stipulated date, they were likely to find him in the company of his wife, and other relatives, the most critical of whom were *bomalome* (uncles). By now *go kokota* would have transformed into *patlo*. At this stage the party, which by now is called *ditlhogo* (heads of delegation) and included women *bommamalome* (maternal aunts), would be told the good news along the lines that, 'Here is the girl, you take her alive and if in the future you are tired of her please return her alive'. In Setswana or Sekgatla rendition, they would be told, '*Ke yo monyana, le mo tsaya a tshela mme ga le sa tlhola le mmatla le mmuse a tshela*'. In this way the girl would be formally engaged according to Sekgatla tribal law and custom. The involvement of women was also meant to confirm the engagement, and also express gratitude to the girl for agreeing to marry their son. The presence of women, who were adept at *moduduetso/mogolokwane* (ululation), may also have been involved in performing that celebratory rite – ululation – in order to signify sealing the deal.

However, the sealing of the *patlo* would continue for a few days, when the delegation of women returned to the girl's place to present her with gifts, sometimes called *matlisiwa*. In olden days, these consisted of *diaparo-tsa-matlalo* (skin clothes), *dibaga/ditalama* (beads) among other articles of adornment, and were presented to the girl's mother in the presence of some witnesses who invariably were relatives. Later the girl would be summoned to witness her *matlisiwa*, referred to as 'her debt' by her mother. The implication of this metaphor was that she was now legally bonded to the boy and his family, and that this demanded her good behaviour. This then made her *ngwetsi* (daughter-in-law) to the boy's people. The custom was that the girl had to take a few weeks before using her presents, otherwise the accusation that she was in a rush to get married would be levelled against her. As indicated earlier, modesty was a key attribute demanded of a potential bride or wife.

All along the boy would be unaware of the developments as he would be far away at *moraka* tending livestock. After the sealing of the *patlo* the boy would be brought home from *moraka,* and one evening his *malome* would take him to the girl's home for introduction to her parents as their *mokgwenyana* (son-in-law). Alongside his *malome,* the boy would be entertained and advised that the girl's home was also his, and that he should never hesitate to visit whenever he was hungry or in need of rest. The *patlo* process was concluded when the girl's parents brewed *bojalwa* (sorghum beer) for the boy's people to come and celebrate with them. This beer-drinking ceremony was called *setlhako* (the sandal), a metaphor reflecting the numerous trips the boy's people would have made to the girl's homestead. This was also an occasion for introductions by relatives from both sides to acquaint themselves with one another, and join hands in future household endeavours as in-laws. Bakgatla have a saying that *mosadi ke wa setlhako*, meaning that a real or respected wife was the one sought through the elaborate *patlo* process.

In most cases the boy would be absent at such merrymaking, and so were his mother and father, who would sometimes be called to attend their own separate and exclusive event the following evening. Attendance was strictly limited to his mother and father, as it was said that 'procreation was an act of two people only'. Schapera says that this special event was called, 'what one lies waiting for', but we have not been able to find its Sekgatla name from informants in 2020, some 80 years after Schapera wrote on the subject. Nonetheless, he says, "It refers to the time when a woman lies on her back waiting for her husband to sleep with her, or for her child to be born; the boy's parents must therefore realise that when the girl herself was conceived and born, her mother sweated and suffered, and so cannot now part lightly with her" (Schapera, 1940:63).

Much of the process outlined above concerning *patlo* has continued among Bakgatla, but been modified in some respects, due to the influence of Christianity and colonial laws. As indicated above, the major difference was freedom of choice of a mate by a boy, sometimes with the girl and even her parents playing the role of prompting 'by all means necessary'. *Patlo* was essential even where the couple disregarded their parents' disapproval, because it was a requirement in tribal law and custom. Although some couples found ways of circumventing the traditional protocol by fleeing the tribal territory, the belief was that defiance of one's parents could lead to serious difficulties or even misfortune in a marriage or one's personal life. Moreover, after defying parental counsel it would be hard for the couple to approach them for intervention. The guiding adage that '*ngwana yo sa utlweng molao wa batsadi o utlwa wa manong*' ('a child who disregards parental law/guidance accepts that of vultures or birds of prey') could be repeated to them in order to deride their folly. In some extreme cases parents totally disowned the recalcitrant couple, and their defiance was believed to lead to *dikgaba* or *sefifi* (curse) owing to the shame and excessive displeasure felt by the parents.

Whereas in cases whereby families involved in *patlo* were fairly close, the long process could be reduced significantly; but there were also instances where it was followed to the letter. It should be noted that sometimes shortening the *patlo* procedure also gave the impression of both a compromised marriage and respectability. It became common for the boy's parents to enquire from him about the girl as well as the likelihood of success for *patlo*. Once it was ascertained that the prospects were promising, the process of assembling a deputation would start and the girl's parents approached as already outlined above. In cases where the 'bride-seekers' were non-Bakgatla from outside the district, they would be assigned a respected local married man and woman, a party called *rraditsela* and *mmaditsele,* respectively, to guide them on Sekgatla procedure.

There was an innovation where sometimes the party was told to be preceded by women, whom in most cases would be *borakgadi* (paternal aunts) or a close relative, accompanied by another lady to meet with the girl's mother. In most cases the female delegates arrived soon after the request had been issued, and they reiterated the request previously made by men in seeking *sego-sa-metsi*. This call could be done about twice or thrice; but if things had come to this stage, it was a good sign, and the ladies would then be advised that the next deputation, on a stated day, should include male representatives, who consisted of the boy's other relatives. The involvement of women was also to demonstrate that the girl was not being taken to the male-dominated *kgotla* but to the *lapa,* the women's domain.

Another innovation was that in occasional cases whereby the girl's father was no longer alive, women were assigned the role of 'seekers' to approach the mother directly from early on in the *patlo* process. With the introduction of Western material culture, towards the end of the process women brought *matlisiwa* that generally consisted, a £1 note, a white blanket with red stripes, a red shawl, a handkerchief, and two lengths of dress material, costing in all between £3 to £4 (Schapera, 1940:62). These monetary gifts demonstrate the encroachment of Western monetary economy. Immediately after the *patlo* started, the boy's parents would bring the *matlisiwa.* With Bakgatla increasingly involved in migrant labour to South Africa, the boy could also go there and purchase goods for *matlisiwa* with his earnings. The completion of the *patlo* would follow the old procedure, but in a modified form, depending on prevailing circumstances.

A significant innovation resulting from Western influence was the introduction of the wedding ring called *mfitshana* or *lepetu* among Bakgatla, and worn on the ring finger of the left hand. However, the term *lepetu* seems unknown among modern Bakgatla, while *mfitshana* appears archaic and rarely used. According to Victoria Segami and Chrizanne Van Eeden, 'The wedding ring is a conjugal symbol of the couple's commitment to one another and to their unity in marriage. Ancient Western cultures consider the ring as a symbol of the sun, earth, and universe. It represents holiness, perfection, and peace' (Segami and Van Eeden, 2020:37). They further observe that 'a wedding ring is a symbol of a person's love and commitment to their spouse. It is a married person's declaration to the world that one is in a committed relationship and is devoted to one's spouse or partner. The ring is still used as a declaration to the world that the couple is betrothed, with a commitment to care, loyalty, and unending love and support'. Perhaps the circular shape of the ring could also be interpreted as infinity or eternity because a circle has no end.

Unlike in the distant past, by the mid-twentieth century *patlo* involved a lengthy lull, sometimes lasting between two to five years before the wedding would take place. The reason for the prolonged delay was that upon engagement, the groom had to look for employment in South Africa, and and sometimes he rarely visited home. This was meant to enable him to acquire wedding clothes and other resources needed for the wedding. Nevertheless, even in his absence the two families continued cooperation on numerous domestic activities, as well as exchanging friendly visits. In the process, gifts in the form of food such as milk, *madila* (a form of soured milk), *bojalwa* and meat, among others, were also exchanged. The boy's family made sure that the girl was well-looked after in his absence. Her parents were not supposed to take her to a *ngaka* (traditional doctor) without their consent. The boy and girl communicated through letters to share their experiences, with a friend or relative helping to read and write in case of illiteracy. Once in a while, he would send her presents that included cash through his parents.

A later innovation among Bakgatla was a meeting for members of the general community, after *patlo,* where announcements and dates for future developments were made. These are usually written down on small pieces of paper or 'diary' that is given to the attendants. The meeting was aptly called '*general'* and, while among others it has been referred to with various terms such as *pitso-ya-morafe* (community meeting) and *phuthego-ya-botlhe* (free for all meeting), it is the anglicised version that has stuck.

Soon after the *patlo* process was complete, the wedding ceremony took place. However, in case of the *peeletso* of a child, the wedding would be considerably delayed by years, while she was still growing up, until she was in her late teens and ready for marriage. In case of misfortune in the form of death of an engaged girl, her parents presented her younger sister or some other relative to the boy's parents for marriage to take place. This substitution or replacement arrangement was called *se-ya-ntlo.* In the case of the boy's death, his younger brother took over with the children from the union considered belonging to the deceased elder brother. Again the processes of replacement were carried out by the boy's and girl's parents, usually with no involvement of the boy or the girl. It was only in situations whereby the first engagement had failed that the *se-ya-ntlo* could not be sanctioned. Nonetheless, with the freedom of choice of mates, the *se-ya-ntlo* custom also declined, but it could be carried out if the remaining spouse accepted it.

Although the engaged couple could live together to the point of having children, and were even regarded as husband and wife, it was not until *bogadi* had been given to the *bagwegadi* (bride's parents), and an elaborate wedding ceremony undertaken that they were considered fully married according to the customary or Sekgatla law. Once the bride had moved over to the boy's place, and became part of his family, the wedding celebration could be undertaken. So important was *bogadi* that if it was not given, the children resulting from the union were regarded as belonging to the *bagwegadi* (mother's family) not their father's people. Informants argued that *bogadi* was not the buying of the girl, but an appreciation of her labour that her family was losing, and the boy's family gaining. In this respect *bogadi* among Bakgatla was not a mercenary or opportunistic transaction. Cattle were preferred for *bogadi,* but the number given was not standardised. The number of cattle was never a subject of discussion, and the boy's people gave any number at their discretion, but these had to include at least one female for reproduction. Bulls, which were perceived as *batlhabani* (warriors) due to their aggressive nature were not acceptable. It was also held that they were likely to lead to marital discord. Providing them as *bogadi* was thus considered an insult. Ideally, every male beast was supposed to be accompanied by a female one, though this was not obligatory. Odd numbers were also accepted, strangely seven was the only exception as it was believed to be an ill omen. Bakgatla also accepted sheep though this was rare. On the other hand, goats could not be given because they were seen as destructive.

The groom's people initiated the process by approaching the girl's parents, asking them to let the boy *go tsena mo ntlung ya mosadi* (enter her hut of the woman). The agreement to do this was followed by the setting aside of the day for *lenyalo* or *mokete-wa-lenyalo* (wedding) festivities to take place. The boy's people were also expected to bring *legong* (firewood) to the bride's place, which would be used for cooking food for the wedding.

The plural for *legong* is *dikgong* (logs), and the singular *legong* meant that only one species of wood or tree should be brought. There were species of trees which were not acceptable for firewood among Bakgatla. For example, *moomane* was not accepted as it was believed that it would make the married couple prone to endless altercations, as the name implied. Another wood species that was not acceptable was *mosetlha* as it was believed that meat cooked with it remained red, implying that it was uncooked. The idea of not mixing different wood species was meant to avoid bringing about confusion to the couple.

On the morning of the agreed day, the groom's people sent a goat to the girl's place to be slaughtered for the planned feast. The afternoon of the same day saw the boy and a number of his age mates accompanied by the original *patlo* delegation going to the girl's place. Here the boys were led to a separate hut to be joined by the bride, and a corresponding number of her female friends. In the hut they were fed with meat, *bogobe ba ting* (fermented porridge), and *bojalwa* after which they went to the *lapa* to join the girls' people, also enjoying food and drink.

An important ceremonial ritual was that of the cutting, drying and slicing of the *lemipi* (peritoneum) of the slaughtered goat into a thin strip hung around the bride's neck, like a necklace. This form of a 'ring' or 'neck-ring' was an indication that the couple was now married. Meanwhile, the merrymaking continued and *moduduetso/mogolokwane* reached fever pitch. At night the pairs of boys and girls returned to their hut to sleep, and the following morning the newly-wed boy and his friends went back to their homes. However, he could return every night to sleep with his wife in her hut, and went back home early in the morning for food and his daily chores. He did this for some time until the wife was pregnant, after which his parents approached *bagwegadi* in order for her to relocate to their place. Following discussions on the matter, festivity was planned while she was in seclusion for a few days to ensure that she gained weight and beauty. Most Bakgatla men had special admiration and preference for plump women, or women with a fuller figure.

The day of the festivity saw the boy and his relatives going to the girl's place to join in the activity. Critically, if *bogadi* cattle had been received, the girl's *malome* volunteered a beast from his herd, which was slaughtered with its *lemipi* divided and hung around the married couple's necks as indicated above. This was a demonstration that the marriage was complete. The distribution of parts of a slaughtered ox was done strictly according to well-established protocol involving different relatives, with the role they played in the whole marriage process being a major factor. For his part, the all-important maternal *malome*, was given the *tlhogo* (head) among other portions, whilst *mabogo* (forelegs) went to junior paternal *bomalome*. For every animal slaughtered for the wedding all these mentioned parts went to relevant recipients. Through *mmamalome*, married women got *ngati* which was a portion of the small third stomach, or omasum, and a piece of fillet; but the ingredients differed from one community to another. Not long after, *malome* could also host a small feast at his homestead to share the *tlhogo* with others, if it had not already been consumed at the wedding. There was also *thupa* in the form of some ribs of beef, and *bojalwa* sent to the village *kgosi*'s *kgotla* (court and seat of government) to notify the authorities that a marriage was in full swing in the community. *Thupa* was consumed by *banna-ba-lekgotla*, men who spent a lot of time at the *kgotla* attending to cases and generally assisting the *kgosi* in his duties.

It is worth noting that despite the centrality of *bogadi* in marriage, it was quite common for its handing over to be delayed, however, , mainly because the cattle were not readily available for one reason or another. Under such circumstances the *lemipi* ritual was not performed until the *bogadi* was delivered.

One important change or innovation has been that young people could get married without having gone through the *bogwera* and *bojale* rites of passage, whose rigour had been greatly reduced, even when conducted. Whereas the *patlo* process had changed slightly, wedding ceremonies borrowed heavily from Western tradition and Christian influence. Unlike in the past, the new development was that a boy could bring the girl to his place even before the boy and girl started living together. Festivities still characterised the new arrangement, but if the girl was pregnant, or had a child at the time of the wedding, the elaborate rituals were drastically reduced. However, some individuals disregarded these and pursued full-scale festivities, particularly if they came from wealthy families. The two families agreed on a date of the wedding, after which the couple and their *batshwari* ('aiders' or best man and best lady) went to a local shop to purchase the wedding gear for the bride. *Batshwari* were appointed by the couple themselves, and these could be very close friends or relatives of about the same age. Daughters and sons of the maternal aunts and uncles were usually the ones preferred for this role. The shopping party sometimes also included older *bommamalome,* whose experience and wisdom were considered important.

The most significant attire were the dress, veil, umbrella, shoes and gloves that were all white, hence the designation 'white wedding'. Flowers for the bride were also highly appreciated. Most of these could also be hired locally from those who had bought these previously for their wedding (and no longer had use for them). The veil and flowers played such a significant role that a wedding with such an outfit was normally referred to as *lenyalo la lesire le blom* (wedding of veil and flower). *Blom* is an Afrikaans translation of flower, a language Bakgatla became familiar with while working in South Africa. If *bogadi* had been given, the wife was also provided with special triangular or kite-shaped nine-and-above carat ear-rings that Bakgatla called *nkitseng* (know me or know that I'm married). In most cases the groom would have brought his clothes with him from South Africa, in the form of a black suit, black shoes, white shirt, hat, and white gloves.

There were two marriage officers, namely the church minister (*moruti*) and the colonial government District Commissioner (*molaodi*). Bakgatla, who had become churchgoers, also had their weddings conducted in the church with the minister presiding over the ceremony. Before, the holy matrimony ceremony was conducted on a Thursday: the couple were accompanied by their fathers or guardians to the priest to register it. It is worth noting that the church in Botswana had previously denounced *bogadi* as "'a shameful' act, which is among 'deeds of the darkness [that] should be thrown away'" (Dube, 2015:5). However, during the time of Kgosi Isang Pilane (1920-1929) *bogadi* was restored among the Bakgatla because it was argued that discarding it at the insistence of the church had weakened the institution of marriage. We are also told that, "It was largely due to him, too, that the Bechuanaland Protectorate Native Marriages Proclamation of 1926 was promulgated, which restored to the Chiefs certain jurisdiction over the matrimonial affairs of tribesmen married under civil law" (Schapera, 1940:24).

Among other marital practices that the church had condemned as satanic was *se-ya-ntlo*. However, regarding *bogadi* the Dutch Reformed Church in Mochudi under the Rev. J. Reyneke (1923-35), the policy … was "to give the tribe a form of national religion, based on the principles of Christianity, but adjusted as far as possible to Kgatla beliefs and aspirations," writes Schapera. He goes on to say that "*Bogadi*, for instance, is now recognised as an essential part of Christian marriage; the initiation ceremonies for boys are no longer frowned upon, but an attempt is made to control and direct them; and national Church festivals have been instituted" (Schapera, 1940:24).

Therefore, after ascertaining their consent to the marriage and depending on whether *bogadi* had been settled, the priest registered the bride and groom's names, including their ages. They would also be advised to attend the church service on the next Sunday to witness his publicising the banns of marriage. Marriages presided over at the District Commissioner's office also followed a similar arrangement. The registration of the planned wedding and banns of marriage at the District Commissioner's office were referred to as *go pega lenyalo,* since there the marriage would be announced on public notice boards, for about 21 days or so, to enable whoever objects to the marriage for whatever reason to lodge their objection. If the stipulated period elapses without any incident in terms of objections there was *pholoso,* or removal of the notice from the boards. There is also what is called *tlhakanelo dithoto,* meaning swearing for marriage in community of property or out of community of property. According to some informants,

*Figure 1:* Sample of a marriage certificate template

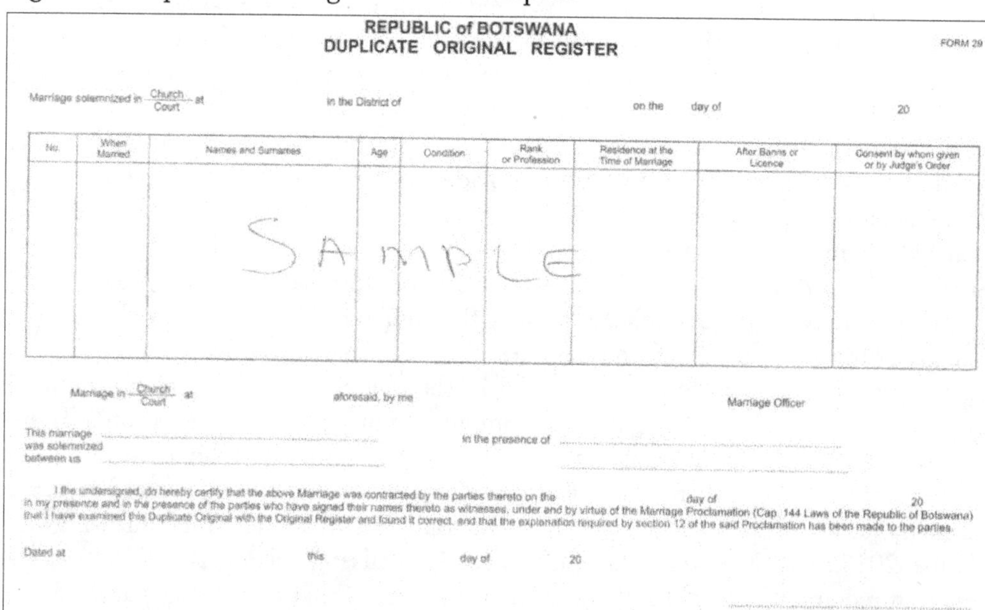
REPUBLIC of BOTSWANA
DUPLICATE ORIGINAL REGISTER

FORM 29

Marriage solemnized in Church/Court at in the District of on the day of 20

| No. | When Married | Names and Surnames | Age | Condition | Rank or Profession | Residence at the Time of Marriage | After Banns or Licence | Consent by whom given or by Judge's Order |
|---|---|---|---|---|---|---|---|---|
| | | SAMPLE | | | | | | |

Marriage in Church/Court at aforesaid, by me Marriage Officer

This marriage was solemnized between us ............ in the presence of ............

I the undersigned, do hereby certify that the above Marriage was contracted by the parties thereto on the day of 20 in my presence and in the presence of the parties who have signed their names thereto as witnesses, under and by virtue of the Marriage Proclamation (Cap. 144 Laws of the Republic of Botswana) that I have examined this Duplicate Original with the Original Register and found it correct, and that the explanation required by section 12 of the said Proclamation has been made to the parties.

Dated at this day of 20

............ Marriage Officer

*Source:* Courtesy of the Republic of Botswana's Department of Civil and National Registration

this was highly misunderstood with marriage out of community of property sometimes leading to suspicions that one spouse could be up to mischief or have a hidden agenda.

It was not uncommon for some people to have their marriage registered at the District Com-

*Figure 2:* Back page of the marriage certificate

DIRECTIONS TO MARRIAGE OFFICERS COMPLETING
DUPLICATE ORIGINAL MARRIAGE REGISTER

**N.B.-Duplicate Original Registers are NOT copies, they must therefore bear original signatures.**

PLEASE ATTEND TO THE FOLLOWING REQUIREMENTS, VIZ:-

1. Verify spelling of names carefully.
2. Complete and sign the Original and Duplicate and Original Register AT ONCE before the parties leave the Church, or other place in which the marriage is being solemnized.
3. See that married couple sign the said record properly, the Bridegroom signing his ordinary signature, and the Bride the name used by her before this marriage; if either party cannot write he or she should make his or her mark.
4. See that besides the Marriage Officer the marriage is solemnizrd in the presence of two or more credible witnesses, who should sign the record or affix their marks thereto if they cannot write.
5. Examine the duplicate with the original, entry by entry, and thereafter sign the certificate of correctness.
6. In the column provided for the record of age of the parties, it is not sufficient to state "major" or "full age" according to Section 13 (1) of the Marriage Proclamation the age must be stated. Where, as is often the case with Africans, the real age is unknown, the apparent age should be written down, e.g., "apparently aged ? years."
7. When one of the parties to the marriage is under the age of 21 (or apparently so) it is not sufficient to state "Consent of Parents", according to Section 17 this consent should be in writing. The written consent may be affixed to the Original Register kept by the Marriage Officer, while the appropriate column in the register both in book, duplicate and copies, should state:
   "written consent of Father / Mother / Guardian A..........B.............. or "written order of District Commissioner.............
   date......................"
8. The body of the form should, where possible, be inscribed in typescript; where this is not possible, all particulars, with the exemption of signatures, should be carefully and legibly written in BLOCK CAPITALS. Thus a clear record will be available for future reference.
9. Duplicate Original Marriage Registers should be despatched to the Secretariat as soon as possible after their completion, with five shillings payable for, and in respect of, the filing in accordance with sub-section 3 of Section 13 of the Marriage Proclamation. Attention in this connection is drawn to Section 23 (1) and (2) of the Proclamation.

   The mark of an illiterate witness on a Marriage Register, whether original or duplicate original, should be attested of certified by the marriage officer. All he has to add is "As witness to mark" or "I certify that the above mark was made in my presence." It is not considered that a Marriage Register is in order where the mark of a witness is not attested or certified in writing. All marks or signs made on a Marriage Register whether by witness of the parties to the marriage must be attested or certified by the officiating marriage officer.
10. In the column provided for "condition" of parties to a marriage, it must be stated whether "Bachelor" or "Spinster," "Widower" "Widow" or "Divorcee". The use of such terms as "Living together as husband or wife," "married in accordance with Tswana Custom" must in no case be used.
11. The reverse side of the Original and the face of the Duplicate Original Registers should bear a certificate by the Marriage Officer that the explanation in terms of the proviso to Section 12 of the Marriage Proclamation (Cap. 117 Laws of Botswana) has been made to the parties.
12. When parties to the Marriage are Africans, as defined in the Republic of Botswana African Administration Proclamation (No.24 of 1956) the certificates required in terms of Section 15 (2) of the Marriage Proclamation should be attached to the Original Register and the certificate hereunder completed.

   I certify that the certificates required by Section 15 (2) of the Marriage Proclamation have been produced and filed with the Original Register.

B. KOOITSE
..........................................
Marriage Officer.

*Source:* Courtesy of the Republic of Botswana's Department of Civil and National Registration

*Note:* Points 6 and 10 need revision as they reflect the colonial period and language as some members of the public have observed.

missioner's office, and also solemnised or blessed at the church with marriage certificates issued (see Figures 1 and 2). The commencement of a wedding ceremony on a Thursday was a tradition initiated by the church and embraced by the district commissioner as well as non-Christians.

Another significant addition to the process was a written invitation card like the one shown in Figure 3.

*Figure 3:* A 1939 wedding invitation card in Mochudi

**The Marriage of**
**MAGANELO D. PILANE,**
**Treasurer, Bakgatla Native Administration, to**
**MAMOREMA,**
**daughter of ex-Rent Chief and Mrs. Isang Pilane,**
**will take place either at**
**Dutch Reformed Church or District Commissioner's Office,**
**Mochudi,**
**on the 21st day of Sept., 1939, at 11 a.m.**

**All Friends, both European and African, are cordially invited to attend.**

**A reception will be held after the ceremony at the residence of ex-Rent Chief Isang Pilane.**

**P.O. Mochudi Village, via Pilane Station, Bech. Protectorate**

*Source:* Schapera (1940:16).
*Note:* 'Ex-Rent Chief' is a typing mistake. It should be 'Ex-Regent Chief'.

The issuing of invitation cards by the tribal elite and royalty, as in the case of Figure 3, could have the effect of closing out ordinary members of the community used to attending these events without invitation cards or even being invited orally. However, people still found their way into the festivity and feasting, and they had to be catered for, more especially at a royal wedding.

Once the boy has delivered *dikgong,* preparations for the wedding got underway involving married women, or their daughters, brewing *bojalwa* and preparing food. They also volunteered in cleaning the yard, and *lekgapho* decoration was done with cow dung on the hut floors, walls, and the *lapa* generally. Rehearsals of songs and dance were conducted in the evenings by a choir of ladies; and according to Schapera, many of the songs had English lyrics and tunes (Schapera, 1940:75). This clearly shows encroachment of European or English influence. The brewery was usually a *leobo* (simple shelter) usually made from tree branches by young men related to the bridegroom. Among other tasks, the young men also made a much neater and well-made *leobo* for VIPs under the supervision of the bridegroom's *motshwari.* As noted above, belief in *boloi* was pervasive among Bakgatla, and nothing was left to chance. Therefore, the bride and bridegroom had to be attended to by a *ngaka* to render ineffective any evil spell that could be cast on them. This practice was embraced by church-goers and non-Christians alike. Schapera writes that, "The ritual varies with the doctor, but generally consists in rubbing a medicinal paste into small cuts made on the wrists and various other joints. The person doctored may also be given a little of paste to eat. The doctor finally smears all the cooking-pots with the same paste, and sprinkles other medicines over the entrances to the compound" (Schapera, 1940:76).

The most important part of the wedding day was the parade that was surrounded by excited people with loud shrills of *mologokwane* by women, and a *leboko* (poem) by *malome* or some other skilled praise poet. An innovation being that Bakgatla women adopted a predominantly blue and white *leteisi* (German print) and a matching chequered *mogagolwane* (small and woollen shawl) tied with a big *kgokelo* (safety pin) and a *tukwi* (headgear). The *leteisi* outfit has also been adopted in other districts of Botswana for various cultural events, to the extent that it has come to be regarded as traditional attire in Botswana.

It is worth noting that *bogadi* has also come to be paid in cash, roughly equivalent to the number of cattle in monetary terms. Financial *bogadi* is referred to as *bogadi-ba-pata* (pocket bride-gift) as opposed to *bogadi-ba-dikgomo* (cattle bride-gift). When bringing *bogadi-ba-pata* the 'commander' of the boy's delegation pegs a twenty, fifty or hundred Pula note to a stick, which he then presents to the girl's *malome*. *Malome* then quietly pockets the note for himself while the cash *bogadi* is given to the bride's parents. The note given to *malome* is not supposed to be drawn from the *bogadi* which must be paid in full.

For the bride and groom, the wedding day was a solemn occasion, and the expectation was that the bride should have tears rolling down her cheeks. This, according to informants, indicated the seriousness of the life she was now entering into, as well as having left her family for her husband's household. In a largely agrarian community the significance of agriculture was portrayed by women darting in front of the bride, sprinkling her with handfuls of sorghum, and hitting the ground with hoes. The bride's arrival was also signified by someone firing a gun. A uniformed communal choir also serenaded the event with their traditional tunes. Nhlekisana (2007:152) tells us that, "Wedding songs are an integral part of Setswana wedding celebration. They are not just sung for entertainment purposes, but talk about issues related to marriage and married life in general". The songs, just like the praise poem, also advise the bride and groom about societal expectations and responsibilities as husband and wife. Once seated in their *leobo,* a preacher prays for the marriage to be a success, and also reads the relevant scripture from the Holy Bible as he preaches to those in attendance. This practice continues to this day.

The festivity would continue with a feast, and additionally, in case *bogadi* had been received, *malome* would slaughter an ox. The distribution of food was done strictly according to protocol, with no one eating before the newly-wed couple and their entourage. With the bride and bridegroom in their elegant wedding regalia, there was no room for the greasy *lemipi* around their necks. This ancient practice had by then been discarded to the annals of history. The distribution of potions of slaughtered animals remains largely the same as in generations gone by. *Malome* has continued receiving *tlhogo*, for example. Much later, however, *thupa* could also be in the form of nominal cash. It was also common for two or more people to share a plate of food, and eat with their bare hands. A number of children also ate from one big bowl. Informants claimed that eating together from the same bowl emphasised communality of the people. Uninvited guests or *bakopi* were also catered for.

Some informants indicated that in the case of marriage of people from the same village, where those involved were familiar with one another and trusted each other, the wife could be allowed to wear *nkitseng* ear-rings, even if *bogadi* was still owed.

## *Go laya* (counselling process) and *go-isa-ngwetsi* (taking the wife to the in-laws)

Before the *bakgwenyana* (boy's people) took the bride to their place there was a crucial ritual of *go laya* (counselling) by married and experienced women carefully selected by her mother. This group, which met in a house or some other shelter was joined by men, and this made the *go laya* process among Bakgatla different to other Batswana. In other words in the Sekgatla culture both the bride and groom's parents witness marriage counselling sessions, and both men and women attend. If the bride is being counselled, the parents of the boy just listen and do not talk, and vice versa. The bride was sternly lectured on her role as a wife, and expectations of her, by way of looking after the needs of her husband, maintaining respect for *bakgwenyana* (her in-laws), cleanliness in her home, and working hard in her *masimo* (fields) for food production. The counsellors also stressed submission to her husband, taking good care of his sexual needs for childbearing, and also to endure adversities and affronts she would experience. It was stressed that her failure to cater for her husband's conjugal rights or sexual needs could lead to him resorting to extra-marital affairs to meet his needs.

The husband was also advised to take great care of his wife by way of cattle farming, cultivation of their fields, and being generally responsible. They were also advised against listening to hearsay and not to make critical decisions concerning their marriage based on people's gossip as this could have adverse consequences for the marriage. The counsellors stressed that any discord in the marriage had to be reported to the wife's parents-in-law for mediation, and not her parents. It was common practice that if the wife bypassed her in-laws and approached her parents, they did not waste time, but returned her to the in-laws. If they entertained her approach this was seen as offensive to the in-laws.

By the time the newly-weds were subjected to *go laya*, the bride would have changed from the white wedding attire to the *leteisi* outfit, complete with a *tukwi*. After the *go laya* process the bridal party would leave, in procession, to the groom's place, a process called *go-isa-ngwetsi* (taking the bride to her in-laws). *Go-isa-ngwetsi* was also referred to as *go mo gatisa motlhala wa dikgomo tsa bogadi* (to make her walk on the tracks of *bogadi* cattle). The following day, they engaged in another feast which signalled the conclusion of the wedding ceremony. The bride officially became part of her groom's family and together with her husband they stayed in their own separate hut.

## Bakgatla Marriage Transformation in the New Millennium

By the new millennium, *bogadi* became a controversial issue as some people opposed it on the grounds that it had now been over-commercialised. In particular, young men claimed that the reason they could not marry was that *bogadi* had become unaffordable. This development was said to have led to a rise in cohabitation numbers, and children born out of wedlock, which caused all kinds of problems. The society had also become excessively consumerist. So serious was this development that President Festus Mogae (1998-2008) complained about it as causing widespread social stress. For instance, in his 2006 state of the nation speech he noted that "suicides and the disturbing crime rate were indicative of the rising social stress levels resulting from the pursuit of ostentatious lifestyles" (Mogae, 13 November 2006). As Gaborone grew rapidly, Kgatleng villages became peri-urban areas. Severe land and housing shortage in Gaborone saw people from the country's capital becoming landlords and tenants in villages such as Mochudi, Bokaa, Morwa, Odi, Modipane, and others. This migration meant that new socio-cultural practices involving marriage were transmitted among Bakgatla. Bakgatla also travelled and worked in other parts of the country, where they embraced new practices.

The emergence of the Internet and social media in the new millennium years intensified ostentatious weddings and marriages, as new ideas and practices were copied and adopted instantly. Furthermore, the emergence of professional wedding planners, and events management services generally have had quite a significant impact on the marriage institution. International practices and cultures were accessible at people's fingertips, and traditional Bakgatla marriage practices and processes have been heavily impacted, as in other districts of the country. Therefore, marriage among Bakgatla has also been greatly influened by the forces of globalization. Items for weddings or marriage can be obtained through the Internet quite easily.

Urbanization also saw the roles and composition of *bomalome* and *batshwari* changing, as well as food protocols. For instance, stories are told of neighbours, friends, workmates and church mates unrelated to the couple intending to marry playing the roles of *bomalome*, sometimes for a fee! The new phenomenon of 'best man', 'best lady' and 'matron-of-honour' who happen to be just friends of the couple, with no blood and marriage relations have increasingly replaced *batshwari*, who were almost always close relatives of those getting married. The new phenomenon involving weddings being held in hired high-end conference centres, hotels and event gardens have also replaced homes as hosting places in some instances. These venues have led to some relatives being excluded from attending weddings in the belief that expenses were being minimised, but the consequence could be disputes and lack of cooperation amongst relatives. Many parents reluctantly acquiesce to the demands of their children in this regard, but if parents had a choice, they would prefer weddings to be held at their homes because of the pride this brings them.

Moreover, most of the time when weddings are held in conference centres and events gardens, professional catering companies are hired, sometimes bringing in exotic meals. The traditional *bojalwa* is almost always absent, and in most cases guests bring their own alcoholic drinks in what is known as 'bring your own' while one or two bottles of Champagne may be placed on the tables for purposes of toasting. The practice of giving *tlhogo* to *malome* and *ngati* to married women does not apply at hotels and garden parties where catering is outsourced. Another issue concerning diet at traditional weddings is that of hygiene. Normally, the animals are slaughtered and skinned by men with their bare hands, and sometimes the dishing of *chotlho*/*seswaa* ('pounded meat') was also done with bare hands, which is against modern hygiene instructions. The carcass is also normally hung from a tree or poles making it susceptible to attracting flies and other pests, as well as meat falling to the ground. There is a Setswana saying that '*motlhopha ntsi ke yo kgorang*' ('one who removes from food a fly, or dirt from falling to the ground and getting soiled, is not starving'), meaning that contaminated food should still be eaten anyway. Big three-legged pots used for cooking food on the fireplace are also susceptible to rust which can pose a health hazard. The possibility of the pots being doctored by a *ngaka* can also be off-putting to some Christians. Whereas self-service arrangements or buffet food has become common in recent times, one is never sure of what goes on behind the scenes in terms of ensuring hygiene. The *bojalwa* is also worked on by women with their bare hands, which is why in some communities it is disparagingly called *maswe-a-dinala* ('finger-nail-dirt'). The sharing of food in one bowl by a number of people has largely disappeared, and nowadays people use cutlery that catering companies are expected to provide.

Traditionally, young men helped in the slaughtering of oxen at weddings, and received *magopelo* (honoraria of pieces of meat) to be taken to their families. However, the outsourcing of service from wedding industry enterprises has meant that poorer, and sometimes unemployed relatives, or members of the community no longer have opportunities for *magopelo*. Again, in the past, preparations for weddings involved not only relatives, but also other members of the community, including total strangers; but the modern outsourcing of services has severely weakened this aspect of social connectedness, which informants point out. Moreover, when weddings are held in conference centres, simple relatives and others from the village may be too inhibited to attend as they would not feel free, owing to the splendour of the facility. They just listen to speeches, eat and drink while seated. Schapera observes that in years gone by, "As the wedding procession approaches the compound, more and more people surround it. Women dance about and trill, children run around and get into everybody's way, men shout, curse and joke" (Schapera, 1940:77). It is not the kind of freedom and behaviour the middle- and upper-classes would appreciate in the twenty-first century hotel wedding.

Furthermore, stories are told of *bogadi* paid by cheques that were dishonoured at the bank, causing great embarrassment. Nowadays *bogadi* is almost always in cash, which can be transferred electronically for convenience. Nevertheless, there are some parents, particularly elderly ones, who still insist on cattle, which are seen as a more dignified *bogadi* than a cash transaction. Stories are told that sometimes the groom would supposedly buy cattle without making payment and the owner would come and claim them causing humiliation and disgrace. Consequently, marriage or 'white wedding' in Botswana has become an arena for ostentation of the haves, and have-nots, in the society.

*Go laya* is also compromised under such circumstances with friends, some of whom may not even be married; playing such a role at drunken bachelor (*stag*) parties and bridal showers. However, this innovation does also play a positive role in marriage by raising funds for couples getting married. The role of *ngaka* doctoring the facilities, which may include the pots and the newly-weds, is also frowned upon by some sections of the population. The non-involvement or limited involvement of parents also leads to dissatisfaction on their part and susceptibility of the couple being unable to nullify *dikgaba*, believed to result from parental and ancestral displeasure. However, the onslaught of the charismatic and prophetic church, or Pentecostal church, phenomenon (also called 'Fire Church' in Botswana) on ancestral worship could be a debilitating factor, more especially that large numbers of unmarried or divorced men and women attend these churches looking for 'miracles' that could hopefully lead to marriage and prosperity.

As demonstrated above, traditional marriage was a protracted process that could take years before *bogadi* was given and the process formally concluded. However, in the new millennium, there appears what the anthropologist Solway (2016) calls "slow marriage" and "fast *bogadi*". By slow marriage Solway refers to the customary practices that have been outlined above, while fast *bogadi* relates to more recent developments involving lavish, and sometimes prohibitively expensive wedding ceremonies called 'white weddings' (Solway, 2016). She writes that "unlike past slow marriage, in which ambiguity characterised the status of the union and the parties, people are now 'officially' single one minute and married the next. The marriage gains public recognition with a white wedding and simultaneous exchange of *bogadi*, which comes to be financially overshadowed by the expense of the wedding itself" (Solway, 2016:312). In her words, parents endorse this development in order to showcase their children's affluence, even if the contribution of the parents themselves could be miniscule.

With Bakgatla, and Batswana generally, increasingly becoming individualistic, this trend seems to dovetail with the fast *bogadi* phenomenon at the expense of the important and entrenched social networks, as well as kin relations, that slow marriage stimulated as they increasingly collapse. "By keeping relationships open and somewhat uncertain, all parties continued to have a stake in maintaining harmonious relations and securing the marriage's stability. Fast *bogadi* upends this" (Solway, 2016:312). It has also become common for couples to join hands in raising funds for *bogadi*, which is different from the past when the groom or his parents or relatives contributed to the expenses. The paraphernalia used at the wedding such as equipment and stage for the disc jockey (or DJ) or a live band, jumping castles for children, drones for photography and video shooting, elaborate cakes, and décor for the marquee tent, and its size, make weddings extremely exorbitant. Sometimes the master of ceremonies may be a popular comedian or radio personality hired from the city. The tent is usually hired if the wedding is held at home and not at the conference centre or event garden (the latter usually has a thatched area and also space for one tent or more). The size of the tent and its elaborate draping design or décor are believed to have become a major status symbol and a powerful statement on the part of the bride and groom, as well as the parents' homestead, if the wedding is held there. In most cases the tent costs far more than what is received in *bogadi* (van Dijk Rijk, 2017). Little wonder that Alexander McCall-Smith titled one of his novels, set in Botswana, *The Saturday Big Tent Wedding Party* (No. 1 Ladies Detective Agency Series). The role of the *ngaka* has declined somewhat, with some couples still utilizing the service while others resort to sprinkling 'holy water' or 'anointing oil' from numerous Pentecostal churches if the couple ascribe their marriage to the power of a prophet trading in these 'holy water' and 'anointing oil' merchandise.

Whereas in the past the bride and groom looked solemn with the bride even expected to shed tears, nowadays they dance actively alongside a group of bridesmaids and groomsmen, sometimes with dance moves that conservative people or elders may disapprove of (Nhlekisana, 2007). Live coverage of the wedding can also be done by individual guests or hired professionals on Facebook among other social media platforms. It is not uncommon for the bride and groom to be in possession of their own mobile phones, using them every now and then during the event. An interesting innovation is that the two are also given a microphone to speak about each other, and how they met. Sometimes the best lady and best man are also given the chance to talk about their friends. The replacement of a communal choir and hosting of weddings in closed conference centres and hotels with elegant invitation cards brings in the element of exclusion (Nhlekisana, 2007). The same concern applies to the role communal choirs play, in which sometimes non-members could join in for added zest, as opposed to employing a live band or DJ.

## The Challenges of Marriage in the New Millennium

There is a serious downside to the glamour-driven innovation noted above. This is exacerbated by the desire on the part of couples to raise the bar against previous weddings they witnessed or heard of. Poorer members of the community are naturally tempted to copy aspects of weddings mentioned above, and in the process overstretch their resources, which exacerbate their already difficult financial situations. The playing of recorded music by DJs has displaced the traditional communal choir whose lyrics contributed to *go laya* the bride and groom (Nhlekisana, 2007). Needless to say, more often than not the expenses outlined above leave the couple heavily indebted since, in some cases, they would have obtained a bank loan to fund the wedding. Unfortunately, this could take a heavy toll on them in the wedding aftermath. Moreover, things could be worsened by death of one of the spouses, as the remaining one shoulders the burden of the loan repayment alone. Informants also talked of some service providers in the wedding industry doing shoddy and substandard work, or cutting corners to reduce costs, which sometimes leave couples frustrated or heartbroken.

Instances, or possibilities, of moral malaise, shame and suicides have even been reported (Livingston, 2009). Among other factors, the impact of this phenomenon has seen a decline in the number of marriages and the sanctity of the institution of marriage in Botswana (Kubanji, 2014). Perhaps, it should be noted that another serious challenge to marriage among Bakgatla and Batswana generally is the government's old policy of separating married couples in the civil service by transferring them to different parts of the country (Ntseane, 1997). This seems to have been a benign practice that was blindly applied to transfers, regardless of people's marital status. Among other concerns, transfers have led to consequences such as temptations for extramarital affairs leading to divorce, suicides or even murders ('passion killings'). We are told that "marriage is also risky for women, especially poor women, who cannot rely upon one man to provide for them and their children" (Solway, 2016:313). Solway also says that "…many middle class women are reluctant to marry, as men's affection and support are seen as unreliable, and their treatment of women disrespectful. There are women with secure middle-class incomes, for example, who have had children but have shunned marriage, taking a lover to get pregnant, but withholding information on the child's existence from him" (Solway, 2016:314).

Although there are instances where kin are requested to make significant financial contributions as well as in kind, there are also other instances where pride or lack of co-operation on the part of relatives may force couples to go it alone. This has the double effect of straining relations between kin members as well as increasing the financial burden and debt on the couple. Nevertheless, involvement and contributions of relatives (some doing so voluntarily) in the planning of the wedding and its execution constitutes continuity in marriage among Bakgatla, and Batswana more generally. Although financial gifts and gifts in kind from well-wishers, through bachelor parties and bridal showers, among others, can be substantial in most cases this is too small to offset the debt accumulated in the process of the wedding. Perhaps it should also be noted that there is added the steep expense in the form of honeymoons, which sometimes are undertaken in South African resorts or exotic overseas places such as Dubai, among others.

The huge costs of wedding and alleged commercialization of *bogadi* are believed to be behind the decline of marriage in Botswana as most couples cannot afford it. Generally, failure to marry leads to many couples living together in what has been described as cohabitation, and as we demonstrate below, this was and is beset by many challenges and problems.

The *bogadi* and high cost of wedding, as outlined above, are said to prevent many who wished to marry from doing so. The result has been couples cohabiting and raising children for many years, if not decades. It has been said that the "…children eventually also cohabit creating a cycle that threatens the very institution of marriage" (Mokganedi, 3 October 2011). A concern emerged that cohabitations presented serious *boswa* (inheritance or estate) crises in cases where one of the spouses died leaving some property behind. Upon becoming President of Botswana in 2008, Ian Khama instituted a commission of inquiry on social ills afflicting the nation, and it was led by Kgosi Puso Gaborone of Batlokwa, consisting of preachers, among others. Among issues raised was problems faced by marriage in Botswana.

Responding to that challenge and also realising that marriage in Botswana was faced with this perceived existential threat, brother David Morwaagole and his sister Annah Morwaagole of Bokaa in Kgatleng made a decision to get cohabiting couples to marry *en masse* in 2011. They called their initiative 'Re A Nyalana' (We Are Marrying). In an interview with the two Morwaagoles, they indicated that they resorted to the initiative after their herdsman at *moraka*, who was unable to marry, cohabited with the mother of his children owing to lack of funds. On realising that this was a widespread problem, the Morwaagoles, who are well versed in Botswana's Marriage Act, as well as the Children's Act, consulted other members of the community and decided to have a mass wedding for customary marriage at the village *kgotla*. They also approached some businesspeople to help with funds to buy rings for the mass wedding ceremony. The organisers had also ensured that *patlo* and other necessary rituals were undertaken, in order for the marriage to be dignified, as well as bringing together the families of the couples.

The first ceremony, which consisted of 11 couples, was held at the Bokaa *kgotla* in September 2011. This unusual development attracted a crowd of well-wishers, tribal leaders, sponsors and journalists among others. "Ululations reverberated throughout the village as bridesmaids and ushers sang '*Mosadi yo montle yo, o ne o mmeile kae*?' ('where have you been hiding this beautiful woman all along?'), and the couples filed into the *Kgotla* to excitedly take their seats" (Mokganedi, 3 October 2011). This was reported to have been a dream come true for many couples, who had lost hope of ever being joined in marriage. The youngest couple was reported to be a 46 year-old bride and her 59 year-old groom, while the eldest was an 82-year-old groom and his 71-year-old bride. The age of these newly-weds shows that some had passed their childbearing age, and in some cases were even great grandparents. Reports state that an awkward moment was when the grooms were advised to kiss the bride, but hesitated since they were not used to doing this in public. "A daring moment by one couple sent the rest into a frenzy of kisses as the crowd cheered them on" (Mokganedi, 3 October 2011). Naturally, the excited newly-weds expressed gratitude to the Morwaagoles and sponsors for making their dreams come true.

The Re A Nyalana project grew with time and it was even extended to other villages in Kgatleng and other parts of Botswana (Williams, 8 April 2015). There was also a drive to involve younger couples in the initiative instead of it being a domain for elderly couples. The success of the first Re A Nyalana wedding ceremony led to the organisers registering it as an official organization, a Society, on 12 July 2012, after 68 couples in different Kgatleng villages benefited from a pilot project (Republic of Botswana, 29 September 2018). Kgosi George Thwane of Artesia became the chairperson, former High Court Judge Gabriel Rwalengera (originally from Tanzania) was the legal advisor, David Morwaagole became technical advisor, while Annah Morwaagole was coordinator. With growth of Re A Nyalana came enhanced organization of the society as it established two regional bodies in Botswana, namely 'Re A Nyalana Society-North' and 'Re A Nyalana Society-South'. By 2015 the programme legal advisor was Attorney Lyndon Mothusi.

With the government of Botswana recognising the critical role Re A Nyalana was playing in reviving the sanctity of marriage and reducing undesirable cohabitation, the organization was officially launched in its birthplace, Bokaa. The guest speaker was the Minister for Labour and Home Affairs, Hon. Edwin Batshu, whose ministry was responsible for marriages. The District Commissioner for Kgatleng, Ms. Wame Samapipi, praised Re A Nyalana and told the gathering that the major problem concerning cohabitation was estate management, whereby the death of a parent led to relatives scrambling and fighting for the property, leaving the children in the lurch, despite the fact that they were supposed to be the main beneficiaries (Disele, 16 October 2012). She also said that individuals who cohabit had less dignity in the community. Most importantly, the District Commissioner advised potential Re A Nyalana couples that, "Botswana common law also does not recognise the paying of bride-wealth, hence they can marry under it"(Disele, 16 October 2012).

Furthermore, Samapipi told her listeners that customary marriage entails *bogadi*, and also said that Re A Nyalana did embrace customary marriages, since its Chairperson was a *kgosi*. In disseminating information on marriage, the organization gave aspirants the choice of common law and customary marriage as per the Marriage Act. According to Samapipi, the primary focus of her office was on older members of society because their relationships or cohabitation had mostly stabilised. "She further said that youth often cohabit for a brief period in urban areas as they sample the joys of unlimited freedom. The family institution is viewed as the basis of society, and is supposed to encompass a man and woman, to be recognised by Botswana law" (Disele, 16 October 2012). Samapipi emphasised *go laya* rites, which she said essentially contributed to better functioning families and communities. During a wedding of eight couples in the village of Molapowabojang in the Southern District in April 2015, the village's Kgosi Kedirile told those in attendance that Re A Nyalana was neither against *bogadi* nor intending to stop it (Letshoo, 13 April 2015).

A government of Botswana Facebook page reported on 29 September 2018 that since the organization's inception it had managed to assist 3,272 beneficiaries in eight districts of Botswana as well as conducting 15 sensitization workshops covering pre- and post-marital counselling. The organization was also credited with raising awareness of the disadvantages of cohabitation, promoting dignity amongst couples, promoting health and morally appropriate social habits, securing professional support and guidance for parents, providing counselling services for the couples, supporting amendments of customary practices, and protecting inheritance rights of women and children (Republic of Botswana, 29 September 2018). It was further stated that "...as a result, there is a recognisable reduction on [sic] inheritance disputes and associated family conflicts. The society has also promoted development of healthy families with the idea that stable homes will provide a conducive environment for child development" (Republic of Botswana, 29 September 2018).

The issue of *bogadi* remained prominent in the national discourse, with the media publicising it as much as possible. Social commentator Mpho Kuhlmann's view was that "the 'price' in bride-price is a four-letter word that can set the bride and groom and bride's families at each other's throats because often times it covers a multitude of sins, from get rich quick schemes to domestic violence" (Kuhlmann, 22 April 2019). The high cost of marriage was also consistent with the economic performance of Botswana and the global economy. For instance, "According to figures released by Statistics Botswana, the biggest dips in weddings in Botswana happened in 2009 and 2011 when the world was experiencing an economic downturn" (Kuhlmann, 22 April 2019). In June 2012 the co-founder of Re A Nyalana, David Morwaagole, made a presentation to *dikgosi* at the Ntlo Ya Dikgosi (House of Traditional Leaders, formerly known as the House of Chiefs) on the rise in the cohabitation rate and the decline in the rate of marriage. *Dikgosi* agreed unanimously that *bogadi* be regulated and standardised, given the very high figures demanded in payment of *bogadi*. Traditionally, eight cattle were the maximum required for *bogadi* in some communities, however, some people had become unscrupulous and demanded far more than that.

At the same wedding ceremony in Molapowabojang in April 2015 the Re A Nyalana legal advisor Lyndon Mothusi told the audience that "the Reanyalana [sic] programme does not encourage divorce because it brings awesome results. He encouraged married couples to always make a will stating how they would like their property to be dispatched upon death of either of the couple" (Letshoo, 13 April 2015). However, despite focusing on older couples with 'stable relationships' by 2019 there were reports that divorce cases were rising among Re A Nyalana 'graduates'. Moreover, Re A Nyalana seems to have been somewhat stigmatised by some sections of the society as *lenyalo la mophako* ('free or social welfare marriage'). Certainly, the otherwise noble initiative does not seem to have attracted the middle class, let alone the country's political class, in order to give it enhanced dignity, even if that could be a popular gesture. Moreover, non-payment of *bogadi* meant that the children still belonged to their mother's family and carried her surname, which in itself carries a degree of stigma. Nonetheless, in the case of a purely civil marriage, a couple can still have the father's surname on the birth certificate.

The popularity and 'supremacy' of the monogamous marriage among Bakgatla and Batswana more generally has long eclipsed polygamy, which has become an endangered species as people frown upon it, feeling it to be a 'primitive' act. Polygamy does exist among some ethnic minorities such as the Bazeruru who are of Shona extraction, originally from Zimbabwe. However, polygamy does have its adherents among some *dikgosi*, notably (the late) Kgosi Kgafela II of Bakgatla-ba-Kgafela and Kgosi Kebinatshwene Mosielele of Bahurutshe in Manyana, among others. Surprisingly, despite promoting polygamy, these *dikgosi* themselves are in monogamous marriages, or even divorced. Whereas in the southern African countries of South Africa and eSwatini polygamy is quite common, in Botswana it is not a widespread practice. Interestingly, about 15 years ago or so, the national television news bulletin covered a Mochudi man marrying a second wife, which demonstrates the rarity of the development. One woman who was interviewed by Botswana Television (BTV) at the wedding justified the marriage on the grounds that monogamous marriage was dubious because men had many *dinyatsi* (concubines or extramarital affairs), and polygamy would curtail that insincerity.

According to Kgosi Segale Linchwe of Mochudi a few years ago, he was part of a Bakgatla delegation that visited one of the Bapedi royals in the Limpopo Province of South Africa, and while holding a conversation with him about marriage, they were astounded to find that polygamy was very rare among Bakgatla. The reason was that among Bapedi polygamy is common, and they responded by asking the Bakgatla men whether they were scared of having more than one wife! Whereas supporters of polygamy also claim that it can help curb infidelity in marriage and the spread of HIV and AIDS in the country, general support for the practice does not seem to gain any traction among Bakgatla.

Christians, which many Bakgatla are, also denounce polygamy on religious grounds. For instance, in an interesting account a Catholic lady, married to a Zezuru gentleman, detailed how during the initial stages of *go kokota* there was a clash of cultures. He was marrying for the first time and the lady's parents requested assurance that their daughter would not be subjected to a polygamous union. As indicated above the Bazezuru are a proudly polygamous community.

## Conclusion

This account has demonstrated how marriage and its rituals or rites evolved among Bakgatla over the generations, from the pre-Christian and pre-colonial periods to the new millennium. The change and innovation that happened along the way was a result of adaptation to the forces of Christianity, modern education, Western material culture and globalization. In the early period, marriage played a critical role in creating and fostering social relations between sets of in-laws and their relatives.

Modernity and freedom of choice for a mate reduced the role of parents in the selection process, and the challenges began to proliferate. Independence for Botswana saw accelerated economic development for the country and emergence of a culture of consumerism that has brought about challenges for marriage, particularly the wedding ceremony, as it became associated with a great deal of pomp and ceremony. However, this came at a great price as it became competitive and exorbitant, and has brought post-wedding financial and emotional stress for the couple involved. The hefty price for weddings and issues of *bogadi* are believed to have led to the value and statistical decline of marriage as an institution, and gave way to cohabitation. Re A Nyalana emerged as a remedy to this development but it has had its challenges.

Finally, arguments for polygamy do not seem to be the answer to the socio-economic determinants within which marriage takes place, or exist among Bakgatla. However, it can be argued that, like most other institutions, marriage still has relevance in Botswana and will remain so for the foreseeable future; but challenges and critics will abound. Therefore, wedding bells among Bakgatla and Batswana generally will keep chiming for generations to come while its death knell is held at bay. Just as the Internet blogger Tumi Modise observes somewhat in jest regarding 'bride-gift': "*Bogadi* has outlived two World Wars, even the worst world recession of our time" (Modise, 12 October 2015). By the same token, marriage among Bakgatla has endured and survived countless pre-colonial intertribal wars, pandemics such as the Spanish Flu of 1918, HIV/AIDS, gender-based violence, economic downturns, and will certainly survive Covid-19. Reports of people attending 'Fire Churches' even outside the country looking for miracles that could lead to marriage among other 'blessings', and some married couples even giving testimonies at these churches, demonstrate continued popularity of marriage among Bakgatla and Batswana generally.

## REFERENCES


Disele, S., 16 October 2012. 'Re A Nyalana to be Launched in Bokaa', *Mmegi*.

Dube, M.W., 2015. 'Translating Cultures: The Creation of Sin in the Public Space of Batswana', *Scriptura* 114, pp.1-11. http://scriptura.journals.ac.za

Kubanji, R., 2014. 'Nuptiality Patterns and Trends in Botswana', *Population and Housing Census 2011: Analytical Report by Statistics Botswana*. Gaborone: Statistics Botswana, pp.224–237. http://botswana.unfpa.org/sites/esaro/files/resourcepdf/2011PHCAnalyticalReport.pf

Kuhlmann, K., 22 April 2019. 'Why the Price in Bride-price is a Four Letter Word', *Sunday Standard*.

Letshoo, G.,13 April 2015. 'Re-A-Nyalana Not Against *Bogadi* - Kgosi', *Botswana Daily News*.

Livingston, J., 2009. 'Suicide, Risk, and Investment in the Heart of the African Miracle', *Cultural Anthropology*, vol. 24, 4, pp.652–680.

Makgala, C.J., 2009. *History of the Bakgatla-baga-Kgafela in Botswana and South Africa*. Pretoria: Crink.

Modise, T., 12 October 2015. '*Bogadi* Stays', *Mmegiblogs*.

Mogae, F., 2006. *State of the Nation Address*. Gaborone: Government Printer.

Mokganedi, M., 'Re A Nyalana in Bokaa', *Monitor*, 3 October 2011.

Nhlekisana, R.O.B., 2007. 'Honey, Let's Waltz the Day Ou: The Effects of Popular Music on Wedding Celebrations in Botswana', *Muziki*, vol. 4, 1, pp.152-162. https://doi.org/10.1080/18125980701754652

Ntseane, D.M., 1997. The Unintended Consequences of Transfer Policy on Dual Career Families in Botswana. PhD Thesis, Brandeis University.

Republic of Botswana, 29 September 2018. 'BWGovernment', https://www.facebook.com/BotswanaGovernment/photos/a.1877334049015911/1877336522348997/?type=3&__tn__=-R

Schapera, I., 1940. *Married Life in an African Tribe*. London: Faber and Faber.

Segami, V.B. and Van Eeden, C., 2020. 'Marital Symbols and the Marriage Satisfaction and Spiritual well-being of Batswana Married Women', *Journal of Psychology in Africa*, vol. 30, 1, pp.37-43, https://doi.org/10.1080/14330237.2020.1722363

Solway, J., 2016 '"Slow Marriage", "Fast *Bogadi*": Change and Continuity in Marriage in Botswana', *Anthropology Southern Africa,* 39:4, 309-322, DOI: 10.1080/23323256.2016.1235980. To link to this article: https://doi.org/10.1080/23323256.2016.1235980

van Dijk. R., 2017. 'The Tent Versus Lobola: Marriage, Monetary Intimacies and the New Face of Responsibility in Botswana', *Anthropology Southern Africa*, vol. 40, 1, pp.29-41. At https://doi.org/10.1080/23323256.2016.1243450

# 4

# BAKGOTHU

*Mr. Allan Manyeneng*

**Totem**: *Tlou* – Elephant

**Clan Poem:** *Leboko la Bakgothu-Nama*

## INTRODUCTION

This chapter focuses mainly on the meaning and importance of *lenyalo* (marriage) amongst the Bakgothu (Nama) of Tsabong, the steps involved in their traditional marriages, the rights and benefits associated with Bakgothu marriages as well as the impact of change on their traditional marriage rites and related activities. It looks especially at the way marriage functions as a rite of passage by means of which society not only preserves and renews its values, but also confers rights, privileges and responsibilities of adult family life to couples. As a rite of passage marriage is, of course, a ritual with a number of stages. Traditionally, the stages must be scrupulously observed in order for a marriage to be considered complete. The chapter will describe these stages and the extent to which adhering to them presents challenges in today's circumstances. As with other cultures in Botswana, Bakgothu culture also faces stresses from the pressure to change with the times. The chapter will provide a brief account of how, both as an institution and as a process, the marriage is evolving and adapting to change in Bakgothu society itself, as well as in the nation at large.

The data for the chapter were obtained primarily from field research which was conducted at Tsabong in March 2018. The field work included interviews with carefully selected elders in the village. They were chosen because they were generally acknowledged to be well versed in the history and cultural traditions of the communities that live in the village and its surrounding areas. Their information was supplemented by findings from online sources.

Among the Bakgothu, marriage is a cultural event that resonates with their religious values, which survive as a collective memory in the minds of the elders and revitalised in the traditions and rituals. For the parents on both sides of the newly-weds, and for the newly-weds themselves, marriage is a great gift and an honour from the ancestors and from God. It is also a rite of passage through which a young couple transits into the responsibilities, privileges and roles of adult life. It is the means through which the foundational beliefs of the community are renewed and passed on to the next generation, such as the rules of inheritance, land being held in trust for the community and future generations, a household being owned by the senior female resident, and the gift of procreation. The couple looks forward to not only being parents themselves but grandparents too, a status every sound parent would love to achieve in their lifetime.

There is a wealth of historical and ethnographic research on the people and languages of Namaqualand, going back to the beginning of the last century and earlier, which has proved extremely helpful. In this chapter culture will be regarded as a resource which a people treasure because it is the source of enduring strength in overcoming past adversity and meeting contemporary challenges. Culture provides continuity and cohesion in community life. The temptation to regard culture as a set of ephemeral practices that can be either jettisoned or easily adjusted for administrative expediency should be avoided. Bakgothu, like other ethnic groups in Botswana, are justly proud of their cultural heritage and are keen to uphold it within the context of a diverse but unified Botswana national culture. This is especially so in relation to their marriage traditions. In the case of Bakgothu, as a fugitive migrant community, upholding their traditions resonates poignantly with their sense of identity and survival as a people with a traumatic historical legacy.

## Brief Historical Background of Tsabong Village and Bakgothu (Nama)

The village of Tsabong is situated in the southwestern part of Botswana – in the southern part of the Kgalagadi District. It is a central township for the Batlharo, Bakgothu (Nama) and the Afrikaner ethnic groups in Botswana. Bakgothu (Nama) are one of the Setswana-speaking people of Namibian origin who also speak their own form of Khoe language, Nama, and Afrikaans. According to some elders at the village, Bakgothu originated from Namibia in the area formerly known as Namaqualand that was then part of German South-West Africa, a colony of Germany from 1884-1914. They came into Botswana in 1905 as fugitives when a combined Herero and Nama commando was defeated at the battle of Swartfontein during an uprising against German colonial repression, in which more than half of the Nama population and 70% of the Herero population perished. The Motswana popular historian, Jeff Ramsay (2018), calls the uprising and its brutal crushing by the Germans in 1893-1908, the "Kalahari Holocaust." They first settled at Lokgwabe village in the northern part of the present day Kgalagadi District. Their proper tribe's name is the *Namas,* signifying their origin from Namaqualand The name *mokgothu* was given to them on arrival at Lokgwabe, and was originally meant to belittle and despise them, hence the name *Bakgothu,* which now has overshadowed their initial Nama name. It was at Lokgwabe village that Bakgothu split into two groups and separated. Some remained at Lokgwabe and its surrounding areas, whilst most of them migrated to Tsabong village, where they presently reside at Matlhatlhaganyane Ward under the leadership of Sub-Chief Mr. Piet Kaartze. Bakgothu venerate the *tlou* (elephant) as their tribe's totem,.

The Nama originally lived around the Orange River in Southern Namibia and Northern South Africa and spoke a central Khoe language called Nama. Hence the area they inhabited was called Namaqualand which means 'land of the Nama speaking people (a combination of Nama and the suffix '*khoe-*' or '*qua-*' which means 'people' in the language). At present they number an approximately 250,000 strong population mainly in the Kgalagadi Trans-frontier Park which straddles the territories of Namibia, Botswana and South Africa. Archaeologists such as Guldermann (2008) and Smith and Ouzman (2004) link them to the large pre-Bantu group of Khoe-kwadi language speakers who not so long ago in the past were widespread throughout southern Africa, including the Cape Provinces of South Africa, and who they argue may have introduced pastoral food production into the area. They lived for centuries as pastoralists alongside the San (*Basarwa*) hunters and gatherers long before the Bantu speaking people arrived. Their own legends speak of an earlier period when they lived in a beautiful well-watered land further up north from where they were driven gradually southwards by encroaching Bantu speaking people. Colonization and subsequent developments further pushed them into the more inhospitable desert parts of the region. Their former homeland of Namaqualand is now part of the Kgalagadi Trans-Frontier Park.

## Understanding Marriage from the Bakgothu's Point of View

With reference to the findings of the field research that was conducted in March 2018 in Tsabong, marriage among Bakgothu (Nama) is a process whereby a man and a woman from two different family backgrounds join hands, in the name of love, and with a common intent to create a family and raise children. Bakgothu are quick to emphasise that above all marriage is not just a union between a husband and wife, but it further unifies their respective families, thus creating a lifetime relationship which even divorce cannot terminate. To a community with a history of nomadic pastoralism and the violent uprooting alluded to above, it is obvious that cultural traditions, including marriage traditions, provide cohesion, continuity and stability to the sense of who they are in otherwise chaotic times. They are unhappy that modernization has tended to detract from such traditional functions of marriage in favour of commercialization, in which marriage is increasingly seen as a cash cow by both those who profit from providing goods and services for the ceremony and from the wealth in cash and kind that changes hands as *bogadi.* Furthermore, Bakgothu argue that owing to their small population, it is generally not easy for them to depart from their traditional marriage customs. It is only when they encounter inter-marriages with other communities that they experience challenges with adhering strictly to their well-known traditional processes.

Although their aboriginal Nama religion appears to have been eclipsed by either Islam or Christianity, which they have adopted, it actually still survives and is manifest in their stories, crafts, arts, singing and dancing, rituals and traditional ceremonies such as trance healings and weddings. They profess a belief in Haiseb, God, who has always existed and inhabits the heavens beyond the skies. Traditionally they always prayed to him with their faces towards the East. He renews himself in cycles of deaths and resurrections. Piles of stones, particularly near ancient paths and waterholes, mark tombs or shrines considered sacred as sites of such resurrections. Haiseb sings wonderful songs based on trees and bushes. Naturally, for a people with a legacy of nomadic pastoral herding and reliant on nature, there is an ecological dimension to their religious beliefs that seeks to regulate their relationship with the environment to ensure its continued fecundity, while at the same time assuaging the effects of its harsher aspects.

However, the religion probably finds its fullest expression beyond such day-to-day ecological and productive preoccupations. For it also addresses itself to transcendental and cosmological themes as well as to social themes such as community solidarity, mutuality, political empowerment and cultural revitalization in cosmological and mystical concerns with transcendence and transformation. These concerns are reflected in the rituals and symbolic language of their cultural traditions, including marriage, which are vehicles that are preserved for transmission to future generations, including their values and world view. They contain guidance on such matters as rules of inheritance, the idea that land is communally owned and is not alienable, and gender roles, for example. Among the Bakgothu too, marriage is fundamentally a rite of passage with religious underpinnings, and its rituals re-enact the symbolic stages, namely: rapture or separation from the old status, adjustment to the new status during the transition, and finally reincorporation into society in a new role peculiar to rites of passage in general.

## Types of Marriages/Weddings

Bakgothu state that they are familiar with three types of marriage processes operating within their community. The said marriage processes consist of the customary marriage process, the District Commissioner's marriage process, and the Christian marriage process.

### The customary marriage

According to Bakgothu informants, the customary marriage process entails the use of indigenous traditional ways of conducting a marriage, i.e., using customary laws, rules and procedures to solemnise the union between a man and a woman as a marriage. According to them, the Sekgothu customary marriage process traditionally allowed parents to look for a prospective wife for their son within or beyond the village. When the boy's parents had thus identified a potential wife, they negotiated a deal in which the girl's parents would pledge their daughter to be married to their son in future, when the youngsters were ready to take the marriage vows. Bakgothu call this preliminary visit process *go kokota*. The phrase literally means 'to knock at the door', but in context it signifies a notice of the intention to submit a marriage proposal addressed to the girl's family. They would in response propose a further meeting for the purpose and inform the young man's parents what they would be expected to bring with them to this meeting. The meeting is referred to as *patlo*, or *go batla ngwetsi*, idiomatically translated as 'bride-seeking'. signifying that the boy's family would have come out in search of a bride for their son. At this point, the two families would agree on a convenient future date for yet another meeting, this time to hold the *bogadi/*lobola (bride-wealth) marriage process. When the date arrived, the maternal and paternal uncles and aunts to the young man would set off in the early hours of the morning to fetch the bride-to-be from her home, where they would be met by the young woman's family delegation. Upon the conclusion of the appropriate formalities, the young woman's maternal aunt would release the young woman to the young man's delegation. At this juncture, a marriage of the two parties became valid, even prior to the issuance of *bogadi/*lobola by the young man's parents. The new husband had the option to pay *bogadi/*lobola outright or at a later date. The bride would be transferred to her in-laws' homestead where she would stay until her new husband could afford to build a house for their new family.

## The District Commissioner's marriage

Bakgothu state that the existence of a District Commissioner's marriage system is well-known in their village. The elders are not fully conversant or comfortable with this marriage process, but acknowledge that it is quite common these days for couples to complete the formalities at the District Commissioner's office prior to proceeding with the traditional customary marriage process.

In terms of the Marriage Act, and indeed as a matter of practice by the District Commissioner's office, couples intending to enter into a marriage need to prove that they have attained the age of majority, i.e., 21 years of age. Where one or both parties are of minority age, parental consent is required before the marriage can be registered. Secondly, the marrying couple must each avail a witness, also of consenting age. Three weeks before the marriage date, both the couple and their respective witnesses report at the District Commissioner's office to register the marriage. Each brings with them their national identity card and completes the necessary marriage application forms. From the registration date to a day before the marriage, the District Commissioner's office advertises the marriage banns (at the places where both parties are known to stay or to have stayed). The essence of three-week bann's advertisements is to give notice of the planned marriage to the general public. This allows other people to know about the marriage and afford a chance to anyone inclined to come forward if he or she knows of any reasons why the duo cannot be joined in matrimony.

A day before the marriage is conducted, the couple, together with their respective witnesses, report to the District Commissioner's office to complete forms that address the issue of whether they are marrying in or out of community of property.

Marriages at the District Commissioner's office are conducted in groups. On the day of the marriage, all the couples scheduled for marriage on the same day, as well as their respective witnesses, convene in a large boardroom. In the event there is sufficient space, their relatives and friends would also be allowed in to witness the event. The District Commissioner commences the marriage proceedings with a prayer before administering some marriage counselling. Counselling entails an overview of the challenges the newly-weds should expect to encounter in their daily lives, as well as advice on the responsibilities and privileges of the new phase of life they are entering. Incidentally, by virtue of their daily routine, which includes meetings and discussions with married couples who have lodged domestic complaints or disputes, District Commissioners are in an excellent position to appreciate the problems of married life and to accordingly render sound counselling. At the end of the counselling session, the District Commissioner proceeds to solemnise the couples' marriages and issues marriage certificates, which completes the process.

## The Christian marriage

Bakgothu elders consulted in this study were aware of Christian marriage practices in their village but believed that they are exclusive to church members. They were not familiar with the requirements of a church wedding. However, it is common knowledge that church marriages among the Bakgothu, like elsewhere in the country, are conducted by duly licensed marriage officers. It is also common knowledge that couples are required to register their marriage with the District Commissioner's office and follow all the processes as stipulated under the District Commissioner's marriage process above, up to the counselling stage, before proceeding with the processes of a church wedding. After the counselling stage, the District Commissioner releases the couples intending to proceed to the Christian marriage process. In their possession would be the necessary marriage documentation from the District Commissioner's office to the priest/reverend's church office. The couple then set a marriage date with the priest, usually a Saturday morning. On the appointed day, the couple and their respective family members or friends, convene at the church for the marriage process. The priest blesses the event before solemnising the marriage in accordance with the church principles. The priest then proceeds to offer some counselling, which also centres on how the couple is expected to carry themselves during their marriage. They would be urged to fear God and raise their children in the word of God. Thereafter, the priest issues a marriage certificate and the two families and the guests retire to the bride's home where a feast is held to celebrate the marriage, and in particular, to receive the bride.

Generally, Bakgothu believe that the customary marriage process prevails over the District Commissioner's and the Christian marriage processes. Young people, even today, prefer to marry in terms of their Sekgothu customary practice. The Bakgothu elders attributed this preference to the fact that owing to their small population as a clan, they are especially loyal to their traditions and jealously guard their marriage and other customary traditions against erosion with time. In their opinion, Sekgothu/Nama marriage practice is preferred to other types because, compared to the other two, it is culturally rich in content, relevant to their daily lives and therefore easy to adhere to, and provides useful guidance on their roles as adult members of the Nama community. Bakgothu nevertheless express concern that there seems to be pressure among their youth to include in their marriage processes aspects of either the District Commissioner's marriage process or the Christian marriage process, as if the traditional one on its own were not enough.

## Marriage Processes in Sekgothu

### Betrothal process (*Peeletso*)

Traditionally the marriage process in Sekgothu began with the betrothal process called *peeletso*. Bakgothu elders state that in former times it involved parents who felt their son was ready to marry, going out in the village or surrounding areas to look for a suitable future wife for him. When they had identified a suitable girl they held discussions with the girl's family to ask them to pledge their daughter in marriage to their son when they both reached maturity. They call the process *go beeletsa mosadi*. The maternal aunt was the chief negotiator on behalf of the boy during the process. Sometimes he was accompanied by the paternal aunt. Bakgothu elders say that nowadays, the young man informs either his maternal or paternal aunt(s), who in turn tells his maternal uncle about his intentions. The young man's parents would then be appraised of the developments, whereupon the maternal uncle, in the company of the maternal aunt, would pay a visit to the home of the identified girl on a preliminary visit.

### Courtship process

Bakgothu informants consulted in the course of this study testify that traditionally the courtship process was not part of the marriage process. Apparently, the idea of courtship between young people with the intention of getting married in future was a foreign and unthinkable idea in olden times. It began to manifest itself only with the informants' generation. They say that courtship as practiced today entails an arrangement where a young man establishes a love relationship with a girl with no intention of necessarily marrying her in future. In due course, however, if their relationship develops into a steady, strong and passionate affair the couple may feel they are ready to get married and start a family. When this happens, the young man first informs his mother and a maternal or even paternal aunt, of his wish to get married. The aunt would in turn inform the boy's uncle who would relay the news to the young man's parents. Not long thereafter, the young man's parents arrange a delegation led by a maternal uncle to the girl's family. The aim of the delegation is to obtain information about the girl's family home and its type of people that their son wishes to get married into. This process is called *go kokota* (to knock at the door), signifying, as explained above, the intention to present a marriage proposal. It results in the arrangement of a further meeting at which the marriage proposal itself will be presented in a process called the 'preliminary visit'.

## PRELIMINARY VISIT PROCESS

In traditional Sekgothu practice, the first preliminary visit process is always performed by a delegation, made up only of married and widowed women from the man's family, visiting the girl's home in the evening of the day mutually agreed by both families. They would set off in the evening, taking along some tea, sugar, milk, water, a pot and firewood, among other things. On arrival at the girl's home the delegation would not announce their arrival or request permission to enter, nor would they wait at the entrance to be invited in, as is normal for visitors. Instead, they would enter the premises uninvited and proceed to find a suitable place to settle within the yard. Members of the girl's family, even though gathered for the meeting, were not allowed to acknowledge the visitors in any way. They did not greet them, talk to them or recognise their presence at this juncture. The visitors were not offered hospitality, and when it was time to sleep, they were left to make themselves comfortable as best as they could somewhere on the premises and go to sleep after making themselves some tea.

The informants did not offer an explanation of the significance of the show of detachment in which the visiting delegation is neither acknowledged nor provided with the usual courtesies and hospitality due to visitors. The attitude, nevertheless, is consistent with the first stage in rites of passage, which consists of ritual behaviours that signify detachment from familiar roles in preparation to enter new ones. It appears it is necessary for the two parties to feign not being acquainted with each other even though they may live in the same locality, in order to properly enter the roles of arranging the separation of the marriage couple from their respective families to enter their new status as adults with their own family.

The next morning, the delegation and the hosting party from the girl's family would meet in the house in their new roles and greetings would be exchanged, not as among old acquaintances even though they might know each other well already, but as strangers meeting for the first time. Introductions would then be performed and the courtesies of welcome extended to the visitors in readiness for the processes of the preliminary visit. The young man's maternal aunt and leader of the visiting delegation would inform the girl's party about the nature of their visit. They would explain that they had been sent by the boy's family to propose marriage between their son and their daughter, by declaring that *'re romilwe ke boora mosimane gotla go rulaganyetsa tseo ya ngwetsi'*. In response the girl's party would ask them to let them know the girl they were interested in and identify her by her full names. The girl's party, particularly the chief maternal aunt, would ask a few questions seeking clarification on points of interest to them before ultimately agreeing to grant their approval to the proposed marriage.

After they have granted their approval, the girl's family must next inform the young man's delegation about the type of *bogadi*/lobola gifts they wished to receive as a token of marriage. Amongst others, this would include a cow with its calf (*kgomo ka namane*) They would also demand foodstuffs sufficient for the wedding feast to be held a day after the *bogadi*/lobola delivery rituals known as *patlo* (bride-seeking). Thereafter, a day would be set for the young man's delegation to deliver *bogadi*/lobola. In the interim, two women from the young man's delegation would have been busy outside the house, preparing the tea they brought with them for the girl's party to drink at the end of the negotiations as tradition requires. In the evening, the young man's delegation, their mission accomplished, would depart and travel back to the young man's home to report to his waiting parents and the party of male members of the family, and how their visit transpired. they would then proceed to make arrangements to undertake the next visit to the girl's family for the *patlo*.

## Bride-seeking process (*Patlo*)

When the day for *patlo* proceedings arrived, the same delegation of women would regroup, in the company of their married or widowed men, to set off from the young man's family to the girl's home. They would be expected to report at the girl's family compound around four o'clock in the morning. At the front gate, it was the young man's women delegation that went into the girl's yard first to conduct the *patlo* proceedings, leaving their men waiting outside the yard. The significance of this arrangement was not explained, but since the women had been at the home before, it was presumably to allow them the opportunity to ritually explain to their hosts who the men they had come with were before the men could also be allowed into the home.

After a while, the men of the visiting delegation would be called in to join the meeting, which was attended by a delegation of both men and women from the girl's side. The men from both sides, not having been included in the earlier preliminary visit, would be briefed by the women delegation on how the preliminary visit proceedings had gone before the men commenced to conduct their *patlo* proceedings. Thereupon, the girl would be summoned to join the two family delegation teams and given a place to sit. She would be seated and asked questions, such as whether or not she knew about the young man's delegation and the purpose of their visit. She would accept knowing them. At this juncture, the girl's delegation would proceed to pronounce that they gave the girl into marriage to the young man, rendering the marriage sealed and valid, even prior to the issuance of *bogadi*/lobola. Ululations would be shouted out in jubilation, and wedding songs would be heard within the neighbourhood.

## Bride-wealth – lobola process (*Bogadi*)

On the day appointed for the payment of the bride-wealth, i.e., *bogadi*/lobola, the young man's delegation would be expected to report at the girl's yard in the early hours of the morning around 4 a.m. They would take with them two live cattle, *viz*., a cow and its calf, together with food stuffs to be cooked the next day during the wedding ceremony. The girl's family delegation would then demand the *bogadi*/lobola, i.e., a cow and its calf, together with the foodstuffs, as advised during the preliminary visit. It was these foodstuffs that would be cooked by the girl's family at the wedding the next day.

Where *bogadi*/lobola was to be paid up outright, the *patlo* process would be conducted at the girl's home, after which the two families and their delegates would meet with the village chief, the *kgosi*, who would commence to register *bogadi*/lobola before proceeding to offer counselling to the newly-weds and issuing a marriage certificate. Bakgothu contend that in the past, there was no issuance of a marriage certificate by the *kgosi*. A note acknowledging receipt of *bogadi*/lobola, by the girl's parents to the young man's parents was sufficient.

Be that as it may, Bakgothu state that customarily it was not mandatory that *bogadi*/lobola be paid upfront after *patlo*. According to Bakgothu, payment of *bogadi*/lobola might not be effected immediately after *patlo* but might be delayed or deferred until the young man or his family were in a position to pay. In that case, the young man's uncle, father or any close relation who was married, could deliver the *bogadi*/lobola cow and calf, or *kgomo le namane*, to the girl's parents. It was also an expectation that *bogadi*/lobola would be delivered together with the whip that was used to drive the cow and calf. Interestingly, Batlharo elders mention that nowadays, due to intermarriages with other tribes, they have adapted to either receiving or demanding eight *bogadi*/lobola cattle as is the general practice amongst other tribes of Botswana. They are however, quick to state that when the marriage process involves parties from the Bakgothu tribe, they usually adhere to the Sekgothu traditional practice of a cow and calf as *bogadi*/lobola.

As soon as *bogadi*/lobola proceedings were complete, the young man's family delegation returned home to deliver the good news to the young man's parents, where preparations for the wedding, *lenyalo*, would commence. They call this process to 'cook for lobola', or '*go apeela bogadi*'. For them, cooking for *bogadi*/lobola is a symbol or token of appreciation to the in-laws for having delivered *bogadi*/lobola for marriage to their daughter.

Bakgothu elders decry the fact that unlike in former times, nowadays *patlo* and *bogadi*/lobola processes are held almost simultaneously. They blame this practice on their parents, who adopted it, particularly due to the emergence of civil law marriages. For this reason, nowadays *patlo* proceedings are conducted early in the morning at 4 a.m., so that later the same morning, at about 7 a.m., the wedding party would be able to move the *bogadi*/lobola proceedings to the *kgotla*. At the *kgotla*, the village chief (*kgosi*), in the company of his subordinates, would continue the traditional Sekgothu marriage process by witnessing *bogadi*/lobola exchanging hands between the young man's and girl's family delegations.

## THE WEDDING CEREMONY PROCESS (*MOKETE WA LENYALO*)

According to Bakgothu, whether *bogadi*/lobola was paid upfront or not, the young man's family would still be required to provide food and a cow to slaughter for the wedding feast. The cow would be delivered and slaughtered a day before the wedding day at the girl's home in preparation for a wedding feast – *mokete wa lenyalo*. It was a tradition that on the eve of the wedding day, a certain portion of meat or cut from the cow, the *motlhana*, was prepared and cooked by an old woman who would then fed it to the newly-married woman. It was believed that eating this portion of the cow made the bride strong enough to bear the strain of childbirth when she became a mother. During the wedding day, ribs (*dikgopo*) from the slaughtered cow were also cooked as a special treat for the newly-weds during the feast. The wedding guests and community members would also be treated to delicious traditional food and lots of home brewed beer. Wedding songs and poems addressed to the newly-weds would be sung by performers from both the groom's and the bride's families in an intensely competitive fashion till late in the evening. During the wedding ceremonies, married women would wear shawls, *ditjale* and *doeks* or headscarves, *ditukwi*. The men would wear suits and hats as a tradition. The bride would wear a white dress and a hat, whilst the groom wore a black suit and a hat. The groom's parents would buy the bride's attire, while the bride's maternal uncle would buy the change of dress that the bride would wear later in the evening during marriage counselling proceedings.

## Marriage counselling process (*Go laya*)

Bakgothu state that the marriage counselling *go laya* was conducted on the eve of the wedding day. Only married and widowed people knowledgeable on Sekgothu marriage traditions were allowed to participate in the sessions. Remarkably, Bakgothu aver that recently married couples were denied attendance during the marriage counselling process – *go laya*. It was assumed that recently married people were still insufficiently experienced in matters of marriage to play a useful role in the sessions. It was explained that only couples who had proved themselves through a sustained period of marriage were permitted to participate in the counselling rituals.

Bakgothu elders have great respect and passion for the marriage counselling process of *go laya*. In their opinion, the quality of counselling has the potential to make or break a new marriage. If 'unsuitable' people such as divorced or unmarried people partook in marriage counselling proceedings it would have undesirable effects on the future of the marriage, whilst married and widowed people assured a bright married life. They maintain that the reason why only married or widowed couples of good standing in society were allowed to partake in the marriage counselling process was because such people were deemed to be stable and level-headed. Bakgothu elders thought that a married couple who are experiencing matrimonial problems should not be allowed to partake in traditional marital proceedings like *go laya*. A senior uncle with domestic issues or marital problems would rather delegate his younger brother to lead the marriage proceedings, and even choose not to attend any of the wedding events at all to avoid bringing bad luck to his nephew's marriage. It is for this reason that Bakgothu would prefer their newly-weds to receive counsel from experienced married couples or widows and widowers who are thought to have no blemish in their own marriages.

## Transfer of bride to her in-laws (*Go isa ngwetsi*)

The transfer of the bride or *go isa ngwetsi* is the next step in the ceremony of marriage as a rite of passage in which the girl is separated both from her family and her old status as a single girl, and incorporated into her new family and status as a wife at her husband's place. To underscore the process of separation from previous statuses and incorporation into the new statuses as adults, Bakgothu believe the newly-weds should set up their own home and begin their family life together at the groom's homestead as soon as possible after the rituals of the marriage process. They say that since 'charity begins at home', the newly-weds have learnt enough from their respective families to enable them to set up their own home and start a family immediately after the wedding. They expect the couple to emulate their respective families' successful marriages and good quality of life.

Consequently, the tradition is that shortly after the wedding ceremony, which would have been held at the bride's family home, the groom's family was expected to immediately arrange for the transfer of the bride to the groom's family home. Bakgothu refer to the transfer of the bride to her in-laws as *tseo ya ngwetsi*, to take the bride to her in-laws. On arrival at her in-laws' homestead, the bride would be expected to straight away commence building up her homestead and creating a new family. Furthermore, this ritual of separation was traditionally enacted through the fact that after her transfer to her in-laws, it was not permissible for the bride to return to her home for visits until after a long time. It was only her husband who would make regular visits to his in-laws, to inform them about how well their daughter was settling down in her new status and home. Bakgothu elders decry the fact that this traditional separation of the bride from her family is no longer observed. They blame modernity and technology for the change because they have made travel and communication so much easier than in the past so that everyone now can travel anywhere and contact anyone anywhere in the world.

Bakgothu elders also observed another recent trend in the conduct of marriages in their community which they did not like. The trend is the practice by young people of duplicating marriage ceremonies by having further celebrations under the church or the District Commissioner's office in addition to the traditional Nama ceremony. According to the elders, the practice is confusing to the young people and destabilises marriages, because the other marriage practices represent different value systems which detract from the importance of their own sacred values. The District Commissioner's practices, for example, are said to be based on secular values and may encourage people to marry for the wrong reasons, such as financial gain, status and materialist interests rather than for love. Young people are tempted to marry a rich person as the means to acquire riches quickly instead of seeking to create their own wealth as a couple and build a decent family.

## Marriage Rites and the Significance of Metaphorical Language and Symbolic Actions

Among the Bakgothu, marriage is a cultural event that resonates with their religious values that survive as a collective memory in the minds of the elders, and is revitalised in their traditions and rituals, like marriage. For the parents on both sides of the newly-weds, and for the newly-weds themselves, marriage is a great gift and an honour from the ancestors and from God. It is also a rite of passage through which a young couple transits into the responsibilities, privileges and roles of adult life. It is the means through which the foundational beliefs of the community are renewed and passed on to the next generation, such as the rules of inheritance, land being held in trust for the community and future generations, a household being owned by the senior female resident, and the gift of procreation. The couple look forward to not only being parents themselves but grandparents too, a status every sound parent would love to achieve in their lifetime.

Bakgothu elders believe that customary marriage changes the social status of a newly-married couple. They say that the marriage counselling process inspires the couple to immediately change from their pre-marriage behaviour and adopt a dignified way of conducting themselves both at home and before the eyes of the society. In this premise, the new husband and his wife are privileged to attend and partake in all traditional ceremonies, marriage proceedings inclusive – e.g., they partake in the *patlo* (bride-seeking proceedings), *bogadi* (lobola, bride-wealth proceedings), *ditsheko kwa gae* or *kwa kgotleng* (domestic disputes as well as those held at the *kgotla*), etc. According to Bakgothu, the married couple is also able to give guidance to the upcoming youthful members of the community who are maturing and also aspiring to get married. On the other hand, Bakgothu say that the married couples earn respect from members of the community, particularly their unmarried friends. The friends are also compelled to readjust their behaviour and give the newly-weds some space to start a family. The siblings of the newly-married couple also start to treat them with greater respect than before as they look forward to attaining the same status in the future.

## FACTORS OF CHANGE AND THEIR IMPACT ON THE BAKGOTHU TRADITIONAL MARRIAGE RITES AND ACTIVITIES

Bakgothu informants have observed that nowadays, parents of the new bride demand *bogadi*/lobola payment upfront from the groom's family whereas in the past it could be postponed and offered at a later date. This is believed to emanate from the fact that in these modern times the young bride's parents view marriage as another way that they can derive financial gain. Unlike in the past when there was a generally agreed and accepted value for lobola, currently it is up to the parents of the bride and the groom alone to negotiate its value.

The elders also note that because of the intermarriages which now seem to prevail in their community, their customary marriage processes have been affected. This has resulted in some confusion amongst the current youthful members of Bakgothu, who now seem to have lost interest in strictly adhering to some Sekgothu cultural practices.

Bakgothu interviewees also allege that the introduction of money as an alternative to cattle in *bogadi*/lobola payment has killed the traditional spirit and essence of this custom in their culture. This custom is underpinned by the belief that cattle as payment for *bogadi*/lobola was meant as insurance so that maternal uncles had resources to contribute towards the care and upbringing of the couple's children in future. The elders say the current preference for money does nothing to prepare the uncles to play such a supportive role because they tend to succumb to the temptation of squandering the *bogadi*/lobola money as soon as they receive it. Often the money leads to quarrels amongst the uncles when they have to share the *bogadi*/lobola payment.

## CURRENT PROBLEMS AND CHALLENGES IN BAKGOTHU'S TRADITIONAL MARRIAGES

Current issues pertaining to customary marriages among the Bakgothu vary and mostly emanate from the fact that the society grows and changes from one generation to another. One of the major issues cited as a challenge in current marriages is youthful couples' inability to engage their in-laws or parents in times of disputes. They tend to prefer resolving their conflicts independently, which often leads to divorce proceedings.

Rapid urbanization and migration from the villages is also viewed as a source of that society's current problems. The Bakgothu elders believe that the youth of their community prefer to settle in urban centres where social amenities are much better than those provided in the rural villages. In the towns and cities relationships are fluid, and Bakgothu youth may get involved with people of other cultures who end up inspiring them to depart from their customs and traditional norms. An attempt to convince the youth against intermarriages can only cause the young people to reduce contact with their elders back in the villages, if not complete alienation.

## Conclusions and Recommendations

Society by nature is not stagnant but dynamic. From generation to generation, certain cardinal aspects of culture tend to change with time, some positively whilst others change for the worst. This explains the predicament Bakgothu elders and their youngsters find themselves in.

It is evident that the initial Bakgothu marriage processes and procedures have changed. They are no longer in a state in which the youth among them still appreciate their customs and traditions. Surely, we cannot go back to the drawing board and advocate a reintroduction of Bakgothu customary laws, norms and practices as originally formulated. The society's dynamic nature compels it to always move forward with developments and not backward. This is shown in the behaviour of today's youth who tend to inter-marry across cultures more often than not. The likelihood of inter-marriages was too remote to consider in former times. The respective cultures of couples who enter into inter-cultural marriages get diluted, although one of the cultures, usually of the groom's, may gain the upper hand as Botswana is a patriarchal society.

We recommend that the House of Chiefs (Ntlo Ya Dikgosi) must investigate strategic ways to retain all the merits associated with customary laws and practices. These can simply be derived from all the good attributes that this particular research project has pinpointed from various ethnic groups' cultural practices. Clearly there is competition or even conflict, between customary processes of marriage and the newer forms practiced in churches and under common law, which should be managed on a national level. The Bakgothu customary/traditional marriage processes appear to be declining in favour among the youth in the community. For instance, the Bakgothu increasingly choose to finalise their weddings with an additional civil or Christian ceremony marriage even after first marrying through their customary norms and processes. The encouraging thing about this trend is that it means that Bakgothu youth are still attached to some aspects of their cultural norms and practices. This trend is not unique to the Bakgothu community *per se* but affects almost all the ethnic groups within Botswana. There is therefore a need to harmonise the customary marriage procedures and practices with the civil marriage laws by distilling and preserving all the good attributes of the Bakgothu (and indeed all other ethnic groups) customary marriage processes, whilst also rejecting and abolishing all its bad attributes. In this way we would be able to retain and preserve most of the relevant customary beliefs, norms, procedures and practices. This may help reduce the current high rate of divorce in the country.

# 5

# Bakwena

*Prof. Mabel Magowe*

## Introduction

The Setswana term *lenyalo* refers to both the institution of marriage and the process of getting married. The purpose of this essay is to describe *lenyalo* in both senses of the term as they occur in the culture of the Bakwena people from the Kweneng District of Botswana. The essay explains the significance of marriage as a cultural institution and the rituals (in the sense of ceremonial activities) that must be performed in order to complete a valid process of getting married in the Sekwena culture.

The data for this essay was collected during one month-long field research in Molepolole and the surrounding villages in the Kweneng District. The fieldwork consisted of interviews with carefully chosen elders from the community who were highly spoken of as knowledgeable in matters of the traditions and history of the Kwena people. The author also drew on her experience and intuition as a member of the Bakwena ethnic group. There is also a wealth of electronic resources, creative writing, biographies and academic research, all of which proved extremely helpful in providing information on the history and traditions of Bakwena, especially in so far as they relate to *lenyalo*.

Theoretically, it must be pointed out, for the sake of clarifying the approach adopted in this essay, *lenyalo* must be understood as a rite of passage. As such it serves the two purposes that are associated with rites of passage generally, namely, to enact the transition of an individual or a group of individuals from one social status to another, and to entertain the community in a celebratory feast to mark the transition. In the case of *lenyalo* the transition involves a young man and woman joining the world of responsible adulthood in the community to live together as husband and wife. Underpinning this essay, therefore, is the idea that the activities of the marriage process are rituals in a rite of passage and can be understood in terms of the three stages of a rite of passage. As originally formulated in ethnography, a rite of passage firstly consists of activities and rituals that signify withdrawal from the old status, and form the 'separation stage'. It is followed by activities and rituals that signify or perform the conferment of new status, i.e., pronouncing the couple as husband and wife. It is a transitional state during which the person or people being initiated are neither in the old nor in the new status. It is sometimes referred to as the 'liminal stage'. Finally, there are the rituals of reintegration when the crisis of the liminal stage is resolved and the initiates return to society in a new role or status. This stage consists of performances of rituals that enact and signify the assumption of the roles, responsibilities and privileges of the new status. Because the transitional stage is known as the liminal stage, it is sometimes convenient to use the term 'pre-liminal" and 'post-liminal" for the stages that come before and after it, respectively.

In practice the activities of the marriage process do not fall neatly into these three stages. Some are ambiguous and may signify one or all three of the stages. However, it is a useful scheme to bear in mind in order to understand the marriage processes beyond the mere chronicling of activities. The stages are especially useful because there is an underlying religious symbolism in the processes which means that the wedding process or *Lenyalo* encapsulates deeply held ideas and values which may not be immediately obvious.

## History and Origin of the Bakwena Ethnic Group

The information presented in this section was mainly obtained from a book by David Magang entitled the *Magic of Perseverance* (2008). Magang's book is a biography of a Mokwena man, and describes the history of Bakwena from South Africa to different parts of Botswana and Lesotho. Another important source was Isaac Schapera's notes on the early history of the Kwena (Bakwena ba ga Sechele) (1980) up to the accession of Chief Sechele I in 1831. The play *Sechele I: A Historical Play* by Barolong Seboni and Petlo Literary Artists is also valuable for the contribution it makes to our understanding of Bakwena traditions with regard to issues like the role of kings, indigenous religious ideas and the institution of marriage (2011).

The overview of Bakwena history below is intended to provide no more than a context for appreciating their cultural traditions, especially wedding ceremonies, and the beliefs and values that underpin them. It is evident from these accounts that the Bakwena have a long and proud history during which they have forged a robust identity as a people with resilient traditions epitomised in King Sechele's assertion in the play, before the missionary, David Livingstone, who had accused him of back-sliding as a Christian convert: "I am a Mokwena, a Motswana. You found me a Motswana, and you will leave me a Motswana".

According to Magang (2008), reflecting generally accepted views on the subject, the history of Bakwena, a people who venerate the crocodile (*kwena*) as their totem, can be traced to the Phofu Dynasty which reigned supreme between the 12th and 14th centuries in the then Western Transvaal (now known as North West Province) of the Republic of South Africa. The Phofu dynasty, it must be explained, was a Tswana chiefdom that emerged among the Bantu speaking people who had first settled in the Limpopo river basin more than 2,000 years ago. Their presence in the area predates the rise and fall of the famous Mapungubwe and the Great Zimbabwe Empires. This means that Tswana speaking peoples did not only exist side by side with the builders of these empires, but were most likely intimately connected to their successive rises and falls. Earle *et al.* (2006) are probably right in asserting that that the Tswana communities that exist today are descended from societies, kingdoms and empires first established in the area as early as 2000 years ago. The Phofu dynasty were thus among the many groups in the region that moved around different places in the region including Botswana, Lesotho and South Africa as a result of famine and tribal wars.

The first known leader of the Phofu group was called Masilo, who had two children; a daughter called Mohurutshe and a son called Malope. Mohurutshe was the eldest but was denied succession to the kingship after her father's death because she was a woman, so she left the group with her followers to form the Bahurutse tribe. Malope, who succeeded their father Masilo, remained with the rest of the group at Mabyanamatshwaana. He had three sons, namely Kwena, Ngwato and Ngwaketse, after whom the three largest tribes in Botswana are named. Kwena had two sons from his first wife, namely Kgabo and Phoketsa. Kgabo had Tebele, who in turn had Mogopa and Kgabo II. Mogopa succeeded Tebele but during his reign there was drought and famine. He and his brother Kgabo, were forced to leave the area to search for better, agro-friendlier environments. They settled at Rathatheng where the Crocodile River or Limpopo meet the Marico River. When the drought ended back at Mabyanamatshwaana, part of the group led by Mogopa went back to Mabyanmatshwaana and lived there for centuries until they were forced to flee from the place because of war, and went on to form the present Kingdom of Lesotho. Kgabo II, who had remained at Rathateng with part of the original group, later crossed the Limpopo River to establish Kweneng between 1600 and 1700. His group later settled at Dithejwane Hills near present day Molepolole village. They invaded Bakgalagadi and lived side by side with them in Kweneng. The group was later joined by the Sechele group who came from South Africa fleeing the feared AmaNdebele of Mzilikazi, who had almost wiped out the main Bakwena group under Mogopa. This Sechele group is probably the same referred to in Schapera (1980).

Currently, Bakwena of Botswana reside in different villages in Kweneng District, in the south west part of Botswana, the capital of which is Molepolole, west of Gaborone, the capital city of Botswana. They also live in other smaller villages such as Lentsweletau, Kopong, Thamaga, Mogoditshane, Medie, Mmanoko, Mmopane, Kopong, Mmatseta, Hatsalatladi, Suping, Boatlaname, Sojwe, Mogonono, Gamodubu and Mmopane in Kweneng East. The other villages in Kweneng West include Letlhakeng, Khudumelapye, Shadishadi, Takatokwane, and Dutlwe.

Bakwena co-exist with other ethnic groups, such as Bakgatla of Kgafela in Kgatleng District in the east, Bakgatla of Mmanaana, Basikwa, and Balete of Gabane in the south east. The latter were moved from their ploughing fields during the construction of the Sir Seretse Khama Barracks of the Botswana Defence Force and the Sir Seretse Khama International Airport, which took most of their land. They were moved to villages like Metsimotlhabe where Basikwa of Ramotswa are found, Mmatseta, Lentsweletau and Kopong. In Kweneng West, Bakwena co-exist with Bakgalagadi in Letlhakeng, Sojwe, Kgudumelapye, Dutlwe and Shadishadi. Most Bakwena farmlands are in these areas.

It is not clear from the traditions and resources consulted in this study the extent to which Bakwena share the belief of a common origin in the mythological Matsieng whose footprint is found at the place named Matsieng. Neither is there evidence of a tradition of a creation myth in which humankind is banished from the presence of the creator due to an original sin, such as the story of Adam and Eve in the Bible. Nevertheless, the Bakwena share with other Tswana groups a belief system centred on *Modimo* and *Badimo*. *Modimo*, the Supreme Being, is the creator of the universe, the giver and taker of life. *Badimo* are ancestral spirits whose function is to link together the spiritual and social lives of families and communities. The cosmological ideas associated with *Modimo* are not embodied in a unified oral epic, like *Sundiata* or *The Mwindo Epic*, but are immanent in the underlying symbolism of their arts, crafts, songs, dances, rituals, ceremonies and even the routines of daily life. God, through the *Badimo*, is depended upon to ensure the survival and well-being of the community, harmony in social relations and the fertility of humans, crops and game. One of these immanent ideas is *botho* and the other is *seriti*. Both reflect a central concern with the community as a whole and link together the social and the spiritual worlds through *Badimo*.

When the Christian missionaries entered the region and introduced Christianity early in the 19th Century, the Bakwena, like other groups, were subjected to great pressure that was inimical to their own traditions and religion. And although Bakwena are now mostly professed Christians, and indigenous religious ideas are seldom invoked, theirs is a kind of syncretism in which indigenous Kwena ideas and practices either exist side by side with Christianity or have found equivalent expression in Christian ideas and rituals. The belief in *Modimo* (the god) and *Badimo* (the ancestors) for instance, despite Christian protests to the contrary, is not impossible to harmonise with Christian ideas about God, the angels and saints. The relationship between the old and the new beliefs is complex and much of the old survives in more ways than meets the eye (Setiloane). It is this type of syncretism that King Sechele I probably thought could be possible when he converted to Christianity and still wished to remain king of the Bakwena. When David Livingstone insisted on him denouncing his polygamous marriages, rain making powers (*go fetla pula*), and many other religious appurtenances of the kingship, King Sechele was extremely compromised and conflicted. He felt that such a conversion was cutting him, as head from the body of his nation, and he navigated a more ameliorative and syncretic approach, as dramatised in the play *Sechele I* (Seboni, 2011). Hence, even in looking at the Kwena institution of *lenyalo* and its practices, it is important to bear in mind that many of the practices and behaviours associated with its processes carry symbolic meanings that hark back to the pre-Christian indigenous Bakwena belief systems.

## Understanding the Term Marriage or *Lenyalo* from the Sekwena Perspective

Participants defined marriage as a fundamental institution through which society perpetuates its existence, involving a union between two people (a man and a woman), and two families. One participant said, *"Lenyalo ke selo se se tlhokegang thata mo motheong wa setho, le wa morafe, gore batho banne teng ba bo ba ipitse morafe o o golang, mme le thaega fela ka bobedi jo bo nyalanang"*. This means that marriage is a big undertaking that is needed for the foundation and perpetuation of a group of people who then grow to call themselves a society. The emphasis on the union of a man and a woman clearly excludes other types of marriages such as cohabitation and same sex marriages which are trending, and polygamous marriages of the old culture. Although ostensibly Christian-based, this idea, according to Mulaudzi (2013), is consistent with those in most indigenous African societies despite some subtle differences in terminologies involved in the process. A good case in point is the exclusion of other types of marriages, such as those mentioned above, from valid marital unions. In other words, the understanding of *lenyalo* in Sekwena is made up of a combination of indigenous Kwena influences, on the one hand, and both Christian and contemporary secular influences on the other.

According to the participants and informants in the study, marriage is the union of a man and a woman, allowing them to build a home and live together as husband and wife in order to raise a family. Mulaudzi (2013) further explains that in contrast to the Western belief in the nuclear family, in Sekwena culture, the newly-weds are expected to show an interest in matters pertaining to each other's extended family and lineage. The building of a home, it was explained by the participants, did not only refer to the physical structures in the homestead but also to establishing harmonious relations with family members on both sides. It meant that the newly-weds themselves must work at fitting in within the extended family systems on both the groom and the bride's side, especially for the women who through marriage generally relocated to the groom's family home.

In addition, building a home also meant having children and raising them. Children were viewed as the critical 'fruit" or positive consequences of the marriage. Hence women who had children outside marriage were not regarded as respectable or exemplary. Likewise, if a woman was unable to bear children within a marriage, she was mocked and given names like *moopa,* or one who was infertile. Wives were usually blamed for infertility in the marriage, and the man would be allowed to have a second woman to bear a child for him. The couple would be encouraged to adopt a child from among the relatives. In some families, the woman's younger sister would be asked to bear children on behalf of her sister for the husband. Hence, central to family life was the ability of the couple to procreate. Perhaps this emanated from the fact that in Setswana in general, children were regarded as wealth because they would work in the fields and tend the cows to increase the wealth of the family. Kaufmann and Meekers (1998) also noted that 90% of Africans depended on agriculture for more than 50% of subsistence labour. This, however, is no longer the case as nowadays children stay in school until they are ready to work and start their own families. The family planning movement that started in the

1970's has also influenced fertility and family size among young couples who are now increasingly choosing to have fewer children. Traditionally the preferred sex for a first-born child was a boy. The birth of a first-born boy child was celebrated, especially by the father, as the arrival of a future head of the family. Hence, first-born male children were commonly named *Kgosi*, meaning chief.

The marriage process was also described in terms that suggest that it is a rite of passage through which the union of two people is socially recognised and solemnised in a ceremony that confers upon them the status of responsible adults in the extended family system of both the bride and the groom's family. The process involves practices and behaviours that signify that the approval and blessings of both the groom and the bride's families have been granted. Without the ritual of 'bride-seeking', for instance, the union would not be respected or considered valid. Failure to observe such rituals also led to conflicts and interference in the young couple's affairs by in-laws. If the bride had not been taken through the *patlo* (bride-seeking) processes, the mother in-law would say '*ga ke a mo rwalela ditlhako kaya go mmatla*', or in English, 'I did not wear my shoes to go and seek her out', thus indicating that she was under no obligation to respect, as an in-law, a woman to whose marriage she did not consent to through appropriate traditional rituals.

The marriage process as a rite of passage is a platform for laying the groundwork for a seamless reincorporation of the newly-weds into society in their new status and role as adults with responsibilities to their families and the community at large. Through the processes of the ceremony the couple is instilled with the cultural values and norms underpinning a harmonious social life. Conflicts, especially between the mother in-law and the daughter in-law, are a well-known phenomenon among Bakwena and among Batswana in general. The rituals of the marriage process contain symbolism that signifies the importance of resolving such conflicts, invoking the values of *botho*. In Sekwena culture as one participant explained, *"Re abo re nyala mosadi, re mo nyalela monna wa gagwe le bo matsalaagwe"*, meaning that the woman is married for the sake of her husband and her in-laws. As in other Setswana societies, it was explained, in Sekwena culture the woman is taken away from her family (*oa nyalwa*), and the man takes the woman into his family '*o a a mo nyala*' or '*o a nyala*'. Hence ownership of the marriage is with the man and his family. The practice of lobola, therefore, does not only refer to the bride-wealth that exchanges hands during the ritual, but, crucially, to the process of transferring control of the bride from her parents to her husband's family to serve their interests as a married woman, wife and mother (Bekker & Koyana, 2014), and 'cling to his wife, and together they shall be one'.

## THE MARRIAGE PROCESSES

### INTRODUCTION

Family roles were clearly explained as central to the marriage. The families, especially the man's parents, initiated the marriage negotiations by meeting the girl's parents. The decision may come from the father of the young man, showing interest in his son marrying into a certain family (he may have even identified the girl of interest). The young man may be the initiator, telling his father of his intention to marry a girl of his interest, as happens in 'modern' culture. In both instances, the father would then take over the processes and start to involve the uncles of the young man. It should be noted that henceforth the couple was not engaged directly in the negotiations, but the male relatives led the processes in collaboration with their wives.

Parents must first recognise that the young man was old enough, mature and ready to get married. One participant said this to illustrate the point: *"Ga go tle mosimanyana fela a bo a re kea tsaya, le batsadi ga ba lebe setshosa fela babo bare o ka tsaya. O tshwanetse gore e bo e le monna yo o kileng a ya mmaeneng, ba itse gore o ka tlhokomela lelwapa"*. Translated, this means that the man must be mature enough, must have worked in the mines and be able to take care of his family's material needs. It should be noted that in the old days the financial capability of a man was based on having had a series of contracts of employment in South African mines (usually of a nine-month duration each), where most Batswana men would work for their livelihood. This enabled the men to meet the requirements of bride-wealth and provided evidence of their ability to care for their families. This was not unique to Batswana. Yabiku *et al.* (2010) describe a similar migration of men from Mozambique to work in the South African mines in order to secure the family livelihood. This was also true of Eswatini, Lesotho, Malawi, Zimbabwe where labour recruited by the Mine Labour Organisation sent men by train to the mines, often on trains, *stimela.*

The family members were usually also involved in counselling and supporting the young couple and assisting in disputes to keep the union intact. One participant remarked that *"tsholofelo ke gore ka bobedi jo bo tlaabo bole boša mo nyalong, ba godisiwe mmogo, ba ratane, ba dirisanye sentle, ba rerisane, babo ba nne le bana le matlotlo a dithoto, babo ba tsofale mmogo ba kgaoganngwa fela ke loso"*. Here the emphasis is on guiding and building the inexperienced couple to grow together, love one another, engage with each other, and learn to live harmoniously together, have children and nurture them, and grow old together till death sets them apart.

Marriage was described by informants as a very serious undertaking built on love and understanding, hence the careful choice of a family that the young man would marry into, to ensure that the marriage lasted for ever. This accounts for the saying *'Lenyalo ga se papadi, ke sennela ruri'*, meaning that marriage is not a game but a serious lifelong connection. Informants also explained that in the past marriages were much more than just the exchange of vows and the paying of the bride-wealth, the rings, clothes, the white dress, and the large wedding ceremonies that are prominent in modern day weddings and are often the focus and source of excitement. One participant decried the fact that, *"Batho ba gompieno ba kgatlhwa ke go phatsima ga mesese e mesweu, e bo e re go sena go phatlalalwa o bo o utlwa gotwe, ke bale, baa lwa, ebile baa tlhalana"*, emphasising that people of this new generation are just impressed by the glamour and extravagance of a white wedding that inevitably ends in conflict and divorce. A good, healthy wedding in Sekwena tradition should involve the family's emotional engagement in the couple's lif, and an imposition of expectations on how to live their lives. Participants interviewed expressed that traditions and customs concerning *lenyalo* have been passed on through the generations.

While the participants emphasised that both parties must work hard to keep the marriage going, they also reiterated the point that the success of a marriage depended more on the woman. Women were expected to assume primary responsibility for the stability of the marriage and to fight hard for its success, often against great odds and at enormous sacrifice. This is corroborated by Ellece (2011) who deduced from the wedding songs of Bangwaketse, a related ethnic culture in Botswana, that a woman was expected to sacrifice everything to ensure the success of a marriage to the point of 'being foolish'. This was illustrated in the remark by a female participant in this study who summed up the woman's role in marriage in these words: *"Mosadi o itshokela mathata otlhe a lenyalo"*. Women also provided labour for the family, especially during the ploughing season. Kaufmann and Meekers (1998) indicate that women provided more than 45% of the subsistence farming in African society, so this is not unique to Bakwena. Women were often encouraged, during a *go laya* ceremony, to regard marriage as a lifetime bond, and were warned of the severe sanctions against women who failed to stay in marriage and chose to separate (*go tloga*), or divorce (*go tlhala*). Such women were treated with scorn. So there is always a great readiness to intervene in the case of conflict, either by the parents and close relatives at the clan level or by the chiefs and other selected village elders from the *kgotla*. It is for the purpose of handling such conflicts that to date there is a *kgosana ya tetlanyo*, or a headman of arbitration for marital issues, who provides guidance and counselling for couples with marriage problems, as a last resort, before it escalates to the courts of law for divorce.

## Identification of future marital partners and the initial interest

Identification of a partner occurred long before courtship between the couple. The family looked around amongst other families who were connected to them by blood or otherwise known to them. The father searched for a girl from the chosen family and encouraged his son to approach the girl. The boy was also allowed to look for a different girl from the same family or closer relatives with the same characteristics as the reference family. This dispels the notion that brides were chosen for sons and that the sons had no choice in the selection. Some participants indicated that the choice of the girl might actually start as early as when she was a child, and hence the practice is called *peo letlhokwa*, which was more like booking the girl when she was still young (usually around the age of 10 to 12 years). The young man was informed about this and encouraged to start showing interest and caring for the girl indirectly through her parents. So as he continued to earn money from the mines, he would start to send clothes and blankets for the wife-to-be to mark his own interest, but would not have contact with her. This restriction was intended to allow her to develop free of the pressure of an intrusive relationship and to prevent the risk of early sexual relations. The parents would groom her and guard her against the interests of other boys or men.

## Courtship

Once the girl was old enough, usually in her teens, she would be considered ready for marriage and the negotiations would then begin. The father of the groom-to-be would signal to the young man that it was time for him to get married. In some instances the young man might also express to his father his readiness to get married. If the *peo letlhokwa* had not been done already, the young man's attention would be directed towards a girl identified by his parents from among one of the families they were connected with, and encouraged to take an interest in her. He would be instructed to get closer to the girl in order get to know her better and let her know about his intentions. At this point in the relationship there would be no sex involved. Sex would be taboo until after marriage arrangements had been completed.

The choice of family was also very important beyond familiarity and friendship. The important characteristics included being well behaved, hardworking, not known for witchcraft, being generally healthy without any overt diseases or disabilities, honest and respectable, and not known to be thieves or crooks. One participant said: *"Rona re ne re nyala mo malwapeng a re a itseng, re itse mekgwa ya bone, go itsa gore ngwana wa rona a seka a timelela ko baloing le magodu"*, meaning that the family would typically marry into a well-known home, with good behaviour, and who were not witches or thieves. Similarly the girl was also chosen because of her physical appearance (beautiful and healthy), typically hard working, involved in household chores, and polite and pleasant. As emphasised by one participant: *"Re leba gore a yo o na le botho, o ka aga motse"*, or we look to see that the girl has humility and can build a home. One man said he was guided by his father to three families from among his close contacts. But the young man rejected the first two because one of them had a history of excessive drinking of alcohol and misbehaving (the girl was not necessarily involved in the bad behaviour, but by association she was not eligible for marriage), and in the second family the women were too short and he did not want short children.

The young man would then use different opportunities like meeting the girl when she went to fetch firewood, water at a borehole or or at playing fields, and there he would start the courtship. The girls would typically be shy and keep their distance from the man, or even run away whenever they noted his interest, making it very difficult for the man to get close to them. But if the identified girl liked the boy too, she would gradually soften in her attitude towards him and allow some interaction. If she was not interested, she would become hostile and would not allow any interactions at all until the man gave up. When all had gone well between the two, the young man would then inform his father that he thought the girl was ready and they had agreed on the marriage. There were variations, however, in relation to who could initiate the initial steps of the marriage process as described above. In some instances the young man started the process. He would first talk to the girl of his choice and only inform his uncle afterwards. The uncle would then convey the information to the father. If the girl was 'agreeable' she would also tell her aunt, who would in turn convey the message to her mother. This is an indication that traditionally it was not easy for a child, boy or girl, to start talking directly to the parents about relationships. Only parents could initiate such talks with the child, and usually it would be one way, with the child being instructed what to do, and little discussion. Even today many parents find it difficult to initiate sexually-related discussions with their children.

## PRELIMINARY FAMILY VISITATION

The marriage negotiations involved a number of visits by different family members from the groom-to-be's side. The first visitation was by his parents (father and mother). The father would inform his wife about the intent of the formal visitation to the girl's family to formalise the intentions to marry their daughter. This first visit in Sekwena culture is called *go itshupa* or to show intention. In Sengwato it is called *go bona lelwapa* or to see the bide-to-be's home, whereas in Sekgatla it is called *go kokota,* to make the first 'knock' at the girl's home. This happened even when the families were known to each other. It was a formal notice of the intention to start the process of negotiating a marriage between their respective children. The young man's father would then talk to the girl's father about the intended visit, and the expectation was that the latter would then inform his wife. It should be noted that the men always took the leading role in the conduct of these early stages of the marriage process. The date was set for this family meeting.

During the visit the main agenda was to inform the girl's family of the interest in one of their daughters, and to ask for her hand in marriage to their son. However, it was a brief visit during which there was no discussion apart from the boy's family simply informing the girl's family of their intentions. The girl's family would simply acknowledge the information with the response, '*Re tla utlwa ka lona*', meaning 'We shall wait to hear from you'. This would be later followed by another meeting in which a delegation of uncles from the boy's family would be sent to the girl's home. This is how the meeting would be arranged. The father of the groom-to-be would inform the boy's maternal uncle, and then the paternal uncle. The maternal uncle was the first person to be informed and would be the lead person for further negotiations, a role that must not be interfered with. In order to check that his role was respected, the uncle would ask if anyone else had been informed. This was because in some instances errors were made where the father would tell his brother first. If the maternal uncle found out that this had happened, it was regarded as flouting his leadership role. He would get very upset, and this would deter him from getting involved. The father would then have to make a strong apology if the negotiations were to continue smoothly. In fact, there is a song in which there is a check to see if the maternal uncle has been informed the right way, and it goes like this: '*A ruri le boleletse malome mo mojaditlhogo, gore setlogolo se a nyalwa mo kgotleng*'. If all is in order then the maternal uncle would inform his wife, who also had a role as *mma malome* or maternal uncle's wife. Then the maternal uncle would inform the paternal uncle. Even if the paternal uncle knew something or had heard about this informally: he would pretend that this was the first time he was hearing of it. These two men, with their wives, would make the second visitation to meet the uncles from the girl's family.

A meeting would then be formally arranged at the girl's family home, and the parents of the girl would be present, since it was their home. During the meeting the maternal uncle would take the lead and inform them of the intent of the visit. The paternal uncle echoed this intention. The response from the girl's maternal uncle would be that '*ga re mmogo re tlaa bolelela ba bangwe re bo re le busetsa phetolo, kana rona re tshwareletse botsadi, re tla ba bolelela*', meaning that they were just holding the fort for the family and they were not the sole decision-makers on the issue of marriage. They would then respond after consultation with the relevant family members. Again, not much would be said as to whether they agreed or not, and no one would want to take sole responsibility for having solemnised the marriage in the event that the marriage broke down. It was common to hear sentiments like, '*ga re batle go ikgolega*'. The meeting would end and the uncles would part ways. Usually it was a very solemn, respectful meeting. The women would be wearing traditional headscarves and shawls, and the men would be wearing jackets and take off their hats during such talks, as a sign of respect for this highly esteemed process.

The expectation was that the groom-to-be would be asked by his parents to confirm his intentions and readiness for marriage, and he would then be advised to start preparing and accumulating requirements for *patlo* and the bride-wealth. Likewise, the girl would also be informed by her parents about the intended visit, and would be asked about her interest in marrying the young man. It was necessary to make this confirmation as it set the stage for continuation with the preparations for *patlo* and the wedding.

The uncles on both sides would then call meetings of their respective extended families separately at each family's house to inform them about the plans, and to begin preparing. The extended family members included the maternal (*mmangwane*) and paternal (*rakgadi*) aunts, grandmothers from both sides (*bo nkuku*), and if there were married siblings and closer members of the family they would also be called to this meeting. From the groom's side this was the delegation that would make the third visit. The girl's family would then send a message to indicate that they had informed their extended family members and the third visit could take place. A date would then be set. The main purpose of the meeting was to get a response on the proposed marriage and start planning. There would also be confirmation that the two youngsters had agreed to get married. Sometimes they would be called to the meeting to confirm verbally. If there was no agreement between the two, this would be communicated and the meetings would be dissolved. There would be no more communication regarding the marriage. However, this was very unlikely given the rigorous steps taken to initiate the process.

The girl's family would acknowledge the marriage proposal and then enquire from the groom's side how they intended to proceed with the marriage by asking the question, '*le nyala jang*?'. The expected response would be an indication of the number of cattle they intended to offer as lobola. Usually this ranged from two to eight head of cattle, depending on affordability. The girl's family would then add requirements such as clothes for the girl, which normally would include blankets, a shawl (*mogagolwane*), headscarf (*tukwi*), dress, underwear and money for shoes. One participant said that there was payment of a sheep called '*nku ya perepetsha*' at the early onset during the negotiations, but all other participants denied this practice in Sekwena culture. Another point of departure was expressed by one participant: that when a man did not have any cattle, or if he had no money to enable him to meet the requirements stipulated, his family would pay all expenses for the wedding on his behalf. This was again negated by all other respondents and one of them said, *"Rona re ne re sa nyadise sekopa, re ne re nyadisa monna yo o tiileng, a ipaakaneditse go nyala, a thusiwa hela mo go tsa bogadi ke bo maloma jaaka go tshwanetse"*. Simply put he meant that they would not get into marriage with a lazy and good-for-nothing groom-to-be in the first place!

## BRIDE-SEEKING (*PATLO*) CEREMONY

This was an organised ceremony at which the members of the groom's extended family, and additional members from the community, would pay a visit to the bride's family to ask for the bride. This is typically referred to as 'asking for the calabash of water' (*go kopa sego sa metsi*). It was a very highly respected and jovial, a very active, occasion on an agreed upon date. However, the man's mother and father did not participate in the *patlo* but would send the uncles, who were usually trusted to do the job well, in collaboration with members of the community and family. If plans were such that the wedding was preceded by payment of the bride-wealth for some time, as in the case where people were still engaged at the farmlands during the ploughing season, the men would perform the *patlo* ceremony and the women would just accompany them to ululate. The women's *patlo* would come at a time close to the wedding day.

The preparations for *patlo* involved assigning someone from the boy's family to guide the delegation from the groom's side as a leader of their delegation (*raditselana*), because he knew the culture of his family better. His role would be to brief visitors on how to present themselves, what to say, and how to respond to questions or comments. This was also done to avoid mistakes in the process of bride-seeking or *patlo*. On such occasions the groom's family members were treated as children and expected to be obedient to the in-laws, normally referring to them as their parents. Non-compliance with such rules would be typically sanctioned through fines, hence the need for guidance. The men would be met at the entrance and ushered into the family home of the bride-to-be to wait at the *lelwapa*, a brick-walled or mud-paved yard in front of the house. This yard was usually prepared and well decorated for the event.

*Patlo* took place in the early morning around dawn, where a large number of people from the man's family performed the bride-seeking rituals. The time is typically referred to as '*mahube a naka tsa kgomo*' because that early the only thing you could see would be the white horns of a cow (*naka tsa kgomo*). This practice has been modified somewhat because people complained about not being able to know the key people who talked to them, and the bride-wealth being paid in the dark. The time was modified to after dawn, but still very early in the morning. The men would walk in a procession towards the kraal (*kgotla*), where their *patlo* would take place, and where the prospective in-laws would be waiting for them. *Raditselana* would lead the way, followed by the maternal uncle, the paternal uncle, and then other extended family members, as well as community members who had been invited. The men would kneel in front of the girl's family delegation at the *kgotla*, and the uncle would start the process by kneeling down quietly. The girl's family would greet them by quietly repeating the words '*Dumelang bana*' or 'Greetings to you, our children'. After that a volunteer would pray, and the man's uncle would start asking for the calabash of water, saying, '*ke kopa sego sa metsi*'. The maternal uncle from the girl's side would reply saying, 'The calabash of water is being given to you with wishes of heavy rains' or, '*Sego sa metsi ke seo rea se lo naya ka pula*'. Sometimes they would say '*Metsi ke ao, a nweng ka pula*' or 'Drink the water with heavy showers of rain'. It should be noted here that rain is a scarcity in the semi-arid country where people rely on arable land ploughing (dry land farming) and animal husbandry for their livelihood.

So rain is always an expressed wish in any community gathering. That is why a woman is referred to as a drawer of water or *'sego sa metsi'* for the husband's family. This may also be interpreted as meaning that a woman is treated as a commodity for the man's family. A marriage celebration was also highly rated and valued if, during some of the processes like *patlo* or wedding celebration, some drops of rain fell. This would usually be accompanied by many ululations.

## PAYMENT OF BRIDE-WEALTH (LOBOLA OR *BOGADI*)

After *patlo*, the groom's delegation would ask for 'permission to go round the corner'. This would be to get the cattle requested as bride-wealth. They would typically just say, '*re santse re bowa fale*'. Some younger men and the uncle would then bring the cows in the numbers required, or more if they really liked the family or had gathered more from the contribution of the relatives. The bride-wealth was an indication of appreciation from the man's family to the family that gave them a bride. Some participants explained that it is not payment for the bride because one can never pay enough for a human being. In addition, some participants said that the bride-wealth was a form of security in case the young family went bankrupt. The couple would be able to go the woman's family and ask for help, so the cattle paid would be sold or given to relieve the financial problems. Another informant added that the payment of young cows (usually around 18 months of age) is security for milk, to make sure that by the time the first child is born and later taken over to the mother's maternal home for weaning from the breast, the child must find the cows having bred and producing milk to drink. This would explain why the preferred cattle for the bride-wealth would be of the age that in Setswana is called *maalolelo.*

There have been changes in the value of the bride-wealth over the years. One participant said from an initial three head of cattle it became four then six, and lately eight, which is now the standard rate. Other participants insisted that in typical Sekwena culture, the cows also had to be paid in pairs. Among the head of eight there is a mix of female and male cattle. They may come evenly distributed or preferably with more female ones. The justification advanced was that the number of cattle must be balanced for a good foundation to start a cattle post (*moraka*). In addition, this would give the family the choice to sell some male ones, or to slaughter some for the wedding. In Setswana culture the cattle that are sold or slaughtered are usually the male ones (*dipholo*) as the female ones are kept as breeding stock.

The cows for bride-wealth were typically contributed by the men in the boy's family. The maternal uncle contributed the one that would lead the herd (*e e di etellang pele*), termed a cow for drinking water, '*kgomo ya metsi*', meaning it is given to the girl's family for the wedding ceremony to enable people to eat and drink. Batswana tend to associate water with eating, especially during large ceremonies. For example, during funeral sessions they would say '*bana ba le diretse metsinyana ka fa morago*' or there is a little water prepared for you at the backyard, meaning that food is served. It should be noted that the word for water is stated in the diminutive ('*-nyana*') because in Setswana culture it is customary to understate the extent of one's own generosity, leaving it to the receiver to be effusive with the appreciation. Of course the choice of water as a reference to hospitality in general may be related to the scarcity of rain water in the country. This same concept is reflected in how the cow that is to be slaughtered for consumption at the girl's ceremony is called '*kgomo ya metsi*'. The water may also refer to the beverages that are provided as refreshment during celebrations.

Among the eight cattle offered for the bride-wealth, the second biggest is referred to as '*kgomo ya kota*'. Usually this cow would be contributed by the paternal uncle or the parents of the groom, and during the session the maternal uncle would make a declaration that '*di a kota*'. The expectation was that during the second leg of the wedding on the groom's side, the girl's family would give the man's family a cow in exchange for the *kgomo ya kota* for their celebration. The concept of *kota* was not very clearly explained, but it seemed to have a sexual connotation related to the union of the man and woman. As one man said, '*Ba e seo, re kota ka ene mosadi yo re ba mo neelang yo*', and he was giggling as he said that. It should be noted that Bakwena, like the rest of Batswana, are not comfortable discussing sexual matters openly; hence many symbols related to sex remain unclear. *Kota* has very clear and explicit sexual connotations though!

Bride-wealth had never been in monetary terms, but was in the form cattle in the past, because they have always been the symbol of wealth in traditional Setswana culture. However, lately there has been a noticeable change to the payment of bride-wealth in cash in cases where people either have no cattle or would have problems with obtaining cows, and with their transportation, because the groom's family may live very far away. Cash is also the chosen medium of lobola payment when there are problems with the transportation of cattle because of cross-border restrictions and disease control cordon fence barriers. Usually, because in Sekwena tradition bride-wealth in the form cows is highly respected, they would ask the groom's family to buy cows from a nearby place, and even offer assistance from people they knew who could sell the cows to them. It was the pride of the family to receive cattle for their daughter. However, there are still families that prefer cash. There is a similar practice among other ethnic groups in South Africa, especially those who live in big towns and cities, where it is impossible to rear cattle.

The other example of departure from traditional cultural practice is that nowadays the young man takes on all the expenses himself and there is hardly any assistance in the form of contributions from his family. Some people argued that this is because of the prevailing poverty in the Kweneng area, or because nowadays young people have gainful employment and can afford to do all that by themselves. But in view of the increased expenses incurred during modern weddings, this cultural practice of family support would come in handy in saving the newly-weds financial strain, which can lead to conflict and even early divorce.

Once the bride-wealth had been paid, the men (uncles) would send two men from the bride's side to inform the women that *patlo* had taken place, the lobola had been paid, and the girl had been given away. The groom-to-be was never part of the proceedings but waited around nearby to be summoned if he was needed. After the *patlo*, if the men from the woman's side wanted to see their son-in-law, he was brought by his uncle to greet the family.

Traditionally, after the payment of the lobola, the groom's family would then request permission to depart, and everyone would wait until the next event of the wedding. This changed over time: today the man's family is invited to join the girl's family to get to know each other over a cup of tea. Another current departure from tradition is that some *patlo* events are so big that cows are slaughtered, and a big feast is made, which only adds to the expense of the whole process.

*Patlo* has been regarded as the epitome (*de jure*) of the marriage. That means if this ceremony has been successful, the couple is considered married. The man's family may return to 'borrow the bride-to-be' or to ask for her to relocate to her marital home before the actual wedding if they need her services, because at this stage she is regarded as their daughter-in-law.

The registration and signing dates would be set and known to the couple and the families. Usually, the couple would go, with just two witnesses, to register at the office of the District Commissioner (DC), or be accompanied by a few family members or friends. The event is called '*go pega*', 'to put up' a name because the notice of their names and their intent to marry is placed on notice boards at DC's offices, at any place that the couple is known to have resided, for all to see. If it was planned to be a church wedding, the announcements would be made on three consecutive Sundays (mostly) by a priest of their church. During this day the families would arrange for a *patlo* by women.

## *Tlhagela* (pre-wedding child) fine

There are instances where the couple already has a child, or the girl brings a child from a previous relationship. This is usually declared during the *patlo* ceremony. Usually the couple would have discussed it before, and the man would have committed to taking in the child (or children) born out of wedlock before the marriage. The parents of the girl would indicate that the woman in question had a child or children, typically referred to as calves: '*o tla ka namane kgotsa dinamane*'. It is interesting how objects like the calabash, and animals like calves, are used to refer to human beings. It was difficult to obtain a response to why this is because no one could give a reason. If the couple had their child or children before the marriage, then the man's family would be fined a cow for breaking into the family home before agreements were finalised. It is called '*tlhagela*' or jumping the fence without permission, and the only permission was the wedding. This was paid prior to the *patlo* and it would be slaughtered, cooked and eaten prior to the occasion at a date set by the family. Invitations were extended to the extended family and closer community members. Currently, because of distance and travel constraints between families, this may come the day before the wedding or even during the wedding. One of the common songs related to this says, '*Kgomo di tsile di tsheletse, ya busupa e supile masupatsela*'. This means that six cows have arrived, and there is a seventh one that is pointed out by the herders, who have better knowledge about that one.. This refers to *tlhagela*, the one paid when the girl already has a child.

## *Patlo* by the women and the symbolism of their songs

*Patlo* for women is similar to that of men but more linked to and occurring closer to the wedding celebration, either before the registration at the office of the DC or on the day of the signing (usually a Thursday depending on the DC's schedule). In other places it could be a Tuesday or Wednesday. The women's *patlo* can also be scheduled for early morning on the day of the wedding.

As with the processes among men, the women from the groom's side who seek the bride would also be given a female guide called *mmaditselena* by the bride's family to assist them in complying with the expected processes. It was also done at dawn and conducted at the bride's home, *lelwapa*, and not in the *kgotla*. The *lelwapa* is a brick-walled enclosed area usually in front of the main house, measuring about three-quarter's of a metre in height, and wide enough to accommodate around 50 women. They would find the other women on the girl's side waiting in the *lelwapa,* sitting on mats and having laid out mats for the groom's entourage as well. The mats are made of empty sacks of mealie meal sewn together to make large carpets. The women would march in twos as they arrived quietly in a well-practiced dance style. In Sekwena culture there is no ululation until you have been given the bride. In other cultures, they come with ululation. They would then sit down on the mats quietly. The girl's side of the family would begin to greet them saying, '*dumelang bana*', or '*dumelang bagwe*' meaning 'greetings to you, our children or our in-laws'. *Bagwe* is a name given to the groom's side of the family. In Setswana, in-laws from the groom's side are referred to as 'children' because they are coming to ask for something very precious and must be obedient like children in order to get what they want. An effort was made to clarify the meaning of the word *bagwe,* but participants were reluctant to give details. However, from connotative expressions it seemed to be tied to some sexual expression. It may come from '*go gwela*' which refers to mating between animals. If this is the case, it would seem that they are given this name due to the prospect that their son is going to have sex with this woman. It is not clear why this activity became dehumanised and linked to mating among animals.

When the *bagwe* were greeted, they were not expected to say anything to return the greetings. They merely acknowledged the welcome with the non-verbal sound 'Mhhmmm'. The greetings would be repeated several times with the same response. After a moment of silence, one person among the visitors, usually the groom's maternal aunt, would stand up and enquire of their hosts whether they were all present. Usually, this question was asked to ensure that the rightful people on the girl's side, from whom they had come to ask for a calabash of water, were all present or represented. These included the maternal aunt (*mma malome*), paternal aunt (*rakgadi*), paternal uncle's wife (*mma rangwane*) and grandmother (*nkuku*). It is noted that in Sekwena culture men or women doing the asking or responding would typically be standing and not kneeling as with other Batswana ethnic groups. Then the *mma malome* from the girl's side would answer that all were present, '*re mmogo mma*'. The *mma malome* from the groom's side would then ask for a prayer, which could be given by anyone with the spiritual motivation. She would pray for a successful wedding and marriage, peace and good relationships between the two families. After the prayer *mma malome* would stand up again to 'ask for the calabash of water' saying, '*re kopa sego sa metsi batsadi*'. The response from the other *mma malome* from the groom's side would then be that they were giving them this calabash with prayers for drops of rain, just like the men had done. After this there would be ululations, singing and dancing to celebrate 'the calabash of water'.

The songs usually contain messages to the bride, the groom, the couple, the mother-in-law and the friends. One of the most common songs is about having been given a calabash of water, and having been given a field clearer (for ploughing) from the man's side. It goes, '*Re se tsere segonyana, sa metsi, re ba file moremedi was tshimo*', and the words are repeated several times. From the woman's side songs entail reminders of her role as a woman. She sweeps the yard of her in-laws so that they eat in a clean place. The song goes: '*Fiela, fiela, fiela ngwanyana, fiela ngwanyana o se jele matlakaleng*'. Generally, Batswana are known for cleanliness, and the role of a woman is to keep the compound clean. The bride is also expected to cook for the family, and the mother-in law is reminded in song to leave the pots alone and give way to the owner (the new wife). '*Heela matsale, tlogela dipitsa tseo mong wa tsone ke yo o tsile*'. This, in a way, is to guard against conflicts from the mother-in-law's interference in the kitchen. Interestingly, during *patlo* the mother-in-law is reminded to teach the daughter-in-law, who may still be very young, about their ways of life, including cooking and other household chores, yet this song warns her not to interfere. The other song referring to the couple would say, '*Hane ba le babedi, bane ba le babedi, bane ba le babedi, wa boraro no*'. This says that there were only two and there was no third person (in the agreement for marriage), meaning that there should not be any interference from any third party (which could be parents, relatives, friends, or even another or previous relationship). The other song that reflects the seriousness and challenging nature of marriage goes, '*Dikuku di monate, lenyalo le boima, rona re a tsamaya o tla sala o di bona*'. Translated this means that the wedding cake is tasty, but the wedding is heavy (challenging), and we are all leaving and you remain with the burden (of marriage).

## Bringing the clothes

Like the men, the women would then say 'We are just going round the corner, we are coming back', or in Setswana, '*Re santse re bowa ha*'. At this time a few lead women from the man's side would go and collect the clothes they had been asked to bring for their bride. The clothes would be wrapped in leather skin or, in modern times, in a bag. The women would carry the luggage on their heads. They were met by the lead women from the woman's side, who would then take the goods from them and also carry them on their heads. Both groups would go into a hut/house where the clothes were going to be checked to make sure they had brought all that was requested. When the clothes presented were not of the required quantity or were of poor quality, the girl's family would express this in no uncertain terms. This was seen as a threat to the integrity of the man's family and they would usually want to outdo themselves to please the in-laws. But usually, the clothes would be accepted without putting up a case. In some instances, the men's relatives would indicate that they would bring what was missing, and they would have to check everything against a list. If an omission occurred, it had implications for their integrity. After that, the man's family might ask to see their daughter-in-law, who would then be dressed up by her in-laws in the new clothes to go and greet the rest of the family. The girl would present herself as a shy, polite girl, otherwise she might be scorned for being too forward.

## TAKING THE MAN TO HIS IN-LAWS (*GO ISA MOSIMANE KO BOGWAGWADI*)

In the evening following the *patlo*, the man would be taken to the girl's house to 'lay feet' at the in-laws home for the first time (*go gata lelwapa*) following the blankets (*go latela dikobo*), which were given by him and his family to the bride. He would usually be taken by his uncle, or someone close to him. In preparation for this, the girl's maternal aunt would demonstrate to the girl how to make a bed for her husband. The man would be ushered to this room where the couple would sleep together for the first time, and perhaps this would be their first sexual encounter. One participant indicated that the girl would have been warned about the man's visit and encouraged to be hostile to him in bed by kicking him off and not allowing him to touch her for the first few days, in other words playing hard to get. On the other hand, the man would be asked to be gentle with her until she gave in. But if she continued to be hostile, he should touch her where it hurts most (press on the breast), saying '*Ha a pala o mo tlabole lebele monna, gore o mo katise*'. This would usually mark the beginning of a sexual relationship between the couple. If *patlo* and wedding took place in one day, the evening would be spared for the taking of the groom to his in-laws.

## THE REGISTRATION AND SIGNING OF THE MARRIAGE BONDS (*GO PEGA LE PHOLOSO*)

This is usually done after three weeks of announcements of the wedding plans by the DC's officer, usually on a Thursday of the fourth week when the names are brought down from all notice boards and that is why the event bears the name *go folosa* meaning 'bring down' the notice. This ceremony is usually planned to coincide with the *patlo* for women. The *patlo* would be done early in the morning to give way to the DC's visit when offices opened, around 8 a.m. The girl, accompanied by some of her family members, would then proceed to meet the groom and his family at the DC's office for signing of the marriage bonds, *pholoso*.

The couple might take their vows on that day and sign a marriage certificate, and the event is called *go saena* or appending signatures on their marriage certificate. At this event the bride and her family would meet with the man's family at the office in a white wedding gown. The man would be in a suit, also accompanied by his family. They would then be ushered into a big hall with other couples and the DC, or his officers, would preside over the event. It was typically a series of events where they explained the Marriage Act, the property rights and the choice of being in or out of community of property. They would also counsel couples at length about marriage and the implications of divorce. After that the couples would individually be asked to take vows, the DC or his representatives would usually read the statements for them, and they would repeat after him. This would be followed by signing of the certificate and then the married couple and their families would depart.

In religious families the wedding vows would not be completed at the DC's office, but the couple would take their unsigned certificate to complete the process in their church. The church for this event would be the girl's family church. The big celebration would follow after the church service on Saturday (Friday or Sunday in case of Seventh Day Adventist Church members). Most Bakwena belong to the United Congregational Church of Southern Africa (UCCSA), the former London Missionary Society before 1980, and they call it 'the big church'. (During funerals, when they want a song from the UCCSA hymn book to be sung they announce that they want a song from it, *go tswa mo kopelong e tona*, which emphasised that it is the hymn book that belongs to the 'big church'.) The other common denomination is the Anglican Church, followed by the Catholic and African independent churches. It is very uncommon to have a church ceremony for a wedding on Sunday in the Bakwena ethnic group. Most of the celebrations are on a Saturday. The church wedding would start with the women, led by the maternal aunts from both sides, bathing and dressing the bride in the morning. The group would then proceed to the church where they would meet the groom and his family. The preaching, exchange of vows and signing would then take place. The church service would be followed by the photo shoots and then the procession to the girl's family home via the groom's home.

## Pre-wedding celebration events

The wedding ceremony is a modern-day event that has now become part of the Sekwena and other cultures in the different ethnic groups in Botswana. This involves the registration of the couple at the DC's office, followed by the white wedding. In the typical Sekwena culture it starts with an agreement of the two families to have the couple register at the DC's office. The families would agree on the dates on which this would start. The office would publicise the intended wedding for three weeks and would give the couple the date for registration and making wedding vows. This would be published at every District office bulletin board countrywide, to give a chance to those who would want to object to the bonds of marriage, giving reasons why the couple should not be married. They were to indicate their objection within the three weeks, after which they would be expected to forever keep their peace. The reasons usually advanced would be if the man had a child with another girl that he had promised to marry and did not honour the promise, or one of them was engaged or promised in marriage to another person. It was rare that at this stage any of the family members would raise an objection to the marriage.

## The wedding celebration (*mokete wa lenyalo*)

After the DC's visit or the religious celebration, the couple and the entourage would then proceed to the in-laws place to greet them and show off the bride in the white gown they had bought for her. There they would be given some drinks, sometimes with some bread, biscuits or scones. The visit was usually just for a few minutes, and they would then proceed to the girl's family where a full celebration would usually be prepared. In these modern days the couple then go for a photo shoot before they reach the girl's home for the wedding. Upon arrival at the bride's home, they would be met with singing and dancing and ushered to a marquee tent laid out decoratively with tables, chairs and sometimes flowers and utensils for eating. They would have a special place where they sit with a group of young friends and relatives as the bridesmaids' and grooms' entourage, on a stage set higher than the rest of the guests.

There would usually be a series of speeches, welcome remarks and introductions from elders of both families. Other speeches would be from the uncles on both sides, who would thank the in-laws on the other side for raising the bride or groom as the case might be. They would also counsel the bride and the groom on expected behaviour in a marriage and on relationships with in-laws on both sides. The newly-weds were advised to focus on their marriage and minimise visits to friends. Other speeches would come from friends and well-wishers. This would then be followed by food and drinks and celebration with dance, song and poems.

## SHARING PARTS OF SLAUGHTERED CATTLE (*DIRWE*)

During the ceremony at the wedding celebration, some of the meat from one of the slaughtered cows would be divided among family members – depending on their contributions to the wedding. This starts with the uncle, who would get the head of the cow, symbolising his leadership role in the upbringing of the girl and through the wedding processes. He also qualified for this if he paid the cow that led others in the offering of the bride-wealth and bought clothes for his niece to change into during the wedding ceremony. His wife would have also bought some groceries (a bag of samp, mealie-meal or sorghum meal, a packet of sugar and assorted teas, cooking oil, etc.). The paternal aunt (*rakgadi*) would get the thigh, called *marage*, because she had carried the girl around when she was a baby and urinated on her thighs. The maternal aunt would get the small intestines, mixed with tender pieces of meat from other parts of the cow. The grandmothers and grandfathers from both sides would share the large intestines mixed with other pieces of tender cuts from different parts of the cow. In Sekwena this is called *mala* or *ngati* because it also has some pieces of the omentum fat (the fatty layer that stretches over the abdomen under the skin). The mother would get the chest of a cow *sehuba*, symbolising her role in breastfeeding. There would be a special pot cooked for men, which included offal mixed with other pieces of meat from different parts of the cow and called *mokoto*. Usually, this meat is served at the *kgotla* after lunch. It is very tasty, and women are forbidden to eat it.

## TAKING THE BRIDE TO HER IN-LAWS (*GO ISA LE GO LAA*)

While the wedding ceremony was going on, other plans would continue on the side, such as bride counselling (*go laa ngwana)* and formally receiving the bride (*go gorosa*) inside the in-laws' house, presumably where she would live henceforth. One woman proudly said, *"Rona Bakwena ga re lae ngwana phatlalatsa, go laa ke sephiri sa rona le ngwana wa rona, sedirelwa motlung ko ga matsalaagwe, re molaela bo matsalaagwe le monna wa gawe"*. This would be done a day after the wedding, early on Sunday when the women would bring the girl back to her in-laws in a process called *go isiwa*. The same group of immediate relatives would take her with all her belongings, including the clothes that were bought for her and the wedding presents that would assist her to start a new home.

Usually these presents would be household utensils like pots, plates, cups, spoons, bowls, etc. for the kitchen, as well as blankets and other linen. Upon arrival, the group would be met by other women from the men's side to take the goods from them and usher them to the room where the bride would sleep with her husband.

The women from the girl's side would then ask for permission to counsel their daughter for marriage. They would talk to her directly about how to present herself to her in-laws as a good woman who was there to unite rather than break the family, and they would use statements like '*Mosadi o aga lelwapa, o kopanya batho*'. She would also be counselled on how to respect and treat them well. They would encourage her to treat everyone equally regardless of social or economic standing. They would talk about some of the challenges like finding people with disabilities, the aged and sick, and emphasise that she was there to treat them all with respect, bathe them and feed them. She would be told to keep the yard and house of her in-laws clean, and to cook well for them, emphasising that laziness was not condoned. With regard to her husband the counselling emphasised respect, submission, obedience and good treatment of a man, especially washing cooking and laying the bed for him. She would also be encouraged to stick to one partner, and bear children for him. The interesting part is where she was told not ask him questions about his whereabouts, '*Monna ga a botswe gore o tswa kae*', even when he came home late at night, and never to interrupt him when he was talking, or raise her voice to him. The common statement is '*Mosadi yo o botho, yo o tsalegileng a lailwe, o buela ko tlase, ga ana mafoko mantsi*'. This means a polite woman keeps her voice low and does not have too many words. She should not even be concerned about his extramarital affairs because he is 'an axe that chops everywhere' or 'a calabash that is exchangeable among women'. In Setswana they would say '*Monna ke selepe, o tsamaya a rema kwa le kwa*' or '*Monna ke phafana, o a hapannwa*'. It is interesting again to find humans being likened to inanimate objects that have no feelings or capacity to make decisions. Again, the words could also encourage women to accept promiscuous behaviour from men, and this could result in extramarital relationships, children born out of wedlock and the spread of sexually transmitted infections. In the era of infectious diseases such as HIV/AIDS this practice can be dangerous and a source of networks that can perpetuate infections.

The man on the other hand would be taken by men for counselling at the *kgotla*, or kraal, in the absence of unmarried men or those who had not gone through the *patlo* events. There was not much disclosure on the part of the men on how the counselling would go or what would be said. But they just said, '*A laelwa mosadi go mo tlhokomela, le go tlhokomela bana, le lwapa le ba masika. Le go itshwara sentle ka ele tlhogo ya lelwapa*'. One would trust that the counselling is similar to that of a woman in terms of good behaviour and treating others well. However, nothing is said about acceptance of sexual activities of a woman, as is said to the woman, and this connotes a disparity in expectations of the woman compared to the man.

Nowadays the couple tends to stay with the man's family for a while until they have built their own home to which they would then move. It is no longer expected that the couple will live with their in-laws, and that the woman would serve the family, except occasionally during visits. Generally, however, it is more common for newly-weds to move directly into their homes in the town or wherever it is they may live and work.

### TAKING THE BRIDE BACK TO HER FAMILY

The girl would not be allowed to visit her original family before she could be taken back by her in-laws. Even if there was illness or death, whether she missed her family or not, she could not go there until this was done. One or two women would take her to her family of origin where she could spend a few days with her parents to have proper separation. She would then be taken back to her marital family. After this she could always go back and forth between the families but she now 'belonged' to her husband and in-laws, and should always ask for permission to visit her original family. If the visits were too frequent the in-laws would complain that she might revert back to her original family for good.

A recent change from tradition is that nowadays there is a lot more flexibility regarding restrictions on the girl's movements, such as visits to her parents after marriage. In fact, it is now common to find the girl and her husband visiting her parents frequently, allowing her space to get used to the new environment while still in touch with her parents. It works well as a transitional strategy. However, some in-laws may get offended by this because once the woman is married to their son she now belongs to their family and is not expected to be too comfortable with her own birth family. They would usually be quick to remind her that the bride-wealth has been paid for her to be one of them.

## ADVANTAGES, COMMON CONFLICTS IN MARRIAGES, AND SUGGESTIONS FOR IMPROVEMENT

Marriage, as described above, is clearly a rite of passage which ends with the reincorporation of the couple into society in its new status as a family. The marriage processes have the benefit of ensuring that the couple have the unwavering support of the entire community during different stages of their lives. This begins with the marriage negotiations and the marriage ceremony itself, and on to the subsequent challenges of responsible adult family life, such as starting a family, raising children and dealing with the hardships of life such as illness and bereavement. They are assured that their children will grow up with a secure sense of belonging in a large extended family setting where families live in a mutually supportive community and share resources.

However, these benefits are increasingly undercut by people leaving the villages to look for work and new opportunities in cities and towns where life is fast paced and impersonal. People are often so absorbed with their own lives they are hardly aware of who their neighbours are and of each other's needs. They often live under conditions of such severe resource constraints that nothing is shared. Children are now brought up by strangers like house helpers, who change frequently. Television and electronic toys have taken over the role of parenting as parents are frequently out of the home due to work commitments. Children also tend to start day care and school early, and the cost of this is that the children lose touch with their parents and miss out on the experience of parents playing the role of primary socialization agent.

Family support systems make a huge contribution to the sustainability of a marriage. Parental intervention at times of conflict has benefited many couples who would have otherwise divorced. Family support is felt more during pregnancy, the lying-in period, sickness, bereavement and other family occasions that need financial and human resource support. However, one should be cognizant of the potential for excessive control in the guise of support by some members of the family, either from his or her side, and recognise the need to maintain a balance in the kind of support offered. It needs to be critical to develop the power to reject undue and unsolicited support that takes advantage of the vulnerability of a couple.

Marriage can also have challenges if the negotiations are met with disagreements and misunderstandings between families, or unexpected financial and time demands that drain the very couple that is supposed to be supported. Some of the problems may be due to differences in socio-economic status, with potential for one partner to depend on the other for their livelihood, and for all the requirements from the family during marriage negotiations. The expenses are further increased where there are two separate wedding events, the first on the bride's side followed by another event for the groom's side on a different weekend. In modern practice combined weddings have replaced this traditional practice, thus cutting time and costs.

Bakwena, like other Batswana, have been able to merge the traditional marriage, common law and customary marriages within one big event. The original Sekwena ceremony, which mainly consisted of just *patlo* and *bogadi*, followed by a small ceremony, has now become a huge and expensive undertaking that involves travel, expensive costumes, food, entertainment and other requirements. Resource constraints often mean that raising the money to cover the cost of a wedding can be a challenge for couples. The prevailing high level of unemployment among young people has worsened the problem. Many couples intending to marry have no incomes and cannot afford the cost of a wedding. The declining socio-economic situation of Batswana in general also does not augur well for couples considering a modern Tswana wedding. The trend is towards a decline in the rate of such marriage celebrations. Another unfortunate consequence of the high cost of weddings is that in cases where one of the partners has the wherewithal to pay for the entire cost of the wedding, he or she may tend to go on to be the dominant partner in the marriage, sometimes resulting in a domineering attitude towards the other partner, characterised by abuse and violence.

Other differences may be due to religious affiliations. Usually, a girl who marries into a family is expected to adopt the man's religious affiliation or church. But this has often caused conflict with some religious denominations where the family would not want their daughter to move to another church. Some churches can be inflexible in this regard. Some women also seeking to assert their independence may try to get the man to change to their churches, which is contrary to established practice and not acceptable to most people. Another disconcerting development for families is the tendency in the conduct of such weddings for church officials to take over all processes and displace relatives. The role of the church and priests is traditionally that of solemnising the wedding ceremony at a church service through prayers and sermons sharing what the Bible counsels for a good marriage, and family members feel it would be best to stick to that role.

An aspect of religion that brought conflict between Bakwena and the missionaries, especially David Livingstone, was polygamy. Kgosi Sechele, for instance, who had a relationship of mutual respect with David Livingstone, was married to four women and this was not acceptable to the missionary, who perceived it as contrary to a virtuous Christian life. David Livingstone expected that, in order to become a Christian, Kgosi Sechele should get rid of three of his wives and remain with one, which he did in 1848. Unfortunately, it appears that he continued to have intimate relationships with Mokgokong, his favourite, who was later found to be pregnant. This tarnished the image of Kgosi Sechele before the man of God, David Livingstone. However, David Livingstone's efforts to get Kgosi Sechele to admit wrongdoing, repent and beg for forgiveness failed because Kgosi Sechele had decided that what Livingstone wanted him to do was tantamount to renouncing his role as King and head of his nation. He saw Livingstone's departure as good riddance to someone who had become irksome to his people and kingdom.

Martens (2009), relates another source of conflict between Christianity and tradition among the Bakwena with regard to marriage. From their arrival Christian missionaries objected to the traditional payment of lobola in African marriages. They associated it with 'buying' a bride, which they concluded was a form of slave trade in women. They consequently treated it as abuse of women and campaigned to abolish it, but without success because the practice was deeply rooted in the culture. It is interesting that the Christian missionaries were able to almost eradicate the practice of polygamy, but failed to abolish lobola, *bogadi,* even though both practices had been deeply rooted in the cultural traditions of the Bakwena. To this day *bogadi* is still a revered tradition, but polygamy has virtually disappeared among Bakwena.

Another source of conflict is when the marriage is across ethnic groups. Some of the expectations may come as a shock to them and they may feel the financial or even the physical and psychological strain, especially from making too many visits. In the current practice a compromise has been made by allowing the use of technology like telephone calls and email for the initial negotiations and bringing all other events of 'bride-seeking', paying of pride price, the wedding and taking of the bride and groom to in-laws to one weekend. This has really made things easier for the in-laws travelling from afar, although this is still very strenuous because of the duration of the whole *lenyalo* process, usually beginning on a Thursday and ending on Sunday.

Some traditional practices such as the use of traditional medicine also have an effect on the peace of the wedding ceremony. An example is the expectation that the place where cooking will take place during the celebrations is to be sprinkled with traditional medicine by a traditional healer from the man's side. This was to ward off those who wanted to bewitch the family and stop the marriage. Others believe that the couple must be joined together by drinking some traditional medicine to strengthen the bond between them. Some people still strongly believe in such practices, and when the other family does not agree it becomes a problem. If one family has a religious orientation it becomes a problem to agree to this, and it has the potential to explode into a big conflict. The conflict may worsen if later in life one spouse from the family that pushed for the practice dies. The common belief is that he/she would have been bewitched from the time of the wedding.

## Conclusion

Marriage in Sekwena is regarded as a good undertaking and an essential part of the culture that brings two families together, and perpetuates the human species through the birth of children into the families. It is also regarded as a blessing from God, and married people are given special respect by the community. They are accorded certain privileges, roles and responsibilities that unmarried people would not have. Marriage negotiations are usually led by the man's parents through the uncles and other relatives. It involves many activities that begin with the intention of the parents of the groom to marry into a selected family. The selection of the family is done very carefully, and the first quality is good behaviour. *Lenyalo* is a communal activity and goes beyond the couple to the extended family, whose involvement is evident through the lives of the couple. This advantage of an extended family should not be undermined. However, it would also be good to take cognisance of the increasing cost of living and the need for the couple to have an independent private life. Meddling in their affairs may cause confusion and is often the source of misunderstanding that may culminate in divorce.

## References


Bekker, J. & Koyana, D.S. (2014). The legislative reconstruction of the customary law of marriage. Journal of Contemporary Roman-Dutch Law, 77(23-37) Available at SSRN: https://ssrn.com/abstract=2487834

Ellece, S.E. (2011). "Be a fool like me": Gender construction in the marriage advice ceremony in Botswana – a critical discourse analysis. *Agenda, 25:1*, 43-52,

DOI: 10.1080/10130950.2011.575584. Available at https://doi.org/10.1080/10130950.2011.575584

Kaufmann, G.L. & Meekers, D. (1998). The Impact of women's socio-economic position on marriage patterns in Sub-Saharan Africa. *Journal of Comparative African Studies*, 101-114. ISSN 0047-2328

Magang, D.N. (2008). *The Magic of Perseverence: the autobiography of David Magang.* The Centre for Advanced Studies of African Societies (CASAS), Cape Town, South Africa.ISBN 978-1-920287-70-2

Martens, J. (2009). 'Civilised domesticity', race and European attempts to regulate African marriage practices in colonial Natal, 1868–1875. *The History of the Family, 14*(4), 340-355.

Mulaudzi, P. (2013). Cultural perceptions and linguistic terminology regarding traditional marriage within indigenous South African communities. *South African Journal of African Languages, 33*(2), 153-158.

Schapera, I. (1980). Notes on the early history of the Kwena (Bakwena-baga Sechele). Botswana Society in collaboration with JSTOR, 12 (1980) 83-87. Accessible at https://www.jstor.org/stable/pdf/40980796.pdf

Yabiku, S. T., Agadjanian, V., & Sevoyan, A. (2010). Husbands' labour migration and wives' autonomy, Mozambique 2000–2006. *Population Studies, 64*(3), 293-306.

# 6

# BALETE

*Prof. Brankie Nhlekisana & Dr. Pearl Seloma*

**Totem**: *Nare* – Buffalo

**Clan Poem:** *Leboko la Balete*

*Ke Matebele a mantsho a ga Masodi-a-Mphela* (Mazulu amampela)

*A ga selala le namane letlhakoleng*
*Di robaroba matlhakola*
*Di a robaroba fela di sa tla go a lala*
*Di tsoga di gopola letlhakola lengwe*
*Namane tse di naka di diobe*
*E re fa e re 'gou', Kgodumo!*
*O e tshabele mogotlhong*
*More wa nare ga o lebalebelwe*
*Mmutlwa ga o tshwane le lonaka, o ka tlhomolwa*
*Mogatsa mmolaya nare o ja a batla seyantlo go sa le gale*
*Kgodumo e maboo mabe, go boa e a gabalala*
*Barwa pataolo tsa mere*
*Barwa motlhana o tlhokile motse!*
*O jelwe ke magakabe le manong*
*Barwa kgodumo ya leselesele*

## INTRODUCTION

The aim of this chapter is to provide descriptions of both the institution of marriage and of the stages that have to be undergone before a union between a man and a woman can be recognised as a valid marriage in Selete culture. As in other Setswana cultures, in Selete *lenyalo* is a term that refers both to the institution of marriage itself as well as to the processes by which people are initiated into the institution as husband and wife.

The information used in this chapter was obtained primarily through field research that was conducted among the Balete in the village of Ramotswa and surrounding area during the months of April and May 2017. A sample of approximately 50 elderly male and female informants was interviewed individually and in small groups using open-ended interview-guide questions. The informants were elders from the community who were generally recognised as knowledgeable in matters of the community's history and culture. In addition to the interviews, recourse was also later made to available secondary sources in the form of books and journal articles, especially those that were readily accessible online.

It is clear from the data obtained that *lenyalo* among the Balete is a rite of passage. Among other things this chapter therefore discusses:

(a) the significance of marriage in Selete society, the steps followed in the proper conduct of the Selete marriage ceremony, and the principal role players in its rituals;

(b) the rights and privileges that marriage as a rite of passage confers on the newlyweds in Balete culture;

(c) the language and symbolism of the rituals of the *lenyalo* processes, since as a rite of passage ceremony *lenyalo* is rich in symbolism that includes representations of the phases of separation, transition and donning of insignia of the new status that are not always obvious even to members of the community themselves; and

(d) the impact of change on marriage as an institution among Balete today, and on the processes of its conduct.

Theoretically this chapter will rely on what is generally known about rites of passage and the three phases into which their rituals' performances are grouped, namely: 'preliminal', 'liminal' and 'post-liminal', also known as separation, threshold and reintegration (donning of insignia of new status) phases, respectively. Reference shall be made to these phases whenever necessary throughout the course of this discussion. Borne in mind throughout this discussion will also be the debate on whether, as a rite of passage, marriage merely preserves and reinforces the traditions of a community or has a more fundamental role as an agent affecting social change (Turner, 1969).

## BRIEF HISTORICAL BACKGROUND

Balete are a Setswana-speaking ethnic group of Nguni descent. Their origins are traced back to the Ndebele people of the Transvaal in South Africa. However, according to one elderly male oral historian in Molepolole, the word *selete* refers to an open hole trap with hidden underground spears. It is believed to have been introduced by people of Nguni origin, and was used for trapping lions and other wild animals that were roaming the areas along the Notwane river up to Otse. Because of this, Bakwena ended up referring to people of Ndebele ancestry who came to live in that region as 'makers of *selete* traps', hence the name Balete. However, according to available historical written records, Balete people settled permanently in Botswana around Ramotswa in the middle of the 19th century. The people are not found only in Ramotswa now, but are also settled in the nearby villages of Taung, Otse, Gabane, Mogobane and Mmankgodi in Botswana. They venerate the buffalo as their group totem and lavishly praise it in their communal clan poem '*Leboko la Balete*'. In the poem they identify with many attributes of the buffalo such as strength, courage and independence, as in the following lines, '*Dirobaroba matlhakhola/Diaroba fela di sa tla go a lala*'. They also identify with its tough black hide which they use to signify their identity as 'Black Ndebeles of true Zulu ancestry' (*Matebele a mantsho a Masodi-a-Mphela* (*Amazulu-a-Mpela*)). They recently made history when in 2003 they broke with tradition and installed the first ever paramount chieftainess in Botswana, Kgosi Mosadi Seboko. She in turn made her mark when later in her chieftaincy she took the bold step of reviving the traditional initiation schools for men and women, which had not been held for almost three decades. So, although proud of their culture and keen to preserve their traditions, Balete are a dynamic people who have tried to march with the times. This dynamic tension between tradition and change is evident in their attitudes towards marriage and their practice of its processes. Some Selete traditional marriage practices have changed over time, while other aspects of their marriage rituals have stood the test of time. This chapter focuses on past and present traditional marriage rites among the Balete of Ramotswa.

## Understanding Marriage from the Balete's Point of View

Research, including the present study, shows that *lenyalo* is a complex institution that people, even within a single community, may understand *lenyalo* differently, depending on their experience, age, gender, historical period and cultural background. Among the Balete, marriage is generally understood as a negotiated union between a man and a woman in which they are expected to live together as husband and wife in a lifelong bond. Traditionally, the union is solemnised through a rite of passage ceremony that consists of a number of ritual steps. The steps must be performed in order for the union to be accepted as a valid marriage. However, there may be variations in both the conduct of the steps and in the relative importance attached to each of them. In modern times, for instance, it has become commonplace to insist on the payment of *bogadi* or 'bridewealth' before a marriage can be considered complete and valid. However, this has not always been the case because in the past and indeed in some cases even today, the payment of lobola could be deferred, done in instalments or even waived altogether without invalidating the marriage. Traditionally for Balete, marriage was not about *bogadi* as such, but was more about the *patlo* (bride-seeking ceremony) with a *serufo* cow. *Patlo* was the defining ceremony of the marriage process, and without it a marriage would never be regarded as valid because it is the process by which the couple would have been carefully matched for marriage through elaborate discussions by families on both sides. Although in some cases the union came as the result of two people who were in love deciding to take the bold step to get married, the formalities of the *patlo* process would still have to be performed.

Regarding marriage as an institution, a range of views were expressed by the informants in this study. First, many of the informants expressed the view that marriage was a cultural arrangement to allow for the natural desire experienced by individuals to live with each other as husband and wife in a lasting relationship when they attained the appropriate age. Although an element of personal choice was present even in the past, marriage was traditionally regarded as a union between two families, which came about through negotiations and agreements in which the personal desires of the couple were superseded by respective family interests. Whether solemnised at the *kgotla*, the church or the District Commissioner's office, the informants emphasised the point that marriage was a ceremony during which the couple took the vows to live together for life as husband and wife under one roof, with or without children.

Second, there is a cross section of the people who take the religious view towards *lenyalo.* According to them, *lenyalo* was established by God since time immemorial as a gift to human beings for the purpose of procreation, and to enhance the couple's dignity (*seriti*). The man and the woman are therefore called upon to ensure that their marriage stands the test of time through perseverance, maturity and cooperation. This is a sacred duty to which they commit themselves in vows (*maikano*) before God and many witnesses.

Finally, there were others who defined marriage from a purely personal perspective as a safeguard against the uncertainties of old age. They see marriage as an institution through which two people that would have grown to love each other deeply from years of living together as husband and wife continue to be there for each other in old age. It is an investment for the future in the sense that the couple are guaranteed to spend their old age as the hub of a network of two extended families as senior citizens and community parent figures. From this perspective, marriage means that two people who love each other live together until separated by death and not divorce, and endeavour to make their home a happy one, not only for themselves and their children but for the community as well.

For most informants, marriage among the Balete of Ramotswa was very important because it was a rite of passage which elevated a person's status in the community as well as moulding his or her character for new responsibilities and privileges. Part of this viewpoint was expressed by one male informant who said, "If you had a tendency to misbehave and return home late at night or use money carelessly with fly-by-night friends, after getting married you come to know that much is expected of and from you as head of the household and as such you shy away from senseless behaviours and become more responsible and respectful to the person you are married to".

Other reasons why the traditional marriage institution was important among the Balete of Ramotswa included the fact that it increased the married couple's dignity and sense of responsibility; *lenyalo* made the two people more honourable in the community and the society at large, for it granted them permission to participate in future marriage negotiations and the liberty to actualise the law of procreation to prolong the husband's genealogy, because, as one male informant aptly put it: "From two people a nation is built not only in number but also in character". Marriage catapults an adolescent girl or boy from the state of childhood to womanhood or manhood, respectively, depending on the type of marriage practised.

## Types of *Manyalo* and their Importance

In this section of the chapter, we shall describe the types of *manyalo* (marriage ceremonies) that are at presently practiced among the Balete. We shall show that these practices are premised on rather different concepts of what marriage is as an institution, and that the three types of marriage ceremonies imply different understandings of the relative importance of the various rituals that go into making up the marriage process. In all cases, however, marriage serves as a rite of passage through which a young couple is initiated into the new status of adults, with both its privileges and responsibilities.

Generally, the Balete recognise two types of *manyalo.* First, they solemnise marriages through a traditional *kgotla* ceremony. Unlike the church or civil marriage ceremonies, the traditional concept of marriage is not validated by a wedding ring. Instead, it is officially validated by the bride-seeking ritual and solemnised by the *kgosi* of the village. Second, there is the modern marriage ceremony commonly referred to as the 'white wedding'. It is officially performed by a District Commissioner's officer and/or a church priest, and symbolised by a wedding ring and a common law marriage certificate. We briefly describe Balete perceptions of each type of ceremony in turn below.

In a traditional Selete marriage it was the responsibility of the groom's parents to initiate proceedings when they felt that their son had come of age. In the past, during the era of the South African migrant labour, a man was considered old enough to marry when he had gone through the *bogwera* initiation ritual and found work as a migrant worker in the mines in South Africa. This type of marriage was celebrated mainly at the *kgotla* in the presence of many witnesses and concluded with the bride-seeking (*patlo*) ritual event at home. In the past, traditional *kgotla* marriages did not have certificates. However, nowadays *dikgosi* issue customary law marriage certificates. Traditional marriages were always in community of property. An out of community of property marriage would not be regarded as an ideal marriage since such an arrangement did not exist traditionally. The *kgotla* marriage was highly cherished among the elderly informants because, as far as they were concerned, it was based on authentic traditional values, including mutual respect and the emphasis on harmonious relations between husband and wife, even in cases where they may be some years apart in age.

A *kgotla* marriage process traditionally began when the groom's parents identified a prospective bride and initiated a parental match-making process that ended in a betrothal (*peo letlhokwa* or *peeletso*). Because parents were particular about the character and trustworthiness of a bride, they always ensured that they chose the bride-to-be for their son from a well-behaved and industrious family not associated with any of the following negative attributes: witchcraft, stinginess, laziness, promiscuity, craftiness, jealousy, infertility, divorce, and a habit of using obscene language and drunkenness, among others. In most cases the process occurred when the prospective bride was still in her teens. The estimated marriageable age for a woman in the past was between 15 and 20 years, while that of a man was estimated to be between ages 28 and 30 years, or even older. Most Balete parents believed that in an arranged marriage love and affection were bound to grow out of the intimate acquaintance and bonding that were expected to take place in an ideal marriage. Often, the girl would not even be aware of or notified about such an arrangement. This situation was expressed succinctly by one elderly woman who went through the same process when she mentioned that, *"Le fa o ne o ka ipiriganya, batsadi fa ba setse ba dumetse gore o nyalwe, o a nyalwa, le thupa o ka betswa ka yone"* (Even if you rolled on the ground crying in protest, once the parents had agreed that you were getting married, you got married. A girl could even be flogged if she refused to comply with her parents' wishes). In most cases the girl was informed about the marriage arrangements only on the day of the bride-seeking ritual procedures, normally at the time of the husband-to-be's return from the mines in South African where he would have gone to work following his graduation from the *bogwera* initiation school.

Generally, this type of marriage was associated with couples who had gone through the traditional initiation schools of *bogwera* and *bojale*. For that reason, it was acceptable for them to submit to the *kgosi's* counselling and guidance. The *kgosi*, too, found it easy to provide such counselling and guidance to the couple because he merely reminded them of things they were taught at the initiation schools about their future roles as husbands and wives. It was for this reason that those informants who advocated this kind of marriage believed that it made one's life more orderly and purposeful since the newlyweds learnt consultation and negotiation skills that shaped their character and instilled in them commitment to the welfare of their respective extended families and the community at large. Again, arranged marriages were believed to be based on high moral standards that were grounded in Selete values and ethics. The woman who was married through this type of marriage was viewed as the 'mother of the ward or the community', hence she could freely participate in future marriage negotiations and give counsel with dignity to other women who would be going through the same process.

In the past, the traditional *kgotla* marriage celebrations were not too costly because the bride usually wore a home-made blue German print dress or a wrap-around skirt with a blouse, a headscarf, and a *mogagolwane* shawl. The couple was also accompanied by two pairs of caretakers, namely, two best men, one from the groom and bride's side respectively, and two bridesmaids, one from the bride's side and the other from the groom's side. Also, no *bogadi* was officially demanded by Balete besides the *serufo* (door-opener) sheep or cow. The groom was initially expected to give one *serufo* sheep (and now a mature cow is given), which ideally was from his maternal uncle to the bride's maternal uncle as a token of appreciation that symbolised the consummation of marriage and partnership.

The second type of marriage identified by most Balete adult informants was what the majority called 'white wedding marriage' or modern European, or Christian marriage (*lenyalo la mosese o mosweu, lenyalo la Sekgoa* or *la Sekeresete*). This is the type of marriage that is usually conducted by a District Commissioner's officer or a church priest. Some informants sarcastically labelled it as a 'mixed masala' marriage because very often it incorporated activities from all the three different marriage practices in its procedures. It is common practice nowadays for a couple to tie the knot at the magistrate's court and be counselled by the magistrate herself or himself, and then go through the traditional bride-seeking and counselling procedures of a Selete marriage (or vice versa), and then go to a local church where the couple is blessed and counselled by a priest whose Christian beliefs might even be against the pre-fortification rituals of a Selete marriage, earlier administered by a traditional doctor.

In this type of marriage, the man identifies a future life partner of his choice who often is the same age or of the same level of education as himself. Most adult informants were unhappy with this kind of marriage because they believed that it brought a lot of confusion since the expectations of the three procedures, already mentioned, were different, and in some cases contradictory. Also, unlike the traditional *kgotla* marriage, the 'white wedding' marriage was found to be too costly at every step taken. For example, the white wedding dress and its accessories are quite expensive. Such marriages also demand *bogadi* of eight head of cattle or the monetary equivalent of at least two thousand Pula per cow, and up to three thousand five hundred Pula for the *serufo* (door-opener) cow. The wedding celebration also requires hiring of a tent and chairs and feasting with different varieties of indigenous and international food, among many other things.

One other feature of the 'white wedding' marriage, which most elderly female informants were unhappy with, was the type of counselling the couple was given by the magistrate. Their concern was that very often the magistrate, when counselling the couple, tends to focus on issues that promote individualism rather than the spirit of communalism, and the fact that the very magistrate who gives counsel to the couple may be a young, educated adult who does not even have any experience in marriage himself or herself. Again, there were those who thought that most young couples nowadays seem to pay attention to the magistrate's advice, which alienates them from their biological parents, rather than encouraging them to follow traditional advice that they are given during the bride-seeking ritual event. It was interesting to learn that, among the Balete, it was taboo to share the contents of the verbal traditional counselling given to the bride and the groom with unmarried people and married couples who had not married through the traditional *patlo* ritual.

## TABOOS ASSOCIATED WITH SELETE MARRIAGES

Several taboos or prohibitions associated with the Selete traditional marriage institution were mentioned by both male and female informants. Taboos here refer to certain actions or behaviours within a given society that are forbidden, and whose violation is believed to be either a bad omen or a cause for a curse to befall the violators. Taboos among the Balete are esoteric symbolicic actions whose hidden significance and meaning are rarely explained to the potential practitioners.

One obvious taboo of Selete marriage that has stood the test of time is the prohibition against unmarried men and women participating in the bride-seeking process and in traditional marriage counselling rituals. No explanation was given for the taboos beyond vague impressions created that the issues discussed during such rituals were private and secretive and were therefore not to be divulged to the uninitiated. Every married person who participates throughout the various traditional marriage steps would also be expected to comply with the traditional dress code; men are to wear jackets when they are at the *kgotla,* while women wear blue German print (*leteisi*) skirts that do not expose the woman's knees, and a headscarf. They also had to drape over their shoulders a blue-checkered woolen *mogagolwane* shawl secured in front with a large safety pin (*kgokelo*) in a vertical position. It is therefore taboo among the Balete of Ramotswa for unmarried women to wear a *mogagolwane* shawl secured with a large safety pin as this may bring a bad omen to the deviant.

Traditionally, wedding celebrations were not held during the period when initiation schools in the mountains were in session. They were also forbidden on Christian holidays such as Good Friday. The villagers were expected to respect that liminal period of betwixt and between that those at the initiation lodges helped to overcome successfully by being taught Selete cultural norms, practices and values of manhood and womanhood, respectively.

In the past, it was also taboo for a woman who already had a child to wear a white wedding dress and a veil. Instead, she was expected to put on a two-piece dress and a hat on her wedding day. It was the custom for the wedding clothes of the bride, the hearth where the traditional beer ingredients for the *patlo* ritual were to be prepared, and where the food for the wedding celebration was to be cooked, to all be fortified by a traditional doctor prior to each event. It was also taboo for any young woman who was on her monthly period to come close to, or touch the firewood of the doctored hearth, or even participate in food preparations for the wedding celebration.

Extra-marital affairs among Balete were also taboo and were never condoned by the society. This was explicitly emphasised by one female informant who said, "During our times there were no certificates because we obeyed instructions; our children nowadays should know that the marriage certificate they get from the magistrate is a 'road-block' to extra-marital affairs".

Again, according to the Balete of Ramotswa, a newly-wed young woman had her own separate house within her parents' yard, and it was taboo for her siblings or any family member to go to the back of this house at any time. The reason given by one informant was that "it was a house which no one was permitted to go around since one may accidentally meet her husband when he comes to visit her secretly at night, or in the early morning hours when he leaves the premises, because the son-in-law was respected in the olden days" (*mogwe o ne a tlotlwa bogologolo*). It was also taboo for the sun to rise while the son-in-law was still sleeping at his wife's natal home. In the past he paid a fine if he woke up late and was seen by members of the wife's family because failure to comply with the societal expectations was tantamount to being disrespectful to the in-laws. The son-in-law was forbidden to take a bath at the wife's natal home. His wife was expected to wash her husband's laundry at his parents' home to ensure that she fulfilled her responsibility as a married woman and did not behave like a concubine.

Again, in the past a Molete man was not allowed to build himself a house before marriage because, as explained by one elderly woman, *"Lapa le thaiwa ke monna le mosadi, ba simolola mmogo. Mosadi wa Selete o batla go itse botlhoko jwa ntlo ya gagwe"*. In other words, it was the newly-married couple that should decide on the foundation and plan to build their house from scratch together. A Molete woman preferred to know the limits or the length and breadth of her house. Because of this restriction, the son-in-law was compelled to sleep at his wife's natal home after marriage and wake up very early in the morning to vacate the premises before he was seen by anybody. He would continue to live that way until, as a couple, they built their own house. This arrangement was meant to assist the girl to be comfortable at her mother-in-law's home, and not be vulnerable to abuse by her older sisters-in-law – since most Balete girls were married during their teenage years.

Besides the taboos associated with marriages, other interesting symbolic behaviours are those attached to certain portions of a slaughtered cow which were given to close relatives who played significant roles throughout the different steps of a traditional marriage.

## Kinship Ties and the Significance of Meat Portions at a Wedding Event

Among the Balete, there were some meat portions from the cow slaughtered for the wedding event which were given to the next of kin who had important roles to play throughout the various steps of the marriage process. A few examples are discussed below as cited by the informants. The examples given mostly tallied with the importance of the role the next of kin played in the marriage procedures, especially in relation to the bride. For example, almost all the informants agreed that the head and the neck of the cow, as well as one of its front limbs, were usually given to the maternal uncle of the bride or the groom, depending on where the wedding was celebrated. The maternal uncle was usually given the head of the cow to symbolise his leadership role, being the one to speak first in all the marriage negotiations and procedures.

Brisket and thin flank (*sehuba le lebala la mpa*) were mostly given to the mother of the bride because she had breastfed her. These two portions were also symbolic of the area where she tied the knot of the baby sling. *Ngati* (caecum, part of the large intestine) was for the paternal aunts, while the tongue was given to the maternal uncle's wife. The tongue symbolised the leading role of a maternal uncle's wife in marriage ritual discussions, which were, and still are, always accompanied by ululations. Moreover, the ear(s) of a cow (often referred to as *lesusu*) was eaten by the married women of the ward where the wedding ceremony was taking place. It symbolises their role of 'keeping their ears to the ground' to monitor the relationship of the newly-wed couple.

The rump portion (*motlhana*) was kept aside for the daughter-in-law or the newly-wed couple itself because it is symbolic of the fact that the recipients are expected to bear children after getting married. There was another piece of meat known sexually as *molomô* which was ritualistically prepared for and eaten by the couple on the wedding day before any cooked food could be distributed to everyone else on that day. This small piece of meat was taken from the front, upper end of the thigh of one of the hind legs (where the thigh intersects with the flank) of the cow slaughtered for the wedding and was usually prepared ritualistically by a traditional doctor and given to the couple. The bride was expected to bite it first and then pass it on to the groom to eat and finish it.

The bond created by the *molomô* meat was a deterrent against extra-marital affairs. The couple was therefore encouraged to engage in a sexually intimate relationship, which some informants euphemistically referred to as 'playing *konkolodi*'. This was particularly important on New Year's Eve (*fa ngwaga di kgaogana*), otherwise the couple might suffer a disease known as *thotse* which could lead to death if such an observance was violated.

The family members eligible for the various meat portions mentioned above were mainly those who were the pillars or backbone of a Selete traditional marriage. They played, and still play, a leading role at almost every step of the marriage negotiations and processes.

## Balete Traditional Marriage Processes

Balete traditional marriage was a process characterised by consultations and negotiations. There were several steps which had to be performed according to the prescribed order. Failure to comply with such an order often brought confusion or gave rise to conflict between the two families which were in the process of building a long-term relationship. All meetings arranged in connection with any of the traditional marriage processes discussed below were usually preceded by an appointment for the two partiess to meet.

### *Peeletso* (betrothal)

Betrothal (*peeletso*) among the Balete was a form of pre-marital engagement of a girl from a well-disciplined family that had been identified, and chosen by the parents of her future husband, who at the time may already be working at the South African mines (*mosimane a sa ile majako*). This kind of practice was associated more with the Selete traditional arranged marriages of the past than with the modern 'white wedding' marriages of today. Once the boy's parents had identified the right female candidate for their son, they sent some 'engagement' clothes, blankets, basic toiletry and some money to her parents to teach her 'to be presentable' (*go mo ruta mokgabo*) now that 'she would soon pass the stage of childhood (*o a bo a tlhagogile mo bonyaneng*!)', as expressed by one female informant. The young woman very often did not know that she was engaged because it was an arrangement between the parents of the young man and young woman. Sometimes when the girl had come of age, bride-seeking ritual procedures might even be conducted by the parents in the absence of the husband-to-be, who might simply send some money to his parents to facilitate the process. However, this type of engagement process, which some informants jokingly labelled 'future wife deposit', often led to some disappointments. There were some male informants who lamented the process because they ended up losing their 'deposited future wives' to other financially well-off men.

There were other informants who also talked about a new kind of *peeletso* that took place when a man had impregnated a girl before marrying her. Moreover, some men sometimes took a long time to marry the mother of their children because they wanted to observe the woman's behaviour, her industriousness and commitment to the relationship. Others believe that this modern type of *peeletso,* where the man choses his own future partner, is secular dating rather than Christian courtship.

## Courtship

Courtship and dating are two different pre-marital relationships based on personal choice. They involve a man and a woman who may end up marrying each other in the future. Courtship in the past, however, did not involve any intimate relationship between a man and a woman, while dating often did. During the courtship stage, once a Molete young man had made up his mind to get married, he would tentatively settle the matter with his fiancé, and then he would inform his biological parents first about his intention to marry 'the daughter of so and so from such and such a ward or village'. One male informant explained that, "Marriage commences first within the household; it starts as a secret shared mainly with the parents and the immediate family members like the young man's maternal uncle" (*Lenyalo le thaelwa pele mo tlung; le simolola e le sephiri sa ditsebe tsa batsadi le ba losika le le gaufi jaaka malomaagwe mosimane*). Thereafter, the young man's father would relay the information to the boy's maternal uncle and hand over the responsibility, thus allowing him to play his rightful role as the family spokesperson, and as head of the delegation of traditional marriage negotiations and procedures.

At this point, the maternal uncle was expected to cross-examine or interrogate his nephew to ensure that he was well prepared and had acquired all the necessary resources needed for the fulfilment of the various steps of the Selete marriage procedures. Once the young man's readiness had been established to the maternal uncle's satisfaction, the immediate family members were expected to make an appointment with the girl's family to pay them the preliminary visit.

## Preliminary and subsequent visits

The preliminary visit to the girl's parents involved direct participation of the biological parents of the boy and the girl in the private discussions about the marriage. In other words, the visit gave the immediate family members the opportunity to discuss the marriage issue informally and to know each other, while at the same time allowing the boy's family to observe the behaviour of the girl's family. The primary objective of the preliminary visit to the girl's home was and still is 'to locate the homestead and the ward of the girl's family' (*go bona lelwapa le kgotla ya goora mosetsana*) as well as to inform the girl's parents about their son's intention to marry their daughter. This first visit also gave the biological parents the opportunity "to discuss informally the *lenyalo* processes in accordance with the culture of the girl's parents, if different from that of the boy's parents", remarked one of the female informants.

However, some informants argued that the preliminary visit to the girl's family in some instances involved the participation of the young man's biological parents and the maternal uncle and his wife, while others said that the delegation that participated in the initial visit was usually made up of the junior paternal uncle (*rangwane*) and junior maternal aunt (*mmane*) as well as the maternal uncle (*malome*) and his wife (*mmamalome*), who usually met with the future in-laws on behalf of the boy's biological parents, as pathfinders. When the maternal uncle and his wife visited the bride-to-be's natal home, one male informant explained that the uncle would say, '*Re tla jaana re setse setlhako sa ngwana morago*' (We come this way following our boy-child's footsteps on the ground). Most informants agreed that the immediate family members were the ones to accompany the boy's biological parents, if need be, since at this stage the discussions would still be tentative and private.

Depending on the outcome of the preliminary visit to the girl's family, if they had informally accepted the proposed marriage, then the first return visit would be led by the *malome* and his wife, as well as the paternal aunt (*rakgadi*), and a few other trusted men and women of the ward (*batsadi bangwe ba lekgotla*), especially those who would be directly involved in the *lenyalo* process and/or contributed to it in one way or the other. It was also explained that the second return visit to the girl's family did not require direct participation of the biological parents from both sides any longer because it marked the beginning of detailed discussions on the marriage requirements and procedures.

After the first return visit, several subsequent visits to the girl's family might follow depending on whether the two families shared the same culture or not. Further visits might involve discussions on the modalities of the various stages of the marriage preparations, setting of dates for the initial registration of names of those getting married (*go pega leina*) and for the signing of the actual marriage contract at the magistrate office (*go folosa leina*) after the three weeks of advertising the marriage banns, date and times of the two bride-seeking ritual events, including the presentation of the *bogadi* and *serufo* cow, as well as the date, venue and type of wedding celebration preferred by the couple-to-be, ideally in consultation with the rightful next of kin.

Once the boy's and the girl's families, in consultation with the couple-to-be, had agreed on the dates for the various steps to be followed, or to be taken at different stages of the marriage preparations, then arrangements would be made to actualise as much as possible all the things that had been agreed upon by the two parties. At this stage, more people were invited to participate in the preparations, including friends, distant relatives, neighbours and ward members on the girls' side and the boy's side, respectively. However, from that point onwards, the main role players (*ditlhogo tsa merero*) at different stages of the marriage preparations and negotiations would be the maternal uncle (*ma-

*lome*) and his wife (*mmamalome*), junior paternal uncle (*rangwane*), paternal aunt (*rakgadi*) and junior maternal aunt (*mmane*) and their spouses, as well as *ralekgotla* where applicable. The participation of immediate relatives in ritualistic events is supported by the Setswana saying mentioned repeatedly by the Balete elders that '*Ngwana segwe o a tlhakanelwa*' (a child is like a sorghum panicle (*seako sa lebele*) that is shared).

Moreover, after the dates had been set for *patlo* and other processes and the two families involved had agreed, the girl's family was expected to start preparing for the bride-seeking (*patlo*) stage and to receive the *bogadi* cattle and the *serufo* (door-opening) cow. At this time, a series of detailed preparations were expected to be completed prior to the *patlo* ritual events scheduled to take place at the girl's family ward on Friday – which was the day on which the couple-to-be would be signing the marriage contract at the magistrate's office. In most cases, it is at this stage that the girl's family would expect several material things from the boy's family, including a bag of sorghum for brewing the traditional beer for the *patlo* event. Additional things often expected from the boy's family were a load of firewood and special thornless branches for constructing an open kitchen shelter (*matlhakolana a leobo*) where traditional beer was to be prepared. They might also contribute a goat whose meat would be used as relish for those brewing beer among other preliminary preparations. Traditionally, it was also during the *patlo* preparations that a traditional doctor would be called to come and fortify the hearth where the sorghum beer would be prepared. For Christian families, the priest would come and pronounce blessings over the hearth.

For most adult Balete informants, the *patlo* (bride-seeking) event (including the presentation of the *serufo* cow) is the very essence and backbone of a traditional marriage contract, not necessarily *bogadi*. This is because, originally, Balete never demanded *bogadi* during *patlo* since it was mostly viewed as a free will token of appreciation of one or two small livestock animals, hence the saying '*bogadi ga bo sekwe*' (that is, one cannot demand *bogadi,* or take someone to court for not honouring it or for violating its attendant instructions).

## *PATLO* (BRIDE-SEEKING )

The *patlo* event among the Balete is performed at two levels. The first one is performed on Fridays by married men from the groom's family very early in the morning around 5 a.m. at the *kgotla* (meeting place) of the bride's family ward. The second level of *patlo* is performed by the married women from the groom's family at the bride's family compound the day after the return of the bride from signing the marriage contract at the magistrate's office or at the bride-to-be's local church. This takes place any time between 10 a.m. and 2 p.m.

Another important event that takes place on the *patlo* day among the Balete of Ramotswa is the traditional marriage counselling sessions (*go laya*), whereby the bride would be counselled by her maternal uncle's wife and other married female relatives at her natal home during the day. Late in the afternoon on the same day, the groom would also be given counsel at the *kgotla* of his family ward or at the *kgotla* where the groom's party was accommodated, if the bride were from outside Ramotswa.

The first *patlo* ritual performance was the one by married men from the groom's party, which commenced as soon as they arrived at the *kgotla* of the bride's family ward. This kind of *patlo* would be performed early in the morning (around 5 a.m. or so) before the bride-to-be left for the magistrate's office. It is important that the negotiations follow the right culturally prescribed order during which the right symbolic language is used. One of the informants supported this observation indirectly when he said, *"Mokgwa wa go baya puo o botlhokwa mo patlong"* (The way you present your words during the *patlo* event is important).

In the early morning hours when members of the groom's delegation arrived at the *kgotla* of the girl's family ward, they would expect to find the girl's male relatives (*bagwegadi*) already seated and waiting for them, and the fire at the *kgotla* hearth already kindled. In terms of spatial movement, the arriving delegation would very often pass behind those already seated at the *kgotla* in silence, and walk towards the chairs they would have been shown to use; if the chairs were not enough, the rest of the groom's delegation would sit down on the ground. The negotiations usually started with a prayer led by someone from the groom's party. One of the male informants explained that *"Mo patlong ya borre, fa ba tsile go kopa segametsi, malome ke ene a tlhulang mafoko pele, mme ralekgotla a bo a a digela"* (At the men's bride-seeking ritual, when they have come to ask for the bride, the groom's maternal uncle is the one who speaks first, while the one to conclude the negotiations is *ralekgotla*, that is, the ward headman or a respected elderly man in the ward).

Consequently, the maternal uncle of the bride-to-be would also be the one to respond first during the bride-seeking meeting, at which the groom's delegation had come to ask for *segametsi* (future daughter-in-law) officially. Since *bogadi* was introduced in the Selete culture, the male-specific *patlo* proceedings were usually followed by the presentation of live *bogadi* cattle or by '*bogadi jwa pata/kgwatlha*' (*bogadi* in monetary form).

The second *patlo* ritual performance was that of married women from the groom's party together with the bride's party, which would take place inside the yard '*bosigo bosele motshegare*' (during day time between 10 a.m. and 2 p.m.), and mostly within a courtyard which was situated in front of one of the houses. One female informant explained that this type of *patlo* ritual event takes place after that of men '*bosigo bo setse bo sele*' (in daytime). In other words, when it actually takes place is dependent upon the time the men conclude theirs at the *kgotla*. As in the case of the male-oriented *patlo* performance, the negotiations of the female-oriented *patlo* ritual would be led by the maternal uncle's wife of the groom. In both types of *patlo*, divorced men and women might participate, but were not allowed to comment on anything during the proceedings. Married men and women whose marriages had not involved *patlo* were not allowed to participate in the *patlo* ritual process, just like single men and women.

Nowadays, those women who participate in the *patlo* ritual always come wearing a uniform made of a royal blue German print skirt (which some call *tšhiba ya letweitshi/leteisi*) and a white blouse, a blue and white checked woollen shawl (*mogagolwane*) and a headscarf. The blue and white checked woollen shawl is usually secured in front with a large safety pin (*kgokelo*) in a vertical position. In support of the above *patlo* dress code, one of the female informants affirmed that *"Basadi ba ya patlong ba apere paka ya letweitshi la tšhiba le le botala jwa legodimo le malausu a masweu le megagolwane e e botala jwa loapi, gape ba rwele ditukwi mme e le ba ba nyetsweng, ba ba mo malwapeng a bone, e bile ba kile ba laiwa le bone"* (Women go to the *patlo* ritual event wearing blue German print skirts and white blouses, a blue *mogagolwane* blanket and a headscarf, but should also be married and not divorced, and must have gone through the traditional marital counselling also).

As mentioned earlier, *patlo* performance would mostly begin with a prayer led by someone from the groom's delegation. Then it was important that the head of the delegation (that is the groom's maternal uncle and maternal uncle's wife, who are the mouthpiece of every ritual event) asked first whether everyone was present before the event commenced. The one who led each one of the two delegations would say, '*A le mmogo batsadi*?' If it were the maternal uncle's wife, she would follow the affirmative response from the bride's team with expressions like, '*Bagolo, ke tla ke tshematshema mo tsatsing go tla go fitlha fano; bomme, re fano go tla go kopa segametsi*'. (Elders, we come a long way in spite of the scorching sun to come to this place; mothers, we are here to come and ask for the bride). *Patlo* in Selete culture involves the presentation of *dilwana tsa patlo* (material items for the bride.) such as a bedtime blanket, German print dress and/or white wedding dress and veil, *mogagolwane* shawl and a large safety pin, headscarf, shoes and essential undergarments. However, in the past only a night blanket and a dress were bought by the groom's parents.

On *patlo* day, homemade traditional sorghum beer would be served together with some food prepared for the groom's delegation, among other participants. After *patlo* proceedings were over at different times, the two *patlo* delegations would be offered some food to eat and a calabash of traditional beer to quench their thirst as a gesture of mutual respect and a cordial relationship. *Patlo* ritual has changed for the better in terms of the time it is performed, as well as the day of the week, which is now set aside for such an activity so as to take into consideration those with paid jobs.

Another important activity during the *patlo* performance event is presentation of *bogadi* cattle, which is followed by *go laya mosadi* (to counsel the bride).

## *BOGADI* (BRIDE-WEALTH)

Several explanations were given by both male and female informants regarding the significance of *bogadi/magadi* among the Balete of Ramotswa. Generally, most Balete adult interviewees viewed *bogadi* as *tebogo* (a token of appreciation), *go phimola dikeledi* (to wipe one's tears), *go intlafatsa* (to make oneself beautiful) or *go supa lorato le kamogelo* (demonstration of love and acceptance) by the groom's parents to the bride's parents.

*Bogadi* was also explained by one female informant thus: *"Bo supa kgolagano ya monna le mosadi e e ka fa molaong, mme ebile gape re ka re ke tlotla e e lebogang ba ba nyalanang"* (It demonstrates a lawful union between a man and a woman, and again one can say it is a sign of respect that appreciates those who are getting married). In the past, as *bogadi* was gradually introduced among or adopted by the Balete of Ramotswa, "it signified unity and a mutual relationship between the two families, and was not a commercial transaction or business as now seems to be the case", as expressed by one young adult male informant. Another female informant raised a similar concern when she said, *"Bogadi jo bontsi ga bo age motse sentle ka go nna jaaka o kare o rekisa ngwana kgotsa o a mo koba"* (Expensive *bogadi* does not bring peace in the household because it is like you are selling your girl-child or you are chasing her away).

However, at the initial time of *bogadi* negotiations, if the groom's maternal uncle feels that the charge is too high, he can plead for a reduction of the number of cattle requested until the two parties reach an agreement. He tactfully uses expressions such as '*Lo re kgamile*' (You have choked us), or '*Bolayang mme le gogeleng moruting*' (You may slaughter but please be merciful), or '*Re fokoletseng tlhotlhwa*' (May you kindly reduce the charge, it is too high). There was a consensus among elderly men that Balete originally did not observe *bogadi* practice, rather they demanded the *serufo* sheep (now replaced by a mature cow). Most elderly informants believe *bogadi* was introduced through inter-marriages and, as a result, Balete found it profitable to copy or imitate those other traditional practices, beginning with what one male informant expressed in English as an "experiential-based retaliation charge for impregnating a girl" (that is, *tlhwatlhwa ya tuelo ya tshenyo!*). Other elderly male and female informants explained that up to the early 1970s, *bogadi* was not at the centre of marriage negotiations as the *serufo* cow was, which is also known as '*pula kgoro/pula lebati/pula ntlo/pula makgabe*'. This initial laxity on *bogadi* is what others think might have given birth to the proverb, '*bogadi ga bo sekwe*' or '*bogadi ga bo na tshekelo*'. In other words, *bogadi* was not compulsory, hence no one could be taken to the *kgotla* or prevented from marrying a woman simply because he did not have *bogadi* cattle to offer, or the actual number of cattle requested from him. This means *bogadi* among Balete did not have a set price or a standard number of cattle as is the case today.

Since the introduction of *bogadi* practice among the Balete of Ramotswa, which some elderly men think was borrowed from Batlokwa and Bakwena people, with whom they interacted with over time and geographical space, the number of *bogadi* cattle has drastically increased. Nowadays, the officially agreed number of *bogadi* cattle for the Balete of Ramotswa and nearby villages is eight, plus the mandatory *serufo* cow from the groom's maternal uncle. This cow is presented to the bride's maternal uncle around 7 p.m. or 8 p.m. on the Saturday evening of the wedding day celebration. The *serufo* cow symbolically opens the door for the son-in-law, thus granting him access to his wife's room, or gives him license to enter his wife's room at her natal home on the evening after the wedding celebration. The girl's maternal uncle is entitled to the *serufo* cow because he would have bought a traditional German print dress for his niece, which she may use as one of the dresses she wears when changing attire on the day of the wedding celebration.

One elderly male informant explained that nowadays there are two types of *bogadi*: '*e bong, bogadi jwa kgomo tse di maoto a mane le bogadi jwa seswa jwa kgwatlha kana jwa tse di sa tshwaiwang*' (that is, the four-legged *bogadi* of cattle and the modern 'pocket *bogadi*, *or* 'those cattle that are not marked on their ears'). This second type refers to the equivalent cost of the number of *bogadi* cattle requested in monetary terms. If *bogadi* is in that form of monetary value, each cow nowadays costs between P2000 and P2500, while that one *serufo* cow can be between P3000 to P3500. Other informants mentioned that the official agreement is that 'pocket *bogadi*' should not exceed P20,000 under normal circumstances, unless the groom's parents decide otherwise. Very often competition led some families to give beyond the agreed maximum number of *bogadi* cattle as a way of distinguishing themselves from other families. However, *bogadi* for a woman already with a child when getting married was different. One female informant explained that *"Bogologolo fa o setse o na le ngwana bogadi bo ne bo fokotswa, mme gompieno ba a bo oketsa"* (In the past, the number of cattle for *bogadi* for a woman already with a child was reduced, while today they increase the number of *bogadi* cattle for such a woman). The difference is in the change of perception. In the past, the focus was more on behaviour, hence *bogadi* cattle for the woman who was still a virgin was higher than for the one with a child. Whereas today, the focus seems to be more on economic expenditure or gain, hence *bogadi* for a woman with a child is often increased because the parents feel they have spent money to take care of both their daughter and her child.

Traditionally, *bogadi* among the Balete of Ramotswa does not discriminate in terms of insiders and outsiders. It was explained that the same number of cattle is charged for both Molete and non-Molete families alike. Even though in the past, when a Molete married Molete, the groom could be permitted to present only the mandatory *serufo* sheep or cow, and not give any form of *bogadi* by taking into account the socio-economic status of the groom's parents.

According to the Selete culture, in the words of one wise old man, it is important that *"kgomo tsa bogadi di a patana sebedi sebedi kana re kare bogadi bo a pana gore bo seka jwa tlhotsa"*. In other words, *bogadi* cattle must always be even or paired so that their total number does not limp (as in odd numbers). Balete insist that all the eight cows must be middle-aged beasts that have never had calves. The even number in this regard symbolises order, friendship and harmony in a marriage.

In Ramotswa, *bogadi* would be presented by the groom's maternal uncle and his team to the bride's maternal uncle and his delegation at their *kgotla*, in the presence of the *kgosana* of the ward. Thus, the overseer of the presentation of *bogadi* would be *ralekgotla* and the uncles of the bride and the groom, among other close relatives. The bride's maternal uncle, on the other hand, would be the one who received *magadi* on behalf of the bride's parents. This activity would very often take place on the Friday on which the marriage contract would be signed by the new couple. Once the number and the identity of the *bogadi* cattle had been verified satisfactorily by the married men at the *kgotla*, the information would be relayed to the married women in the yard. Mostly in the past, more than today, *bogadi* cattle were praised by the maternal uncle to express joy at seeing his niece getting married. The focus of the praise would be in mentioning the different colours and ear marks of the cattle, while the women, led by the maternal uncle's wife, would be ululating in appreciation of the *bogadi* cattle and the maternal uncle's poetic rendition.

If *bogadi* was in the form of money, the groom's maternal uncle might dramatise driving cattle. He would split one side of a freshly cut stick and insert a two hundred Pula note in that cleft stick. As soon as he approached the *kgotla*, he would lift the stick with

P200 in his right hand and recite, '*Ke a tsena, ka tse di sa tsamayeng; ke a tsena ka tse di sa tshwaiwang*' (I have arrived with those that cannot walk; I have arrived with those whose ears are not marked).

Furthermore, one elderly man also explained that, *"Bogadi jwa tse di sa tshwaiwang kgotsa jwa kgwatlha bo amogelwa le go bonwa ke batsadi le ba lesika le le gaufi jaaka bomalome mo ntlong, fa jwa dikgomo tse di maoto mane bone bo bonwa ke botlhe ba ba teng kwa kgotleng"*. In other words, *bogadi* in the form of money is not revealed openly to the public, rather it is received by close relatives such as maternal uncles and the parents inside the house, while *bogadi* of four-legged cows is shown or displayed to everyone at the *kgotla*.

Although *bogadi* is now part of the marriage procedures of the Balete, some informants think that *"bo baya ba bangwe ka fa mosing"* (it disadvantages other people), because nowadays a man cannot marry a woman without having to give *bogadi*. There are some informants who gave examples of *lenyalo* of a close relative which was cancelled or postponed to another date until the groom's party was financially prepared to give *bogadi*. In cases where marriage negotiations were already in progress when the wedding was postponed, once the money had been secured, the negotiations were expected to start all over again. This has now become a challenge to most young men who want to get married. For instance, before leaving for further studies outside the country. Consequently, to ask to marry a woman without *bogadi* in modern times is no longer common among Balete of Ramotswa as was the case in the past, because some of the brides-to-be are the ones now insisting on *bogadi* and not necessarily the parents. The presentation of *bogadi* to the girl's party is usually followed by the *go laya* stage.

## *GO LAYA* (TRADITIONAL MARRIAGE COUNSELLING)

Among the Balete, *go laya mosadi* (traditional marital counselling for the bride) used to take place in the morning at the girl's natal home after the men's *patlo* event; that is, prior to the introduction of magistrate marriages, while *go laya monna* (traditional marital counselling for the groom) was conducted by his close relatives in the morning at the family *kgotla*. This practice was reiterated by one male interviewee who stated that *"Mosimane o ne a laiwa ka Labotlhano phakela thata ke boora mosimane kwa kgotleng ya gabone"* (The young man was given counsel on Friday morning at his family *kgotla* by his relatives). He further mentioned that *"tlwaelo ke gore borre fa ba tswa go batla mo mosong, ba gorogela kwa kgotleng ya gabone, go bo go bitswa mosimane yo o nyalang go tla go laiwa"* (The tendency is that when men return in the morning from the *patlo* event, they go straight to their own *kgotla* and then the boy who is getting married would be called to be given traditional marital counselling). In the case where a Molete man was getting married to a woman who was not a Molete, the young man would be given counsel by his relatives at the *kgotla* of the village ward that would have given them accommodation.

Nowadays, it is common for *go laya monna* to take place late in the afternoon after the couple has returned from signing their marital contract at the magistrate office or the local church. In the case of the bride, one female interviewee explained that *"Mosetsana o laiwa ka labotlhano motshegare mo lwapeng ke ba gabone fo pele ga bo matsalaagwe"* (The girl is given marital counsel at mid-day by her relatives at her natal home on Fridays in the presence of her mother-in-law).

The reason why *go laya* is important is because *"go ruta go re o kgone go ikakatlela fa diphefo tsa botshelo di tla kwa go wena. Go laya ga mofuta o ke sephiri sa ba ba nyetsweng. Mme fela nkare, mosetsana le mosimane ba rutwa gore ba itshole jang mo lenyalong, ba tsenelele merero le gore tiro tsa bone ke eng. Ke gone kwa o fiwang maele a botshelo jwa lenyalo ka kakaretso"* (Traditional counselling teaches you to hold on when the storms of life come to you. Counselling of this type is an esoteric exercise of married people. But I can just say, the girl and the boy are taught how to behave in their marriage, that they should participate in similar events themselves, as well as to know the roles they play. It is during counselling that one is given the maxims of marital life in general).

*Go laya mosadi,* in most cases, starts after *dilwana tsa patlo* (material things bought for the girl by the boy's parents), already mentioned under *patlo* sub-heading, have been received and viewed privately inside the house by the closest relatives of the bride-to-be. One female interviewee mentioned that *dilwana tsa patlo* may include *"dilwana tsa lenyalo tse di rekelwang monyadiwa jaaka mosese o mosweu le lesire, palamonwana, ditlhako, dilwana tsa ka fa teng, mosese wa 'tšhentšhi', mosese wa ga malome, mosese wa ditumediso wa leteisi, le kobo e lekgarejwana le tlaa khurumediwang ka yone ka nako ya fa go laiwa"* (things that are bought for the bride, such as the white wedding dress and the veil, wedding ring, shoes, undergarments, the dress she would change into, maternal uncle's dress, German print dress for greetings, and the blanket that the young lady would be covered with throughout the counselling session).

On the *patlo* day, before the counselling session started, the girl's maternal uncle's wife (*mmamalome*) and her paternal aunt (*rakgadi*) would be the ones responsible for bringing her out of the house totally covered with a heavy night blanket, so as not to be seen by, nor to see, her in-laws, who would also be seated in the courtyard. The two next of kin would then help the young woman to sit down on the skin kaross which was spread on the floor of the courtyard of that house. One elderly woman explained that *"Fa o laiwa o bewa fa gare ga boora monna le boora mosadi o bipilwe ka kobo e e bokete ya bosigo o sa bonwe o bo o lebisiwa kwa go matsalaago"* (When you are given counsel, you are placed between the groom's delegation and the delegation from your side, entirely covered with a heavy night blanket so that no one sees you, and then you are made to face the direction where your mother-in-law is sitting).

*Go laya mosadi* (traditional marriage counselling of the woman), according to Selete culture, is done at the girl's natal home. During counselling, the girl's maternal uncle's wife, as the 'head of the negotiations' (*moja ditlhogo*), would be the one who counselled the girl first; thereafter she might be followed by senior daughters-in-law, the junior maternal aunt (*mmane*) and the paternal aunt (*rakgadi*). It was explained that '*Balete ba laya ba khubame*' (Balete give counsel while kneeling) to show respect and humility, thus leading by example. Throughout the counselling session the young lady would only hear their voices and not be allowed to see those speaking to her.

In addition, the young lady would be given counsel to take care of and respect her mother-in-law and father-in-law, and to be responsible and accountable for her own actions. Again, as aptly stated by one of the female informants, *"Mosetsana o laelwa go aga motse le go latlha ditlhopha tsa bonyana"* (The girl is given advice to build and keep the family together as well as to part ways with her childhood aquaintances). Interestingly, the actual counselling process seems not to have changed much today when compared to the past, since the session is still attended only by married men and women. In some cases, divorcees and widows/widowers may be allowed to attend such an activity, but they are not allowed to give any verbal advice. The belief is that if they are allowed to speak, their unfortunate circumstances of loss and grief may befall the newly-wed couple. Once traditional marital counselling was done, the couple would then be ready for the Saturday or Sunday wedding ceremony.

## *MOKETE WA LENYALO* (WEDDING CEREMONY)

Traditionally, *mokete wa lenyalo* (wedding celebration) among the Balete of Ramotswa is supposed to be held twice. The first celebration nowadays takes place on Saturday at the bride's home, which is the day after the couple have signed their marital contract at the District Commissioner's office, or at the local church. The second wedding celebration takes place at the groom's home the following day or week, also on Saturday or Sunday. Even though everybody is welcome to attend a wedding celebration among the Balete, it does not mean that people are not formally invited to weddings beforehand. Invitations may be passed out by word of mouth as well as by cards. Family members and close relatives of the bride and the groom may extend invitations, directly or indirectly, to distant relatives, friends, neighbours and other members of their respective wards where they reside.

Early in the morning on the day of the wedding celebration, the groom's maternal uncle's wife and his paternal aunt deliver the bride's wedding dress and its accessories to her natal home. It is their traditional role to do this, and to help her to put it on properly.

Any wedding celebration nowadays would be incomplete without a bride dressed up in a white wedding dress and a veil. Similarly, the groom is expected to turn out in a suit of the colour of his choice. Unlike in the nineteenth and twentieth centuries when Balete newly-weds would have at most four witnesses each, that is, two bridesmaids and two groomsmen, nowadays they may have up to eight or more. At the time when they had four, one bridesmaid and one best man would be from the bride's family and the other set of two from the groom's family.

However, in the past when the bride already had a child, she was expected to wear a two-piece attire and a hat rather than a white wedding dress and a veil, as is the case today. Again, in former times the bride and the groom changed clothes only once while nowadays they may change clothes up to three times on the day of the wedding ceremony. Another common practice nowadays is to have a time slot for taking photos. As explained by one female informant, *"Go na le nako ya gore banyalani ba ye go itsaya ditshwantsho kwa mafelong a mantle jaaka kwa Boatle, mme ba a bo ba ntse ba patilwe e bile ba le mo tlhokomelong ya bo bommamalome le borakgadi ba bone"* (There is a time when the couple would have to go and take pictures at beautiful spots like at Boatle, and all that time they would still be in the company and care of their maternal uncle's wives and paternal aunts).

On the day of the wedding ceremony, household chores and responsibilities are shared among rightful next of kin, friends, ward members and neighbours, especially during the preparation of food. One of the key female informants pointed out that *"go ipaakanyetsa mokete wa lenyalo, borre ba tlisa dikgong, ba tlhaba dikgomo tsa mokete, ba tlisa matlhakolana a leobo kana a go aga lelwapana le le apaelang dijo, ba apaya nama; mme gape mongwe wa bone ke ene a itsiseng batlamoketeng masika a banyalani"* (in preparation for the wedding ceremony, men bring firewood and slaughter cows for the event; and they also bring *motlhakolana* branches for building the traditional kitchen shelter or court-yard where the food will be prepared; they also cook meat; also one of them introduces the relatives of the couple to those who have come to the wedding ceremony).

It is important to note that, in the past, most Selete traditional wedding ceremonies involved other private ritual practices that were performed with the aim of fortifying the couple's marriage against witchcraft, or nowadays against satanic spirits. For instance, *"Leiso le ne le thaiwa ke ngaka ya setso go tshaba boloi, mme jaanong mokete wa lenyalo le segofatswa ke moruti wa kereke. Malatsing ano bontsi jwa Balete bo thaya lenyalo ka Sekere-sete go kobela kgakala mewa e e bosula"*, as explained by one elderly woman. In other words, traditionally the hearth was doctored or fortified by a traditional diviner to protect the couple against witchcraft, but nowadays a wedding ceremony is blessed by the church priest. These days many Balete people fortify *lenyalo* the Christian way in order to ward off evil spirits.

Another important practice which was common in the past among Balete, and is still practiced by some, is the *molomo* ritual. One male informant confirmed this practice when he said, *"Mo GaMalete go na le 'molomo', e leng namanyana ya kgomo e e apeilweng e e jewang ke banyalani. Nama ya 'molomo' e ne e fiwa monna le mosadi ba ba sa tswang go nyalana; mosadi o ne a ngatha nama eo pele a bo a e neela monna go e ngatha. Bangwe ba re nama ya 'molomo' ke yone e e tsalang boswagadi fa mopati wa motho a ikela badimong"* (Among Balete there is the *molomo* ritual, which is a cooked piece of meat from a cow which is eaten by the married couple. *Molomo* meat was given to the man and the woman who are newly wed; the wife was the first to take a bite of that piece of meat, and then passed it on to her husband to take the last bite).

Some informants say that *molomo* ritual meat was the thing which gave birth to *boswagadi* (widowhood disease) when one's spouse goes to the place of the ancestors. There were other informants who strongly believed that this type of meat was the final seal of the marriage contract between the bride and the groom, hence it was indirectly linked to future prohibitions and observances in their marital relations.

Among Balete, like in most patriarchal societies, the wife takes the husband's surname and is expected to leave her natal home and go and reside with her mother- and father-in-law. Although this practice was common in the past among Balete of Ramotswa, some elderly male and female informants explained that it was informally modified for various reasons. One of the reasons advanced was the fact that most Balete women married at a young age and as a result they were somehow abused by their unmarried older sisters-in-law who would not hand over to her the money her husband sent from working in the mines in South Africa.

## TRANSFER OF THE BRIDE TO HER IN-LAWS (*GO ISA MOSADI KWA GA BO MONNA*)

Among the Balete of Ramotswa, when the bride was escorted to her in-laws towards the end of the day of the wedding ceremony, she was usually accompanied by her maternal uncle's wife, her paternal aunt, and her junior maternal aunt in the case of the wedding taking place within the same locality. Otherwise she would be taken to her in-laws on the day the wedding was celebrated for the second time at the groom's home. Moreover, besides the bride's escort carrying all her belongings, she was also given a traditional broom and a lantern to carry along. Very often the bride's delegation would find some food prepared for them by the in-laws upon arrival.

Later in the early evening of the same day, however, she would often return to her natal home if her husband had not yet built himself a house. Although she would be residing at her natal home, this did not deprive her of her rights and privileges or make her forget about her responsibilities as a daughter-in-law. During the day, on a regular basis, she would go to her in-law's home and perform all the necessary household chores, including washing her husband's laundry as well as cooking for him.

This new practice that encourages the bride to stay at her natal home until such time that her husband has built their own house has now taken root in the Bamalete culture. It was introduced for different reasons. Some of the reasons were explained by one elderly female interviewee thus: *"Go rulaganngwa jalo go re go babalele monna wa gagwe ka o tlaa patelesega go etela mosadi wa gagwe ka lefitshwana nako tsotlhe go fitlhelela ba ikagela ntlo e e leng ya bone golo gongwe go sele. Go pateletsa monna go re a iteke thata gore ba ikagela motse wa bone ka pele, e seng jalo o felela e le 'ratseleng' wa nako tsotlhe"* (It is arranged that way so that it makes the husband uncomfortable, since he is compelled to visit his wife at night at all times until he manages to build his own house somewhere else. The informal arrangement compels the husband to work hard and build himself a house as soon as he can; otherwise, he ends up being given the nickname 'the one who is always on the road).

It was found necessary that the bride return to her natal home after the wedding ceremony because most Balete women got married at a young age. For that reason, it was necessary that the screening of the bride's behaviour was done at her natal home by her mother and other married next of kin. The young bride's biological mother was responsible for giving hands-on advice as well as correcting and training her until she was mature enough to stand on her own and manage her own home. She would also remind the young bride of the advice she was given during the counselling session.

But when a Molete woman gets married to a non-Molete man, once the bride is taken to her in-laws late in the afternoon, she then stays for good at her in-laws' home. We may assume that this practice might have been encouraged by the *serufo* (door-opener) cow transaction.

## TAKING THE GROOM TO THE BRIDE'S HOME (*GO ISA MONNA KWA GA BO MOSADI*)

In the Selete culture, as explained by one male informant, *"Mosimane le ene o a isiwa kwa ga bo mosetsana"* (the young man is also taken to the girl's natal home). On the night of the wedding ceremony, the groom is often expected to visit his bride at night at her natal home; that is, at the time when the *serufo* cow from the groom's maternal uncle is presented to the bride's maternal uncle. At other times, the groom's maternal uncle may present the *serufo* cow to the bride's maternal uncle in the form of money rather than the actual cow. An explanation for this night-time visit by the groom was given by one elderly male informant who pointed out that *"…fa mosimane a sa aga o kopa boroko kwa goora mosadi; mme o solofelwa gore a tsene ka lefifi a bo a tsoge makuku a sa bonwe. Le mororo go le jalo, monna yo ga a tshwanela go tsholela bana kwa bogwegadi"* (…if the young man has not yet built himself a house, he may ask for temporary accommodation at the bride's natal home; however, he is expected to visit the wife at night and leave very early in the morning without being seen by anybody. That notwithstanding, this man is not supposed to have children while his wife is still living at her natal home). In other words, the groom is partially and privately accommodated by his bride at her natal home until he gets tired of what one informant called a 'hide-and-seek arrangement' and decides to look for a plot and build his wife a house. This arrangement was introduced as a semi-punishment for those who got married before having their own houses.

The night when the groom was escorted by his maternal uncle to his bride's natal home, he was also given an axe and a blanket to take with him – the two items which some informants believe affirmed symbolically his status as a lawful husband. For that reason, he was expected to present the blanket to his wife officially that night in the presence of the private delegation as witnesses.

As already explained in the previous sub-headings, the *serufo* cow is also known as *pula kgoro* (door opener) or *pula ntlo* (house opener). It is therefore the presentation of the *serufo* cow that gives the husband the license to sleep at his wife's natal home, even though he would be doing so secretly, to avoid being seen by his in-laws and other family members and neighbours. Traditionally, the groom was expected to avoid the embarrassment of being seen by the public leaving his wife's natal home every morning, or being penalised by his in-laws for being disrespectful by waking up after sunrise. For these reasons he would visit his wife at night and leave the yard very early in the morning before sunrise, as already mentioned.

Balete of Ramotswa also have what one female informant explained as *ditumediso* (ritualistic greetings). She elaborated by saying: *"Letsatsi le le latelang mo mosong go na le ditumediso, malome le mmamalome wa mosimane ba tshwanetse go ya go lekola booramosadi gore ba letse jang"* (The following day there are some ritual greetings to be done, and the groom's maternal uncle and his wife are the ones to visit the bride's family in the morning to find out if they slept well at night). *Ditumediso* is an important aspect of Selete marriage procedures, so much so that they even have a special *ditumediso* German print dress for the daughter-in-law within the *patlo* package.

Regardless of all these private or secretive traditional marriage processes, which are loaded with meaning, the groom was also free to visit his in-laws openly during the day to go and ask for food whenever he wanted to.

## Marriage Rites and the Significance of Metaphorical Language and Symbolic Objects and Actions

Traditional Selete marriage and its processes, like in other Setswana speaking cultures of

Botswana, is full of metaphorical expressions and symbolic actions. Most of these metaphorical and symbolic expressions and actions are usually evident during various marriage negotiations. For example, Balete of Ramotswa, rather than talk of *ngwetsi* (bride), they use the word *segametsi* (the one who fetches water). Another interesting expression is '*phuti tlaa o je letlhodi*' (literally meaning 'duiker come and eat the lentils') often used by Balete to refer to someone who got married to a man who did not give any form of *bogadi* for her. Again, when Balete are negotiating the reduction of *bogadi* cattle for a woman soon to be married but already with a child or children, they would say, '*Batsadi bolayang mme le gogeleng moruting ka re fitlhela kgomo ka namane mme re batla go e tsaya ka namane e e seng ya me.*' In other words, 'We kindly plead with you to consider reducing the number of *bogadi* cattle because the woman we want to marry already has a child and that child is by another man, not the one who wants to marry her'.

Other forms of metaphorical language used in marriage negotiations are uncommon proverbs such as '*Ngwana segwe o a tlhakanelwa*' (A child is like a sorghum panicle that is shared), while others are symbolic ritual actions such as *molomo*, *thotse* and *boswagadi* illnesses, among others. Other symbolic objects and actions have already been explained, directly or indirectly, elsewhere in this chapter, such as the *serufo* cow, among others. One can therefore speculate that coded language used during marriage negotiations helps to separate the uninitiated from the initiated, as well as amateurs from seasoned Balete married men and women who are conversant with their traditional dos and don'ts of the past and the present. It is also this kind of language, among other things, which makes Selete marriage processes interesting and unique.

## Rights, privileges and benefits associated with traditional marriage practices

The significance of *lenyalo* among the Balete of Ramotswa cannot be overemphasised because it seems to be what determines as well as dictates the rights, privileges and the benefits of being married men and women within Balete communities.

Married men and women among Balete of Ramotswa enjoy more rights and privileges and benefit from traditional marriage practices, compared to the unmarried men and women. Married men and women of good character in the Selete culture are the ones used as models of behaviour to be emulated by the newly-wed couples, hence they are the only ones permitted to participate in marriage negotiations and allowed to offer verbal advice whenever necessary. The benefits associated with traditional marriage practices are usually reciprocal in that the beneficiary must also be a contributor. For example, the maternal uncles are entitled to the *serufo* cow, but they should have also contributed significantly to the welfare of their nephews and nieces in the process.

## Problems and challenges in traditional marriages today

Among the Balete people of Ramotswa, as in other cultural groups in Botswana, there are problems and challenges that married men and women experience and/or encounter, directly or indirectly, in their marriages over time. Marriage problems and challenges are not new. Even in the past young Balete men and women experienced or encountered challenges in the marriage process, such as unnecessary delays in concluding marriage negotiations or lack of financial support from close relatives, among others.

One major challenge of the past expressed by most elderly women in Ramotswa was that of arranged marriages, which some of them feel deprived the girl-child of the right to choose her life partner. One elderly woman who lived through such an experience expressed her feelings thus: *"O ne o batelwa monna wa ngwaga tse 90 wena o sa le monnye le boboko bo ise bo tii, mme o felele o mo amogela fela ka o itse le go betswa o ne o ka betswa gore o bo o felele o mo ratile o rata le o sa rate"* (A man of 90 years was chosen for you while you were still young and not yet psychologically mature, but because you had no choice you had to accept him, knowing that if you did not, you may be beaten until you complied and learnt to love him whether you liked it or not).

Other informants, however, think arranged marriages among Balete were better because the young women were compelled to respect their elderly husbands as well as comply with societal expectations. This is unlike today where young men and women tend to marry their age mates.This observation was reiterated by one elderly woman who stated that *"tlhalano e ntsi gompieno e bakwa ke go re monkane le monkane ba a nyalana"* (many divorce cases today are a result of the fact that age mates marry each other). Not only that, but both may be educated and holding jobs and financially independent when they get married; so when they are in the house it is like 'having two bulls in one kraal', as remarked another elderly female informant. Most elderly interviewees, regardless of gender, were of the view that this issue of equality in almost everything is what triggers marital conflicts that lead young couples to divorce within a short time. As far as other informants were concerned, nowadays young people come into marriage to experiment rather than to stay. In the past, as mentioned earlier, the husband was always ten or more years older than his wife. This meant that the Molete man always had the upper hand in family matters because he was the only one working in the South African mines, for instance. The husband, therefore, was the person who wielded financial power in the household and as such his wife was completely dependent on him for almost everything.

Consequently, if a man had agreed to 'offer' (not to 'pay') *bogadi* and somehow failed to honour his words or for some reason he was unable to afford it, no one could take him to court for that, hence the saying '*bogadi ga bo sekwe*'. Unlike today, in the past *bogadi* was given to the bride's family as a symbolic expression of satisfaction and appreciation for the 'gift' (the woman) who the young man had been allowed to marry and live with for the rest of his life. However, in olden times *bogadi* was not practised among Balete people of Ramotswa. But as time went by, some families opted to emulate other cultures they interacted with and started asking for one or two *bogadi* cows informally as a sort of compensation for their honourable and schooled girls. The family that could not afford *bogadi* was not penalised or victimised in any way, however. Some informants think *bogadi* today has become an exploitative business because the number of cattle demanded is too many, and if it is in monetary form, the cost of one cow is also too high, as already mentioned elsewhere in this chapter.

Another female informant gave an interesting enigmatic example of *bogadi* vis-à-vis married couples' behaviour today. She had this to say: *"Ka 1978 fa ke nyalwa mo ga*

*Malete, kgomo ya bogadi e ne e le P300 fa ya sefuro sa ga malome e ne e le P500, gompieno bogadi bo a tura, e bile bo humanegisa monna*" (In 1978 when I got married in ga-Malete, one cow of *bogadi* was charged P300 while the *serufo* one for the maternal uncle was P500, but nowadays *bogadi* is expensive, and even makes the man poor). The reason advanced was that in the recent past *bogadi* charges were on the lower side, yet the people were able to endure marriage for a long time, while these days *bogadi* is very expensive, but people do not last long in the marriage due to lack of endurance and accrued *bogadi* related debts.

Other problems and challenges are related to the erosion of cultural values, especially concerning conflict resolution procedures among married couples. According to Selete culture, when there was any conflict in the household, the wife was expected to inform her mother-in-law and/or his husband's maternal uncle's wife, while the husband informed the wife's biological father and/or her maternal uncle. In modern times, however, most young couples hardly consult their in-laws when there is any conflict in their marriage. Instead, some of them prefer to talk to their friends and biological parents, failing which they would rather go to the magistrate or the District Commissioner to resolve the matter alone.

The last problem is that of cohabitation. Some of the male and female informants bitterly complained about the tendency of some of their sons and daughters who work in towns away from their natal village of Ramotswa, who practice '*go nna mmogo*' (to cohabit) or '*go ruana*' (to rear each other), before they marry. One female informant gave an example of her son who was cheated on by his girlfriend with whom he had lived for a very long time, and had children with, out of wedlock. In this case, the problem started when her son and his girlfriend decided to get married and the girl took her son's credit card without his consent to hire an expensive tent and chairs for the first wedding celebration of her family's side, while the boy was left destitute and had to be assisted by his relatives to raise his *bogadi* cattle. It is for similar reasons that some informants view some of the modern marriages as 'validation of cohabitation' because the couple would have been living together anyway, or already viewing themselves as husband and wife because they have raised their children together, though not officially married in accordance with traditional Selete marriage procedures.

Balete of Ramotswa, like other citizens of Botswana, feel that their marriage institution has been affected by change over time and space, directly or indirectly.

## THE IMPACT OF CHANGE ON TRADITIONAL MARRIAGE RITES AND ACTIVITIES

Balete traditional marriage rites and activities, like elsewhere in Africa and the world at large, have been impacted by change in many ways. However, only a few worrisome changes were specifically stated by the interviewees, while others were mentioned in passing in their conversations regarding the Selete marriage procedures and processes. Most of the changes that have impacted or are impacting Balete marriage rites and activities negatively, directly or indirectly, are those related to language use, socio-economic issues, moral values, *lenyalo* processes, cultural expectations and human rights issues, among many others.

First and foremost, Balete like other Setswana-speaking ethnic groups, note that their language is gradually changing due to the influence of internal and external forces. Through this research, we have observed evidence of semantic shifts in their vocabulary today, especially regarding the use of the Setswana word for the bride and the groom. The majority of those interviewed, consciously or unconsciously, referred to the bride as *monyadi* (literally, the one taking a step to marry) rather than *monyadiwa* (the one who is being married), as was originally the case in the Setswana language. *Monyadi* was the term originally used for the groom rather than the bride. Interestingly, the groom would mostly be referred to as *mogwe* (son-in-law), or only associated with the variation of the terms in question when using the inclusive term *banyalani* (that is, a couple or literally, those who have married each other). One informant who also noted this gradual semantic shift saw this as evidence of how people think today, because they no longer know who marries who – for they think the status of men and women is equal in a marriage, and yet that is not so according to Selete culture. Among the Balete, the husband is senior because he is the head of the household.

One other obvious change is the fact that in the past the parents were the ones who arranged their children's marriages, while today the children are the ones who choose a life partner for themselves. In the past also, as stated by one female informant, *"Monyadi o ne a nna mo ntlong beke tse tharo fa leina le santse le pegilwe, o ne a tswa mo tlong fa leina le folosiwa kwa ga molaodi; mme gompieno moo ga go yo ka bana ba rona ke bone ba ithulaganyetsang manyalo ka madi a tswa kwa go bone"* (The bride-to-be was kept inside the house for three weeks while waiting to sign the marital contract at the Magistrate office; today that practice is no more because our children are the ones involved in their marriage arrangements because the money for the preparations comes from them).

One other change is that some Balete girls now get married after they already have children, while in the past no man was interested in a woman with a child by another man. There was also the *peeletso* practice that did not involve any intimate relationship; hence a young woman was expected to safeguard her virginity until at the time of marriage. This is the reason why the bride with a child was not allowed to wear a white wedding dress and a veil, because a veil was symbolic of virginity. Due to a shift in moral values in society, nowadays a white dress and a veil is no longer a symbolic object as in the past, but more of a theatrical property of a glamorous 'drama' which often ends with a divorce within a short space of time, as observed by one key informant.

Another interesting change, mentioned by some Balete interviewees, is the fact that the most important and honourable role player in marriage procedures, the maternal uncle (*malome*), has become more often a paid theatrical figure than a real uncle, as one informant complained: *"Gompieno go rekwa batho go tshameka karolo ya bomalome"* (Today, there is a tendency to buy/hire people to act out the role of a maternal uncle). This tendency is gradually encouraging youngsters to treat marriage lightly and find it easy to get into and out of marriage. They get married without consulting their parents and divorce at a whim without seeking advice from their close relatives before going to the High Court, or taking the law into their hands and walking out of a marriage. Many female informants expressed unhappiness regarding the role of unmarried magistrates in conducting wedding ceremonies and providing counselling to the newly-weds. The feeling is that such people do not have the requisite experience for this role. There was also concern among the informants that some of the advice provided during the magistrate's court weddings was divisive because it encouraged individualism instead of family and community building values. Instead, as lamented by one elderly woman, there is excessive preoccupation, in this type of counselling, with the relationship between the daughter-in-law and mother-in-law, even in families where there are fathers-in-law. This stereotypical idea that mothers-in-law abuse daughters-in-law is something that most of the women informants were unhappy about.

Balete of Ramotswa are not happy about the fact that *lenyalo* these days is very expensive. For instance, *bogadi* cattle have increased in number as well as the equivalent cost of one *bogadi* cow in monetary terms is increasing almost annually, as stated above. Besides the escalating cost of *bogadi*, the white wedding clothes for the bride are also costly because *banyalani* nowadays tend to have an escort of many bridesmaids and groomsmen. The expenditure of wedding ceremonies is also high when compared to the past, because today young couples spend much money on expensive venues or retreat grounds, instead of just holding the ceremony at home. Others prefer to hire large tents, chairs and decorative objects even when they are not financially stable simply to impress friends and other invitees, as observed by one elderly woman. Because of this tendency, nowadays, in some of the pre-marriage meetings, the couple-to-be often demand contributions from everyone present, while in the past only close relatives such as *bomalome* and *borakgadi* were the ones who offered assistance out of goodwill, and not out of compulsion as is the case in some situations. Sometimes those getting married may even go to the extent of hiring catering companies instead of allowing relatives to cook food for the wedding ceremony at home, thereby giving them the opportunity to be a productive participant in a family occasion by offering a helping hand. Other elderly informants lamented the fact that close relatives of the bride and the groom, in situations where catering is outsourced, are often treated like visitors at their own children's wedding ceremonies. They think that this alienates and deprives them of their cultural roles and privileges.

Another worrisome change is the increasing number of divorce cases among the young couples in Ramotswa. According to some of the elders in Ramotswa, divorce was an abomination in the past because any divorcee was stigmatised and treated by the community as an outcast. A divorcee could no longer participate in marriage negotiations because it was feared that he or she may bring bad luck to the ongoing marriage procedures. Nowadays, however, it seems such stigma is no longer a deterrent for a divorce. Most of the young couples tend to omit or ignore some of the traditional steps of *lenyalo* in Selete culture. There are young couples that prefer to pay more attention to the magistrate's advice than to the advice they are given by their families during the *patlo* ritual.

One key informant who expressed his worry concerning these current changes stated that one word which is synonymous with many of these challenges among Balete is '*ditshwanelo*' (human rights). "The word *ditshwanelo* has given birth to the abandonment of cultural values and appropriate etiquette, and instead endorsed protected lawlessness and lack of respect for husbands and wives in *manyalo* today", remarked one *kgosana*.

However, one other informant clarified this point by explaining that most young people have misunderstood or misinterpreted the word *ditshwanelo* to mean taking the law into their own hands or doing things the way they like. This, to the extent that most of them cannot differentiate rights from privileges (which are context-based temporary rights that can be withdrawn from the person at any time if he/she acts inappropriately). Another of the *dikgosana* said that *ditshwanelo* are not a new phenomenon, as Balete have upheld or even exercised such rights in the past. There was consultation and respect for age differences and culture-specific gender roles which were taught at initiation schools for boys (*bogwera*) and for girls (*bojale*), respectively.

## Conclusions and Recommendations

Our research has shown that the Balete of Ramotswa practice three major types of *lenyalo*. The first is the traditional Selete marriage ceremony conducted at the *kgotla*. The second is a combination of the above with a civil marriage ceremony conducted at the magistrate's court or District Commissioner's office. Lastly, the third combines the traditional wedding with a religious ceremony at a church. However, most elderly interviewees do not distinguish between the last two and see them as one and the same type of wedding, which they identify as 'a modern white wedding', regardless as to whether the marital certificate was signed at the magistrate's court or the church.

Another finding from the research is that even though *lenyalo* and its processes are constantly evolving, and changes are inevitable, some aspects of traditional marriage procedures and practices have stood the test of time. The observance of the *patlo* and *go laya* rituals has been especially resilient, as have been the compulsory rituals of the *serufo* cow. Others, however, are either gradually fading away or undergoing change, in some cases for the better and in others for the worse. Among the changes that the informants regret is the high divorce rates among young people. Another is the fact that *lenyalo* has become too expensive for ordinary Balete to afford. There is also concern about the tendency among Balete to copy the traditional practices of other cultures without knowing their true significance.

In terms of recommendations, over half of the 50 married men and women interviewed in Ramotswa have expressed concerns and dissatisfaction about *lenyalo* today compared to the way it was conducted in the past. For that reason, they suggested some of the following recommendations:

(a) There is a need for *magosi* or *dikgosi* in Botswana to agree, control and enforce '*seelo sa kgomo tsa bogadi le tlhotlhwa ya tsone fa e le tse di sa tshwaiwang,*' as expressed by one informant. In other words, it is necessary to standardise the number of *bogadi* cattle as well as the equivalent in monetary terms.

(b) People should be made aware of the dangers of embracing or copying wholesale other people's cultures, such as with '*dilwana tsa patlo tse di ntsintsi, le bogadi jo bo kwa godimodimo, jalo jalo*' (countless *patlo* clothes often required, expensive *bogadi* charges, and the like).

(c) Traditional marriage counselling should also impress upon newly-married couples the fact that they should not neglect their parents after marriage. It is not uncommon to find cases of *mmangwana* (the bride's biological mother) ending up destitute in old age, because of neglect by their children, as lamented by some elderly female informants.

(d) Traditional marriage counselling should not be a one-off event, but should continue even after the signing of the marital contract. Balete, and other peoples of Botswana, should introduce post-marriage counselling after a specific period.

(e) Other informants would like families to be allowed to make choices, such as allowing their children to hold wedding ceremonies in neutral places like halls where hired security is often involved (to prevent the theft of family items when *lenyalo* is held on domestic premises).

(f) *Magosi* and parents should address the problem of cohabitation by introducing *kgotla* seminars and debates that focus on such issues in every locality in gaMalete and elsewhere in Botswana.

# 7

# Bangwaketse

*Mr. Allan Manyeneng*

**Totem**: *Kwena* – Crocodile

## A Brief Historical Background of Kanye Village and the Bangwaketsi

Bangwaketsi originate from the Bakwena ethic group of Molepolole, but they never resided there. They split from Bakwena at Phuthadikobo in the current Kgatleng region, in the 1600s. This was advent to a conflict between the two brothers Kwena and Ngwaketsi. Kgosi Ngwaketsi then left his elder brother (Kgosi Kwena) and settled at Magagarape. Incidentally, Kgosi Kwena had a son called Motshodi, who remained in the current Kgatleng region as Kgosi Kwena migrated further into the current Molepolole village.

## Understanding Marriage from the Bangwaketsi's Point of View

Bangwaketsi elders mention that, traditionally, marriage was perceived as an establishment of a new and lifetime relationship between both the families of the bride and the groom. They maintain further that marriage brings together almost all relatives of the newly-married couple, to the extent that even post the death of either spouse or a divorce for that matter, this bond remains forever, particularly owing to birth of the children of the marriage who would naturally and actively interlink between both the maternal and paternal families.

## THE TYPES OF BANGWAKETSI MARRIAGES/WEDDINGS

The elders amongst Bangwaketsi state that, initially in olden times, and prior to arrival of the missionaries, Ngwaketsi marriage processes entailed their traditional *kopo/patlo*c (bride-seeking) and the *bogadi* (bride prize) as discussed hereunder. Upon the arrival of missionaries, they brought along the Christian marriage process, which then ran parallel with the traditional Ngwaketsi marriage process. They also mention that it was when Botswana attained independence in 1966 that the civil marriage process was introduced. on an equal footig Bangwaketsi further understand that the civil marriage process is executed by the State through a District Commissioner under the civil law of marriage. Both the elders and youthful Ngwaketsi couples identify with three types of marriages within their tribal territory, *viz.* the *customary* marriage process, the *Christian* marriage process, and the *District Commissioner's* marriage process. Bangwaketsi elders associate much with the customary marriage process but also take note of the fact that nowadays, their customary marriage process is almost always followed up with yet another marriage process – at the District Commissioner's and/or the Christian marriage process.

### CUSTOMARY MARRIAGE

According to Bangwaketsi, during former times, a father and mother would consider searching and identifying a suitable potential wife for their up-growing son. Unlike today, the search was usually conducted within close relatives, such as cousins from the maternal or paternal side of his parents. The parents may also search further into daughters of their close friends and associates, should a need arise. In all the foregoing scenarios, the intention is to come up with a quality daughter-in-law, who was brought up from a family of good repute, i.e., *mekgwa ee mentle*. Upon identifying a certain family, the young man's parents would approach the girl's parents to break the news of their future marriage intent. In the past, the girl's parents would, upon receiving such news, choose either to agree or disagree to the future marriage proposal. Bangwaketsi are quick to mention that where a young man's family are known for bad repute, the girl's family would decline the proposal.

In the event the girl's family accept the marriage proposal the young man's family, the latter would straight away return home to engage their son's immediate uncles and aunts further. This entails the delivery of a male sheep, *nku ya mokwele* and a headscarf for the girl as a token of appreciation of the bride. At an appropriate time for marriage, a date would be set by parents and relatives of the young couple for *bride-seeking*, *kopo* (or *patlo*) and other marriage processes to follow.

Interestingly, Bangwaketsi elders also speak of yet another cultural approach to marrying their sons, which started around the 1920s (as mentioned above). During that time, the young man's parents would start to observe his approach and interest in girls. This observation would be when he was of marriageable age, around 26 to 30 years of age. Inasmuch as the parents would be interested in seeing and learning where their son may have female interests, they were equally quick to advise him against his interests where they perceive poor upbringing from a family he wishes to marry into. Should the parents agree to their son's choice of wife, they would immediately approach the girl's parents to express their intent in having their daughter as a bride, *ngwetsi*. Equally, if the girl's parents agree to the proposal, a marriage engagement is completed. The aforementioned *mokwele* and other marriage processes would follow accordingly.

## Christian marriage

Bangwaketsi believe that the Christian marriage process was brought about by missionaries, when they migrated into southern Africa many years ago. They are clear that the Christian marriage process found the Ngwaketsi customary marriage process already in place. Subsequently, both marriage processes co-existed amongst their community to date. In particular, the Ngwaketsi elders associate the Christian marriage with their folks who are mostly church-goers with various church denominations in the Ngwaketsi region. The elders are of the view that only a church minister or reverend who has been granted a marriage license is permitted to solemnise a marriage. A marriage license is obtained from the Ministry of Home Affairs, upon the reverend qualifying or satisfying the Minister that he qualifies to undertake the marriage process.

Like all other districts within Botswana, before the marriage is solemnised by the priest or reverend, the marrying couple are required to first register their marriage with the District Commissioner's office. They will then follow all the processes as stipulated under the District Commissioner's marriage process below, but only up to the counselling stage. After the counselling stage, the District Commissioner would release those couples intending to follow the Christian marriage process. Thereafter, the couple would proceed to the priest's church office in possession of some matrimonial documentation from the District Commissioner's office addressed to the priest.

The couple would then set a marriage appointment date with the priest, usually scheduled for a Saturday, or any preferred or convenient day. On the agreed date, the couple, together with family members, friends and neighbours from both parties, would convene at a church, or even at any designated place to witness the Christian marriage process. The priest would bless the event before solemnising the marriage in terms of the church principles. Thereafter, the priest would proceed to offer some counselling sessions to the couple, which also centres on how the marrying couple is expected to carry themselves during their marriage life. Like the District Commissioner, a priest is usually inundated with disputes and complaints from married church members. In general, he, or she, has experienced of dealing with previous marriage problems and so is a suitable person to offer sound counselling in this regard. The marrying couple is urged to fear God and raise their upcoming children with love and care, through the hand of God. Thereafter, the priest issues a marriage certificate. The two families, relatives and friends would then retire to the bride's home, where a feast would be held to celebrate the marriage.

## District Commissioner's marriage

Bangwaketsi recognise the District Commissioner's marriage process as a product of 'civilization' brought about by the government/state. They believe that this marriage process is always preferred by their youthful marrying couples, who are quick to subsequently merge the Ngwaketsi customary marriage process with it at all costs. The elders and the youthful married couples agree that this caused the two marriage processes to be administered in parallel for the same marriage. Ngwaketsi elders associate this marriage process with the youthful couples and that it attracts the latter as it centres on material property and wealth. The elders also feel that the marriage officers at the District Commissioners are usually incompetent to solemnise marriage processes since most of them are very young, unmarried and indeed inexperienced on matrimonial matters. They rather prefer the Christian marriage process because their marriage officers (the priests), are usually married and accompanied by their wives at such proceedings. Ngwaketsi elders also feel that the District Commissioner's marriage process excludes parents of the marrying couples from partaking in the marriage process apart for being witnesses.

As is the case with such marriages countrywide, the Marriage Proceedings Act regulates marriage processes to be adhered to as and when couples intend to marry. Couples intending to marry are required to provide documentary proof that they have attained the age of majority, that is, 21 years of age. Where one or both parties are of minority age, parental consent is required before the marriage can be registered and concluded. Secondly, the marrying couple must each avail a witness, also of consenting age. Three weeks before the marriage date, both the couple and their respective witnesses are to report at the District Commissioner's office to register the marriage. Each shall bring their national identity cards and complete the necessary marriage application forms. From the registration date until a day before the marriage, the District Commissioner's office advertises a marriage though a system called 'banns'. Theses are publication on noticeboards, at the places where both parties are known to stay or to have stayed). The essence of a three weeks banns advertisement is to give the public at large an opportunity to know of those who are getting married, and whether anyone has any cause as to why the couple cannot be joined in matrimony. Reasons to stop a marriage from proceeding may be because one of the parties is already married, or one has promised a different partner marriage and is thus banned from continuing with this proposed marriage, an so forth.

A day before the marriage date, the couple, together with their respective witnesses, report at the District Commissioner's office to complete documentation that addresses issues on whether or not they are marrying in or out of community of property, i.e., the nature of how they are going to administer their estates.

During the day of marriage, the marrying couple, together with other couples scheduled for a marriage ceremony that day, together with their witnesses, will convene in a large boardroom. If there is enough room, relatives and friends are also allowed in to witness the marriage proceedings. The District Commissioner commences proceedings with a prayer, before conducting a detailed public counselling session. Counselling here entails most of the good and bad events that married couples generally go through, some on a daily basis. Incidentally, owing to the nature of their daily work, which also entails meetings and discussions with married couples who have lodged domestic complaints or disputes, a District Commissioner is in a privileged and sound position to appreciate exactly what marriage life connotes. Upon completion of thorough counselling, the District Commissioner would accordingly solemnise the marriages, whereafter, issuance of a marriage certificate completes the process.

## Marriage Processes

### The betrothal process (*Go baa lotlhokwa*)

In the Customary Marriage Process chapter above, it is mentioned *inter alia* that parents of a young man take time to identify a suitable woman for marriage to their son. Also, the Ngwaketsi elders speak of a period from the 1920s when a young man's parents would allow their son to identify his potential wife and his parents to approve or disapprove of his choice. When this identification of a bride is completed, with a visit to the girl's home by the young man's parents, and both parties having agreed to a future marriage proposal, a marriage engagement is sealed with *nku ya mokwele* and a headscarf for the girl. This marriage process is termed *go baa lotlhokwa*, betrothal marriage process.

Subsequent to this process, the young man can be sent on a regular basis to visit the girl's family, at times delivering a portion of meat from a goat slaughtered earlier on at his parents' home, or bringing a of firewood load or some clothing for the girl. This would go on until the aspiring couple reaches appropriate marriage age, when the *kopo* (*or atlo*) marriage process and other marriage processes would follow to finality of marriage process.

### The courtship process

In terms of Ngwaketsi culture, courtship processes only started in the 1930s, when young men and women were going through a transitional period from a young man being found a suitable wife to the young man, but independently finding his own wife. Bangwaketsi therefore relate courtship to a special relationship between a young man and his 'lover girl', which, depending on the strength of its prosperity, may culminate into a marriage relationship upon passage of reasonable time.

Bangwaketsi elders state that this relationship does not usually or necessarily involve or concern the parents of the two lovers until such a time comes when the young man starts considering his intent to get married, and engaging his parents accordingly. The elders mention, further, that courtship gives their youthful couples latitude in choosing a wife or husband from all sectors of the society, even internationally. They view this modern approach as a common recipe for the prevailing high rate of divorce, since the couples do not necessarily have sufficient background information about the families they are marrying into.

The elders further mention that courtship at times dies before the marriage stage, and in a worst case scenario, the girl may end up being impregnated. In such situations, the girl's parents would approach the young man's home to break the news of pregnancy. Upon the young man accepting responsibility for the pregnancy, he is expected to pay damages in the form of two cattle. In the event the young man expresses intent to have custody of the said child, he is expected to pay eight head of cattle, which represents and is equivalent to the costs of *bogadi*. According to Bangwaketsi, the *bogadi* price is actually a token of appreciation by a man to the woman's parents, for having born children to their daughter.

## PRELIMINARY VISIT PROCESS (*GO KOKOTA*)

As is the case with most Tswana marriage cultures, Bangwaketsi believe that it is upon the young man's parents being satisfied with their choice of a potential bride that a preliminary visit is arranged, *go kokota*. This involves a visit to the girl's home by the young man's father and mother, at times in company of one of the uncles and aunts. They would arrive at the girl's home to meet up with her parents, where the young man's parents would break the news about their intent to take their daughter as future wife to their son. In the past, the young man's parents took total control over the preliminary visit process. The elders mention that this was purely because parents were the ones advancing *bogadi* (cattle) and costs of a wedding feast with none or minimal contributions from their young man – probably because he would have earned the *bogadi* through working for his family at home, fields and cattle post as he grew up into a manhood. Ngwaketsi elders are quick to mention that nowadays, it is the young man who chooses whom to marry and even if his parents may not necessarily be happy with the choice of bride made by their son, they would still partake in marriage processes, primarily to satisfy their son's wishes and just hope for the best. At this juncture, the young man would have equally accumulated sufficient funds to pay for *bogadi*, to buy a wedding ring and to fund the marriage feast.

When time is ripe, the young man's parents would inform his maternal uncle about their son's marriage intent, and the uncle would equally visit his sister's home to further discuss the marriage prospects, *go rera tseo*. Thereafter, the maternal uncle would go around and invite all other married paternal and maternal uncles, aunts as well as appropriate relatives, to discuss and conclude as a team that should lead the preliminary visit process. Simultaneously, parents and relatives of the girl would be aware of the impending preliminary visit by the other party. In the premise, they would equally be preparing their delegation to meet the young man's delegation in discussions.

At an appropriate date and time, the young man's delegation would set off to the girl's home. Greetings and introductions would be exchanged before the young man's uncle or father breaks the news of their intent to take their daughter into marriage. The Ngwaketsi elders emphasise that more often than not, this is never a tough interaction between the two families, except on very rare occasions where the girl's family disapproves of a marriage due to unsuitable behaviour traced to the young man's upbringing.

Where the girl's delegation agrees to the marriage proposal, both parties would now zone into marriage processes, and whatever demands and expectations from both families, to conclude the Ngwaketsi customary marriage process.

Subsequent to this visit, the young man's delegation would shortly return to the girl's home to deliver a sheep, *nku ya mokwele*, together with some clothing for the girl, such as a dress, underwear clothing, a headscarf, which all represent a token of marriage engagement, i.e., *go isiswa dilo tsa peelelo*, meaning, to deliver engagement gifts.

At this point, the young man would be occasionally sent on errands to the girl's home, at time to deliver some firewood or a chunk of meat after his father would have either slaughtered a sheep, goat or cow.

## THE BRIDE-SEEKING PROCESS (*KOPO/PATLO*)

In terms of the Ngwaketsi culture, bride-seeking, which they refer to as *kopo* and not *patlo*, is strictly attended by married people and widows. According to the Ngwaketsi elders, *patlo* in culture connotes a situation whereby a married woman had fled to her in-law's home upon abuse by her husband, and in turn, her in-laws would inform her parents or the husband to leave their home, *go batlela ka kwano*, hence *patlo*.

The elders maintain that divorced persons are not allowed to attend marriage proceedings since they are deemed to be unfit to offer the marriage entrants any form of marriage counselling, *go laya*, in the advent of their failed marriages. Like most Tswana cultures, even a widowed uncle or aunt would not lead the marriage proceedings. They are required and indeed expected to appoint an alternative uncle or aunt to step in their shoes and lead the marriage delegation and proceedings. However, they are still allowed to be in attendance at the marriage proceedings.

Three weeks prior to the *kopo* event, the marriage intent is registered, either with the kgosi (tribal chief or king), or at church or a District Commissioner's office. In fact, it is the *kopo* marriage process, *tseo*, which Bangwaketsi, like most ethnic groups much appreciate as comprising a complete marriage even before the *bogadi* price is issued.

Unlike most Tswana *kopo/patlo* proceedings, the Ngwaketsi *kopo* is conducted not in the early hours of the morning but at noon. Latecoming by the young man's *kopo* delegation would always attract a penalty fee of P200 or more.

It is only three weeks after the marriage has been registered with the tribal authorities that the *kopo* process kicks in. According to Ngwaketsi culture, usually at noon, the young man's *kopo* delegation, led by the maternal uncle, m*alome*, in his capacity as the chief negotiator and head of the marriage delegation, would arrive at the girl's home.

The chief uncle, *malome*, would walk ahead of the men's delegation in silence and report at a *kgotla* just outside the girl's family home. In the interim, close but away from an entrance of the girl's yard, the young man's women's delegation would remain under the command of the maternal uncle's wife, *mma malome*, and the paternal aunt *rakgadi*. The chief uncle would then proceed in silence with other male marriage delegation team straight to a *kgotla*. They will be met by the girl's marriage delegation team, which would be seated around a fire place awaiting their arrival. The young man's team would kneel down upon arrival, whereupon one of the girl's marriage delegation team would greet them about twice before they respond, *dumelang dira*, meaning 'greeting enemies'. Upon responding to the greetings they are asked what they want. The young man's chief uncle would respond to say that they have been sent by the young man's parents to look for a wife: *"Re rumilwe ke boora Modise gotla go ba batlela ngwetsi or sego/metsi mo goora Baagi"*. This translates to: "We've been sent by the Modise family to find a wife for their son, from the Baagi family". The girl's chief uncle would demand to know which girl in particular they are interested on, and the man's uncle would mention a name, which would be confirmed by her uncle, whereafter the girl's uncle would confirm existence of such name and agree to a marriage proposal. In the event that the young man happened to have impregnated the girl at some stage in the past, her chief uncle would announce this event as an offending and thorny issue for the young man's delegation. A penalty would be imposed in the form of a cow, termed *kgomo ya tlhagela* for the young man's family. '*Tlhagela*' means that the young man had previously unlawfully broke in and entered through a back yard into the girl's family compound to sleep with her, and bearing the said child. The *tlhagela* cow would be immediately slaughtered upon receipt and prepared into a delicious meal to be enjoyed only by the married men and women from the girl's relatives upon departure of the young man's delegation. After this the young man's chief uncle would immediately request to be given a short break, *goya go bofa setlhako*. This is an opportune moment to go out and bring the *bogadi*. Equally, this moment facilitates their women counterparts to also conduct their women's *patlo* process with the girl's women delegation.

Under the leadership of a wife to the young man's uncle, *mmamalome*, the women's team would go through to the yard where they would find the girl's women team waiting for them, seated in the yard. Greetings would be twice offered by the girl's *mmamalome*, and the same process as the one conducted by their men's team would follow until the girl's aunt releases her in marriage. An aunt from the young man's team would then request water to drink, whereupon the girl's aunt would stand to bring the girl, with a calabash of water, to quench her in-laws' thirsts. The 'asking for water' process is actually meant to be an opportune moment for the girl to be seen or come into contact with her in-laws. They would also deliver some clothing, blankets, etc., as presents for the girl.

At this juncture, the *kopo* proceedings are complete, giving rise to a new marriage between the two families. Women from the girl's side would start ululating excitedly in joyous moods over the granting of the new bride. Both the men and women from the two families would then meet over tea where marriage songs would also be sang.

## THE BRIDE-WEALTH PROCESS (*BOGADI*)

In terms of the Ngwaketsi culture, as is the case with most Tswana ethnic groups, *bogadi* does not bring about a valid marriage: it can only be through *kopo/patlo*. This means that one can be validly married through *kopo/patlo* even where *bogadi* has not yet been delivered. For them, *bogadi* is paid as a token of appreciation of the children born into the marriage, and may be paid out later on when the couple's children are of youthful age.

Immediately after the *kopo/patlo* process is completed, and in the shortest time, and upon the women also completing their *kopo/patlo* process, the young man's chief uncle would return leading the *bogadi* cattle upfront, whilst the other men would drive them from behind. As the uncle walks closer to the girl's homestead, he would shouts in jubilation, calling upon the girl's mother and aunts that he is bringing in *bogadi* cattle and needs to be 'called upon' to collect his bride, otherwise he'll return home with the cattle, '*mma mpitsa kea tsena ka kgomo e tshweu, hao sa mpitse ke boa ka tsone*'. The chief uncle would then lead his entourage to the girl's *kgotla* where they would report to the girl's men's delegation that they brought *bogadi* cattle and ask for a bride, *sego sa metsi* or *ngwetsi*. In turn, the girl's chief uncle would receive the cattle in the company of his delegation. At this juncture, the chief uncle would select one or two cattle out of the *bogadi* as his share, leaving the rest to the girl's family. The elders mention that the chief uncle would get two cattle when *bogadi* was eight cattle, that is *di tlhwaile*, otherwise he gets one cow, where *bogadi* is six cattle, *di tsheletse*. In return for having taken one or two cows, the chief uncle would give out a big fat cow to the young man's delegation, now called *bagwe*, the in-laws, since the *kopo* process, which validates marriage, would have been completed. Ngwaketsi elders mention also that by virtue of his status as the chief uncle, the latter is customarily expected to contribute a cow to top up *bogadi* cattle called *kgomo ya ketelela pele*, a cow that leads *bogadi* cattle.

Shortly after *bogadi* has been delivered, the girl's father would also give a cow, called *kgomo yoo rraatso*, a cow contributed by the bride's father. This cow is killed immediately upon being presented before the male delegations from both parties. The skinned carcase of the dead cow, laid on a side, is shared between the two families. Its upper part is allocated to the young man's delegation (*boora mosimane*) to take along on the way back home, whilst the lower part of the cow remains for the girl's family (*boora mosetsana*). The lower part of the meat, which remains with the bride's family, is further divided and shared between the two families – it is called *kgomo ya motlhakanelwa*, literally meaning a cow that is to be shared between the two families. It symbolises a token for uniting the two families through the marriage of their two children. Another portion of meat from this lower side of the cow, *sekgwana*, is then jointly cooked by maternal aunts from both families, who thereafter deliver same to paternal aunts respectively. The paternal aunts would first serve the meat to the bride and groom before serving the married attendants from the two families, starting with the groom's family. As mentioned above, the *sekgwana* meat symbolically unifies the two families through a marriage of their children. Another portion of meat from the bride's part, a *motlhana* meat portion, is reserved to be taken along by the bride when she is transferred to her in-laws shortly.

On the evening of the *bogadi* day, at the young man's home, the male delegation team would gather at the family *kgotla* to offer marital counselling to the newly-married young man – this is called *go laya monna* (this process is explained further hereunder). The following day after the *kopo* process is finalised, the young married girl would be taken to her in-laws home by her delegation.

Ngwaketsi elders explain that before the 1950s, *bogadi* had no fixed prize at all – four cattle and sheep would suffice to find one a wife. In Ngwaketsi custom, a father would provide the *bogadi* where he is well off. Otherwise his close relatives may contribute some cattle or sheep where necessary. Bangwaketsi elders are quick to mention that, since the young man in those days spent most of his boyhood looking after his family cattle, the crops at the lands, and doing other family errands as and when the need arose, his father would, naturally, also contribute *bogadi* for his son. Nowadays, the young man is responsible for all the necessessities required to complete the customary marriage processes. The young man is expected to work hard in order to raise enough money to pay *bogadi*, which starts with at least a minimum of eight cattle. The young man currently also has to provide for the white wedding costs, such as their wedding rings, their clothing, food stuffs, transport costs etc., which now make a marriage very demanding and expensive on today's young men, who now find it difficult to accomplish. Yet, in today's world, without *bogadi* and its ingredients, no marriage would go through. The Ngwaketsi elders mention that leaving all marriage financial responsibilities to a young man has caused today's young men to shy away from marrying and choose to just cohabit with their loved ones, something very common nowadays amongst the upcoming parents.

## THE WEDDING CEREMONY PROCESS (*MOKETE WA LENYALO*)

Bangwaketsi elders mention that the wedding ceremony process came about through the arrival of missionaries with their Christian marriage process. Initially, a meal enjoyed by both families at the girl's home after receipt of *bogadi* was sufficient to conclude the Ngwaketsi marriage process and transfer the bride to her in-laws. The process entails buying or wearing a veil, wedding costume for the bride and a black suit for the groom, as a token of celebrating a wedding ceremony. This process starts at church before a priest and is called *mokete wa lenyalo*, a wedding celebration. It is also an attribute of the Christian marriage process commonly solemnised by a priest of a church.

The wedding ceremony process follows at any arranged time after the *kopo* and *bogadi* marriage processes have been accomplished. It is arranged by both the families, of the bride and the groom. Ngwaketsi elders maintain that the wedding ceremony process was and remains not mandatory, and would be staged depending on the financial affordability of each family to undertake or not. This event commences usually in the morning at church. The bride would wear a beautiful white veil dress and head crown whilst the groom puts on a black suit and hat. The priest would solemnise and bless the marriage at church in the presence of relatives from both parties. The wedding procession would then relocate to the bride's family house where, earlier in the morning, a cow would have been slaughtered and preparation of meals for a feast commenced. The groom, his family, relatives and friends would be invited to join the groom's relations at a feast. Members of the community are usually welcome to also join the feast. Introduction of close relatives and guests from both families would also be made at some point during the course of the feast. This is said to mark the beginning of a new relationship between the bride and groom's families and relatives, as a lifetime bond. Together with meals, traditional beer is served and traditional wedding songs are sang by choirs from both the bride and groom's families at alternate times. These songs would usually have a message relating ideal marriage lifestyles to either the bride or the groom, at times to both of them. A gifted relative, usually an uncle or aunt, would throw in a poem or two to either the groom or the bride, followed by ululating voices from senior women from the village.

During the course of the feast the girl's maternal uncle is offered the head from the slaughtered cow, called *ditlhogo tsaga malome*, the uncle's head-gift. This is just a token of appreciating the very big role played by a maternal uncle in the up-bringing of his neice and nephews. In terms of Ngwaketsi culture, it is a great offence to deny a maternal uncle such a privilege.

On the following day, a similar wedding event is held at the groom's family home.

Here, no church ceremony is involved. The proceedings commence with the arrival of the bride and her family guests, together with community members. As at the bride's home, food would be served together with traditional beer, and the singing of wedding songs by choirs from both families. As was the case at the bride's home, the groom's maternal uncle here is equally offered a cow's head as a token of appreciating his role as an uncle.

At this juncture, a date is agreed upon at which the bride will be transferred to her in-laws to commence her new family life. This process is called *go isa ngwetsi kwaga matsalae,* to take the bride to her in-laws.

## The marriage counselling process (*Go laya*)

As is the case with most ethnic groups nearby, Bangwaketsi elders take their traditional marriage counselling process (*go laya*) very seriously. This is a platform where the newly-married would be exposed to the marriage dynamics – how to handle or approach marriage life in a very successful manner, and avoidance of possible unnecessary future divorce. As stated above, on the evening after the *bogadi* process, the young man would be summoned to his family *kgotla*, where his married and widowed male delegation team would be seated ready to offer marital counselling. Starting with his maternal uncle (the chief uncle), men would take turns to advise the young man on marriage dynamics – the dos and don'ts of a married man. He would be strongly warned against hanging around with former unmarried friends and to choose new appropriate friends from the married male locals. The elders would inform him that he has now graduated from being a boy to a married man, must start going about with married men and also conduct chores associated with family men. Only the male delegates from the young man's side attends this process at the young man's home *kgotla.*

Bangwaketsi elders mention that, on the other hand, the newly-married girl is only offered marriage counselling at her in-laws' residence the day she is transferred there. In the presence of her in-laws, her female marriage delegation team would seat her down on the floor and offer her some marriage counselling. In turns and starting with her chief aunt, they would advise her on how best to attend to her husband and the upcoming new family. She would be advised against keeping friends, that her friend is her husband. She is informed that the short light shoulder blanket, *tsale*, is worn and pinned by her chest with a safety pin to symbolise how she must keep all her domestic matters – good or bad, to her chest and never to share them with other community women, but only with her husband. Also, she is advised to always wear a headscarf, *tukwi,* in public as it signifies her marriage status as a woman. During this process, the groom's women delegation would just be attentive and watching, with clear vision to observe whether indeed their daughter-in-law would, in future, take heed of the counselling advice. Only the married and widowed women are allowed attendance of this process.

## The transfer of bride to her in-laws process (*Go isa ngwetsi*)

In terms of the Ngwaketsi marriage culture, transfer or delivery of the bride (*go isa ngwetsi*) to her in-laws is usually undertaken a day after the *kopo* or when the wedding process is completed. This marriage process is termed *go isa ngwetsi kwaga matsalaye*, to deliver the bride to her in-laws. In the morning hours, the bride, together with her marriage delegation team, led by the chief maternal aunt, would proceed to her in-laws' home. In their possession would be all her personal possessions, as well as the newly brought *kopo* clothing, bedding, and other wedding gifts she received. The bride would carry a calabash of sorghum beer, whilst her chief aunt carry *motlhana*, T-bone, meat portion that was reserved from *kgomo ya motlhakanelwa* apportioned the day before. The bride would be expected to cook and serve the *motlhana* to her in-laws on the day of her reception. The bride's family marriage delegation, both men and women, would travel to deliver their daughter to the groom's place. The married women delegation would be carrying along with them the marriage gifts the bride was presented with during the *kopo* proceedings. Usually, a few married men and women from both her maternal and paternal sides, uncles and aunts always inclusive, would suffice to form an appropriate team to deliver the bride. They would be singing some wedding songs, which send to the bride some themes or messages on how to maintain a positive marriage life.

Upon arrival at the in-laws' yard, the bride's women would be carrying her suitcases and bags on their heads with the chief aunt in front and the bride midway between them. They would follow in a straight line into her in-laws' yard. When they enter the groom's yard, they would be greeted and welcomed by the groom's women delegation team with great and joyous ululations. As they enter the yard, they are met with ladies stamping sorghum, some sweeping the yard whilst one lady would be laid on some prepared blankets in the yard with a baby, to symbolise how they expect their bride to do all these tasks, including bearing children. The groom's team would then proceed to receive the goods from the bride's delegation team and take them into a house or room specially designated for the bride and the groom. Thereafter, the women from both families would be seated with the bride sitting on a goat skin carpet, *phate ya podi*, to sit on. In turns, some of the groom's women team would sit next to the bride in a bumping fashion – this is called *go rurubatsa ngwetsi*, meaning, to assure the bride that she is welcomed and must get settled with her in-laws. At the same time, a female delegation from the bride's side would start to offer some marriage counselling to their daughter, starting with the chief aunt, whilst her in-laws would be watching and listening. Thereafter, the bride is ushered to the special house or room where her belongings were put, upon receipt. In this house or room, the chief aunts from both the newly-married couple would remain with the bride for a short time, particularly with view to demonstrate to her how a matrimonial bed is prepared for a husband. Ngwaketsi elders mention that it is in this room that the bride is also exposed to how a husband is handled in bed. She would also be seriously warned against sharing the matrimonial bed with any other person but for her husband.

Thereafter, the process is concluded, with a small meal before the bride's delegation returns back home leaving her with the in-laws. As soon as she has been delivered to her in-laws, the wife becomes part of the new family and would soon adapt to their way of life.

At this juncture, the bride is allowed to cook the *motlhana* meat and sorghum grain she brought along. When ready for serving, the groom's chief aunt would guide her with serving the meal – as she dishes and serves, and she is simultaneously told the names and relations of those close family relatives she is serving, this being an opportune moment for her to get accustomed to her new family.

### The bride taken back to her natal home process

The Bangwaketsi elders are quick to state that in terms of their cultural practice, there is no process like the taking of the bride back to her natal home. As soon after the bride has been formally transferred to her in-laws, her mother must, within reasonable time, pay her a visit at the in-law's place, *mma mosetsana go gata kwaga matsale.* This visit is symbolical as it sets her daughter free to now start paying visits to her parents' home to attend whatever communal callings that may arise, such as bereavements, marriage, and other social events. Failure to make such a visit by the bride's mother would deny her daughter an opportunity to visit her home in the event any social calling arising back home.

## Bangwaketsi's Marriage Rites and the Significance of their Metaphorical Language and Symbolic Actions

### The rights, privileges and benefits associated with Bangwaketsi's traditional marriage practices

Ngwaketsi elders view their customary marriage rites, metaphorical language and symbolic actions as significant in many respects. Like most Tswana ethnic groups, the elders maintain that these values emanate from the initial Tswana traditional language usage.

### Marriage rites

The Ngwaketsi marriage rites, for instance, prohibit unmarried people attending traditional marriage processes. Such are strictly attended to by the married persons. Divorced persons and those undergoing marital conflicts are equally barred from attendance. The elders believe that the divorced and the ones with troubled marriages have potential to bring bad luck or ill advice to the newly-weds if they are allowed to attend and participate in such rituals. As for the unmarried, they are deemed to be immature and not conversant with matrimonial issues, and unqualified to offer any form of marital counselling to the newly married. Even in cases where the unmarried are friends to the marrying couple, they are disqualified since they are deemed likely to mislead the couple because they know nothing about marriage dynamics.

### Metarphorical language

Ngwaketsi elders view their marriage metarphorical language as a new communication skill that is meant to inspire and equip the newly-weds with metarphorical phrases meant to easily guide them against taking wrong life decisions. For instance, the metarphorical phrase *mosadi oa bapalwa* would translate to mean that a woman represents a man's investment, whilst the phrase *mosadi tshwene o jewa mabogo* means that a man does not necessarily get attracted to a woman's beauty, but mainly becomes concerned with her inner personal self. Another metarphorical phrase known to Bangwaketsi concerns their preferring to befriend a widow as opposed to a divorcee: *letswele la motlhalwa gake le tshware, nka mpa ka tswara la moswelwa.* They associate the divorced with bad luck, bad faith and ailment, hence *tlhalo ke bolwetse.*

## SYMBOLIC ACTIONS

There are several Ngwaketsi symbolic marriage actions. Amongst them is a process where a bride's father, upon receipt of *bogadi* cattle prize, would slaughter and donate a half portion of its meat to the in-laws, at the same time preparing a special meal with some of the remaining half carcas for enjoyment by marriage delegates from both families. This cow is called *kgomo yoo rraatso.* As noted from above, the essence of this cow is to unify not only the newly-weds, but also their two families into a new lifetime relationship. The elders mention further that the relationship further manifests itself by virtue of the birth of the couple's children who happen to be naturally related to both families.

The symbolic phrase *goya go bofa setlhako* is a statement mentioned by the young man's chief uncle immediately after they have been granted the bride at the end of the men's *kopo/patlo* marriage process, i.e., just after being allowed to marry the girl during the *kopo/patlo* process. The chief uncle to the young man would announce that they wish to be released briefly, so that 'they go out to tie the shoe lace", *goya go bofa setlhako.* This brief excuse allows the young man's delegation to briefly get prepared to either drive in the *bogadi* cattle or to bring in *bogadi* money if such is agreed as the *bogadi.* To the girl's male marriage delegation, this phrase is an indication that the young man's male delegation now wishes to start the *bogadi* marriage process since the *kopo/patlo* marriage process would have been completed. This further clarifies that in the event such a phrase would never be mentioned after the *kopo/patlo* marriage process; it would be assumed that there is no immediate issuance or delivery of *bogadi* as it would have been deferred to a future date owing to whatever reasons.

As stated above, during the transfer of the bride to her in-laws, they cause her to sit on a goathide skin carpet (*phate ya podi*). Women from her in-laws' side would sit beside her in a bumping position, which elders say symbolises an act of assuring the bride that she is most welcome and must relax and feel at home. This symbolic action is termed *go ruruhatsa ngwetsi*, to stabilise the bride.

The Ngwaketsi elders also speak about *kgomo yaga malome ya ketela pele.* This refers to a cow donated by the maternal uncle, the chief uncle, to his marrying niece. It is meant to accompany and top up the *bogadi* cattle. In attempts to explain the foregoing, the elders go further to add yet another metarphor to say that *ngwana o mogolo kwa gaabo mogolo*, which translates that a child is superior at their maternal family's home. They explain that children commonly tend to get much closer to their mother's relatives than their father's, naturally making them grow closer to their maternal uncles, who happened to be always available to offer them life skill guidance, more often than not. It is along this same line of thought that in a similar manner, when a Mongwaketsi father slaughters a cow, he would always, as a symbolic action, offer or assign its head to the children's maternal uncle, hence *kgomo yaga malome ya ditlhogo*. The elders also appreciate that traditionally, when a marriage has gone sour, it is the children's maternal uncle who would go out of his way to take care of them. This further explains why after payment of the *bogadi* cattle, the maternal uncle would always have an opportune moment to take for himself one or two cattle from the *bogadi* cattle, *go thiba kgomo yaga malome ya bogadi*. One of such cattle must be female so that it starts bearing calves that would mature, multiply, and assist the uncle to feed his nieces and nephews should a need arise.

*Ditlhogo tsaga malome* are therefore a token of appreciation to the uncle for taking good care and bringing up the niece or nephew. This would explain why a husband would always offer his children's maternal uncle the head of a cow, sheep, etc. whenever he has slaughtered a beast. The uncle is also offered a female *bogadi* cow with an assumption that in the event his married niece encounters a future marriage misfortune of whatsoever nature, an uncle would have accumulated sufficient cattle from *bogadi* to be able to fend and maintain his married sister's children/household.

## Factors of Change and their Impact on Ngwaketsi Traditional Marriage Rites and Activities

Bangwaketsi elders are concerned against the notable cultural dilution brought about by the Civil or District Commissioner's marriage process. On the contrary, apart from mostly preferring their Ngwaketsi traditional marriage process, the elders' second preference is the Christian marriage process. The elders are primarily concerned that most marrying officers at the District Commissioner's office are not only young but unmarried. For this reason, they view such officers as unqualified to solemnise and offer marriage counselling to the newly-weds as they lack experience on marriage modalities. Besides, Ngwaketsi elders are adamant that the District Commissioner's marriage officers are mostly interested in promoting the acquisition of financial and material wealth amongst the marrying couples, and shy away from instilling traditional marriage guiding principles, hence the prevailing high rate of divorce cases countrywide.

The elders also feel that unlike in the past, nowadays people, particularly women, get married not out of passion but mostly due to the temptations of financial and material gains. They maintain that this trend has caused most marriages not to last but to end tragically. This they say sadly negates the essence of a marriage.

The elders also lament the youthful couples now having a right to choose their partners independently of parental guidance. They believe that this has caused the youthful couples to overlook the importance of knowing the background of one's potential in-laws, causing the youth to even marry outside their communities into the international community, which they term *go nyalela ba dichaba.* This negative change resulted with their now married youth only learning the hard way when they eventually disapprove of the strange and foreign traits displayed by their partners or families, hence their resolution to a divorce. Incidentally, and as is the case with most ethnic groups researched, some of the Ngwaketsi elders who participated in this particular research happened to have lived during the transitional period when the choice of a wife by a young man's parents was fading being replacemed by individuals now having an independent choice of a marrying partner. In fact, some of the elders involve in this study had their partners chosen by their parents, whilst others did choose partners for themselves. Unlike currently, the latter group are quick to mention that though they chose their own partners, their parents played a pivotal role in influencing them to choose wisely, hence their prolonged marriages, compared with the current youthful couples. With the transfer of married couples, *bogadi* is now preferred in monetary terms as against issuance of cattle.

Furthermore, the Ngwaketsi elders also noted some change in the trend: *bogadi* is now being managed by the current ounger generation. They mention that upon the arrival of the Civil Marriage process, a financial and economic price tag was attached to the *bogadi.* This perpetuated a strong favour for a *bogadi* cattle to now commonly be substituted with the equivalence of cattle in monetary terms. For instance, in olden times, cattle were a major trade currency, not only for a *bogadi* for marriage, but also for purposes of general bartering of goods and merchandise. In the past, four cattle and four sheep would be sufficient to pay *bogadi.* Also, the cosmopolitan lifestyle, nowadays experienced within almost all the main villages of Botswana, totally distracted youthful Ngwaketsi from appreciating the values attached to the Ngwaketsi customary marriage processes.

Unlike previously, nowadays the parents of a bride would over and above the payment of *bogadi*, demand for provision of a double bed, blankets, clothing, food stuffs, etc. On the contrary, Bangwaketsi in former times only demanded cattle and blankets made from animal skin, *diphate*, as a token for a *bogadi.* Owing to the current steep material costs of *bogadi*, the elders are of the opinion that this new practice has now caused a number of able young men to shy away from committing themselves into marriage and have now resorted to cohabitation with their female lovers. They just cannot afford the current extraordinarily high *bogadi*, and have now resorted to cohabit with their lovers as an alternative measure to the current unaffordable monetary *bogadi.*

Another change identified by the Bangwaketsi is that in the past, it was the young man's parents, uncles and aunts who would assist in payment of their son's *bogadi.* But because payment of *bogadi* was deferred to the time when the young man was now a father of maturing children, and having worked hard to raise a family and accumulated cattle (some initially given to him by his father), the husband was able to afford payment of *bogadi.*

The elders lament that, worse still, today's marrying couples not only marry under the customary marriage rites but commonly proceed to arrange for yet another marriage process under either the Christian or Civil marital processes.

## Prevalent Problems and Challenges in Bangwaketsi's Traditional Marriages Today

There are a number of existing problems and challenges regarding the Ngwaketsi traditional marriage today. They include a high rate of divorce cases amongst the youthful married Ngwaketsi couples, unlike in the olden days. Ngwaketsi elders lament that in terms of their culture, and indeed as the Bible commands, marriage can only be terminated by the death of one of the spouses, no more no less. They maintain that their previous marriages within close relations were everlasting because it was easy and quicker for the parents or relatives of the married couples to intervene and assist the couples whenever there were matrimonial conflicts. Besides, the couples were in the past married and staying within very close proximity of their parents and other relatives – so it was easier and convenient for families and relatives to know or tell when any couple are having a marriage problem. Currently, it is not practicable to come in and assist fighting couples. This is so because the newly-married couples are now total strangers from different societal and ethnic backgrounds. Also, the newly-married couple now stays far away from their close relatives, making it very difficult for close relations to sense or identify when the couple have problems. All these problems are associated with the current cosmopolitan life styles experienced by the youthful couples.

Like other Tswana ethnic groups, Ngwaketsi elders also mention that the abolition of initiation schools, (*bojale* for girls and *bogwera* for boys) has greatly interfered with and degraded the proper upbringing of their youth into responsible elders as they grew into adulthood. Their youthful couples are now copying the negative and wrong cultural practices acquired from the international community, owing to globalization, and more particularly the internet. This the elders believe, has greatly compromised the essence of a beautiful and good marriage life today.

The elders further question the civil marriage process. They feel that the District Commissioner handles the marriage process unilaterally instead of mutually with the marrying couple's parents. They further feel uncomfortable that unmarried marriage officers are not qualified to solemnise or even to render marriage counselling when they have not gone through a marriage themselves. This to them is a recipe for the prevailing high divorce rates. To them, the marriage process must be strictly left to married people as they are rich with marriage life experience.

## Conclusions and Recommendations

As is observed with other ethnic groups researched, it is evident that advent to the coming of the missionaries and Western civilization to our country, many cultural practices, not only in marriage processes but in life generally, have diluted and distorted the marriage process of the Bangwaketsi. Since we all appreciate that society everywhere is dynamic and not static, it can only make sense that the Ngwaketsi marriage culture has been degraded by effects of globalization. This calls for Ngwakesti elders as well as their youthful married couples, to join hands in reviewing their ethnic marriage processes.

The rationale here would be to come up with appropriate standardised ethnic processes that would serve their current marriage set-up without necessarily offending both the cultural and the cosmopolitan lifestyles as they co-exist today. For instance, an Ngwaketsi delegation may approach the state and advocate for use of only married persons to solemnise and offer counselling to marrying couples. The standardization of *bogadi* in terms of the number of cattle to be paid. This would assist in ensuring that exorbitant *bogadi*, which threatens to impoverish newly marrying couples, is reduced a view to accord newly-married couples to expend more of their hard-earned money in starting a matrimonial home than in paying high *bogadi*.

Lastly, the codification of the Ngwaketsi traditional marriage processes would go a long way towards preserving their ethnic practices, at least for the benefit of upcoming young generations. This will assist in ensuring that not all is lost in terms of how the Ngwaketsi marriage process are, or how they used to be. Besides, the codification of this would assist the Ngwaketsi to further look into how their elders used to conduct cultural matters, as well as how they can amend civil law to suit the current generational lifestyles without offending its cultural aspects.

Therefore, the current House of Chiefs must further be engaged in these issues, so that they are attended to, not only for Bangwaketsi but for all Tswana, and other, ethnic groups.

# 8

# BANGWATO

*Mr. Allan Manyeneng*

**Totem**: *Phuti* – Duiker

**Clan Poem:** *Leboko la Bangwato*

*Ba Ga Mmangwato ba ga Mabiletsa;*
*Ba kile ba biletsa Sekgoma ntwa;*
*Sekgoma le ene ka ele ngwana wa bogosi;*
*Le ene a ba e biletsa.*
*Ka hakgamala kago sala ke eme.*

## INTRODUCTION

The justification for this study on the subject of *lenyalo*, as a cultural institution and practice is, under prevailing consensus, the most crucial role that cultural traditions in Botswana have played in the country's exceptionality as a prudently managed economy and a stable democracy. The link between national economic development and cultural traditions was flagged by Stephen B. Lewis Jr., Emeritus Professor of Economics at Carlton College in the United States. Lewis was at one time special economic advisor to both Presidents Masire's and Mogae's governments, but is probably more widely remembered as editor of President Masire's memoirs, *Very Brave or Very Foolish, Memoirs of an African Democrat*. He argues that Botswana's meteoric rise from being one of the poorest countries in the world to a medium-income country within a few decades since independence is closely related to how its founders built the new nation on those parts of traditional culture which were compatible with, or essential to, democratic development. In other words, in addition to science, mathematics, engineering and technology, the bedrock of Botswana's phenomenal development since independence in 1966 is the contribution of those areas of national life that the humanities cultivate and study, i.e., cultural institutions and practices, such as *lenyalo.*

*Lenyalo*, in Sengwato, as in other Setswana-speaking communities in the country, refers to two related aspects of marriage in their culture. Firstly, it refers to the institution of marriage itself which is revered as a divinely ordained coming together of a man and a woman as husband and wife for the purpose of building a family. Secondly, it refers to the traditional rituals that are performed in order to solemnise and finally celebrate the union in the community. It is important to note that over and above its immediate purpose as a rite of passage, whereby two people are initiated into new roles as responsible adults in the community, marriage practices also constitute a social renewal ritual during which society takes stock of itself. Research to improve understanding of how rituals like *lenyalo* enable a community to review and rededicate itself to its values and sense of identity in a changing world is crucial. This is especially the case if we want to give cultural traditions an appropriate role in modern national development along the lines Professor Lewis suggests as pointed out above.

*Lenyalo* and its practice among the Bangwato is part of a deeply entrenched traditional belief system which continues to shape their sense of who they are and their understanding of both the social world and the spiritual world, as has been done for generations in the past. *Lenyalo* as a ritual, therefore, is a critical national resource that must be carefully studied and documented if the nation wishes to leverage its role in national development. The values and sense of identity engendered by this belief system are relatively stable and predate the overarching national identity that the government has endeavoured to forge since independence in 1966. Government's effort to construct a cohesive national identity from the traditions of the various communities in Botswana has sometimes been viewed by some communities as a threat to their individual sense of identity and deeply held values and beliefs. They fear that the government's goal is to create a homogenous application of one ethnic group's cultural practices on others. It is important to allay such anxieties by making sure that the identity, belief systems and practices of each community are understood and respected in the creation of a united but diverse national cultural space. It would, for one thing, avoid errors such as those in the past when an attempt was made to ban weddings during certain times of the year because that was another community's ploughing season.

It is also important to understand that culture is not a collection of fossilised habits but a living dynamic entity, which is constantly changing to adapt to new situations. So, when references are made to a people, in this case Bangwato, being justly proud of their culture and being committed to guarding jealously against its dilution, such references relate equally to the people's justified pride in their culture's flexibility and ability to respond to change constructively. There is certainly enough pressure to change in the form of increased opportunities to live outside the box of one's traditional geographical home. People travel to other parts of the country and beyond, people inter-marry across cultural traditions and raise their children in cultural contexts which are a far cry from those of their homes. The World Wide Web and other technologies have expanded the world view of the average Mongwato. The challenge here, obviously, is how to retain one's sense of cultural identity while still maximizing the benefits of working and living with people from other cultures. In cross–cultural marriages, for instance, there may be conflict around the retention or rejection of *bogadi*, which may be seen from one perspective as trade in human beings, to overstate the case a bit. The exchange of wedding rings also may be significant for one party while to another it might be merely an expensive formality whose meaning does not go deeper than the sparkle of the jewelry and the jaw-dropping price tag.

Part of what needs to be done is to understand the symbolic significance of practices and objects used during the process of *lenyalo*. The tendency is to see them as mere formalities to get the marriage over and done with and to ignore their deeper significance. The practices and objects used in the various processes of *lenyalo* are coded with lessons that are relevant to the success of the marriage itself, and for the cohesion of the community into which the newly-weds are initiated as responsible adults. Thoughtful conversations about traditional cultures are essential to ease the complications that arise when cherished customs appear to be recklessly abandoned and new-fangled ones are embraced without much reflection.

It is also apt to remind ourselves that marriage is essentially a religious ritual. It is a rite of passage through which the union between a man and a woman is solemnised and consecrated as a marriage. It consists of stages in a ritual integration of the couple into the fabric of society in accordance with the people's religious belief system. So even though *lenyalo* may have immediate and easily recognisable secular purposes, it plays the deeper role of renewing and affirming the ancient pact between the human and the divine under which marriage is a gift from God to humankind bestowed at creation. In the Setswana religious belief system marriage connects people to a spiritual world which is inhabited by *Modimo* in the heavens at the top of the hierarchy and the living parents of an individual on earth, hence the profound respect for elders in Ngwato culture. So. the traditions and practices of *lenyalo* are not superficial and disposable formalities but are the glue which holds together the family, the community and its institutions on earth and bonds them with the ancestral spirits and *Modimo* in heaven. As has been pointed out in a related context, even though a private affair, marriage has serious public consequences and attempts to interfere with its sanctity should not be easily countenanced.

## Information Sources and Data Collection

The data used in this chapter were firstly gleaned from such literature review as was possible only online in the situation of COVID-19 related restrictions. Seminal works consulted include work on the Bangwato by historians Parsons, Makgala, Bennett and others. Ethnographer Schapera and theologian Nkomazana, among others, were vital in helping build a picture of traditional Ngwato society at its point of contact with the Christian world introduced into the country by missionaries and traders, mostly in the

19th century. The bulk of the data, however, was obtained through field research conducted among the Bangwato in Serowe and surrounding areas. The analysis of the data led to this chapter, part of the research covering the marriage practices of as many ethnic communities in Botswana as possible in this book. Telephonic and in-person interviews were conducted with key people such as headmen, village chiefs, senior citizens and other individuals acknowledged as well-versed in matters of *lenyalo* and the culture of the ethnic community in general. Snow-balling was used to identify further interviewees and to identify and recruit participants for workshop-type group discussions.

For this chapter the view adopted in analysing the data is that marriage is a rite of passage, and as such is a fundamentally religious ritual. The missionaries introduced Christianity to the country in the early 19th century and were able to convert so many people, often through *dikgosi*, that at present the majority of Batswana are professed Christians. It does not, however, follow from this that Africans have forgotten their indigenous religious beliefs and traditions. The missionaries had little control over the different ways in which the early converts perceived and adapted Christian teachings, in much the same way that churches today do not lord over their followers. It seems that even when converted and nominally profess Christianity, Africans retain their indigenous religious beliefs largely intact. Since Africans did not write, crucial ideas and concepts were encoded and passed on from generation to generation through the activities of rituals such as *lenyalo* itself, as well as others such as *bogwere* and *bojale,* rain-making, supplications and funerals. Understanding the symbolism of the practices and language of the process of *lenyalo* will help us understand what deep meanings and social tensions it serves to address as a ritual. When we understand the spiritual basis of *lenyalo* and the indigenous beliefs it encodes we will also be in a position to appreciate how African beliefs and traditions do find expression even in the ceremonies of imported Christian and Western style civil marriages. Carefully studied, the practices and language exhibited during *lenyalo*, whether customary or Christian, may be discovered to have resonances that go back even to the legends of Matsieng, Tintibane, Thobega and the other divinities of Lowe's cave at Rasesa, where the first humans are said to have emerged from the ground and where Thobega contracted the first ever marriage when he married Tintibane's daughter, and from where Matsieng was led to a place of women, presumably to find a companion fit for him too.

## A Brief Historical Background of Serowe Village and the Bangwato

Serowe has not always been the Bangwato seat of power. When the kingdom first came into its own under Kgari, who ruled from 1817 to 1828, their seat of power was in the Shoshong Hills. However, it was his son Sekgoma I who built his capital at the site of the present village of Shoshong. A power struggle subsequently ensued between King Sekgoma I and his son, Khama III. Sekgoma was a staunch traditionalist and wanted to revive the glory of his father, King Kgari. Khama III, on the contrary, was an overzealous convert to Christianity and clashed with his father because of this. He refused to submit to the marriage arrangements that had been made for him and decided to marry a woman of his choice in a Christian marriage ceremony. Khama moved the capital to Palapye when he became king. However, Palapye did not prove an ideal location and in 1902 he moved the capital again, this time to its present site of Serowe.

The subject of marriage looms large in Ngwato history, and marriages mark key moments in the rise and development of the Ngwato kingdom. According to various sources, the Ngwato were a scion of the Kgabo–Kwena that had earlier broken off from the parent Kwena group which had settled at a place called Ratheng along the Crocodile River. The Ngwato themselves did not break away to form a separate chiefdom until after the Kgabo–Kwena group had long moved to the present day district in Botswana and settled around the Dithejwana Hills. They were a subordinate lineage group under the Kwena of Molepolole when Motshodi, the grandson of Kgabo-Kwena was *kgosikolo* (paramount *kgosi*) from 1740 to 1770 with their own leader, Mathiba. The breakaway happened during the reign of Motswasele I, who was Motshodi's successor. It happened because of a war over marriage. Apparently, a Mongwato woman, who the Ngwato had tricked Motswasele out of marrying, nevertheless deserted her Ngwato husband to marry Motswasele anyway. Mathiba and the Bangwato launched an attack on behalf of their jilted countryman called Mongwe. They captured some Kwena women, stripped them naked and left them to find a place to hide their shame in a maize field. The Kwena launched a counter-attack to avenge the insult and drove Mathiba and his Bangwato out of the land in a battle which has since been dubbed 'the battle of wives and skirts'. Mathiba fled to a place called Ngwari in the area around present day Shoshong. The account is apocryphal, but the fact that it survives in folk memory points to the importance among Bangwato of marriage in the foundational myth of their kingdom; and also the perception that marriage may be a private affair, but has public and even historical significance.

There are other key events in recent Ngwato history in which marriage played a vital role, but it is not the place of this chapter to go into them. It will suffice, therefore, to make the point only in the present broad strokes. Firstly, the foundational event of the kingdom that is alluded to above, is sparked by a conflict about marriage. Secondly, the conflict between Sekgoma I and his son, Khama III may be a religious one, but there is little doubt that what brings it to a head is the issue of marriage. Lastly, there is the world famous marriage of the late President Sir Seretse Khama to an English woman. Despite the world wide hue and cry about the issue of race that the marriage gave rise to, in Serowe itself the race of the late president's bride was not the issue. In Serowe the issue raised by the marriage was more about women and commoners playing a decisive role in a power struggle in the kingdom, because the support for Seretse Khama was led by women commoners who perceived that his uncle may have been using the marriage to a foreigner and a commoner to exclude him from his inheritance. These three events are key moments in the history of Bangwato because they mark crucial transitions from one status to another. The first memorialises the tensions and stresses of the experience in the transition of a lineage group to the status of an autonomous kingdom. The second similarly encapsulates the tensions and stresses that were experienced in the transition from a pre-colonial society to colonial subjugation. The last encapsulates the tensions of the transition from colonial rule to independence.

In some accounts of Ngwato history, it was during Mathiba's flight from the war with Motswasele that he experienced the event that led to his Ngwato group adopting the *phuti* totem. It appears that after the split from the Kwena at Molepolole, Mathiba was pursued up to the northern Kgatleng boundary at Ngwari. It was at Ngwari that when his pursuers had him nearly cornered that he found a hiding place under a *motlhakola* shrub but startled a buck that was grazing nearby so that it bounded away in flight. The pursuers, mistaking it for him, immediately gave chase, thus leaving him behind to escape. From Ngwari he went further north to Lephephe where he founded a separate chiefdom in 1780. He attributed his narrow escape to the buck and decided to adopt it as his chiefdom's totem. This is how it has come to be that the Ngwato to this day venerate the *phuti* as their totem.

At Lephephe, Ngwato birthed Makgasane, whose younger brother was Moleta, whose younger brother was Mokgadi. The latter ruled on behalf of Mathiba, who grew up as a Mokwena. He moved to Otse, Shoshong with his five wives. Mathiba birthed Khama I and Khamane. Khama I birthed Kgari, who birthed Macheng and Sekgoma. Kgari was killed during the Mashona wars at Motopo Hills. Kgari birthed Khama II, who died a young man. Sekgoma birthed Khama III, who went with Sebele and Bathoen to London, seeking British protection for Bechuanaland. Sekgoma II, elder to Tshekedi, gave birth to Seretse Khama.

## Understanding Marriage from the Bangwato Point of View

According to the Ngwato elders, a marriage connotes a union between a man and a woman with a clear intent to stay together as husband and wife, and raise their children into responsible members of the community. According to their understanding, it is against this background that in marriage not only is a new family born to the community, but the establishment of numerous relationships is also achieved. The relationships here entail the in-laws and their relatives, as well as the bearing of children in the marriage, which is viewed as building a strong relationship between the two marrying families. *Lenyalo* in Sengwato may be seen as a religious ritual that can be understood as a rite of passage, since it marks the transition from the status of a relatively carefree youth to a responsible and privileged adulthood. Like all rites of passage its activities can be divided into three sequential stages as follow.

(a) **Separation stage,** which consists of activities that symbolise and reconcile the tensions and stresses of separation from the old status. In the case of marriage this consist of ceremonies and symbolic acts that may help the initiate deal with the loss of the security and comfort of his or her parental home, and to resolve the tensions and strains to which the separation may give rise.

(b) **Threshold stage,** sometimes referred to as the liminal or in between stage. It consists of activities and symbolic representations of the sense of isolation and insecurity that the individual may experience as the result of belonging to neither the old nor the new status. The activities of this stage emphasise and attempt to resolve the strains and stresses of longing for the past and trepidation about the future, i.e., the tension from the opposite pulls or pushes of the old status from which one has been expelled and the new one to which one has yet to be welcomed.

(c) **Reintegration stage,** celebrating the admission as a member with new status. The ceremonial activities of this stage are rich in symbolism that emphasis not only a new sense of belonging to a special group but both the responsibilities and privileges of the new status as well. However, despite the emphasis on joyful alacrity of donning the credentials of the new status, there are tensions to be resolved at his stage too, particularly with the need for restraint and humility in asserting the prerogatives of the new roles.

It is important, however, to point out that the stresses and tensions to which the rituals and language of *lenyalo* draw attention, and are designed to resolve, have correspondences in the history of the society that is marked by similar transitions from one historical period to another. It is therefore necessary to understand the significance of *lenyalo* in Sengwato culture, not merely as relating to the tensions and stresses of marriage itself, but also to the life of the community as a whole. This is the sense in which marriage is a social renewal ritual in Sengwato.

## Types of Marriages

As in other communities in the country, three types of marriage traditions coexist among the Bangwato. These are:

(a) **Customary marriage** that is conducted in accordance with Sengwato customs and traditions at a *kgotla*.

(b) **Religious marriages** that are conducted in accordance with a preferred religious tradition, which among the Bangwato is predominantly Christian.

(c) **Civil marriages** conducted in accordance with the stipulations of Botswana common law as set out in the Marriage Proceedings Act No.18 of 2001.

The first is indigenous while the other two are both importations, introduced into the country by Christian missionaries and settlers during the processes of colonization, mainly in the 19th century. The first (and the second in some cases) are potentially polygamous, but the third is strictly monogamous. Furthermore, it is illegal to enter into marriage to a second person under one system while still married to another under either of the other systems. However, it is perfectly legal to go through a second ceremony under any system with the same person. In general, Bangwato, like other Batswana, tend to believe that there is a deep religious aspect to marriage and will, in addition to fulfilling the secular requirements of a civil marriage, undergo either a customary or a Christian ceremony to satisfy that aspect. Described below is a brief assessment of the attitudes of Bangwato towards each of the marriage processes.

## SENGWATO CUSTOMARY MARRIAGE

Bangwato in Serowe and elsewhere in the country believe that the practices they perform during customary weddings are ancestral traditions that have been passed down to them through countless generations. Observing the traditions is a matter of honour and upholding the integrity of their identity in a changing world. There is no 'manual' of Ngwato traditions and customs to guarantee that these practices are properly observed, so they rely on what has been retained and preserved in the collective memory of the community, and the writings of historians and missionaries of the the time. The older generations are revered as custodians of these surviving traditions. The traditions are a crucial resource because they are more than mere formalities to be observed at a wedding. They are a storehouse of indigenous knowledge that is reaffirmed and re-energised with every wedding ceremony.

The first step in a Sengwato marriage ceremony is the identification of the future marriage couple. Traditionally, the young man's parents set off the process by identifying a suitable girl as a possible bride for their son when they felt he had come of age. This was normally an easy enough job because the girl was identified from among relatives or friends in a close-knit society in which families had a measure of each other's standing. The suitability of the girl was not based on her personal attributes primarily, but on the regard in which her family was held in the community. A family with a wholesome reputation was deemed guaranteed to raise girls with the requisite *mekgwa le maitseo,* behaviour and manners, befitting a good wife. Girls from such families, regardless of their personal attributes, were coveted prospective brides.

Traditionally, when a suitable girl had thus been identified, it was up to the father of the young man to approach the girl's family and broach the subject of a possible match. In considering the proposal, the girl's family similarly placed a great deal of stress on the social standing or reputation enjoyed by the young man's family. Young men, sometimes regardless of their personal attributes, if they came from families with unsavoury reputations such as for sloth, practice of witchcraft and antisocial behaviours, had remote prospects of being accepted as possible future sons in-law. If the two families were in agreement and the match was considered suitable, the two families would then embark on their respective preparations for the customary marriage process.

The process consisted of several carefully orchestrated ceremonies which had to be scrupulously observed to ensure that the marriage is a properly conducted one. The process included, but is not restricted to *patlo, bogadi* and *mokete wa lenyalo*. *Patlo* is the most important of the processes: without it no marriage would be considered properly conducted or valid. It is followed by *bogadi* which some people even think is the main process in completing the marriage process. However it can be delayed, paid in instalments and even waived. It is not a requirement for the transfer of the bride to her marital home the way *patlo* is. Another variation in tradition is that increasingly marriage partners no longer necessarily come together via graduation from the traditional initiation schools, namely *bogwera* and *bojale* for men and women, respectively.

Since the introduction of Christianity in the early 19th century, and abetted by the overzealous crusade on its behalf by King Khama III, some modifications have been exhibited in the conduct of the rite, especially among Christian converts. Khama discouraged the practice of parents identifying future marital partners and arranged marriages. He felt that this avoided the trend among young people to blame divorces on poor marriage matches by parents. Another modification, also going back to the time of King Khama III is with regard to *bogadi*. Instead of the stipulated payments in cash and livestock, Khama III instituted the requirement that the man build a house or a granary and fill it up with sorghum grain (*sesowa*) in the girl's parents yard as a token of appreciation of the role they played in raising a wife for him. The move was also intended to help men from underprivileged families who could not afford the stipulations of conventional *bogadi*. Similarly, it is not essential to the formalization of a marriage, and could be foregone or undertaken in the form of a simple meal shared by parties from both families.

This would complete the Ngwato customary marriage processes, with the girl now having graduated to become a married woman, transferred to her in-laws to start a new family and build relationships amongst her husband's community. Further details of the Ngwato customary marriage processes are explained in later sections. Ngwato elders also maintain that during the olden times, the traditional initiation schools – *bogwera*, young men's initiation schools, and *bojale*, girls' initiation schools – played a vital role in preparing young men and women to become responsible and resourceful parents of tomorrow.

## Christian marriage

Bangwato elders are of the view that the Christian marriage process, as brought about by missionaries long ago, naturally found the customary marriage process already in place. As with most Tswana ethnic groups, both marriage processes have co-existed in their community to this day. Bangwato appreciate that a Christian marriage process involves a priest as a marrying officer, as opposed to their marriage culture where the couples' parents and their married relatives jointly participate in assuring that the new family they are about to conceive stems from a well-thought out and sound foundation.

Both the Ngwato youth and elders are conversant with the marriage laws of the land, common law, and state that before a marriage was solemnised by a priest, the marrying couple would be required to first register their marriage with the District Commissioner's office. They would then follow all the pre-marriage processes as stipulated under the District Commissioner's office, but only up to the counselling stage. After the counselling stage, the District Commissioner would release the couples intending to follow the Christian marriage process. Such couples would proceed to meet the priest at the church office, in possession of matrimonial documentation from the District Commissioner's office addressed to the priest.

The Ngwato elders mention that the couple would then set a marriage date with the priest, usually scheduled for a Saturday, or any preferred or convenient day. On that date, the couple, together with family members, relatives, friends and neighbours from both parties, would convene at a church or at any designated place to witness the Christian marriage process. The priest would bless the event before solemnising the marriage in terms of the church principles. Thereafter, the priest would proceed to offer some counselling to the couple, which centred on how the marrying couple was expected to carry themselves during their marriage. Like the District Commissioner, a priest is usually inundated with disputes and complaints from married church members. In the process, he is experienced with marriage problems and is thus eligible to offer sound counselling in this regard. The marrying couple would be urged to fear God and raise their upcoming children with love and care, through the hand of God. Thereafter, the priest would issue a marriage certificate. The two families, relatives and friends would then retire to the bride's home, where a feast would be held to celebrate the marriage.

## District Commissioner's marriage

According to Bangwato married couples, the District Commissioner's marriage process came about with colonization when Botswana became a state. The Ngwato elders associate the District Commissioner's marriage process with youthful couples who are deemed to be attracted to it, regardless of the consequences. As with most other Tswana ethnic groups, the Ngwato elders are quick to note that after a valid Ngwato customary marriage process, their youthful married couples would take another step and remarry under civil, or common law. The elders also observed that their youthful couples were mostly interested in the property and financial aspects of the civil marriage as stipulated in the Marriage Proceedings Act. Whilst the youthful couples appreciate the essence of this Act, their elders find it distasteful, since the marrying officers are usually unmarried men and women with no concept of what married life entails, and yet, inexperienced as they are, they solemnise and offer marriage counselling to the newly-weds. This practice, in the views of the elders, works against their customary marriage processes, which prohibit unmarried persons from participating in marriage processes. The Ngwato elders also view the marriage process at hand as being a 'one-marriage-officer' mission, whilst their customary version collectively involves several seasoned elderly minds.

As is the case with such marriages countrywide, the Marriage Proceedings Act regulates marriage processes. Couples intending to marry are required to provide documented proof that they have attained the age of majority, 21 years of age. Where one or both parties are of minority age, parental consent is required before the marriage can be registered and concluded. Secondly, the marrying couple must each avail a witness, also of consenting age. Three weeks before the marriage date, both the couple and their respective witnesses are to report at the District Commissioner's office to register the marriage. Each shall bring their national identity cards and complete the necessary marriage application forms. From the registration date to a day before the marriage, the District Commissioner's office will advertise the marriage though a system called 'banns' (at the places where both parties are known to stay or to have stayed). The essence of a three weeks bann advertisement is to give the public at large an opportunity to know who is getting married and whether anyone has any reasons why the couple cannot be joined in matrimony. Reasons to stop a marriage from proceeding may be that one of the parties is already married, or one has promised a different partner marriage and is barred from continuing with another marriage, and so forth.

A day before the marriage date, the couple, together with their respective witnesses, report to the District Commissioner's office to complete documentation that addresses whether they are marrying in or out of community of property, i.e., the nature of how they are going to administer their estates.

During the day of marriage, the marrying couple, together with other couples scheduled for a marriage ceremony that day, along with their witnesses, would convene in a large board room. If there is enough room, relatives and friends would also be allowed in to witness the marriage proceedings. The District Commissioner would commence proceedings with a prayer, before offering detailed counselling. Counselling here entails most of the positive events, as well as negative ones, which married couples generally go through daily. Incidentally, owing to the nature of their daily work, which entails meetings and discussions with married couples who have lodged domestic complaints or disputes, District Commissioners are in a privileged and sound position to appreciate exactly what marriage life connotes. Upon completion of thorough counselling, the District Commissioner would accordingly solemnise the marriage, whereafter, issuance of a marriage certificate would complete the process.

## Marriage Processes

### The betrothal process (Peeletso ya mosadi/Go baa lotlhokwa)

As alluded to above (under Ngwato Customary Marriage Process), in the past the Ngwato parents would, upon a son graduating from the traditional *bogwera* initiation ceremony, *go rupa*, search among their relatives for a suitable young lady to become their son's wife. The current Ngwato elders are quick to maintain that their deceased parents were in fact married to their close relatives, as was the norm then. Upon identifying an appropriate candidate for a wife, the young man's parents would set out to visit the girl's family home to expressi their desire to take the girl into marriage with their son. All things being equal, the girl's family, being satisfied with the other's family background, would accede to the marriage proposal. The Ngwato custom calls this traditional first marriage process *peeletso ya mosadi*, engagement of a woman for future marriage. The elders further emphasise that the betrothal process is sealed between both families with a presentation of some clothing for the girl, such as a dress, underwear, blankets – all classified as *mosese wa lotlhokwa* in Ngwato culture. Also presented were other basic commodities from the young man's family. According to Ngwato culture, in the past a man was ready for marriage at about 30 years of age, whilst a woman was considered mature enough for marriage when she commenced her menstrual cycle, then around 17 years of age.

Shortly thereafter, the young man's parents would revisit the girl's family, this time in the company of his maternal uncle and their son. The latter would have been pre-briefed, mostly by his uncle, to be on the lookout for a potential wife at their intended destination. On arrival, and after the usual greetings, the girl would offer the young man a calabash of water to drink, and he would later be informed that he was to marry the girl who had offered him water earlier on. At the time, such an arrangement was unquestionable by the young man. He would customarily accede to the marriage arrangement.

One old Ngwato woman mentions that she never fell in love with her husband. She was 17 years old in 1951 when her husband's parents paid her parents a visit at home. Upon their departure, she was summoned by her parents, who informed her that the visitors were impressed with their family's child-rearing principles and therefore wished to take her as their son's bride. They started buying *mosese wa lotlhokwa* to signify their future marriage, carried out the *patlo* process in 1952 and her *kgoroso* to her in-laws was undertaken in 1953 when she was 19 years old. The old woman maintains that even her two sisters were married in the same way.

## THE COURTSHIP PROCESS

According to Bangwato, courtship as a stage in the marriage process in their society only started about forty years ago. They understand courtship as a private love relationship between a man and a woman which may, but not necessarily, lead to marriage. For various reasons, in recent times young men and women have increasingly preferred to be at liberty to find their own marital partners, and resented the practice of parentally arranged matches. Although not entered expressly with marriage intentions in mind, depending on the stability and potency of a relationship, courtship may culminate in a marriage proposal. Even though not directly involved, parents generally keep a keen eye on the development of their children, and will be aware of these courtship relationships. They will proffer advice and opinions on their children's choice of partners, especially towards the beginning of the relationship. Their approval or disapproval of any prospective partner would always be based on their appreciation of the girl's or boy's family background. Where the couple feels ready, and make up their mind to marry, it is normally the man who makes the proposal to his lover and accordingly commences proceedings to engage her for marriage.

It is only at this point that the young man informs either his maternal uncle or father about his marital intentions. When this happens, the processes of a regular customary marriage are set in motion. The young man's parents, with close relatives – uncles, aunts, and so forth. now collectively take over the proceedings and implement the Ngwato customary marriage processes to finality.

The Ngwato elders consulted confirm that the process of courtship was already in practice in their youth but not all of them took advantage of it. In fact, some of them attest to the fact that their own marriage partners were identified for them by their parents in accordance with the norms of a traditional arranged marriage. However, they acknowledged that the move towards courtship as a preferred mode of identifying marital partners was a global transformation which some Bangwato were happy to embrace. It was a welcome development because, for the first time in their culture, people had the opportunity to marry partners of their choice from within the community and beyond. However, the elders consulted felt there was a downside to the practice.

While it created opportunities for people to go beyond the close-knit circle of family and friends to identify potential marital partners, it raised the spectre of cross-cultural marital conflicts, especially since people could now identify their partners not only from other parts of the country but other parts of the world. The elders felt that this practice leads to situations in which marital problems are difficult to deal with because of gaps in the cultural backgrounds of the couples and their respective in-laws. They see the practice as the source of acrimonious matrimonial disputes and divorce cases which prevail in society today.

Furthermore, courtship does not always end in marriage. Sometimes this creates problems because children are born into the relationship either before marriage or before it ends. Where a courtship ends prior to marriage, but the girl was impregnated by her lover, the girl's parents approach the young man's home to break the news of the pregnancy. When the man accepts responsibility for the pregnancy, he is expected to pay what is called 'damages' in the form of one or two head of cattle, *kgomo ya tshenyo/kgomo tsa go diga lebele*. If the young man further expresses an intention to have custody of the child, he would be expected to pay eight cattle, which represents and is equivalent to the costs of *bogadi*. This is a practical resolution of the problem. but it is not ideal because the best place to raise a child is in a home with both its parents.

## Preliminary visit process (*Go kokota*)

Unlike the betrothal marriage process, Bangwato elders maintain that the preliminary visit marriage process kicks in at the moment when both the young man and woman are now mature and ripe enough to be joined into holy matrimony. In the past, it was upon the young man's parents being satisfied with their choice of a potential bride that a preliminary visit was arranged, i.e., *go kokota,* which literally means to knock at the door. This involved a visit to the girl's home by the young man's father and mother, at times conducted in the company of one of the maternal uncles and aunts. In the olden days, the parents of a young man would travel to meet with the girl's parents at her home, where the young man's parents would break the news about their intent to take their daughter as future wife to their son.

Bangwato elders are quick to clarify that in the past, the young man's parents would know and appreciate that an agreement for them to marry another's daughter did not entail a payment of *bogadi*/lobola as is the practice with most Tswana ethnic groups, but just an erection of a grain storage house or *moduko/sesowa* at the girl's house. As discussed under Customary Law above, Kgosi Khama III abolished *bogadi* with a view to make marriage affordable to all, without payment of cattle but just the building of a *sesowa*. It was just after the preliminary visit and indeed an agreement to a marriage by the girl's parents being sealed, that the young man's parents would commence to build a *sesowa* at her parents' yard and fill the same with sorghum grain. However, the Ngwato elders lament that currently, and owing to societal cultural changes, they have now copied and aligned to the common Tswana *bogadi* cattle process of demanding six to eight cattle as the bride-wealth.

## THE BRIDE-SEEKING PROCESS (*PATLO*)

In terms of the Ngwato culture, the *patlo* process would have been preceded by the *go kokota* marriage process, now giving the young man some visitation access to his future in-laws' family home – at times through errands from his parents to the girl's parents. As soon as the young man was ready for marriage, he would be instructed by his parents to go and build *sesowa* and yard at his future in-laws' homestead. Thereafter, some men, uncles inclusive, would visit the girl's home to confirm the quality of the *sesowa*, after which the uncle would hand over the *sesowa* to the girl's parents. The women from the young man's side, his mother and aunts inclusive, would then follow up with a load of sorghum in a cattle-drawn trailer to fill up the *sesowa* to the brim.

Immediately thereafter, married male relatives, close friends and associates would visit the girl's home, led by the paternal uncle, to look for the bride – *go kopa metsi*. They would have brought a cow to be delivered to the girl's home, i.e., *kgomo ya metsi*, to signify bride-seeking, which would later be slaughtered for the wedding ceremony. Upon arrival at the girl's home in the morning, they would find a group of seated men of similar backgrounds as them, awaiting their arrival for the *patlo* process. The young man's paternal uncle would greet the girl's marriage delegation and inform them that they had come to ask for water, '*re tlile go kopa metsi*'. At this juncture, a paternal uncle from the girl's side would respond by availing his nephew to them, i.e., *kelo rolela metsi, ke rebola ngwetsi*. This would complete the men's Ngwato *patlo* marriage process. Thereafter the marriage would be registered at the *kgotla* a few days before the young man's married women's delegation undertook a similar visit to conduct their *patlo* marriage process.

The young man's women delegation would visit the girl's woman delegation and find them seated and waiting for them. They would exchange greetings before the paternal aunt requested a calabash of water from the girl's delegation. The girl's aunt would respond by availing the girl for marriage, at the same time warning the young man's delegation that the bride was still young and immature, therefore she must be taught the household chores wherever she was going to be raising a family.

## THE WEDDING CEREMONY PROCESS (*MOKETE WA LENYALO*)

According to the Ngwato culture, the wedding ceremony is particularly meant to facilitate the transfer of the bride to her in-laws' household, that is *mokete wa setapa o isa kgorosong ya ngwetsi*. On the morning of the wedding day, paternal aunts from both families would meet at the bride's home to dress her up for the wedding ceremony. In times past, the bride would wear a white dress with a veil – the white dress signified that she was pure and without a child at the time of marriage. A man would wear a black suit and a hat. The two families, their relatives and friends, as well as members of the community, would converge at church for the marriage solemnization and blessings by a priest/pastor. During the relevant time, some married men from the groom's side would, in the morning, present at the bride's home a cow for slaughter for the wedding. It was called *kgomo ya metsi* because it was meant to request water, *e tsile go kopa metsi*. A cow designated for the *kgomo ya metsi* ritual must be a female. Another cow would be presented by the bride's maternal uncle and it was called *kgomo ya ga malomaa mosetsana ya tlhogo*.

If the uncle was unable to provide the cow, the bride's father or paternal uncle could do so. The two beasts would be slaughtered and cooked for the feast during the wedding festival.

Upon slaughtering of the cows for the feast, the groom's male marriage delegation would be offered the right-hand half of the carcass, *letsogo*, to cook where they were accommodated. They would cook the meat and specially prepare its hoof, holding it on a stiff stick (*lomapo*), for presentation to the *kgosi* at the bride's home *kgotla*, where her marriage delegation team would respond with greetings to the groom's delegation, at the same time shouting the *pula* (rain!) slogan which advocates for peace. According to the Ngwato culture, this signified that the groom's family had managed to make peace with the bride's family and established a new relationship, *mogwe o digile mogwegadi, jaanong o mo hentse, o amogetse tlhako oe jele, ke thebe.*

The general wedding feast would continue for the rest of the day with food and drinks served, wedding songs and poems narrated, as well as dancing and ululations by the old and the young, the married and the unmarried, all in a joyous mood over the newly-formed family relationships.

As is the case with most Tswana cultures, the bride's maternal uncle would be offered the head from the slaughtered cow, called *ditlhogo tsaga malome*, the uncle's head-gift. This is a token of appreciation for the very large role played by a maternal uncle in the upbringing of his nieces and nephews, as well as leading the marriage proceedings from beginning to end.

At the end of the wedding day, some leading people from the two marriage delegation groups would meet briefly to arrange for both the counselling (*go laya*) and transfer (*go isa ngwetsi*) of the bride processes.

## The marriage counselling process (*Go laya*)

To the Ngwato elders, their traditional marriage counselling process (*go laya*) is cardinal as it prepares the newly-married couple to transit smoothly into marriage without disturbance from the immature lifestyle they have been leading. Amongst other things, Bangwato expect the counselling to expose their newly-weds to all sorts of marriage dynamics. This entails counselling on how to handle or approach marriage in a successful manner and avoid divorce.

According to Ngwato culture, the marriage counselling process would be conducted upon the bride's transfer to her in-laws. On arrival at her in-laws' home, the bride would be seated in the middle of the room on an impala skin mat, next to her mother-in-law. The impala mat signifies that the bride has beaten other girls through marriage, *phate ya phala, gore o phala banyana ba bangwe*. She would also be dressed by her mother-in-law, with a headscarf (*tukwi*) and short shoulder blanket (*tjale*) pinned with a safety pin at the front. Her mother-in-law and other women would sit close to her and jostle her, as a way of assuring her to feel at home and relax, *oa kibelwa*, meaning, she is being settled down. In the event her mother-in-law was widowed, the groom's maternal aunt would take over the role of settling down the bride (*go kibelwa*).

At this juncture, the chief aunt and maternal aunts from the bride's side would bring a calabash of food for the in-laws, comprising cooked meat and sorghum meal. The bride would in turn serve this food to her in-laws. As the bride's relatives now returned home, she would be offered some sorghum grain to pound and cook. Her mother-in-law would put pots on the fire and allow the bride to start cooking a meal. When the meal was ready, the mother-in-law would bring the pots into the house so the bride could start serving all the relatives present at the homestead.

### THE TRANSFER OF THE BRIDE TO HER IN-LAWS PROCESS (*GO ISA NGWETSI*)

In terms of the Ngwato marriage culture, the transfer or delivery of the bride to her in-laws would usually be undertaken on the evening of the wedding day, a day after the *patlo*, or after the wedding ceremony was completed. This marriage process is termed *go isa ngwetsi kwa ga matsalaye*, to deliver the bride to her in-laws. During the material time, the bride, together with her marriage delegation led by the chief maternal aunt, would proceed to her in-laws' home. In their possession would be all her personal possessions, as well as the newly brought *patlo* clothing, bedding, and other wedding gifts she was presented with. Also in their possession would be a calabash of cooked meat and sorghum meal, to serve to her in-laws upon arrival. They would sing wedding songs upon arrival, whose message would primarily be to alert the girl to be of good manners and to represent her family well, or to take heed of negative attitudes she was likely to come across at her new home or settlement.

### THE BRIDE TAKEN BACK TO HER NATAL HOME PROCESS

The Bangwato elders are quick to state that in terms of their traditional marriage practice, the father and mother of the bride do not attend the bride-seeking (*patlo*) and transfer of bride (*go isiwa ga ngwetsi*) processes. They remain at home and do not even eat food from the fireplace where festive food was cooked. They can only eat food from the said fireplace in the evening after their daughter has been transferred to her in-laws. It is against this background that the bride must, the following day after being delivered to her in-laws, be returned to her family. This allows the girl's mother to accompany her daughter back to her in-laws, with a view to seeing where her daughter resides. The mother thereafter leaves her daughter at her new home and returns to her homestead.

## BANGWATO MARRIAGE RITES AND SIGNIFICANCE OF THEIR METAPHORICAL LANGUAGE AND SYMBOLIC ACTIONS

### RIGHTS, PRIVILEGES AND BENEFITS ASSOCIATED WITH BANGWATO TRADITIONAL MARRIAGE PRACTICES

As is the case with all other Tswana ethnic groups, the Ngwato elders view their customary marriage rites, the metaphorical language, and the symbolic actions as significant for various reasons. The elders maintain that, amongst others, these values are vital to educating the newly-married about the essence of a prosperous marriage.

## Marriage rites

The Ngwato marriage rites prohibit any unmarried persons from attending their traditional marriage processes. Strictly, only the married are allowed to attend and to participate in the proceedings. Those who are married through civil marriage law, bypassing the traditional marriage process, may attend but will not be given an opportunity to have a say during the customary marriage proceedings – they just sit, watch and listen. Also, the Ngwato marriage rites do not allow divorced persons and those going through matrimonial disputes or conflicts to attend their marriage proceedings. The elders believe that the divorced and those with troubled marriages have the potential to bring bad luck or poor advice to the newly-weds if they are allowed to attend and participate in such rituals. Children as well as unmarried people are deemed immature and not conversant with matrimonial issues, therefore they are disqualified from attendance and offering any form of marital counselling to the newly married. Even in cases where the unmarried are friends of the marrying couple, they are disqualified since they are deemed likely to mislead the couple because they know nothing about marriage dynamics.

## Metaphorical language

The Ngwato elders are quick to mention that their metaphorical language is not only confined to marriage processes but to general life situations. As regards their marriage metaphorical language, they find it a useful tool in terms of inspiring the newly-weds to adhere to positive principles of life as they bear and raise children, as well as their interaction with members of the community at all levels.

For instance, the metaphorical phrase: '*go baa lotlhokwa*', marital engagement of a young woman had its own connotations. The young man's parents would *inter alia* present some clothing such as a dress, underwear, headscarf and a blanket to the engaged woman. This engagement would become a promise to marry the girl in the near future. Members of the community would come to learn that their sons had to look elsewhere for a bride in the event they had intended to approach the engaged girl. There would also be gifts offered by the young man's family to the young engaged girl. Such gifts are described as '*pula ntlo*', to open a house, or '*gore mosimane atle a kgone go etela mosetsana*', to facilitate the young man's regular visits to the girl's homestead. This is meant to confirm that each of the couple really love each other, and are geared up for possible child-bearing and marriage.

Another metaphor Ngwato elders associate with is related to their strong belief that a woman represents a man's investment, hence the phrase '*mosadi tshwene o jewa mabogo*', which means that a man doesn't necessarily get attracted to a woman's beauty, but is mainly concerned and attracted to her inner self. The elders mention that in the past when wives were chosen by parents for their sons, any complaint by a young man against the ugliness of a wife chosen for him was met with a metaphorical response: '*mosadi tshwene o jewa mabogo*', meant to impart to the young man that as a matter of fact, what they desired for him was not the physical beauty of a woman but her heart – her inner personality, attributable to the desirable upbringing she received from her parents.

### SYMBOLIC ACTIONS

Bangwato have numerous symbolic marriage actions that they cherish and preach to their newly-weds. For instance, upon receipt of *kgomo ya metsi* during the *patlo* marriage process, the girl's family would slaughter the same, and offer the right hand portion to the young man's delegation to cook. Upon cooking this portion, the young man's male delegation stuck a stiff stick to the hoof and bone of this cow and presented it to the girl's male delegation as a token of appreciation for the girl's male delegation's hospitality. In turn, the girl's male delegation would accept the cooked hoof and shout out the Tswana cry, *Pula!!!* – signifying a lifetime of peace and prosperity created between the two newly marrying families.

Also, it is a required symbolic action that a married woman must wear a headscarf and a short shoulder blanket when in public places; this signifies that she is untouchable as a married woman, *mosadi o rwala tukwi abo a apara tjale mo sechabeng*. Furthermore, the mother-in-law's symbolic seated action beside the new bride during bride transfer (*go isiwa ga ngwetsi*), is meant to remove any potential fears and negativity from the bride, and to assist her in really feeling welcome at her in-laws' homestead. The Ngwato elders maintain that, from experience, this gesture enables the bride to quickly adapt into the new family environment and take up her duties as a new wife.

There is a process where a bride's father, upon receipt of *bogadi* cattle, would slaughter and donate a half portion of its meat to the in-laws, at the same time preparing a special meal with some of the remaining carcass for enjoyment by marriage delegates from both families. This cow is called *kgomo yoo rraatso*. As noted above, the essence of this cow is to unify not only the newly-weds but their two families into a new lifelong relationship. The elders mention that the relationship further manifests itself by virtue of the birth of the couple's children, who are naturally related to both families.

The Ngwato elders further advise that the bride's parents do not eat meals during the wedding day. They only eat meals in the evening, after the wedding, when their daughter had been formally transferred to her in-laws. It is believed that otherwise the parents would bring bad luck to their daughter's new marriage.

The Ngwato marriage culture has some beef portions specifically preserved for married men. These portions are called *mokoto* and comprise a combination of the backbone upper portions of a cow and the tripe. This meat is well cooked and pounded before being served to the married men from both families at the family *kgotla* on the evening after the wedding feast. Symbolically, the Ngwato elders say it is meant to commence, seal and promote positive relationships between the men from both families.

## CHANGE AND ITS IMPACT ON THE NGWATO TRADITIONAL MARRIAGE RITES AND ACTIVITIES

Bangwato elders lament that unlike in former times, the parents nowadays have no major role to play in terms of identifying an ideal wife for their son, and vice versa. They observed that during their time, parents would conveniently identify good child-rearing traits from a particular family and use them as a yardstick to get their sons or daughters married. Nowadays, it is the son who independently identifies his future wife and starts the courtship marriage process. The Ngwato elders state that even if the parents may raise concerns about the family their sons wish to marry into, it becomes a non-starter to attempt convincing them otherwise once they have made up their minds. This goes against their intended purpose of guiding their sons and daughters into quality marriages, hence, according to the elders, the current high divorce rate amongst their tribe.

Ngwato elders also view the District Commissioner's marriage process as exclusive of the parents of the marrying couple, as evidenced by the District Commissioner's unilateral administration of marriage. Some marriage officers of the District Commissioner's office are unmarried, and therefore do not qualify to solemnise and offer marriage counselling as they are not experienced in that field. This, the parents view as a contributing factor against a sound and well-founded marriage, which therefore defeats the intended purpose of their traditional marriage counselling process. Owing to this lacuna, the current youthful marriages are sadly short-lived.

The Ngwato elders further believe that inter-marriages between other Tswana ethnic groups, as well as the international community, have totally diluted their customary marriage process to the extent of almost eradicating it. This trend, together with the metropolitan lifestyles currently enjoyed by the youthful married couples, make it even more difficult for the elders and relatives to easily observe whether the newly-weds appropriately run their marriage lives. This has contributed to the current rise in divorce cases since their youthful married couples only realise later that the foreign marital conditions do not match their Ngwato culture, and now become a challenge to their children.

Also noticeable from the current cosmopolitan lifestyles enjoyed by the youthful married couples, are the economic imbalances they encounter in cities, towns and townships, where a lot of material competition causes debt and financial conflicts amongst couples, often ending in very sad divorce cases. In some cases, the elders observe further that some couples do not marry out of passion but mainly due to the material wealth of their love partner. This, the elders maintain, also has a negative impact on the sanctity of the current marriages.

Ngwato elders reveal that during their time, there was no *bogadi* for their marriages. *Patlo* and the building of a *sesowa* house sufficed to validate their customary marriages. This, to them, allowed the couples to easily get married and use their hard-earned funds to start a new family, instead of paying their funds to the girl's family as bride 'price'. This caused their newly-weds to start a new family with a financial setback. Financial constraints would cause quarrels amongst couples, and lead to marital separations or even divorces. Currently, they view the payment of *bogadi* through cattle or by monetary terms as a financial attraction that tempts their people to divert from the valuable traditional Ngwato marriage norms, leading to the current instability in marriage.

The Ngwato elders are also worried that since the replacement of their traditional initiation schools (*bojale* and *bogwera*) with modern education, it is difficult to teach or convince their children about the value of their traditional marriage processes. They have observed that the youth simply take the ethnic marriage processes as primitive, and some even choose to cohabit without getting married, whilst others enter into civil marriages without even involving their parents.

Lastly, the Ngwato elders are bewildered to see their youthful marrying couples combining the Ngwato traditional marriage process with the civil marriage (District Commissioner's marriage process). They view this combination as being born of a desire by the youth to acquire more wealth, as emphasised by civil marriage law, as opposed to their traditional marriage laws which place emphasis on love and family commitments.

## Problems and Challenges in Bangwato Traditional Marriages Today

Bangwato, both old and young, admit that there are prevalent problems and challenges within their ethnic group. These entail, *inter alia*, inter-marriage with other ethnic or international communities, ever-rising costs of *bogadi*, lack of parental guidance during the newly-weds' early marriage life (mainly caused by distance between the newly-weds and their parents/relatives), use of multiple marriage processes by the married youthful couples, government's use of unmarried Marriage Officers at the District Commissioner's offices, and so on.

On the issue of inter-marriages, Bangwato observe that in former times, marriage was an arrangement between two very close families. Even the setting up of a new home for the newly-weds was within reasonable reach for families and relatives of the married couples. As and when conflicts arose at a matrimonial home, it was easy for the close relatives to pick it up and hastily intervene to restore peace. On the contrary, Bangwato feel that this is no longer the case. Currently, due to modernity, their youth find themselves interacting with people, not only from other Tswana ethnic groups, but even globally. This has naturally caused their youth to establish love relations with people of different cultures, ending up with unsuccessful marriages as the newly-married couples end up mismatching in terms of upbringing and backgrounds. At times, a cosmopolitan lifestyle even causes some of their youths to unilaterally enter into marriages at the District Commissioner's office without parental knowledge and consultation. The elders however concede that owing to the irreversible effects of modernity and globalization, there is little they can do to persuade their youth to adhere to Ngwato cultural practices generally.

When raising their concerns regarding the ever-rising costs of *bogadi*, Bangwato generally feel that the price must be standardised countrywide. They base their reasoning on the fact that already they experience intermarriage with other Tswana ethnic groups, who also have varying *bogadi* 'price' tags. This causes unnecessary disputes and resentments amongst potential in-laws who feel the exorbitant *bogadi* price is a 'rip-off' for their sons. They maintain that this alone can cause a marriage to start off from a very bitter or unfriendly stance that may have a negative impact on the newly-weds' relationships.

As regards the use of multiple marriage processes, the Ngwato elders would ideally prefer their youths to choose between marrying either under the traditional Ngwato marriage process, or the District Commissioner's, and not to mix the two processes, as is currently the case. This, they believe, would assist in reducing the confusion the married couples experience when they attempt to manage their marriages with a combination of two or three (if church is also involved) varying marriage processes. They argue that, on that note, those who would enter into the Ngwato marriage process sincerely and in good faith should, even when living in cosmopolitan regions, always revert to the village for consultation as and when they experience misunderstandings. This, they believe, would go a long way towards saving most marriages today.

The Ngwato elders wish to advocate for government to stop assigning unmarried Marriage Officers to solemnise marriages and render counselling to newly-weds. They argue that without the instincts acquired by virtue of marriage, unmarried Marriage Officers lack the necessary skills to properly and appropriately solemnise and counsel the newly-weds. To the elders, this is unfair to the youthful married couples as it sets their marriages on a shaky foundation.

## Conclusions and Recommendations

It is evident from the aforegoing remarks that many factors have led to what Bangwato tend to see as a devaluation of their customary marriage traditions. Bangwato see modernization and globalization as major causes of the changes that the Ngwato customary marriage processes have undergone in recent times. From my interactions with the Ngwato elders, in the course of research work on this chapter, it became clear that they were affected by the change in the status of *bogadi,* as a case in point. The practice of *bogadi* was part of the Sengwato traditional marriage process in the past, but was abolished under the reign of *Kgosi* Khama III. According to them the *Kgosi* had abolished *bogadi* in order to enable all classes of people in his kingdom to afford marriage, irrespective of their economic background. He only demanded that a man prove himself worthy of marriage by erecting a habitable structure at his potential in-laws' yard, and fill it with sorghum grain. After the Khama's demise, it appears that Bangwato gradually reverted to the practice of *bogadi*. The informants see this as a regression in their traditions to an unpopular past practice. They attribute its apparent resurgence to the forces of both modernity and globalization that have led to a rise in inter-marriages with people from other cultures, both within Botswana and abroad, where *bogadi* is still a strong tradition.

Another area in which the Bangwato feel change has undermined the integrity of traditional marriage processes, has to do with the fact that three types of marriage processes exist side by side in Botswana. This fact has led to the tendency among Batswana of all ethnic communities celebrating the same marriage at least twice, first under the marriage processes of one's own ethnic group, under the processes of a civil marriage, and again qith a church wedding. It was not readily obvious from the informants why they objected to the practice, even though they were emphatic that one must get married only once and under one marriage process. Celebrating the same marriage twice under two or more processes sequentially should not be allowed, they argued. Even for reasons of cost alone one must agree that their objections make sense, because multiple celebrations under different traditions have the potential to double or treble the cost of a wedding. One reason why people might do it anyway may be that the processes serve different purposes. The customary marriage process may satisfy a couple's strong spiritual need to identify with their ancestral traditions and to bond with their respective extended families. The civil marriage ceremony may in turn satisfy the equally powerful desire to identify as members of sophisticated national or even global elite. It may well be that there will in future be a critical mass of people who would like the Marriage Act reviewed, with the aim of strictly directing marrying couples to choose from among the three marriage processes, and not to have them in combination to celebrate the same marriage.

Be that as it may, it is also evident that, like all other Tswana ethnic groups, Bangwato culture is generally dynamic and evolving. From one generation to another since time immemorial, Bangwato have reviewed their traditions and adapted them to fit in an ever-changing world. They look to do things differently all the time to improve the efficacy of their traditions, as well as to respond to pressures to change as the result of inter-ethnic pressure.

One issue that seems to require urgent review is that of *bogadi*. A proposal may have to be advanced to Ntlo Ya Dikgosi on the issue. Consultations and conversations need to be held nationwide to consider the possibility of coming up with a national policy on *bogadi*. Such a policy would not only stipulate the minimum and maximum amounts that can be charged for *bogadi*, but also provide guidelines on a reasonable budget for items such as clothing and household effects which form part of the *bogadi* package.

Similarly, it appears, it may be necessary soon to recommend to the Ntlo Ya Dikgosi to consider guidelines to harmonise the many and diverse traditions of Botswana so that the government's ideal of a diverse but united national culture is based on a sound knowledge of each individual tradition in the country. It would not be constructive to try and forge a national culture by expanding the hegemony of any one group over the rest. Studying and codifying all Tswana traditional marriage beliefs and customs is important. It should be done, but not in the spirit of paring away the distinctive features of each ethnic group to create identical traditions in the country. Tswana marriage processes and procedures are not very different from each another, but it is in the distinctiveness of each that their value to national culture resides. The main challenge will always be how to encourage a culture of tolerance and receptiveness to other cultures so that even cross-cultural marriage celebrations are performed in seamless, conflict-free atmospheres

Finally, pressure to provide support for the revival of traditional initiation schools is probably due. It is obvious that the Tswana traditional initiation schools (*bojale* and *bogwera*) taught a plethora of useful life skills and nation-building habits of thought and attitudes to the youths of the past, and contributed demonstrably to the stability and happiness of marriages. It may be worth our while to borrow a leaf from their modalities, while at the same time learning from their pitfalls. There are important lessons to be gleaned from the way initiation schools were organised and from what they taught that could be useful to present efforts to inculcate a spirit of harmonious and tolerant coexistence among the diverse cultures that make up the nation.

# 9

# Barolong

*Mr. Allan Manyeneng*

**Totem**: *Tholo* – Kudu

**Clan Poem:** *Leboko la Barolong*

*Re namane tsa tholo,*
*Re ja mogope re o lala…*

*Re batho ba mogogoro wa lošo,*
*Batho ba ga Gogomela…*

*Re bo'Mmina tshipi ha go le tlala,*
*Ha go le kgora re bina tholo…*

*Tholo e e thupana thekeng,*
*E e reng go utlwa lengolo e tlole,*
*Go bona lerole e tlolele godimo…*

*Tholo eo e sa latelweng ka motlhala,*
*Eo e bonwang ka bojang go thetekela…*

*Re batho ba ga Morara-a-Noto,*
*Tshipi e ncho, Noto-a-Morolong…*

*Ntsha sehuba morolong,*
*Go tle go bonale kwa o tswang gone…*

*Tlhago ya gago e tswa kwa go Tshesebe-a-Modiboa,*
*Tshesebe yo o hetotseng ntlha,*
*Ntlha ya lerumo la segosi…*

*O tswa kwa go Setlhare-a-Monnyane,*
*Setlhare sa metswe e e ko teng,*
*E e rileng go anama ya hudusa Magoge,*
*Magoge le morahe wa Bakaa…*
*O tswa kwa go Nakedi-a-Masepe,*
*Nakedi e e bobowa bo ntlha…*

*Source:* www.facebook.com/1120666381326877/photos/a.1122825264444322.1073741827.1120666381326877/1245973642129483/?type=3&theater). *Last accessed 25 May 2022*

## A Brief Historical Background of Goodhope Village and the Barolong

Barolong originate from Tanganyika, the current Tanzania in East Africa – to date, there still remain their relatives who still speak the Tswana language in the current Republic of Tanzania. From a certain O.S. Phibion's writings on the Internet, he discusses the nature and origins of Southern African Musical Traditions, he mentions in passing of "…Barolong tribe also found in…Wakaranga – A Bantu speaking Community east of Lake Tanganyika…"

Just before 1400, Barolong migrated from Tanganyika to Thabancho united under the leadership of Kgosi Morolong. Whilst at Thabancho, Barolong got dismantled by the then prevailing Mfecane warfare, which show them spreading over the Northern Cape region around the Setlagole, Taung, Ganyesa and Morokweng region. Around 1760, just after Kgosi Tau I's death, Barolong split once more, this time due to internal conflicts amongst their royal kraal. A fight ensued amongst the deceased Kgosi Tau I's four sons, i.e., from four of his five matrimonial homes (the fifth house did not bear a son), *viz.* (a) Ratlou, (b) Tshidi, (c) Seleka & Rapulana, as well as (d) Makgetla & Maleme. This ended with them taking different ways with their followers to form wards. The current village of Goodhope, a capital village of Barolong in Botswana, initially emerged as a cattle post for Kgosi Lotlaamoreng I. The current Barolong Farms came about as part of the 48 farms owned by the Barolong tribe under the leadership of sub-chiefs appointed by Kgosi Lotlaamoreng in 1885. Some of these farms entailed Bodibe, Madibe, Mmashutlhe, Khunwana, in the current South Africa, as well as Goodhope, Mokatako, Hebron, Pitsane and most parts of the Barolong Farms in the current Botswana.

## UNDERSTANDING MARRIAGE FROM THE BAROLONG'S POINT OF VIEW

According to research findings, Barolong in the olden days viewed marriage as a joint venture between close relatives and at times within family friends, with view to start a new and meaningful matrimonial bond between their beloved children. Owing to well-known practise of good behaviour, habits and positive upbringing of children by some particular house-holds, i.e., *mekgwa e mentle yago godisa bana*, relatives would prefer to choose for their son or daughter, a wife or a husband, from such a maternal uncle's house. The main purpose for close relations being to impress, preserve and maintain upon their children, qualities and principles of good and sound style of family leadership and child upbringing amongst themselves. This caused Barolong to more often than not, end up going no far but within the wars, when they wish to marry their sons or daughters. In fact, they maintain that during the material times, most families did maintain good standards of child upbringing – because where a child showed signs of disrespect, uncles and aunts, together with other close relatives and friends were usually engaged to assist in disciplining a culprit. It was also believed that with such relative intermarriages, resolution of disputes between the married couples mostly easily achieved – unlike where they marry across the tribes, where they were uncertain about the other tribe's style of family upbringings.

Also, Barolong elders mention that initially, marriage was perceived as a sound natural God – created source for procreation of children and multiplication of his people. Traditionally, a Rolong household would on average bear close to ten or more children. Since subsistence farming was their main source of living, i.e., where cattle, small-stock, poultry etc. farming was coupled with the ploughing of fields to sustain a family, the more the children a family had the better, since they assisted in providing labour force. Simultaneously, the experience such children get exposed to renders them life-time talents and attributes that further transform them into future and responsible adults/parents.

On the other hand, the youthful married Rolong couples explain that nowadays, economic life demands they experience in the cosmopolitan world impedes against them bearing more than three children per family. They mention that owing to cosmopolitan life, their children are unfortunately not exposed to the traditional Rolong village type of farming lifestyle. They attend modern schools in townships/cities and interact with children from various tribal, national and international regions. Hence, a dilution of the initial Rolong marriage processes amongst other things. They therefore end up with the current inter-marriages we experience today.

However, Barolong elders are quick to point out that the basic Rolong traditional marriage started transforming into the current set up when the missionaries arrived in Southern Africa, bringing with them a combination of the Christian as well as their ancestral types of marriage processes. They also mention that the Civil/District Commissioner's marriage process which also emerged and ran parallel with the Rolong Customary marriage process, was a contributory factor to a dilution in the initial Rolong marriage. To them, it was upon arrival of both the Christian as well as the Civil Marriage processes that the initial Rolong type of marriage process got diluted to the current status.

However, the Rolong elders are comforted by a fact that generally, the Rolong traditional marriage process is just minimally diluted, as most current youth religiously undergo the traditional process before choosing whether to go an extra mile and fuse it with the civil or Christian marriage.

## THE TYPES OF BAROLONG MARRIAGES/WEDDINGS

Currently, Barolong recognise an existence of three types of marriage processes, *viz.* the customary marriage process, the Christian marriage process, and the District Commissioner's marriage process. Barolong elders are of the opinion that as was the case in the past, to date, the Customary marriage process emerges as the most practised by their community. They are further mindful that the current married youth always prefer to employ both the traditional Rolong marriage as well as the Civil marriage process to run parallel, some even ending with the Christian marriage process as the second or third process within a single marriage.

### CUSTOMARY MARRIAGE

According to Barolong elders, in the past a customary marriage process would commence with a young man's parents identifying an ideal potential wife from close relatives such as the maternal uncle's daughter (a cousin), i.e., *ntsalaye.* Alternatively from a close family friend's home, where the latter were found to be of ideal family attributes. Through the betrothal marriage process -peeletso, an agreement would be sealed about some prospects of a future marriage between their children when they reach maturity age, i.e., go baa lotlhokwa. This stage is reached after the young man's parents would have earlier on, searched around the tribal community, particularly those of close relations, and identified for their son or daughter, an ideal family to marry from. At a ripe time, around 18 to 20 years of age, or after the boy and the girl have enrolled and passed the initiation ceremony stage, i.e., *bogwera* for the young man and *bojale* for the girl, the young man's parents would send a delegation of married uncles, aunts, and close relations to the girl's home to arrange for marriage, i.e., *patlo* proceedings, which Barolong refers to as *goya go batla ngwetsi*, or to seek the bride. It is the maternal uncle, i.e., *malome* who leads the delegation of men and women to arrange for, negotiate and seek for a bride for their son. A maternal uncle from either the young man or the girl's side is the chief negotiator, followed by the uncle's wife, i.e., *mma malome*, who usually leads the marriage proceedings from the women's side, on issues that only affect women during all the marriage proceedings.

In terms of the Rolong custom, like it is the case with most Tswana tribes, a delegation from the young man's side is called '*bagwe*', whilst that from the girl's side is called '*bagwagadi*'.

Barolong are quick to mention that unlike in the past, currently the chief, upon registering the marriage, issues a marriage certificate as well as a document to the young man's family acknowledging receipt of *bogadi* by the girl's family. The *kgosi* would thereafter offer some counselling sessions to the groom and the bride.

## Christian marriage

Barolong are of the opinion that the Christian marriage process came with the missionaries, finding their customary marriage process in existence. The two types of marriage then co-existed running parallel for each marriage. They also believe that this type of marriage is usually practised by those who are regular church members of various denominations A church priest, minister or reverend (pastor hereafter) who has been granted a marriage license is allowed to solemnise the marriage. Prior to this, the church marrying officer must have registered his credentials with the Ministry of Home Affairs, where a Marriage Officer's License is issued (assuming he qualifies).

Secondly, the marrying couple would still be required to register their marriage with the District Commissioner's office. They will then follow all the processes as stipulated under the District Commissioner's marriage process above, but only up to the counselling stage. After the counselling stage, the District Commissioner releases those couples intending to follow the Christian marriage process. In their possession, the couple will have marriage documentation from the District Commissioner's office. The couple would then set a marriage appointment date, usually scheduled for Saturday or any preferred marriage day. On that date the couple, together with family members, friends and neighbours from both parties, would convene at a church or at any designated place, to witness the Christian marriage. The pastor would bless the event before solemnising the marriage in terms of the church principles. Thereafter, the pastor proceeds to offer counselling sessions to the couple, which centre on how the marrying couple is expected to carry themselves during their marriage life. Like the District Commissioner, a pastor is usually inundated with disputes and complaints from married church members. This based in the premise that he is experienced with previous marriage problems and suitable to offer sound counselling in this regard. The marrying couple is urged to fear God and raise their upcoming children with love and care, through 'the hand of God'. Thereafter, the pastor issues a marriage certificate. The two families, relatives and friends would then retire to the bride's home, where a feast would be held to celebrate the marriage.

## District Commissioner's marriage

Barolong are of the belief that the District Commissioner's marriage system is a product of 'civilization'. They are content that at least their youthful married couples still respect and always first go through the customary Rolong marriage processes before finalising it through the District Commissioners' marriage process. They say this causes the two marriage processes to be administered in parallel for a same marriage.

As is the case with such marriages countrywide, the Marriage Proceedings Act regulates marriage processes to be adhered to as and when couples intend to marry. Couples intending to marry are required to provide documentary proof that they have attained the age of majority, that is, 21 years of age. Where one or both parties are of minority age, parental consent is required before the marriage can be registered and concluded.

Secondly, the marrying couple must each avail a witness, also of consenting age. Three weeks before the marriage date, both the couple and their respective witnesses are to report at the District Commissioner's office to register the marriage. Each shall bring their national identity cards and complete the necessary marriage application forms. From the registration date until a day before the marriage, the District Commissioner's office advertises a marriage though a system called 'banns'. Theses are publication on noticeboards, at the places where both parties are known to stay or to have stayed). The essence of a three weeks banns advertisement is to give the public at large an opportunity to know of those who are getting married, and whether anyone has any cause as to why the couple cannot be joined in matrimony. Reasons to stop a marriage from proceeding may be because one of the parties is already married, or one has promised a different partner marriage and is thus banned from continuing with this proposed marriage, an so forth.

A day before the marriage date, the couple, together with their respective witnesses, report at the District Commissioner's office to complete documentation that addresses issues on whether or not they are marrying in or out of community of property, i.e., the nature of how they are going to administer their estates.

During the day of marriage, the marrying couple, together with other couples scheduled for a marriage ceremony that day, together with their witnesses, will convene in a large boardroom. If there is enough room, relatives and friends are also allowed in to witness the marriage proceedings. The District Commissioner commences proceedings with a prayer, before conducting a detailed public counselling session. Counselling here entails most of the good and bad events that married couples generally go through, some on a daily basis. Incidentally, owing to the nature of their daily work, which also entails meetings and discussions with married couples who have lodged domestic complaints or disputes, a District Commissioner is in a privileged and sound position to appreciate exactly what marriage life connotes. Upon completion of thorough counselling, the District Commissioner would accordingly solemnise the marriages, whereafter, issuance of a marriage certificate completes the process.

Barolong elders associate the District Commissioner's marriage process with the current 'civilization' and youth, who greatly emphasise material wealth. For this reason, they are of the view that it does not really concern them because, unlike the current youth, they only married in terms of the Rolong traditional marriage process, which, for some, entailed having to be found a wife or husband by their parents, although most lived during the the transitional period when parents chose for their children, but most chose a partner for themselves. The elders therefore view the District Commissioner's marriage process as an aspect that encourages youth to be materialistic in their marriages, moreso that they must make a choice between being married through the in or out of community of property regimes.

## The Marriage Process

### The betrothal process (*Go baa lotlhokwa*)

As discussed earlier above, the customary marriage, which Barolong refer to as *lenyalo la Setswana*, a Setswana or traditional marriage, was in the past arranged by the parents of both a young man and a young woman, long before their children attained the puberty stage, through a betrothal marriage process. It is called *go baa lotlhokwa* in the Rolong culture. Unlike nowadays, in the past there was no chance for a young man to consider identifying a young woman for marriage. It was the duty of a young man's parents when he is between 9 and 16 years old, to identify a girl from amongst the families within the community as a potential wife. Parents would look for this ideal potential wife from a family that they believe to have generally upheld good and desirable habits, *mekgwa ee mentle*. As is the case with most other Tswana tribes, Barolong maintain that it was, previously, particularly important to scrutinise the background habits of potential in-laws before choosing a daughter-in-law or before allowing the young man to marry their daughter. This was premised on a belief that where a family is known to be of bad or undesired repute, such as practising witchcraft, theft, promiscuity, back-biting, etc,. it is presumed that their offspring would repeat such bad behaviour as they mature into adults – a totally undesirable environment for a family and child upbringing, they said. In this way, they were attempting to avoid their sons or daughters getting married to the wrong type of families in their community.

According to Barolong, when a potential daughter-in-law has been identified for a young man by his parents, they would in no time visit the parents of such a girl to arrange for a future marriage. An agreement to marriage betrothal by the girl's parents would seal a marriage engagement between the two families. This arrangement is called *go baa lotlhokwa*, to engage the girl in marriage. Periodically as he grows up, the young man would be sent on errands to the girl's home, at times to deliver a chunk of meat when his parents had slaughtered a cow or sheep, or even a sack of maize, sorghum, or any harvest from the field. Just after such arrangement, the young man's parents would provide a live castrated male sheep termed *nku ya mokwele,* an engagement sheep, as a present to the girl's family, or as a token of marriage engagement. Also gifted to the girl is a headscarf for her to wear. The *mokwele* sheep is strictly eaten and shared by the girl's family, excluding the young man's.

As the young man progresses into manhood, his parents would intensify sending him on errands to the girl's home. Strategically, the girl's parents would have by then, erected a hut for their daughter at the back side of the yard, isolated from the main family house. This arrangement facilitates for young man starting to sneak into the girl's hut during night to see the girl, or the girl's mother offering the young man sleep over (when sent on errands), as the rain is coming.

Barolong elders mention that the betrothal arrangement has since died out – during their youthful times – and then the current courtship marriage process evolved. Courtship in current practice is where current lovers, i.e., a young boy and a girl, establish a love relationship that culminates in their marriage.

## The courtship process

Barolong believe that in terms of current life styles, a young man simply falls in love with a girl of his choice, even from another part of the world, and establishes a relationship if he wins the girl. This happens in their youthful teenage years. Unlike their forefathers, the youth today are not particularly concerned with the girl's or young boy's parental background and good or bad family habits. Upon passage of limited time, usually two years in a relationship, after the young man has now satisfied himself that his love partner qualifies as an ideal future wife for him, and having acquired sufficient funds to pay *bogadi* and its ancillaries, he would approach either his parents or maternal uncle to express his intent to marry. Where an uncle is informed by the young man, he would approach the young man's parents and inform them accordingly.

## THE PRELIMINARY VISIT PROCESS (*GO KOKOTA*)

Acccording to the Barolong elders, a preliminary visit was in the past arranged when the young man's parents were satisfied that their son is ready for marriage. Currently, it is the young man himself who takes the initiative to tell either his uncle or parents about his intent to marry a certain girl – usually upon being also satisfied that he has accumulated sufficient funds to pay for *bogadi* (as mentioned above), to buy a wedding ring and to fund the marriage feast.

At an appropriate time and date, knowing that their young man is mature, or has graduated from a *bogwera* initiation ceremony, his father and mother pay an unexpected visit to the identified girl's family home. Upon an exchange of greetings with the girl's parents, the father would break the news that they have come to ask for their daughter's hand in marriage, at the same time mentioning the names of the appropriate girl in question. Though rare, the girl's parents may decline the proposal for whatever reasons they may have. More often than not, declining would be based on bad manners or habits associated with the young man's family, *mekgwa ee maswe* (as mentioned above). Otherwise, where the girl's parents agree to the marriage proposal, the two parents would straight away commence discussions on the nature of their children's marriage as well as the logistics involved. In Rolong culture, this preliminary visit process is called *go kokota*, to knock at the girl's home with marriage prospects.

Upon this meeting, the two families would each start informing their respective relevant close relatives, such as maternal uncles, paternal uncles, and aunts and break the marriage news. A date would soon be set when the young man's uncles from both the paternal and maternal sides, as well as their respective aunts, at times in company of other close relatives, would deliver an engagement gift in the form of a large castrated sheep, to the girl's family home (as mentioned above). At the girl's home, they would be met by an almost an equal team of relatives, i.e., the girl's uncles, aunts and close relatives. The maternal uncle, as a team leader, would present the *mokwele* sheep to the girl's male delegation at their *kgotla*, where her maternal uncle, *malome*, would receive it on behalf of the girl's family. By custom, the sheep must be immediately moved to the back yard, before it urinates, and thereupon get slaughtered. The meat is well cooked, and served only to the married couples present from the girl's family. It is usually eaten after the young man's delegation has returned home. Barolong elders also mention that meat from the sheep's chest is nicely prepared for consumption by both the young man and girl in the evening of the same day. On that evening, it is expected by Rolong custom that the young man must, in the evening, pay a visit to the girl's home, usually accompanied by an uncle or friend who would later leave the young man there to spend the night. It is at this juncture that both the man and the woman are fed with the sheep chest delicacy. Symbolically, this is said to work so that the couple get settled and composed, *batle ba retibale dipelo*. The Rolong elders further mention that since the chest of the sheep is somehow fatty, some of its fat was smeared all over the girl as ointment, with a view to aiding her during penetration overnight, since in former times they would have reached this stage still virgins – unlike as is the case with the current youth.

A sheep was and is still preferred to a goat. In fact, as a norm, a sheep is insisted upon because it is naturally regarded as a quiet creature as compared to an ever-shouting goat. Symbolically therefore, Barolong are of the view that the sheep, as a symbol for *mokwele* would inscribe on the mind of the girl, a sense of always keeping secretive their sensitive matrimonial house-hold issues, and not to let them out to her friends or close relations.

Barolong elders state that during their parents' time it was not necessary, during preliminary visits, for the two families to discuss in detail the marriage logistics since they were both conversant of what the Rolong marriage process involves. The reason for this being that they intermarried with close relatives – it was common for a son to take his maternal uncle's daughter in marriage. This is called *go nyala ntsalake*, to marry my cousin. Also, the elders decried that detailed discussions today are held because the current youth intermarry within various tribes and societies locally, and even internationally. Barolong elders are however quick to highlight that in fact, it was during their youthful years that a transition from parents choosing a wife for their son to them having to independently choose their own lovers began. This explains why, from the current research, some of the Barolong elders had their spouses chosen for them by their parents, whilst most of them had the privilege of independently choosing their own spouses. They lamented further that in their case, they still benefitted from wise advice from their parents, even before they chose their lovers, unlike the current youth who do not take heed of parental advice in such matters.

## The bride-seeking process (*Patlo*)

The bride-seeking process in Rolong custom is strictly attended by married people and widowed ones. Divorced persons were and still are barred from attendance as they are assumed to be unfit to offer the marriage entrants any form of counselling, *go laya*, due to their failed marriages. Even a widowed uncle or aunt would not lead the marriage proceedings and may have to ask an alternative uncle or aunt to step in their shoes and lead the marriage proceedings delegation. He is allowed attendance of the marriage proceedings though.

To date, the Rolong *patlo* proceedings are strictly held in the early mornings, between 4 a.m. and 5 a.m. Failure to observe these time periods would always attract a penalty, such as payment of money – these days the penalty is P200.00.

In the early hours of the *patlo* proceedings' day, the maternal uncle, *malome*, in his capacity as the chief negotiator and head of the marriage delegation, would lead a team consisting of married men and women to the girl's home. Close to an entrance of the yard at the girl's home, the women would remain under the command of the maternal uncle's wife, *mma malome*. and the paternal aunt, *rakgadi*. The maternal uncle would then lead the men's delegation into the yard and proceed straight to the *kgotla* in silence. They find the girl's marriage team, also of the same composition, seated and waiting for them around fire. The young man's delegation would be kneeling down in silence. Thereafter, the chief uncle to the girl would greet them about twice saying: greetings enemies, *dumelang dira*. After the second greetings, one of the young man's team would stand up to pray. After the prayer, the girl's uncle would enquire what the young man's team want, to which his uncle would respond, saying they have been sent by the young man's family to look for a bride for them, at the same time mentioning the name(s) of the girl they wish to marry, for example, *'re romilwe ke boora Marumo go tla go ba batlela ngwetsi mo goora Medupe. Mosetsana yo, o bidiwa Boipelo'*. The chief uncle would in turn respond to confirm the existence of a girl with such name(s). He will further agree to release the said girl to the young man's team, but at the same time lodging a concern that the girl was their only pillar of strength as she has all along been working tirelessly to attend to the family's daily household chores (currently he would say, the girl has been taken through formal education and is learned through my financial expenses; now you are denying me her material services).

Since they would now have been granted the bride, the young man's team would request to be excused away for a short while – which is termed *goya go bofa setlhako*. This interlude period is usually meant to accord the young man's women team to equally participate with their counterparts at the girl's home to conduct their *patlo* as well.

In the event that the young man happened to have impregnated the girl at some stage in the past, her chief uncle would announce it as an offence and impose a penalty in the form of a large sheep termed *nku ya tlhagela* against the young man's family. '*Tlhagela*' means that the young man had previously unlawfully broke and entered through a back yard into the girl's family compound to sleep with her, thus bearing the said child. With such allegations of having intruded, *tlhagela*, the young man's delegation would present a large sheep to the girl's male delegation as penalised. The *tlhagela* sheep would be immediately slaughtered – upon receipt, and prepared into a delicious meal to be enjoyed only by the married men and women from the girl's relatives, upon departure of the young man's delegation. This ends the young man's male delegation *patlo* marriage process and gives way for their women counterparts to also conduct their women's *patlo* process with the girl's women delegation.

Led by the wife to the young man's uncle, *mma malome*, the women's team would go through to the yard where they would find the girl's female team waiting for them, seated on the yard. Greetings would be twice offered by the wife to the girl's uncle, and the same process as the one conducted by the men would follow until the girl's aunt releases her in marriage. An aunt from the young man's team would then request water to drink, whereupon the girl's aunt would stand to bring the girl with a calabash of water to quench her in-laws' thirst. The asking for water process is meant to be an opportune moment for the girl to be seen, and to get her into contact with her in-laws.

At this juncture, the *patlo* proceedings are complete, giving rise to a new marriage between the two families. Women from the girl's side would start ululating excitedly in joyous moods over the granting of the new bride. Both the men and women from the two families would then meet over tea where marriage songs would also be sang.

However, in the event that *bogadi* is also delivered that morning, tea will be deferred and the young man's women's delegation would also ask to be excused for a while to give their men's team an opportunity to revisit the *kgotla* to now deliver *bogadi*.

## The bride-wealth presentation (*Bogadi*)

In the event that *bogadi* is to be delivered immediately after the *patlo* proceedings, the young man's marriage delegation would, just after being granted the bride, *ngwetsi*, request to be temporarily excused so that they go and fetch the *bogadi* cattle or money left under guard nearby, *re kopa go ema ha, re boha setlhako*. Shortly thereafter, the young man's delegation would advance the girl's male delegation at the *kgotla* driving the six or eight *bogadi* cattle. The chief uncle would lead the rest, shouting out the names and colours of the *bogadi* cattle as his team companions drive them along. The uncle would shout out proudly and loudly, telling the girl's delegation that he is coming into their homestead, bringing the *bogadi* cattle, and that he wants the bride and they must make way for him. In the process, the girl's women team would also come out of the yard into the street joyfully making ululations to receive *bogadi* cattle. At the *kgotla*, he would invite the girl's chief uncle to receive the cattle, whereupon the sticks that drove the cattle would be thrown towards the said cattle by the young man's team, so the girl's men team could use same to drive the *bogadi* cattle into the family kraal. This completes the *bogadi* process for men.

Thereafter, the young man's women's team, led by her chief aunt, in a line, would also revisit their counterparts at the girl's yard, this time head-loaded with gifts, e.g., blankets, and suitcases with clothes, to deliver to the girl's women's team. These gifts would have been sourced by the young man's women's team as per a shopping list, initially provided by the girl's parents during the preliminary visit process. At the yard entrance, the girl's chief aunt would lead her team in a line, to receive the gifts, also head-loading them, and taking them to into the house. In times past, gifts bought for the girl entailed clothing, a headscarf, *tukwi*, and a small shoulder blanket, *tsale*. Inside the house, both women teams would get seated to allow the young man's chief aunt to open the suitcases and individually show and display the gifts presented to the girl from her in-laws, and also confirming that they are as per the provided 'shopping list'. In the event there are any missing items of gifts, the young man's women team would be penalised and compelled to remedy the situation. As she shows the clothing gifts, the young man's chief aunt would also summon their new bride and remove her headscarf and short shoulder blanket to dress her with the new ones they just brought along as a symbol that she now belongs to them and must dress according to them. This completes the Rolong *bogadi* marriage process, where men and women from both parties would then meet over tea and biscuits, with a possible feast later in the afternoon, or at a future date, to celebrate the marriage.

Shortly thereafter, the parents of the bride and the groom, a few men and women (usually uncles and aunts), in company of a few other close relatives, as well as the bride and the groom, would approach the village *kgosi's kgotla* to register the marriage, *go folosa lonyalo kwa kgosing*. At this event, the girl's delegation would declare receipt of *bogadi* cattle or money to the *kgosi*, who would in turn issue to the young man's delegation, a note of acknowledgement of receipt of *bogadi*, signed by the girl's representatives and the chief. The chief would also offer some marriage counselling sessions to the newlyweds before issuing them a Customary Marriage Certificate.

Barolong elders regard *bogadi* as a token of appreciation by the young man's family to the girl's family, for having raised the bride for them whom they are now marrying. In terms of the Rolong culture, only six young cattle are worth the *bogadi*. Besides, eight sheep were equally acceptable to pay *bogadi*, or even a combination of two cattle and four sheep. Barolong elders are quick to point out that nowadays usage of cattle to pay *bogadi* is increasingly dying out. This they attribute to social developments and globalization which now seem to emphasise much on monetary value, as against any other life assets. Money has replaced cattle as a token of *bogadi*, and only under rare situations would one come across cattle being presented as *bogadi*. Lately, P2500 to P3000 is an agreed standard equivalent to a single *bogadi* cow, which sums up to about P20,000 to P24,000 for the current eight cattle charged as *bogadi*.

At this stage, the *bogadi* marriage processes are said to be satisfied. However, it would be up to the girl's family to decide whether or not to prepare a feast in acknowledgement of receipt of *bogadi*, *go apeela dikgomo tsa bogadi* – where the girl's family would choose a day to prepare a feast inviting the young man's family and relatives to celebrate the marriage. Alternatively, the chief uncle, who would have by then had been awarded a share of one or two *bogadi* cattle, may equally prepare a feast.

As was mentioned above, Rolong culture does not insist on the immediate issuance of *bogadi* upon completion of the *patlo* marriage process. In fact in the olden 'good' days, a Rolong man would simply marry through the *patlo* marriage process (which indeed is still a valid marriage without *bogadi*), establish his new matrimonial home, and raise their children together with his wife. *Bogadi* would become a husband's greatest concern only when his children start attaining the age of maturity, i.e., just as they get ready to enrol with the customary initiation schools, or the young man at the cattle post is now maturing into a man. It is at that juncture that a husband would have accumulated more than enough cattle or sheep to afford to pay *bogadi*. In particular, he would be willing to pay *bogadi* also because, in the event one of his daughters getting married without him having paid *bogadi*, he would not be competent to receive *bogadi*. Traditionally, the *bogadi* rights would automatically be transferred to his daughter's maternal uncle. Be that as it may, Barolong elders mention that the latter embarrassing situation (uncle retaining the *bogadi*) would have been a rare occurrence because previously patriotic love amongst relatives would cause a husband's father, paternal or maternal uncles and aunts, close relatives or their combination, to contribute sufficient cattle to cater for *bogadi* on his behalf. Barolong decry that this practice is currently history since a young man today is unequivocally expected to raise enough funds to cater for all the marriage proceedings, inclusive of *patlo*, *bogadi* and wedding (*mokete wa lenyalo*) costs, hence some reluctance by young men today to enter into marriage processes and choose to simply cohabit with their women lovers.

At this juncture, the *bogadi* marriage proceedings are said to be fully completed, giving possible rise to wedding ceremony preparations, *mokete wa lenayalo.*

## The wedding ceremony process (*Mokete wa lenyalo*)

According to Barolong culture, the wedding ceremony before the arrival of the missionaries, who brought along the veil wedding costume for the bride and a black suit for the groom as a token of celebrating a wedding ceremony, which would commence at church before a marrying priest. In Rolong custom, it is called *mokete wa lenyalo*, a wedding celebration. It is also an attribute of the Christian marriage process that it iscommonly solemnised by a church priest.

The wedding ceremony process would follow any time after the *patlo* process, and is arranged between families of both the bride and the groom. The Rolong elders allude to this process not being mandatory, and would depend on the financial affordability by each family to undertake it or not. If the event starts at church, the bride would be wearing a beautiful white veil dress and head crown, and the groom would put on a black suit and hat. The priest/pastor would bless the marriage at church in the presence of relatives from both parties. Assuming that solemnization was conducted at the District Commissioner's office, the procession would then relocate to the bride's family house where earlier in the day, a feast had commenced. The groom, his family, relatives and friends would be invited to join the groom's relations over the feast. Members of the community are usually welcome to also join the feast. Introductions of close relatives and guests from both families would also be made at some point during the course of the feast. This is said to mark the beginning of a new relationship between the bride and groom's families, and relatives for a lifetime bond. Together with meals, traditional beer is served, and traditional wedding songs are sang by choirs from both the bride and groom's families at alternate times. These songs usually have a message relating ideal marriage lifestyles to either the bride or the groom, at times to both of them. A gifted relative, usually an uncle or aunt, would throw in a poem or two to either the groom or the bride, followed by ululating voices from senior women from the village.

During the feast, at both the bride and groom's homes, their respective maternal uncles are respectively offered a head from the slaughtered cow, called *ditlhogo tsaga malome*, the uncle's gift head. In terms of the Rolong culture, it is not only unthinkable but offensive to deny an uncle such a privilege.

On the following day, a similar wedding event is held at the groom's family home. Here, no church ceremony is involved. The proceedings commence with the arrival of the bride and her family guests, together with community members. Just as at the bride's home, food would be served, together with traditional beer and the singing of wedding songs by choirs from both families.

At this juncture, a date is agreed upon at which the bride will be transferred to her in-laws to commence her new family life. This process is called *go isa ngwetsi kwaga matsalaye*, to take the bride to her in-laws.

## THE MARRIAGE COUNSELLING PROCESS (*GO LAYA*)

Barolong elders seriously respect the traditional marriage counselling process. This entails a congregation of married and widowed couples from both marriage families to offer counselling to the bride and groom. In Rolong custom, men conduct their part with the groom at the family *kgotla*, whilst the women would do likewise with the bride at the home compound at her in-laws' home. This process is called *go laya banyalani*, to offer counselling sessions to the newly-weds. It is undertaken in the morning, just as the bride is officially taken to her in-laws' home.

According to the Rolong elders, only married and widowed couples are preferred to offer counselling to the newly-married couple. It is believed that owing to the immense experience from their past married life, they are best placed to relate to the newly-weds what marriage really entails. After the counselling process, the two families now decide on a date to be set so that the bride is formally transferred to her in-laws' homestead. It is at her in-laws' place that she would stay until her husband affords to build her a house within the same ward.

At the family *kgotla*, the groom's marriage delegation, in the presence of the bride's marriage delegation, would commence the proceedings with the chief uncle leading the way. Whilst the groom would be seated at the centre of the *kgotla*, his men would inform him on the importance of a prosperous marriage and how it is achieved – that he is now a grown man and must stop being found in the company of his old unmarried friends,, and start adopting appropriate married men as his new friends who would lead him rather mislead him into an ideal marriage. Inside the groom's yard, women from the bride's family would, in the presence of her in-laws, equally offer counselling sessions to her on the prospects of making an ideal married lifestyle between herself, husband and family. The counselling sessions usually take an hour or less to be done with.

## THE TRANSFER OF BRIDE TO HER IN-LAWS PROCESS (*GO ISA NGWETSI*)

A transfer of the bride to her in-laws' home is usually undertaken in the morning hours. The bride's family marriage delegation, both men and women, would set off carrying along the marriage gifts she was presented with during the *patlo* proceedings. A few men and women from both her maternal and paternal sides, uncles and aunts always inclusive, suffice to undertake this process. She would also bring along her basic personal belongings.

At the in-laws' yard, the bride's women would carry her suitcases and bags on heads into the in-laws' yard in a straight line, with her chief aunt at the front, the bride also amongst them. They would be received by the groom's women's delegation with ululating voices of joy and marriage songs. The groom's women would receive the goods into a house set aside from the main house. Inside the designated house, the aunts from the bride's side would prepare a bed for the newly-weds, also coaching the bride on how to prepare the matrimonial bed, as well as how to treat a man in bed. She would be strictly advised that their bedroom is not a child's play area but a private one exclusively reserved for her and the husband to have rest or sleep. In the interim, the men from both families would be seated at the groom's family's *kgotla*, awaiting the women to complete the process as it is predominantly women-driven.

Thereafter, the process is concluded, possibly with a small meal, before the bride's delegation returns back home leaving the bride at the in-laws' family home. As soon as she has been delivered to her in-laws, the wife becomes part of her in-ls' family and immediately adapts to their way of life.

### The bride taken back to her natal home process

In terms of the Barolong, there is no process of the taking of the bride back to her natal home. As soon as she has been formally transferred to her in-laws, her mother must, within reasonable time, pay her a visit at the in-law's place, *mma mosetsana go gata kwaga matsale*. This visit is of cardinal importance as it serves as a symbol of releasing her daughter so that she may undertake visits back to her home as and when any event requires her attendance. Failure to make such a visit by the bride's mother would deny the latter the opportunity to visit her home in the event of any social-calling ariseing way back home.

## Barolong's Marriage Rites and Significance of their Metaphorical Language and Symbolic Actions

### The rights, privileges and benefits associated with Barolong's traditional marriage practices

Barolong elders are very particular about their customary marriage rites as well as the significance of their metaphorical language. In terms of the Rolong marriage rites, only married or widowed couples are allowed to participate in any of the marriage processes. These may include, but be not limited to the following: the preliminary visits, bride-seeking, bride-wealth proceedings, counselling sessions, and so forth. Divorced couples, as well as those currently involved in heated matrimonial disputes, are not supposed to partake in marriage proceedings. It is believed that the divorced and those with troubled marriages have the potential to bring bad luck or to ill advise the newly-weds if allowed to attend and participate. Unnmarried people were equally unaccepted at marriage proceedings as they are deemed to be immature and not conversant with marriage issues. Even if such people were friends to the marrying couple, they were deemed to be likely to mislead the couple as they do not know anything about marriage dynamics; hence their exclusion.

The significance of Rolong metarphorical language and symbolic actions emanates from initial Tswana traditional language usage. For instance, *goja sehuba sa nku ya mokwele*, eating the breast of a *mokwele* sheep was specifically reserved for the bride and the groom. As mentioned above, a *mokwele* sheep is offered by the groom's family to the bride's family as a symbolic action for engagement of the girl. The sheep is delivered shortly after the preliminary visit to the girl's family, where it is immediately slaughtered and all cooked for the married present marriage delegates to eat and finish the same day. The sheep's breast, which has a lot of fatty meat, is specially prepared for both the bride and groom to feast on in the evening when the groom has been allowed a night's visit to spend with the girl at her home. After the engaged couple has eaten the said meat, *rakgadi* and *mmamalome* would smear the girl with fat ointment from the meat all over her body. This was meant to make sexual penetration smooth as the couple would have met as virgins, unlike with current youth who break their virginity at an earlier stage, and without parental knowledge or involvement. Again, the elders were of the belief that when the new couple ate the fat from the said *mokwele* their hearts and feelings would settle down, *go retibatsa maikutlo a banyalani*, so that they quickly get to know and love each other at first contact.

The above goes hand in hand with the symbolic gesture of betrothal, *go baa lotlhokwa*, which literally means to earmark a girl for future marriage when she is mature enough, as explained above. The essence of betrothal is an assurance by her family that that the girl will be specially reserved and groomed for future marriage by the family of a young man who initiated a marriage proposal.

As regards the symbolic language of *goya go bofa setlhako*, this was a phrase used and understood to mean that an interlude break is requested by the groom's men delegation during the *patlo* proceedings. The break was necessary so that the young man's male delegation can be temporarily excused to go and get prepared to deliver *bogadi* cattle, or to facilitate their women counterparts to also proceed with the women's *patlo* proceedings, which are held separately by women from both parties immediately after their men have completed their *patlo* process.

The Rolong elders are particular about their bride having to wear a *jale*, a short shoulder blanket, pinned together with an up-pointed safety pin underneath, close to her chin, and a *tukwi*, a headscarf. The significance of wearing a shoulder blanket is for the girl to learn to always wrap together, and keep to herself, her matrimonial matters, issues, concerns, problems, and so on. These, she is not supposed to talk about with her friends and associates but to keep to herself and only discuss with her husband. The up-pointed safety pin tying the short shoulder blanked stays up to give the girl forward direction on her movements. On the other hand, the headscarf is always put on to protect a woman's head, since a woman's head is supposed to be always covered – as is also stated in the Holy Bible.

*Ditlhogo tsaga malome*, the cow that the maternal chief uncle is allocated after *bogadi* cattle are received, has a significant role. Traditionally, a child would be more acquainted with his or her mother's relatives than the father's. This gives the child an opportunity to grow up playing with or visiting their maternal uncle's children more often. In this regard, the child gets more help and life skills from the maternal uncle's side than anywhere else. *Ditlhogo tsaga malome* are therefore a token of appreciation to the uncle for taking good care of and bringing up the niece or nephew. This would explain why a husband would always offer his children's maternal uncle the head of a cow, sheep, etc., whenever he has slaughtered a beast. The uncle is also offered a female *bogadi* cow with the assumption that in the event his married niece encounters a future marriage misfortune of whatsoever nature, an uncle would have accumulated sufficient cattle from *bogadi* to be able to fend and maintain his married sister's children/household with.

## Factors of change and their impact on Rolong traditional marriage rites and activities

Barolong are clear that their customary marriage processes and procedures have to some extent changed. In particular, they attribute such changes to factors such as societal change. They maintain that, initially, their forefathers married within the clan. A man was found or chosen a wife by his parents, and vice versa. Upon arrival of the missionaries and the introduction of Christianity, young men and women adopted some Christian customs, *inter alia* a choice by one to independently identify a lover and future marital partner. In fact, the research reveals further that amongst the current Rolong elders, some are amongst the last generation that had their marital partners chosen for by their parents.

The Rolong elders also notice some change in the trend of *bogadi* now being abused by the current generation. With the arrival of the civil marriage process, an economic price tag has been attached to *bogadi*. Traditionally, *bogadi* was not used to gain financial or economic power *per se*. It was a token of appreciation to parents of the bride, for having groomed and raised a wife for their son. The reason why a married Rolong male parent would later on become eager to pay *bogadi* as his children grew into maturity was to prove his manhood capability and also to pay for their mother's maiden name, thus maintaining his family name. The elders state that, nowadays, parents of the bride perceive *bogadi* as monetary repayment for the education they provided their daughter. Also, the current parents would rather prefer to be paid money instead of cattle as *bogadi*. This they attribute to the cosmopolitan type of lifestyles that society currently finds itself with. Economic value is not much associated with cattle but with easily transferable money. Although equally regarded as valuable assets, acceptance of cattle, or their preference as *bogadi* price, is owing to their expensive and stressful maintenance trends.

## Prevalent problems and challenges with Barolong's traditional marriages today

The existing problems and challenges regarding the traditional Rolong marriage are diverse. The elders talk of a high rate of divorce cases amongst youthful married couples. Unlike in the past, where Rolong couples were close relatives, it was easy for them to resolve their matrimonial disputes and sustain their marriage life – their parents were always available to assist with resolution of their matrimonial disputes. Nowadays this is not easy as young married couples spend most of their married life in urban areas, where they work and interact with other couples from diverse cultural backgrounds, which are intertwined with the Christian, or civil, or both types of marriage.

Another noticeable problem is identified as lack of parental guidance of newly-married youthful partners. In the past, married couples lived within close range of their relatives, and learnt how to survive or deal with any societal challenges. Nowadays, married couples stay afar from their parents or relatives. Cosmopolitan economic pressures cause them to face life independent of their parents and relatives, and they have no one but themselves to assist in case of any type of life-challenging difficulties, hence their ultimate resort to divorce, even over small issues. They are confident that the traditional *bojale* and *bogwera* initiation schools used to play a vital role in moulding the youth into responsible adults and parents of the future. The current mainstream education is viewed as a double-edged sword, because whilst it brought along desirable changes into the current society, it equally brought along some confusion among the youth who are unable to distinguish between wrong and right type of behaviour.

Rolong elders further decry 'civilization', which caused the current married youth to restrict child procreation to two or three children per family. It is against the stressful economic background that the youth are now compelled to reduce the number of children per family, unlike in the past where a family would have close to ten children.

The Rolong elders also find it unthinkable that the civil marriage process is able to engage unmarried Marriage Officers to solemnise current marriages. This to them is very offendsive, because they regard marriage as an institution that can only be a success if appropriately commenced with people of the right calibre, being the equally married and experienced persons. They therefore attribute the current high rate of divorce cases to improper counselling from unmarried Marriage Officers.

## CONCLUSIONS AND RECOMMENDATIONS

Clearly, many factors have caused a devaluation of an ideal Rolong customary marriage. In particular, westernization and globalization seem to be the main causes of change in traditional marriage life and processes. As some would put it, society is dynamic and not stagnant. This on its own would readily explain why from one generation to another, society would continue to change the way things are done, with a view to improve the efficacy of life. This has not only affected the marriage processes of the Rolong people but all societal groups of people, universally.

In the end, the only recommendation one could make is to urge the current House of Chiefs to consider a codification of all the basic Tswana traditional marriage beliefs and customs. This could be possible because, generally, most Tswana marriage processes and procedures are not very different from one another. Not only should this be done with marriage processes but must be undertaken with regard to all other Tswana traditional processes pertaining to other societal aspects, such as the conduct of funerals, initiation schools like *bojale* and *bogwera*, as well as all other cultural trends that have the potential to improve the current bad trends visible in today's society. This can be greatly achieved through a diligent selection of all the good customs, norms, practices and behaviours which were or are still in practice. Such wealth of trends must be codified or documented, with a view to reintroduce them into today's society. This is so because there still exists a plethora of good, effective and efficient customs, not only about marriage but about all aspects of life.

# 10

# Batawana

*Eagilwe Segosebe*

## Introduction

This chapter focusses on the institution of *lenyalo* among the Batawana of Ngamiland. The data used for the compilation of this chapter was collected from selected representatives of some Batawana wards (*Goo-Seetsho; Mabudutsa; Mabudutsana; Molapisi; Segongwana; Kubung; Kgosing* and *Borolong*), which culminated in the production of this work. Selection of subjects was purposive and largely guided by age and cultural knowledge. In other words, elderly people, or those identified as knowledgeable by informers, were selected for interviews or discussions.

## Historical Background

Batawana are an ethnic group of Ngwato origin that ceded from the latter in around 1795 or 1800. The Batawana ceded from the Bangwato due to disputes over succession in the Ngwato chieftaincy. Therefore, like the Bangwato, Batawana revere a duiker (*phuti*). Due to the patriarchal culture of the Batawana, all offspring born of Batawana males have *phuti* as their totem. One should hasten to note that the Tswana-speaking Batawana are not a monolithic community. Rather, the community from time immemorial was constituted by other Tswana-speaking groups who revere animals of their mother ethnic groups. For example, there are Batawana of Batlokwa, Bakwena, Barolong, Balete origin and others.

Upon seceding from the Bangwato, Batawana went to settle in the Ngamiland District among other African tribes that they found in the area. These included among others, the San, Hambukushu, Bayeyi and Basubia. These other minority groups of Ngamilanders, whose occupation of Ngamiland is not adequately documented, has attracted little or no interest from both historians and human rights activists in the area.

## Batawana Marriage Social Context

The evolution of marriage among the Batawana was influenced by the space they occupied, and contact with other non-Tswana speaking Batswana in Ngamiland, since their separation from the Bangwato and the environment in which they found themselves. Separation of Batawana by large distances from other Tswana-speaking Batswana naturally lead to changes in the way they do things through cultural transformation. Similarly, the new environment in which they came into contact and interacted with non-Tswana speakers who practised their own cultures led to a two-way acculturation. Consequently, the evolution of marriage practices must be understood in this context. What this means is that marriage practices among the Batawana may, to some extent, exhibit what appears a divergent practice from that of other Tswana-speaking Batswana. This should be understood as a function of cultural change in the context of a new environment and subsequent cultural diffusion.

By coming into contact with non-Tswana speaking Ngamilanders, Batawana lost some of their cultural practices and adopted the practices of other Ngamiland communities among which they lived.

## The Importance of Marriage

According to the interviewed informants, marriage is an arrangement or a union created by God to bring a man and a woman together. The marriage process among the Batawana epitomises consultation (*morero*). It brings a man and a woman to cooperate and live together and make a family, as it grows the extended families of the bride and the groom. A family carries the responsibility for social reproduction. Marriage is a testimony that the groom and bride have grown into adulthood and that they are responsible enough to live together in harmony. Marriage broadens the pool of relatives and friends. This is important when carrying out certain tasks that require more hands. Those interviewed asserted that marriage helps to: build homes and households; facilitates cooperation in executing community tasks; brings friendship among the families of in-laws; legitimises the union between a man and a woman; and finally creates a conducive environment for raising children by both parents.

The informants spoke of the importance of being married – to be accepted in certain undertakings of social activities. For example, bachelors could not attend consultation meetings on marriage. The only exception to this rule is unmarried women whose daughters are getting married, as provision is made for them to attend talks pertaining to their daughter's marriage. This flexibility is facilitated by draping the mother with a shawl that gives her the ticket to attend the meeting. However, in the past she was not allowed to say anything or make any comments, but presently some families allow them to talk. Otherwise, unmarried people had no entitlement to attend such gatherings, let alone have a say in them, because they had not been counselled in marriage practice and law. Consequently, they have no right to offer advice in that regard. In the marriage processes such relatives are usually only restricted to the preparation of food and other tasks where that would be required of them. This is corroborated in the quotation by a *Mmegi* staff writer below, who suggested that being married signifies social status, which allows one to access activities exclusive to married persons, such as meetings. Many of the issues raised herein are still true in contemporary Botswana. The quotation is an illustration in this regard:

> In the past, the institution was so highly regarded in that it could determine one's status in the community and society at large. Single women of age were shunned as *mafetwa* and [it was] every parent's wish was to marry off his or her daughter. A man of age who was likewise not married was also poorly regarded and banned from attending meetings and events exclusive to married men. For example, bachelors were not allowed to attend *patlo* (an event where potential in-laws visit a would-be bride's place to ask for her hand in marriage) and during *kgotla* meetings they had little say at times risking being humiliated publicly during debates because of their marriage status. (Seretse, 2009).

Families on both sides have high expectations of the outcome of a marriage. They wish that the organization of the wedding be smooth and run peacefully, to make a memorable occasion. They would want to see the new family grow and prosper, live in harmony together, bear children, and develop a strong bond of friendship that only death can destroy. Families wish the union to be a permanent relationship, and one that will not bring disrepute to their families, but one that other people will envy and regard as examplary.

## THE MARRIAGE PROCESS

### COURTSHIP

In the past it was the responsibility of the parents to find a wife for their son. This was done when their son was away at the initiation school. Both parents on the bride's and groom's side desired that their daughter and son respectively marry in a family with good social standing and conduct. As a result, parents took it upon themselves to ensure that their children married in families identified by them and not by the bride and groom to be. Generally, families that were taken to be lazy, aggressive or violent, or witches, were avoided.

The arrangement for marriage adopted one of two approaches that were practised then. The first approach was for the parents of the groom-to-be to identify a family to which they would want their son to marry into. Normally such a family would be well known, or may even be a member of the extended family (e.g., a cousin). They would then approach the prospective daughter-in-law's parents to express their interest in having their son marry in the family, in a process called *go seba/ditshebo* (literally meaning going to gossip with the prospective in-laws). This would constitute the preliminary visit.

Following the gossip procedure, the bride-to-be's family would respond by indicating that they would revert to the visitors after due consultations with other members of the family. During this period the bride's family would assess the groom's family's social background to determine if they would want their daughter to be married in that family.

There was a variation in this approach to arranged marriages, which applied to cases where the bride may not yet be born or may still be young. The parents of the groom-to-be would, in a similar way to the above, identify a family into which they would want their son to marry into. For this approach however the groom to-be is engaged in a process called *peelelo* (betrothal) until such time that the bride has grown and is ready for marriage. In this case the groom-to-be's family would start caring for the unborn baby from pregnancy until he or she has grown up. After the girl 'bride-to-be' reaches the marriage age, her parents would send word to the prospective in-laws advising them that their daughter was ready to get married.

Another variation on arranged marriages was where the parents identified a family that they liked and directed their son to look for a wife within that family. After identifying a girl who he would like to marry, the son first informed his mother, who would in turn inform his father. The mother would then visit the girl's mother to gossip with her (*go ya ditshebong/go seba*). She would tell her that her son had identified one of her daughters and would like to marry her. After the visitor had left the mother informed her husband about the purpose of the boy's mother's visit. Word would be sent to the boy's family that they would revert to them in due course. In the meantime, they would carry out a background assessment of the boy's family. If their conduct and social standing is acceptable, word would be sent to the boy's family to the effect that they would waiting to hear from them.

When all consultations are complete, and parents on both sides are agreeable to the marriage, they would inform their son or daughter that they had found a husband or wife for him or her, respectively. The groom's family would then propose the date of the marriage. If agreed upon, marriage arrangements would then be undertaken, as discussed later. It would seem that, in the first version above, courtship and romance were not a necessary antecedent for two people to join hands in marriage. The way courtship was practised is well articulated in the Tswana proverb that says *mosadi tshwene o jewa mabogo,* which speaks of the importance of utility of the woman to her in-laws. Courtship was therefore not a necessary antecedent to marriage, but social acceptance ws. This is in agreement with the findings of Senekane (1995: ch. 1, section 1.1.1.3) concerning the Tswana of Oodi District quoted below:

> Courtship and romance love were not considered to be of great importance. Marriage was looked upon as a process. The affection of the spouse was expected to develop over the years after the wedding and was not considered a prerequisite for the making of a marriage agreement.

The second approach also applies to the contemporary period. The young man finds a young lady who he wishes to tie the knot with and informs his mother, who in turn informs her husband. The father would call a meeting (*morero*) of close relatives and inform them that his son had found a girl that he wished to join hands with in a marriage. A history of the girl's family is assessed to determine if it is the right family to marry into. After the family satisfied itself that the girl's family's conduct and social standing were admirable then the boy's mother would visit the girl's mother to gossip and inform her that her son had found her daughter and would like her to join hands with him in marriage.

The girl's mother would later relay the news to her husband. She would inform him that so and so's mother told her that her son has interest in marrying their daughter. Her husband would then break the news to close relatives. A consultative meeting (*morero*) would be convened. In this meeting, the girl would be called to confirm that she knows the boy who wants to marry her, and whether she had agreed to the proposal. If she is agreeable to the proposal, the meeting would agree to closely observe and assess the boy's family's social background and standing to determine if all will go well for their daughter by marrying into that family. If the bride's family are happy with the social background of the groom's parents, they will give a green light for marriage arrangement to go ahead.

A variant to the 'gossip' process (*ditshebo*) is where close relatives of the boy go and see the prospective in-laws and to 'show themselves'. Normally this would have been done by the parents of the boy, especially the mother. Nowadays even close relatives can be involved in this process. For some reason the latter process seems to be gaining ground. Close relatives such as paternal and maternal uncles and aunts are the ones who take part in this process. It is, however, not uncommon for parents of the boy to go and meet the parents of the girl so that when they send relatives for bride-seeking (*patlo*) the in-laws would know them already. Going to gossip may not be widely prevalent in many contemporary families. After visiting the in-laws and all is well with the bride to be's family, preparations could now start – on the side of the bride's family to receive the groom's family when they come on the bride-seeking (*patlo*) errand, while the latter would prepare to go to the bride's family to formally request that the bride-to-be and groom-to-be be allowed to join hands in marriage. This would then be followed by bride-seeking (*patlo*) and wedding arrangements.

Nowadays courtship has shifted from parents to the two lovers. The parents' desire to have their offspring marrying in families known and beloved to them is now a thing of the past, and unheard of. The groom is now free to find and propose love and marriage to the girl he wishes to marry. After finding the girl he informs his mother, who in turn informs his father. Consultations (*morero*) follow and subsequent steps are pursued, as above. This change has meant that courtship is carried beyond the boundaries of the extended family and distant relatives. As a matter of fact, intermarriages take place across tribal and racial boundaries. A major change in the *patlo* is that many families do not practice the gossip process, it may be confined to a few families, if it still exists.

## BRIDE-SEEKING (*PATLO*)

Those who are involved in the bride-seeking process are the paternal and maternal uncles and aunts. But unlike in other Tswana-speaking tribes of Botswana, where the maternal uncle plays a major role, among Batawana the paternal uncle is the one who plays the major role. According to the respondents this is a matter for the ward's tribesmen and not for the maternal uncle who in fact represents the in-laws and comes from another ward. However, some families put the maternal family upfront, a procedure that prevails elsewhere among other Tswana tribes. At any rate it is regarded as important that the maternal uncle attends and contributes to all consultations (*morero*) even where the paternal uncle is in charge, as he represents the boy's or girl's mother's kin. Only married people took part in this process. Unmarried people are not allowed.

Bride-seeking among the Batawana is carried out early in the morning, but not when it is still dark. Those who come for the bride-seeking must be visible and identifiable to avoid giving the daughter being sought to 'hyenas'. In actual fact this may only be symbolic and cannot be a real concern because a representative of the bride's family is assigned to join the groom's party in the *patlo*, in order to guide them on what is expected of them when they approach the in-laws. Usually a man (*rraditsela*) and a woman (*mmaditsele*) are assigned to the groom's party for this purpose. It is noteworthy that these two are not supposed to be spokespersons of the visitors, but they could coach them on what to say and provide them with guidance on what to do on approaching the in-laws' place, and what to do once they are inside.

Traditionally the bride-seeking process took a total of four days and was conducted in the afternoon, according to an elderly informer. The four days are still being practised, although some families have started easing away from this tradition due to the time constraints of working people. The four days of *patlo* were arranged as follow, in the past. The first two days were allocated to men. On the first day the men requested fire (*molelo*), literally and symbolically meaning one who makes the fires. This infers that they requested someone who will come and make fire for their son at his new home, so that he does not stay in the dark. At this first visit the host would simply respond by saying *ga re mmogo*, suggesting that some of the critical relatives were not in attendance, and therefore no definitive answer could be given. On the second day the men would request *sego sa metsi*, literally meaning someone who will come and draw water. In this case the new bride is expected to draw water for her in-laws. To this, the host would respond by saying *metsi re a a lo naya*, meaning that they are acceding to the request, that is, allowing their daughter to get married.

The third and fourth days were set aside for the women relatives. On their first day (the third in the *patlo* process) the women declare that they are following on from the visits of the men (*borre*) to request for *sego sa metsi*, literally the one who contains water. It is not uncommon to hear local women saying 'we have come here on the trail of our men' (*re tsile mo motlhaleng wa banna ba rona*). This may be confusing because the men are neither necessarily theirs nor their husbands. It should be *bo rre* without the possessive '*ba rona*'. They are told that it is as they heard from the men (*bo rre*) who came before them on the same errand, meaning that the *sego sa metsi* is released to them. They express their gratitude and leave. On their second day (fourth in the whole bride-seeking process) the women come to bring gifts (*dilwana tsa malebogo*) to the in-laws as a way of expressing gratitude for being awarded *sego sa metsi*. In all the occasions, including visits by men, the visitors always ask for permission before they leave. In Setswana *ba kopa tsela,* literally meaning they request the road. The hosts respond by saying *tsela re a e lo naya*, meaning that permission is granted. On the fourth day refreshments are served before the visitors leave.

Traditionally those participating in the bride-seeking exercise leave quietly, but do not necessarily walk in a line when they leave the boy's family compound as it is seldom observed, a function of cultural interactions. On arrival at the compound of the girl's family, they approach silently and walk quietly to take their positions in the space reserved for them in front of the host, facing them. The host greets them as a way of allowing them to deliver their message. They make their request to have their son join hands in marriage with the identified daughter of the family. After receiving a response from the host, they ask to leave. They are given such permission, and they leave. When the delegation arrives back home, they do not form a line, and they are not greeted as is occasionally observed in some such occasions. The greetings referred to here and above are associated with traditions of other tribal groups in the district, which were copied due to a prolonged period of cultural interaction.

In Setawana penalties are not common during *patlo,* except in extreme cases of misconduct by the visitors. This is, however, preempted by assigning a relative as a guide (*mmaditsele and rraditsela*) to both the women and men's sides to assist the visitors to execute *patlo* according to the expectations of the host. Other than that, the only time that penalties were or are applied is during *tlhagela*. Symbolically, the meaning of *tlhagela* is that the boy jumped over the compound at night to see his fiancée while the in-laws were not properly covered and as such saw them undressed because they were not aware that he was around. This remains true to date. *Tlhagela* is applied only when the young man impregnates the girl between *patlo* (i.e., after the family of the girl agreed to the marriage) and the actual wedding. Outside this period no penalties are applied. If the girl gets pregnant before *patlo*, then the family of the boy pays for the damage, *tshenyo* in Setswana.

Contemporarily, there are conspicuous changes in how *patlo* is carried out. For example, due to work-related time constraints, *patlo* takes place over two days as opposed to the original four days described above. Therefore, the requirements of the *patlo* are executed in a total of two days for both men and women. This means that *patlo* can be accomplished over the weekend and allow participants to go back to their places of work. But change has not been accepted by all without grumbles. There are still families that do not want to let go of the old tradition, but the winds of change are upon them.

Major changes, as indicated above are that:

(a) courtship is now a domain of the boy who finds the girl he loves and informs his parents that he would like to marry her;

(b) intermarriages go beyond confinement around the extended family and transcend ethnic and tribal boundaries;

(c) *ditshebo* are no longer extensively practised, or may be confined to a few families if still practised;

(d) outrunners from the groom-to-be's family are sent to go and identify the family to the bride-to be's family (*go itshupa*); and

(e) *patlo* takes place early in the morning as opposed to the afternoon, as was the case in the distant past according to one of the informers.

## PAYMENT OF BRIDE-WEALTH (*BOGADI*)

Payment of *bogadi* among the Batawana is a mixed bag. Some older people suggest that *bogadi* used to be demanded in the distant past and was paid accordingly, while others say it was never paid. But the overall understanding among the elderly folks is that *bogadi* was paid in the past. What is clear is that for a long time Batawana have not practised payment of *bogadi* for many decades. For example, for two women married in 1934 (the younger one) and 19xx (for the older one), no *bogadi* was paid. Therefore, until just over two decades ago (i.e., since 1996) contemporary Batawana have had nothing to do with payment of *bogadi*.

There are two perspectives regarding the conditions of *bogadi* payment according to those suggesting that it used to be practised. One perspective is that it was paid accordingly, and as demanded, by the in-laws; the other is that the payment was paid based on the ability of the groom-to-be's wealth and social standing – so payment was determined by what the latter could afford or was willing to pay. Those who suggest that *bogadi* was never an issue among the Batawana suggest that there was only an offering of one beast from the groom's family to the bride's family, which essentially was a thanksgiving offering (*kgomo ya malebogo*), as a show of gratitude for the fact that they were given permission to marry the bride-to-be. This beast was called *perephetsa*, and it was meant to be slaughtered and eaten.

Payment, according to some informers, was made through ploughing of a field for the in-laws. For example, the boy's family would plough a field for them,and inform the parents of the girl to come and take care of it, and the latter would work on the field and harvest the crops for themselves. According to one of the informants, crops harvested from a field provided and ploughed by the groom-to-be's family constituted payment of *bogadi*. Over time this form of payment was replaced by payment with cattle.

It is not clear when exactly the *bogadi* paid in the past was stopped, but there is a general understanding that it was stopped by Kgosi Moremi. He stopped it to reduce disputes among families related to the payment of *bogadi*. In particular, where a man married into a poor family and paid *bogadi* accordingly, disputes arose if the marriage did not work out properly. In this case, the bride's family were expected to reimburse the groom's family the *bogadi* that was paid, failing which the bride could not be released to go back to her natal home. Thus, her parents would have to pay back, or she would do by staying at her new home and endure emotional and other abuse. Therefore, Kgosi Moremi is said to have abolished *bogadi* on account of abuse of the poor married to wealthy families.

It is worthy of note to point out here that during the interlude after the payment of *bogadi*, the sequencing of *patlo* in relation to the civil marriage procedures was exactly the reverse of what was prevailing among other Batswana groups where *bogadi* payment was a requirement. In the latter case the *magadi* are paid after civil marriage procedures are concluded at the magistrate court or church (i.e., after the fact). Because the marriage practice among the Batawana for a long time negated *bogadi* payment, it was unheard of that the civil marriage could be concluded before the *patlo*. The *patlo* had to be executed first and a marriage contract agreed to by the in-laws prior to its execution at the District Commissioner's office. Failure to do so could attract dispute and cause the marriage contract to be scorned by relatives, if not the community at large, because the newly wed would be regarded as having entered a marriage contract without the blessing of their parents.

As fate would have it, just over two decades ago (i.e., since 1996 as observed by the author) the Batawana reinstated or started demanding payment of *bogadi* from the boy's family. On why this was the case, informers suggested that this was done to protect their resources, because when their sons married outside the district, they paid *bogadi*, yet when their daughters got married outside, they received nothing in return as they did not demand *bogadi*. It was for this reason that *bogadi* was reinstated in *goo-Tawana* or among the Batawana of Ngamiland in 1996 or thereabout. The normal time for payment of *bogadi* is in the morning.

Hand-written insertions by the chief's representatives at the top part of the undated notes captioned below (Figure 1) suggest that they were written in 2011 and put into effect in 2012. For reference purposes this undated document (sourced from the Batawana Tribal Administration (BTA) in September 2020 ) is referred to as 'Social Val-

***Figure 1.***

Effect from 2012

**DITSHWETSO TSA SETHO/BOTHO (SOCIAL VALUES – NGAMILAND DISTRICT**

***Figure 2.***

2.4.2 ✓ * Mo ga Tawana kgomo ke P2000.00, bogadi ja rona ke kgomo tse (6) ka P12000.00 mme a sa fete fa.

* Go tsala ngwana ke kgomo tse pedi (2) ka P4000.00.
Dikotlo ke kgomo tse nne (4) ka P8000.00.
Tshenyo ke kgomo tse nne [illegible]

ues – Ngamiland District' by borrowing from its title and the inscribed date of effect. It will therefore, for purposes of this chapter, be referrred to as the BTA (2012) after its date of effect.

Section 2.4.2 of Figure 2 is in apparent reference to the payment of *bogadi* and other family maintenance requirements/charges. For example, *bogadi* was charged six beasts, maintenance four beasts, damage (payment for children born outside wedlock) four beasts. In all cases the price of each beast was fixed at P2000.00. Currently the official number of *bogadi* beasts requested (based on a *kgotla* meeting resolution) stands at eight and the price per beast remains P2,000.00 amounting to a total of P16,000.00. This is in stark contrast with what prevails in other parts of Botswana where *bogadi* is either based on the BMC market price of a beast or the education attained by the bride to be.

Only the following additional clothing items are bought for the bride-to-be:

(a) a blanket (*kobo*);

(b) a cloth material for the bride's dress (*phatsa*);

(c) a reel of cotton thread (*tlhale*);

(d) a headscarf (*tuku/tukwi*); and

(e) money to pay the tailor (*madi a moroki*).

Like elsewhere in Botswana, there are variations in the actual amount of *bogadi* requested, based on variables such as the number of head of cattle demanded, or the monetary value attached to the beasts. This adds an expense to marriage requirements, and may be partly responsible for the prolonged co-habitation of young couples before getting married. The latter is a common occurrence across the country, one might point out. Currently, the groom-to be has to pay *bogadi* of tens of thousands of pula as a precondition to get permission to marry their loved ones. Consequently, the young grooms-to-be suffer an escalating financial burden when they contemplate getting married. Fortunately, under Batawana wedding pocesses there are not many other gift exchanges such as *kgomo ya patlo, serufo, motlhakanelwa* and others. There is, however, a beast donated from each side on the eve of the wedding feast. For instance, on the eve of the feast that takes place at the bride's home the groom's family will donate a beast and vice versa. On the morning following the delivery and reception of the bride at the groom's family home the previous day, the groom's family donates a male sheep to the bride's family as a symbolic gesture to cover her trail. In Setawana it is called *nku ya serwalo.* It represents what in the Western culture is a cake. A sheep is also symbolic of a quiet and peaceful coexistence.

It should be noted, before ending this section, that *bogadi* procedure has its own protocols in terms of who participates and has a share in it. Those involved in the *bogadi* procedures are parents in conjunction with the uncles, in particular the maternal uncle to represent her sister, coming on account of representing motherhood. The maternal uncle gets a share in the *bogadi* paid, and returns the favour by donating a cow that will be slaughtered during the wedding feast.

## THE MEANING AND FUNCTION OF *BOGADI*

When confronted with the question of the meaning and importance of *bogadi*, informers gave varying, albeit interesting, insights that demonstrate the prolonged pause in the payment of *bogadi* that went on for many decades as alluded to earlier. There is one perspective that one might describe as conventional. According to this perspective *bogadi* is important as it:

(a) testifies that an agreement has been reached for the daughter to get married to a man or has been given away for marriage in another family, or has a husband-to be;

(b) demonstrates the commitment of the groom-to be towards marriage;

(c) acknowledges the investments and related costs that the bride's parents undertook to raise their daughter; and

(d) shows gratitude by the groom-to-be that his fiancée was properly raised on his behalf. This perspective is perhaps informed by the distant past experiences, during which *bogadi* payment was practised and a couple of recent decades during which *bogadi* was reinstated.

The other perspective was apparently informed by the intermission in the payment of *bogadi*. For obvious reasons this perspective did not appreciate the meaning and value of *bogadi*. According to them *bogadi* has neither function nor meaning. For example, asked about the meaning and function of *bogadi* one of the respondents succinctly responded, *"ga bo kae sepe ka lenyalo la bogadi le tshwana fela le le go sa ntshiwang Bogadi"*. This literally means that payment of *bogadi* has no special meaning or function, as marriages where *bogadi* has not been paid are similar to those where *bogadi* has been paid.

The practice of *bogadi* payment among the Batawana exhibits epochs of payment and non-payment. While it was paid in the distant past, there was a prolonged period of non-payment of *bogadi* that ran for many years, until ove a couple of decades ago when it was reinstated in 1996 or thereabout. The form of payment also changed from a ploughed field to cattle to the current monetary payment (as the alternate form of *bogadi* payment). Another change is that while in the past the value in whatever form requested for *bogadi* was the same for all people, or depended on what the groom's family could afford or were willing to pay, this has changed. Nowadays there are variations in the amounts requested by families. Families charge as they wish, some leaving room for negotiation. In particular, variability is evident among the diverse ethnic groups, which may have influenced family decisions. But the Batawana have largely adhered to the official number of *bogadi* cattle and other clothing items required for the bride agreed at the *kgotla* since *bogadi* was reintroduced, as indicated earlier.

## THE WEDDING CEREMONY

Traditionally the wedding ceremony was in two parts, executed over two days. Weddings were generally hosted at home by in-laws on both sides. The festivity started at the bride's place with singing, merrymaking, and preparation of food, which consisted mainly of abundant meat and starch. Lunch was promptly served at mid-day. On this day the groom's people are received as guests. On the second day the festivity will be moved to the groom's home where they would receive the in-laws. At the end of the day the bride is brought to the groom's place while there is still daylight. It was taboo to deliver the bride at night.

In actual fact the festivities started on the eve of the wedding ceremony. On that night, several goats were slaughtered and cooked overnight. The meat was cooked so well that it was well shredded (called *seswaa* in Setswana). On the eve of the wedding children spent the whole night singing. Children, who would be celebrating the night with songs, would be fed the meat cooked overnight, in the morning. This meat called *diphiri* or *nama ya diphiri* (literally hyena meat or meat for hyenas) would be served to the children early, at dawn. There was no invitation. Every child who could make it would be fed to their fill. As they were fed in the dark they could not be discriminated or harmed because they were not easily identifiable. When it was time for everyone to wake up, the children would go and sleep at their homes. The beauty of the *diphiri* was that when preparations for food and other tasks begin in earnest in the morning there would be no disturbance from children. As meat takes long to ingest, children would only feature in the afternoon when the bulk of the tasks were completed, and they could receive attention again.

In the past food was prepared by members of the extended family. Everyone brought their pot(s) to come and cook food for the visitors. Each relative received certain cuts of meat, as required by tradition, which they would prepare. Meat composed an assortment of beef, goat, lamb and chicken. They would also prepare pots of starchy food. Thus, food for feeding the visitors would be served from pots prepared by relatives. At the end of the day when everybody had been fed to their satisfaction, the cooks would carry the remaining food in their pots to feed members of their families who could not make it to the wedding, such as young children and the elderly. Food preparation and feasting was important at the occasion, not only because the in-laws received visitors on the day, but it was also symbolic of social status. The idea was to preserve this image of the family.

In terms of the dress code, attention was focused on the newly-weds and their attire. Nobody really paid much attention to other people. There was no prescribed dress code, and anybody could dress the way they pleased because the ceremony was hosted in the homes, not elsewhere.

Considerable changes have taken place in the way wedding ceremonies are held nowadays. In some cases weddings are hosted away from homes in specifically prepared locations such as hotels, wedding gardens, or hired canvas tents that are hoisted near the home. Food catering companies or groups are hired to cook and serve food to the visitors. Visitors are only accepted to participate in the festivity if they carry invitation cards. Families soon found out that the new system leaves out children and the elderly. To address this problem some cooking is still done at home to serve those who for one reason or other are unable to go to the hotels or such places. There is no more *diphiri* meat prepared for the children who are generally overlooked by those distributing invitation cards. It is an acceptable norm for people to come to the festivity through invitation only. One can hazard to suggest that the kids are the unfortunate victims of this new system. It is not uncommon to see invitation cards that are categorically unwelcoming to kids. As the *diphiri* are slowly disappearing from the picture, children suffer a double blow in terms of enjoying the food, and as children are literally turned away if they do not carry an invitation card

Nowadays prescribed dress codes for best ladies and men are the norm. They dress elegantly in specially designed and expensive suits and dresses. Special uniforms made of German print (*leteisi*) are also recommended for invitees who are willing and able to afford them.

## Counselling of the bride and send-off

Counselling in marriage is best described as an ongoing process, since informal counselling takes place as soon as the parents feel that it is time for their son or daughter to get married. At this time there will always be advice as to what getting marreied means. Informal lessons about manhood or womanhood are offered by close relatives. Formal counselling takes place after the wedding festivity.

The bride's relatives gather to counsel their daughter (i.e., after the wedding festivity) where she is advised about the dos and don'ts of marriage e.g., regarding general conduct in marriage, relationships with her in-laws, spouse, friends and the extended family members, as well as her role in the ward, particularly when there are social tasks to be performed. This is done just before she is taken to her new home. Only married members of the extended family both men and women are allowed to participate in this formal counselling. Instead, they meet together in the *lelwapa* (coutyard) for this occasion. Everybody who attends has to be properly dressed, as in men wearing jackets and women wearing a headscarf and a shawl on their shoulders as a sign of respect for this last and critical stage of *lenyalo*. Unmarried people and divorcees are forbidden from attending the meeting. The former because they themselves have not been initiated into marriage, and the latter for fear that their involvement in divorce might cast a bad omen on the newly-weds.

It is a fairly common practice among the Batawana for the bride's mother, who all along remained in the background for the most part, to send word to the groom's mother through those taking her daughter to her new home. She is usually afforded the first opportunity to counsel her daughter, together with a message to the groom's mother. She would send a firm message to the in-laws to the effect that she expected her daughter to be loved and treated with respect, and that she should be taught what is expected of her and be given advice to allow her to grow in marriage without abuse. The message is normally brief and to the point and is conveyed by any good speaker. Men and women are not separated but work as a team in counselling.

After the formal counselling the bride is taken to her in-laws by women in procession (*ngwetsi ea bopelediwa*), a splendid and awe-inspiring occasion to watch as mothers gracefully walk their daughter to her new home. They slowly walk her out of her parents' home in a somber mood, and pick up pace a little beyond the home compound to save time. Nowadays cars are used in between to cut the distance and save time. They would disembark as they approach the groom's home and continue the procession slowing the pace as they approach to the in-laws home. As it enters the compound of the in-laws, the procession of those bringing the bride will do so silently. The mood in the air, especially of those watching the procession from the compound but are not sitting in the *lelwapa* where the bride would be received, is indescribable.

There is excitement that is subdued by the requirement to be silent to respect of the arrival of the bride. One can only guess that the silence is symbolic of peace and respect in the marriage. The pace is reduced to that of a snail, and with the deeper silence combined, an air of anxiety and suspense is created before the bride arrives to the hands of her mother in-law, who sits her on a mat next to her (explained below). The visitors are shown to their seating places. Designated members of groom's party stand up to receive the bedding materials brought by the bride's party. The mother-in-law will then rise to remove the shawl that the bride is wearing and drape her with one specially prepared for her. A message from the bride's mother is delivered to the groom's family, who acknowledge its delivery and respond by indicating that the outcome of any marriage is determined by the will of God. After this the bridal party leaves in a procession, as they came, and head home.

It should be pointed out here that traditional preparations to receive the bride included providing a specially prepared skin where the bride would be made to sit next to her mother in-law. Due to what one believes to be a product of cultural exchange, Batawana no longer make use of the skin. Instead, they use a mat prepared from certain riverine reeds that are dried, entwined into a mat (*moseme* in Setswana) and carefully rollled up, and rolled out on the day the bride is received by her in-laws.

## COUNSELLING OF THE GROOM

After hearing the message from the groom's party and following their departure, men will summon the groom to the side for a counselling meeting. Male relatives and friends gather to counsel the groom where he is similarly advised about the dos and don'ts of marriage, e.g., regarding general conduct in marriage, relationship with his in-laws, spouse, the extended family and friends, as well as his role in the ward, particularly when there are social tasks to be performed. Above all he is informed about the message from his mother in-law regarding treatment of her daughter. Only married men are allowed to participate in this formal counselling. All men who attend have to wear a jacket and everybody sits on the ground as a sign of respect for this almost last and critical stage of *lenyalo*. At the end of the counselling, he is taken by the assigned person to the *lelwapa* to see his wife.

## TAKING OF THE BRIDE BACK TO HER NATAL HOME

After the bride was sent off to her in-laws' home it is a requirement that she be taken back to her natal home to greet her parents on the third day. For example, if she was sent off to her in-laws on Saturday afternoon, she would pay a visit to her parents on Monday morning, accompanied by two senior women in the family. This visit is important because it is the one that allows her to freely visit her parents as and when she chooses thereafter. If this is not done, she will not be allowed to visit home. It is usually a short and happy visit with ululations. Those bringing her will greet as normal and pronounce that they had brought her to step foot at her parent's home. She would come at a later date to pick up stuff that she wishes to bring to her new home. No feasting occurs during this visit, but if there is food left they will be served. Some families may prepare for the visit and provide drinks and the like.

After the visit she goes back to her in-laws' place for the final procedure of the marriage, where she would cook sorghum porridge. The porridge may be cooked with fresh milk (*logala*) or sour milk (*sebube*). When the porridge is cooked and ready for serving, elderly women will bring several dishes to her to serve her in-laws. There is a dish for everyone in the family (parents, uncles, aunts and so on). The mother-in-law is served the sticky portion (*bogogo*) at the bottom of the pot. This is so that whenever she dishes food, she must always leave some in the pot for her husband. She will dish a little amount into all the dishes because there is not a lot cooked to start with, but just enough for everyone to get one spoon or two. The number of dishes is representative of relatives of the groom and the procedure is symbolic of the fact that she is expected to occasionally serve them some food. This is also an occasion for the bride to get to know members of her new family.

## Factors that Have Influenced the Changes in Marriage

According to the informers, factors that influenced the changes in marriage include improved incomes, and lifestyles. Improved incomes and personal rights provided under our democratic system, such as children's rights, are others. In the past decisions ere made communally with the help of the extended family. A case in point is the demand of escalated amounts of *bogadi* by some families, which is seen by others as due largely to greed, inclined to make profit from the marriage of daughters. Another factor is seen as the competition among the newly-weds to have the most expensive wedding ceremony. Acculturation also played a part due to exposure to other non-Tswana speaking groups in the district.

## Consequences of the Changes to Traditional Marriage

As a consequence of modern trends, celebration places are hired outside the home, where food is expensive, and entertainment is provided (as opposed to traditional songs that used to entertain guests) resulting in very costly wedding ceremonies. The attire for the wedding couple is very expensive. In addition, the groom has to buy clothes for the increased members of the bride's extended family. *Bogadi* is now paid in beasts and money and not a field as was the case in the past. The consequence of these changes is often poverty for the young family, as some of them take loans to finance these extravagant weddings. The situation gets worse where the marriages do not work out well, and breaking up, against the background of outstanding loans. In the case of Batawana some changes were due to socio-political decisions, as when Kgosi Moremi abolished the payment of *bogadi* to protect the fundamental rights of married women to go back to their natal homes if the marriages did not work out. The overall effect of the changes has seen a proliferation of unstable marriages, gender-based violence, divorces and in extreme cases killings.

Now the boys are responsible for courting the girls they wish to marry, a responsibility that in the past used to be the domain of parents. The bride is responsible to the husband and no longer to the ward or extended family. Intermarriages among the extended family members in the past allowed for social control and guidance: this promoted respect between the newly-weds. Hence, this resulted in fewer conflicts, disputes, break ups, and stable marriages that lasted.

## Possible Solutions to Hardships Brought to Marriages

Respondents suggested that the only way that marriages could be saved from destruction is through trust, love, honesty, loyalty, patience, respect, consultation, forgiveness, good conduct and self-restrain, accepting one's capabilities, and avoiding unnecessary competition with others. They suggested for the community to reflect on their marriage processes, and as portrayed in the Bible, to go back to the 'cross-roads' and choose the right path that will redeem marriages and bring stability to them.

## Reference

Seretse, G. 2009. Traditional Marriages. https://www.mmegi.bw/index.php?sid=7&aid=193&dir=2009/October; last opened 6/12/2019.

# 11

# BATLHARO

*Mr. Allan Manyeneng*

**Totem**: *Tshwene* – Baboon

**Clan Poem:** (*Leboko la Batlharo*)
*Re baga Mokgatiti wa lewa!!!*
*Tshwene ke naiwa mmele;*
*Makopo gaa naiwe.*
*Ditshwene ha dia masimo;*
*Di etelelwa ke tshwenegadi pele.*
*Rotwe otla kwa morago -*
*Atla a di retolola.*
*Ke hudile, ka tlatsa, ka relela, ka wa;*
*Maje a gaetsho a borethe mogokwane!!!*

## BRIEF HISTORICAL BACKGROUND OF TSABONG VILLAGE AND THE BATLHARO

Tsabong (formerly spelt Tshabong) is a village located in the south-west of Botswana in the Southern part of the Kgalagadi District. It is a central township for the Batlharo, Bakgothu and Afrikaner ethnic groups in Botswana. Batlharo are one of the Setswana-speaking people of Bantu origin. According to some elders at the village, Batlharo originated from South Africa. They are in fact Bahurutshe in origin. Batlharo parted with the Bahurutshe of Lehurutshe village in South Africa before relocating to Kurumane under the leadership of Kgosi

Motlhware, hence known as Bahurutshe *ba ga Motlhware*, 'the Bahurutshe of Chief Motlhware's clan' at some stage. Batlharo mention that their totem, a baboon (*tshwene*), as well as their culture's poem, both resemble that of the Bahurutshe tribe, for they are one people by origin. They are also known as Batshweneng, a name derived from *tshwene*.

In 1845, Batlharo ultimately migrated to Tsabong village, seeking shelter away from the raging Batlharo/Boer wars. Some even moved further into the Kang/Tshane area of the northern Kgalagadi District. Batlharo explain that the name *Tsabong* is derived from the Setswana verb *go tshaba*, which literally means to run away from danger, hence its initial name *Tshabong*, as they were *running away* from the wars to a place of shelter. The village comprises a population of about 9000 residents (Batlharo inclusive), mostly cattle and small stock farmers. Batlharo youth are in the majority, whilst the old age group is limited in number. leaving behind a few who are either married or widowed, whilst a few remained unmarried, but well conversant with their culture. Most of the youth community is not married, but have chosen to form cohabiting relationships. Besides, most youth available were not very conversant with their traditional marriage processes. Batlharo's ward, *kgotlana*, in Tsabong is called Legonono. (In all, there are ten wards in Tsabong, which represent various ethnic groups that make up Tsabong village. Amongst others are the Bakgothu (Nama), the Khoisan, the Ovaherero, the Bangologa and the Afrikaners, to mention a few.)

## Understanding Marriage from the Batlharo's Point of View

Those who were interviewed in Tsabong, as part of the information collection for the writing of this chapter, indicated that marriage among Batlharo is a union between a man and a woman. They said it evolved from the time after God created Adam and Eve. They view the essence of marriage as being to ensure that human beings live an organised lifestyle distinct from all other animals. The beauty of marriage to them is also that it extends to involve and create a new and lifetime relationship between both the groom's and bride's families. Marriage is a necessary transformation that either a man or a woman must pass through before they die. It is the foundation, or forms the genesis, of establishing a community, because married couples procreate children, which translates into a continuity of existence of a society from generation to generation. However, Batlharo elders are quick to point out that nowadays, and unlike during their grandparents' time, marriage has lost its essence. The elders believe that the current youthful married couples experience quite an alarming rate of divorce cases due to non-compliance with cultural practices. For them, 'civilization' is the root cause for the current youth's departure from practising cultural norms, hence the prevalence of marriage breakdowns. Other research records derived from the Botswana National Archives express the same view as above about how Batlharo view marriage.

## The Types of Marriages/Weddings

Batlharo identify with three types of marriage processes, *viz.* the *customary* process, the

*District Commissioner's* process and the *Christian* process. The Batlharo elders at Tsabong are of the opinion that previously, and to date, the customary marriage process emerges as the most commonly practised by their community, followed by either the District Commissioner's or the Christian type.

## Customary marriage

In terms of the customary marriage process, Batlharo say that in the past, a young man's parents would arrange and agree with the girl's parents through the betrothal marriage process, on prospects of a future marriage between their children (*go baa lotlhokwa* or *peeletso*). This stage is reached after the young man's parents would have earlier on searched within the community, or even searched somewhere outside their community, and identified for their son an ideal family to marry from. At a ripe time, say 18 to 20 years, the young man's parents would send a delegation of married and widowed uncles, aunts, and close relations to the girl's home to conduct *patlo* proceedings, that is, proposing for the girl to be married to their son, which Batlharo call *go kopa sego sa metsi*. According to Batlharo, the maternal uncle is, in hierarchy, the chief reference point when it comes to either the marriage issues affecting either the young man or the girl's marriage processes and discussions. He is then followed by the paternal aunt. This process of requesting a young woman in marriage is called *patlo*, which is derived from *go batla mosadi*, 'to seek a woman for marriage.' A delegation from the young man's side is called *bagwe* in Setlharo, whilst that from the girl's side is called *bagwagadi*. Details of the customary marriage process of Batlharo are explained under the headings below.

## District Commissioner's marriage

Batlharo are familiar with the existence of the District Commissioner's marriage system. They are, however, generally not very conversant with details regarding how the said process operates. I have, however, the privilege of acquired knowledge on how the marriage processes of this marriage system operate. That is so by virtue of my profession and also by reason of my being married through the same process.

As is the case with such marriages countrywide, the Marriage Proceedings Act regulates marriage processes to be adhered to as and when couples intend to marry. Couples intending to marry are required to provide documentary proof that they have attained the age of majority, that is, 21 years of age. Where one or both parties are of minority age, parental consent is required before the marriage can be registered and concluded. Secondly, the marrying couple must each avail a witness, also of consenting age. Three weeks before the marriage date, both the couple and their respective witnesses are to report at the District Commissioner's office to register the marriage. Each shall bring their national identity cards and complete the necessary marriage application forms. From the registration date until a day before the marriage, the District Commissioner's office advertises a marriage though a system called 'banns'. Theses are publication on noticeboards, at the places where both parties are known to stay or to have stayed). The essence of a three weeks banns advertisement is to give the public at large an opportunity to know of those who are getting married, and whether anyone has any cause as to why the couple cannot be joined in matrimony. Reasons to stop a marriage from proceeding may be because one of the parties is already married, or one has promised a different partner marriage and is thus banned from continuing with this proposed marriage, an so forth.

A day before the marriage date, the couple, together with their respective witnesses, report at the District Commissioner's office to complete documentation that addresses issues on whether or not they are marrying in or out of community of property, i.e., the nature of how they are going to administer their estates.

During the day of marriage, the marrying couple, together with other couples scheduled for a marriage ceremony that day, together with their witnesses, will convene in a large boardroom. If there is enough room, relatives and friends are also allowed in to witness the marriage proceedings. The District Commissioner commences proceedings with a prayer, before conducting a detailed public counselling session. Counselling here entails most of the good and bad events that married couples generally go through, some on a daily basis. Incidentally, owing to the nature of their daily work, which also entails meetings and discussions with married couples who have lodged domestic complaints or disputes, a District Commissioner is in a privileged and sound position to appreciate exactly what marriage life entails. Upon completion of thorough counselling, the District Commissioner accordingly solemnises the marriages, whereafter, issuance of a marriage certificate completes the process.

Batlharo elders do not particularly favour the District Commissioner's marriage process. This is because it does not engage parents of the marrying couples in any way, something which makes them have doubts about the authentic nature of the District Commission's marriage process. What makes them elated though is that their youngsters never dare marry under the District Commissioner's process without first going through the customary marriage process. The elders only view the District Commissioner's marriage process as an aspect that encourages youth to be materialistic in their marriages, more so that they have to make a choice between being married through the *in* or *out of community of property* regimes.

## CHRISTIAN MARRIAGE

Batlharo believe that the Christian marriage process exists amongst their community and is practised by their tribesmen who are regular church members at various church denominations in Tsabong. They are not really conversant with its processes. I had an opportunity to enquire on this process through my church Minister of the Methodist Church Southern Africa – Gaborone Circuit. First the church marrying officer, the priest or a reverend, must register his credentials with the Ministry of Home Affairs, where a Marriage Officer's License would be issued, assuming the priest qualifies.

Secondly, the marrying couple would still be required to register their marriage with the District Commissioner's office. They will then follow all the processes as stipulated under the District Commissioner's marriage process above, but only up to the counselling stage. After the counselling stage, the District Commissioner would release those couples intending to follow the Christian marriage process. The couple will be in possession of marriage documentation from the District Commissioner's office to take to the priest/reverend's church office. The couple would then set a marriage appointment date with the priest, usually scheduled for a Saturday morning. During the marriage day, the couple, together with family members, friends and neighbours from both parties, would convene at church to witness the marriage. The priest would bless the event before solemnising the marriage in terms of the church principles. Thereafter, the priest would proceed to offer some counselling sessions to the couple, which also centres on how the marrying couple is expected to carry themselves during their marriage life. Like the District Commissioner, a priest is usually inundated with disputes and complaints from married church members. He, or she, is experienced with couselling on marriage problems and suitable to offer sound counselling in this regard. The marrying couple is urged to fear God and raise their upcoming children with love and care, through the hand of God. Thereafter, the priest issues a marriage certificate. The two families, together with their companions, then retire to the bride's home, where a celebration feast would be held. In particular, the feast is a demonstration of an appreciation by the girl's family, for receipt of the bride-wealth, lobola (*bogadi*).

An observation made by the Batlharo elders is that over and above marrying under the customary marriage practice, the youth go further and duplicate their marriage process by remarrying through the District Commissioner's office, or even through the church route where they are Christians. According to the elders, this stems from the established Civil marriage process, which they deem as not making marriage sacred any more. They say that the youth nowadays marry for wrong reasons, such as for the gain of material things, recognition, security, etc., instead of marrying for passion, creating joint wealth as a couple, and the building of a decent family.

## The bride taken back to her natal home process

In terms of the Batlharo marriage culture, there is no process whereby a daughter-in-law is taken back to her natal home. As soon as she has been delivered to her in-laws, the wife becomes part of her in-law's family, and dances to their way of doing things. More often than not, her husband would make several visits to her parents' home, at times the wife also accompanying him to see her parents. In terms of Batlharo culture, a son-in-law (*a mogwe)* is, *inter alia*, expected to take good care of his in-laws. This explains why he would make more regular visits to his in-laws than their daughter. Equally, a daughter-in-law is expected to do the same with her in-laws, hence her almost constant stay with them.

According to some extracts accessed from the *Native Laws & Custom of Batlharo of Kgalagadi* (as related by the Junior Native Tribunals at Tsabong and Bogogobe), dated 1936, (ref: S.211/4) from the records of Botswana National Archives, the following are mentioned with regard to the Batlharo marriage practice: at page 3: "...after birth of the first child, '*kgomo ya dithari*' is paid by the parents of both parties by producing one ox each, which are slaughtered and eaten by both families and their relations together." At page 4 thereof, the record goes on to state, "At any time after this, '*bogadi*' must be paid by the husband to his wife's maternal uncle. '*Mokwele*' may also be given on agreement between parents regarding the prospective marriage of their children. This binds the contract, and if it is broken by the girl or her parents, *'mokwele'* must be returned. '*Mokwele*' is not returned where the girl dies before she becomes of age to marry". Further, on *bogadi*, the record states, "'*Bogadi*' is not payable if there are no children. There is no fixed time when '*bogadi*' should be paid. The '*bogadi*' should be paid to the wife's eldest maternal uncle".

The National Archive's records continue to mention, with respect to Batlharo, "'*Bogadi*' is a form of contribution towards the wife's brothers in return for the children which she has borne to her husband, and also a form of recompense to them in respect of the future payments of which they may have to make, as the maternal uncles of such children". The records further reveal that "It is presumed that the husband has repudiated payment of '*bogadi*' and his wife's maternal uncles are entitled to demand payment, when he fails to give the neck of a beast slaughtered by himself". Upon receipt of *bogadi*, the chief maternal uncle may apportion some to the wife's father and brothers as well. The older maternal uncle also has a duty to share some *bogadi* portion with his younger brothers (the younger uncles).

The records further show that where the husband dies prior to paying *bogadi*, his own maternal uncle becomes chiefly liable. However, the paternal uncles or even his father may assist with the *bogadi* payment as well.

## Marriage Processes

### The betrothal (*Peeletso*) process

The customary marriage, which Batlharo refer to as *lenyalo la Setswana,* a Setswana or traditional marriage, was in the past arranged by the parents of a young man long before he attains puberty, through a betrothal process. In Setswana this is called *go baa lotlhokwa*. Unlike nowadays, there was no space for a young man to identify a young woman and think about marrying her. It was the duty the parents of a young man (about nine to sixteen years old), to identify a girl from amongst the families within the community as a potential wife. Parents would look for an ideal future wife from a family that they believe to have generally upheld a good and desirable background. According to Batlharo, it was vital to make a scrutiny of a potential in-law family's background, before choosing a daughter-in-law or before allowing the young man to marry one's daughter. This was premised on a belief that where a family is known to be of bad or undesired repute, such as practising witchcraft, theft, promiscuity, back biting, etc., it is presumed that the offspring from such a family would repeat such bad behaviour as they mature into adults – a totally undesirable environment for a family and child upbringing, they said. In this way, they were attempting to avoid their sons or daughters getting married to the 'wrong type' of people in the society.

When the young man's parents are satisfied with the identified potential daughter-in-law's background, they would accordingly inform the young man's maternal uncle. Together with him, the parents would visit and inform the girl's parents of their future intent to take their daughter in marriage to their son. This in fact is an engagement of the girl for a potential future marriage, which Batlharo call '*go baa lotlhokwa*' literally meaning 'to earmark a girl for future marriage'. To cement this process, the young man's family would provide a live cow or sheep termed *kgomo or nku ya mokwele* (a *mokwele* cow or *mokwele* sheep), as a present to the girl's family or as a token of marriage engagement. This *mokwele* cow or sheep is also known as *kgomo kampo nku ya ditumalano*, a cow or sheep pertaining to an engagement agreement. Also gifted to the girl is a headscarf for the girl to wear. The *mokwele* cow or sheep is strictly eaten and shared by the girl's family, excluding the young man's. As the young man progresses into puberty stage, his parents would start occasionally sending him on errands to the girl's home. Strategically so, the girl's parents would have by then, have erected a hut for their daughter at the back side of the yard, isolated from the main family house. This arrangement facilitates the young man to start sneaking into the girl's hut during nighttime to see the girl, or the girl's mother offering the young man sleep over (when sent on errands), as the rains are coming. It is at this juncture that where the two youngsters happen to fall in love, the courtship level would have been achieved. A Motlharo elderly man is quick to mention that even if the two couple seem not to be interested in each other, at an appropriate time, the young man's parents would arrange with his uncles and aunts, from both the paternal and maternal sides, to commence the *patlo* marriage process with the girl's family.

Batlharo maintain that this type of traditional Setlharo marriage process has since died out. The elders said that it was during their parents' era that the betrothal marriage process ended. It is the courtship marriage process that evolved in their youthful times. This is where, currently, lovers (a young boy and a girl) establish a relationship that culminate with their marriage.

## The courtship process

With today's life style, a young man simply falls in love with a girl and establishes a relationship if he wins her. This would be around the ages of 15 to 16 years old. Upon passage of time, usually two to four years in the relationship, after the young man has now satisfied himself that his love partner qualifies as an ideal future wife and having acquired sufficient funds to pay a *bogadi*/lobola prize and its ancilliaries, he would approach his maternal uncle expressing his intent to marry. Depending on his close relations when he grew up, the young man may even choose to inform his paternal uncle or his mother for that matter. Upon receipt of the news, the uncle would summon the young man's parents and inform them accordingly.

## The preliminary visit process

Batlharo elders mention that nowadays the maternal uncle would ask the young man if he has accumulated sufficient funds to afford *bogadi*/lobola prize – encouraging the young man to pay *bogadi*/lobola and its ancillaries outright. This they view as a departure from cultural norms where *bogadi*/lobola was only paid upon the birth of several children of the marriage. In terms of Batlharo, as is the case with most Tswana-speaking cultures, a maternal uncle, followed by a paternal aunt, is the chief negotiator where marital issues arise pertaining to their neice or nephews. Together, the maternal uncle and paternal aunt would agree on inviting one or two other very close relatives (from both the paternal and maternal sides) to accompany them on paying a first visit to the identified girl's parents. Batlharo call this process *go bona lelwapa*, which means, 'to come to see the girl's homestead'.

The young man's delegation would be met by the girl's parents. They would exchange greetings, whereupon the chief maternal uncle would state the nature of their visit, i.e., that they are being sent by the young man's parents pertaining to their intent to take their daughter into a future marriage. At this juncture, the girl's parents, on hearing about their daughter's marriage prospects, would stop the young man's delegation from any further discussions on the matter, and pronounce that there are 'main, vital parents' to their daughter, who are not available to assist in marriage discussions'. They will plead that the discussions be deferred to an appropriate time and date where concerned parties from both families would be present. However, in the event that the girl's parents do not like the boy or his parents, they would immediately decline the marriage proposal, and vice versa.

The girl's parents would remain at home, rounding up the relevant maternal and paternal uncles and aunts to prepare for the next visit. At the next meeting, both families, being represented by uncles and aunts from both sides, the young man's delegation, through the maternal uncle, would formally inform the girl's delegation of their intent to marry a certain named girl from the family. The girl's maternal uncle would in turn respond to confirm the existence of a girl of the names mentioned, and that indeed they are willing to give her in marriage. Further discussion would arise, such as whether the groom intends to pay *bogadi/*lobola outright or at a future date, whether or not *bogadi/* lobola is paid in terms of live cattle or is to be paid in monetary terms; and the nature of clothing to be purchased by the groom's family. In the olden days, clothing bought for the girl entailed a headscarf, *tukwi* an*d* small shoulder blanket, *tsale*. Another vital question to determine the meeting outcome would be whether or not the girl was previously impregnated by the young man.

Thereafter, a possible and convenient future date is agreed on for the *patlo* process to be held. It needs to be pointed out that even without the outright payment of *bogadi/*lobola by the groom, Batlharo would still recognise marriage as indeed being validly constituted through the *patlo* process alone. This attribute is prevalent and shared by most Tswana-speaking cultures, even today. Where *bogadi/*lobola is paid outright, Batlharo demanded only two cattle or four sheep as bride-wealth. The wealthy are allowed to exceed the normal *bogadi/*lobola limit if they able to, but must avail the cattle or money in even numbers, i.e., not 1, 3, or 5 but 2, 4 or 6, etc. However, currently monetary payment for *bogadi/*lobola is allowed and the worth of a cow is measured in terms of the current market price of a one and half year old cow.

In the event that the young man had previously impregnated the girl in question, a penalty is imposed against the young man's family by the girl's maternal uncle. The penalty is usually in the form of a grown-up cow, called *kgomo ya tlhagela*, 'a penalty cow', paid by the young man's parents for his previous intrusion into the girl's yard. At the end of the preliminary visit, *go bona lelwapa*, the young man's family delegation would retire back home where the young man's parents would be informed of the deliberations held at the girl's home. This would now kick-start preparations for the *patlo* process.

Batlharo elders decry that nowadays, over and above the *bogadi*/lobola cattle, the young man's parents are provided with a long shopping list to purchase clothing for the girl, her mother and her maternal uncle. This entails a headscarf, *tukwi*, a German print dress, *leteise*, money to buy shoes, a shoulder blanket and a safety pin. As for the food-stuffs, they will demand tea, sugar, bread flour, oil, milk soft drinks, whisky and beer from the young man's delegation. All the listed items must be brought along at the upcoming *patlo* event.

## The bride-seeking process (*Patlo*)

According to Batlharo, bride-seeking, or *patlo* in Setlharo, is strictly attended to by the married and widowed couples who are familiar with the Setlharo customary marriage. It is a taboo for the married couples going through serious matrimonial issues to attend the *patlo* process. Equally, the divorced and unmarried people also do not partake in marriage proceedings. Batlharo elders say that they jealously guard against such, to protect the newly-weds' marriage from bad luck. It is believed that the married couples of good social standing, as well as the widowed ones, qualify to attend *patlo* proceedings because they are viewed as seasoned in terms of what marriage entails. They are therefore perfectly suited to render marriage counselling to the newly-weds. Equally, the widows and widowers are presumed to be also eligible to attend because their marriages only got terminated through death – God's will, and not through other undesired causes, like divorce or desertion.

As for the divorced couples, they are considered impure to take part. This is because divorce is viewed as a bad luck experience. The divorcees are assumed to be likely to render bad counselling to the newly-weds, as experienced from their failed marriages. The unmarried people are barred from attending the *patlo* process because they are considered still immature and without any marriage experience. They are therefore viewed as unsuitable to offer any marriage advice to the newly-weds – rather, they are taken to be likely to encourage bad behaviour of the newly-married couple. This explains why, after marriage, the newly-wedded are always advised during a counselling process, to cut any serious friendships or close relations with their former unmarried friends and associates, i.e., to choose new friends from the married class as their social status is viewed to have advanced to a sacred level.

At the commencement of the *patlo* marriage proceedings, the young man's delegation – appointed married and widowed uncles, aunts and close relatives – would already know the *patlo* process expectations and requisites of the girl's family, from the previous preliminary family discussions at the girl's home. In former times, a Setlharo young man's delegation would arrive at the girl's home in the early hours of the morning, at around 4 a.m. (currently they start the proceedings at 5 a.m.), knocking at the girl's family front yard gate. The girl's family delegation would be equally awaiting their arrival at the girl's home. After three to four knocks, the boy's delegation would be allowed into the yard and into the house. Men do not meet at the family *kgotla* as is the case with most Tswana ethnic groups. Instead, they mix and discuss the *patlo* proceedings together with their women in the house. During the *patlo* proceedings, the young man's delegation would be led by the chief maternal uncle. They will be seated and exchange greetings with the girl's delegation. However, at this juncture, the girl's delegation would remain mute, unresponsive to the greetings, until a *pula molomo* fee is paid to them, i.e., a fee of P50 in the past, and currently P100. In the views of Batlharo elders, the *pula molomo* fee symbolises that the young man's delegation are strangers to the girl's family, so they cannot just enter their premises to seek for a wife without first persuading them with something of value.

Upon receipt of the *pula molomo* fee, initial greetings by the young man's delegation would be responded to by the delegation from the girl's family. The chief maternal uncle would then proceed to announce to the girl's delegation that they have come to seek a bride, *ngwetsi*, for marriage to their young man, for example: 'We have been sent here to seek a wife in marriage to the Mogotsi family' (*Re rumilwe gotla go kopela boora Mogotsi ngwetsi*). The girl's chief maternal uncle, or one of his companions, would in response ask for the name of the girl requested, to which the young man's chief maternal uncle would state the name. The maternal uncle would then pretend not to know of such name, and about twice or so, may even bring in a different female youngster from the house to confirm if she is one of them. This would be just an attempt to either confuse them or to find out if indeed they know who their future bride is. But ultimately, the chief maternal uncle would pronounce to the young man's delegation that indeed the girl they are seeking is available, and he would accordingly give her to the young man's delegation in marriage.

At this juncture, the young man's delegation would further announce that they have brought a present in the form of a *mokwele* cow as a token of engagement of the girl into marriage, '*kgomo ya mokwele*'. Batlharo say that the *mokwele* cow was traditionally gifted to the girl's family during the betrothal proceedings. This was due to the fact that it was initially *symbolising a marriage engagement bond* between the two involved families. The Batlharo elders decry that, because the youngsters now choose their own lovers, and decide as to when they get married, a *mokwele* cow is currently gifted to the girl's family immediately after the latter has been offered as a bride to the young man's delegation during the *patlo* proceedings. Batlharo ere of the opinion that during the *patlo* proceedings, a *mokwele* cow, i.e., an engagement gift, is actually gifted to the girl's family as a token or symbol of sealing the marriage engagement bond. The *mokwele* cow would be immediately slaughtered upon receipt, cooked and eaten at the girl's home by all those who are present at the *patlo* event, apart from the young man's family delegation.

In the event that the young man had at some stage impregnated the girl during their courtship, which at times did happen, an aunt from the girl's women delegation would, during the *patlo* proceedings, inform the boy's family about the incident. This would be prior to agreeing to a request to offer the daughter in marriage. At this point the boy's delegation would accept that he had committed the offence, *tshenyo,* meaning damages, or *ntsa e jele matlalo* – literally meaning that, 'your dog has eaten our hide'. In terms of Batlharo tradition, where a young man impregnates a young woman at a pre-marriage stage, he is liable to compensate the girl's parents with a cow, *kgomo ya tlhagela*. This cow is usually brought and paid out at this stage – before the girl's delegation proceed to a stage to offer their daughter in marriage, as discussed above.

According to Batlharo elders, it is at the tail end of *patlo* process that the groom's delegation would furnish gifts to the bride in the form of a headscarf and *tsale*, a small shoulder blanket, during former times. Currently the gifts have multiplied to also include a dress, shoes, a half-sleeved top and some earrings for the bride. The bride's shoes are not bought by the groom *per se*: he provides money so that the bride buys them herself – it is believed that in the event the groom buys his wife a pair of shoes personally, this would cause the bride to ultimately elope and run away from her matrimonial house in due course. Batlharo elders decry that, unlike in times past, the girl's mother is currently additionally gifted by the groom with a dress and more. Moreover, the bride's maternal uncle is also gifted with a long winter coat and a hat.

The elders are also concerned that, nowadays, large groups of people from the young man's side would come to seek a bride, some even having matrimonial issues or being unmarried. Also, the girl's parents demand clothing and food stuffs from the young man's family to prepare for a wedding feast after the *patlo* process, something unknown during their forefathers' time. Besides, they now conduct both the *patlo* and *bogadi*/lobola simultaneously, inviting financial stress on the marrying couple who now finance their marriages from their pockets.

Upon completion of the Setlharo marriage process, the groom is called son-in-law, *mogwe* by his in-laws, whilst on the other hand, the bride is called daughter-in-law, *ngwetsi*, by her in-laws. The daughter-in-law addresses her husband's parents respectfully as father-in-law and mother-in-law, that is *matsale* (singular) or *bo matsale* (plural). On the other hand, the son-in-law, *mogwe*, would address his wife's parents as father-in-law and mother-in-law as *mogwagadi* (singular) or *bagwagadi* (plural).

## The bride-wealth (lobola) process (*Bogadi*)

Batlharo elders are quick to explain that in terms of their culture, as soon as *patlo* proceedings are completed, even prior to the issuance of *bogadi*/lobola, bride-wealth, a valid marriage is deemed to be concluded and sealed between to two involved families. What they would then do is to register the *patlo* proceedings with the tribal authority, the village chief (*kgosi*) for formal record.

A married girl would, as soon as it is practicably possible, be released to her in-laws' family to start up her new family life. Where the *bogadi*/lobola prize was paid outright, the bride would be delivered to her in-laws in the early hours of the very next day. She would stay with her in-laws until her husband completes the construction of their new homestead. Usually, the husband would build his wife a house within his family's ward. In terms of Batlharo culture, it is assumed that subsequent to marriage, the husband would work to the best of his ability, procreating children with his new wife, and building a new family. Simultaneously, he will be taking care of his in-laws, at the same time accumulating sufficient number of cattle to pay up the bride-wealth, *bogadi*/lobola, at an appropriate time. Batlharo also mention that in their culture, *bogadi*/lobola comprises only two cattle, four where the groom is wealthy or who holds himself in high esteem. Four sheep are also sufficient where cattle are unavailable. Because there was no formal employment in the past, the maternal uncle and the young man's parents used to assist by paying the two *bogadi/*lobola cattle for their son (more so that the son would have grown up taking care of the entire family livestock anyway). But where the family was not well off, the young man would end up having to work harder to accumulate the two cattle or the four sheep for *bogadi/*lobola.

Batlharo view *bogadi/*lobola as symbolising a young man's token of appreciation to the girl's family, for having contributed immensely to quality bringing up a wife for him, the wife who ultimately bore children for him. On the other hand, they believe *bogadi/*lobola is meant to buy 'the name' of children born into the marriage so they use their father's names (husband's name). This explains why *bogadi/*lobola, is paid up later on – five to six years down the line when the couple is assumed to have at least produced off-springs. Unlike among most Tswana, *bogadi/*lobola becomes due upon the birth of two to three children of the marriage, and not immediately – during the *patlo* process.

Unlike in the past, Batlharo say that currently, *bogadi/*lobola prize comprise of eight cattle – seven cows and one ox. Nowadays the maternal uncle gives the seven cows to the girl's parents and remains with the ox. The ox retained by the maternal uncle is called *kgomo ya lesori/masori.* He is accorded the ox as it is assumed that its value would afford the maternal uncle to buy the girl, his neice, a dress change during the wedding day, *mosese wa setlogolo waga malome*,. The maternal uncle also provides a cow for slaughter during the wedding. Accompanying the *bogadi/*lobola cattle during the process is a *seme* from the young man's delegation, i.e., a whip that drove down the *bogadi/*lobola cattle to the in-laws' place. The whip is actually symbolic, in the form of a bottle of whisky or any expensive alcoholic beverage with status. It is the maternal uncle who also takes over the *seme* gift from the young man's delegation.

Further, Batlharo are quick to mention that a married man who fails to pay *bogadi for gis wife is* not entitled to receive the same in future, for his daughters when they get married. Instead, it is his daughters' maternal uncles who would receive *bogadi/*lobola under such circumstances. For this reason, married Batlharo men are always willing and eager to end up paying *bogadi/*lobola so that they do not feel worthless at their future daughter's marriage and *bogadi/*lobola events. The elders also mention that *bogadi/*lobola nowadays are eight cattle, as opposed to the original two or four. Besides, *bogadi/*lobola is also payable in monetary terms. The monetary price for each cow equates to the current market value of a cow in the region – which is currently P2000.00 per small *bogadi/*lobola cow.

Batlharo elders do mention further that, initially, there was no clothing provided by the young man's family as gifts during the *patlo* process, except for a *tsale* and a *tukwi* – a headscarf and a small shoulder blanket provided to the bride. However, currently, some clothing and blankets are also required as part of the *patlo* gifts for the bride, her mother and the maternal uncle.

As stated above during the customary marriage process, the chief (*kgosi*) in the village is always approached to wed the couple when *bogadi/*lobola is involved. The *kgosi*, in the company of his subordinate chiefs, would register *bogadi/*lobola, offer counselling sessions, and issue a marriage certificate.

## The wedding ceremony process (*Mokete wa lenyalo*)

According to Batlharo, a wedding ceremony would usually be held at the newly-married girl's house hosted by her parents. It was usually conducted as a token to symbolise appreciation of acceptance of *bogadi/*lobola cattle by the bride's family. As they put it '*...seya bogwe se tletse, se bowe se tletse*' - in simple terms, '...were giving back to the in-laws, as much as they have provided for us through *bogadi/*lobola payment'. Batlharo mention that, traditionally, there was no particular day reserved for weddings. They would be held on any day and at any time to suit both the groom's and bride's families. A wedding day would be scheduled as soon as the *bogadi/*lobola process has been accomplished.

On the wedding day the groom would wear a black suit with a white shirt and black hat, whilst the bride would put on a white or beige two-piece costume with a hat. A cow will be slaughtered, some maize is cooked, and there will be some traditional brew. All members of the community are welcome to enjoy the feast, together with special guests from the groom's family. After the normal formal introduction of families from both sides, food and drinks are served, whilst various choirs from both the groom's and bride's families would take turns singing wedding songs and ululating. A talented uncle or aunt would also recite a poem or two to either the groom or the bride. The songs sang at the wedding were not just noisy but related various messages to the newly-weds. Some songs reveal and advise on how a married woman or man is expected to behave, some songs even expressing the beauty of being a married couple. This event usually ends in the evening when delegations from both families would secretly retire into a private house to offer some counselling to the newly-weds.

## The marriage counselling process (*Go laya*)

According to Batlharo, marriage counselling is of paramount importance. This is because marriage counselling serves to generally assist in guiding the newly-married couple on how to administer their marriage jointly and in harmony. As mentioned above, only the married couples and the widowed enjoy the privilege of attending and offering counselling to the newly-married couple. *Go laya* (counselling) is conducted in the evening of the wedding day (or on the day appointed by the two families where the young man only performed the *patlo* process without outright payment of *bogadi/*lobola). This process is called *go laya* – to offer counselling to the newly-married couple. It is believed that owing to the immense experience from their past marriage lives, they are better placed to relate to the newly-weds what marriage really entails. In the presence of her in-laws, the bride's family (the uncles then the aunts), would address the bride as to what is expected of her as a married woman – that she takes good care of her husband, cuts off unmarried friends, watches her tongue, and does not share her bedroom matters with the outside world, and so forth. As soon as they are done, the groom's family would equally offer him some counselling, almost the same advice as one offered to his wife, but with variations here and there. Counselling would normally take about an hour or less. After the counselling process is done, the two families now decide on a date to be set so that the bride is *formally transferred* to her in-laws' homestead. It is at her in-laws' place that she would stay until her husband affords to build her a house within the same ward.

### The transfer of bride to her in-laws process (*Go isa ngwetsi*)

Batlharo are quick to state that for them the most important part of their marriage processes is the *patlo* process (bride-seeking). They generally do not attach much effort to the process of transferring the bride to her in-laws. In Setlharo, this process is called *go isa ngwetsi kwaga matsalaagwe,* to take the bride to her in-laws' homestead. The bride is brought to her in-laws by her maternal uncle's wife (as chief aunt) in company of other aunts and close relatives. This entails a group of about four to eight married or widowed elders – the maternal uncle's wife with other aunts and uncles, and some close relations. Like at all other marriage proceedings, the divorced and unmarried are strictly not welcome to this event.

During the scheduled date, the bride's transferring delegation team would arrive at the groom's home in the early hours of the morning, around 5 a.m. In olden times, a bride was never transferred to her in-laws at noon as is the case nowadays. This was viewed as bringing a curse to her new home that can cause possible marriage breakdown. At the entrance of her in-laws' yard, the bride's delegation will be met with a group of married men and women (uncles and aunts), ululating and singing songs of reception to the new daughter-in-law. The bride's delegation would be ushered into the yard, walking on a straight line, some carrying the bride's belongings on their heads and passing them over to the bride's in-laws as they reach the house by the courtyard. Apart from her normal clothing and personal belongings, the bride would also have the new clothes gifted to her by the groom during the *patlo* ceremony. Besides, in the event the bride had some livestock gifted from her family, e.g., some cattle or small stock, they would be taken along to her in-laws during the transfer period.

Thereafter the bride would be shown her new bedroom. The husband's maternal uncle's wife would train the bride on how to make up the matrimonial bed. She would be strictly advised that their bedroom is not for child's play but a private area exclusively reserved for her and her husband to have rest or sleep. The uncles' wives from both couples would prepare fire for the bride, and also coach her on sweeping formats and other household chores. Batlharo believe that setting a fire signifies to the bride the essence of making tea and food for her husband before he sets off in the mornings.

## Batlharo's Marriage Rites and Significance of their Metaphorical Language and Symbolic Actions

### Rights, privileges and benefits in traditional marriage

In terms of the Setlharo custom, marriage brings honour and respect not only to the newly-married couple but to their respective parents and families as well. The social status of the newly-weds immediately changes from being ordinary residents to being adults and parents with dignity. They can even partake in tribal discussions or court processes at the *kgotla*. Batlharo mention, further, that due to this transformation the married couple now have a privilege and indeed a social right, to participate in future marriage proceedings, such as during the marriage preliminary visit process (*go kokota*), the bride-seeking process (*patlo*), the marriage counselling processes (*go laya*), attendance of matrimonial disputes, complaints and resolutions, and so forth. Batlharo believe that marriage also transforms the newly-married couple into lifetime friends, such that they complement one another and live together symbiotically, for the benefit of both. As one Motlharo woman puts it, "A married person always has someone (a spouse) to take care of, to be reminded of, or to discuss life issues with, whilst an unmarried person lacks these qualities".

## FACTORS OF CHANGE AND THEIR IMPACT ON TRADITIONAL MARRIAGE RITES AND ACTIVITIES

Batlharo explain that the introduction of both the civil marriage as well as the Christian marriage systems overshadowed the Setlharo marriage system. This is evidenced from their youths' current practise of not having faith in *patlo* as the ultimate marriage process, preferring to go a step further and combining *patlo* with a civil or Christian marriage – marriage duplication through at least two different marriage processes.

Secondly, the introduction of monetary value to payment of the bride-wealth *bogadi/* lobola has turned marriage into a business opportunity for the girl's family. In the past, *bogadi/*lobola was received by the chief maternal uncle, who would share this with his younger brothers, parents of the bride, and paternal aunt. Nowadays, it is the parents of the bride who determine the value of *bogadi/*lobola, some even demanding it in the form of money as against cattle. This is because in terms of value, families prefer to receive money rather than cattle, since management of cattle and their survival and security pose more risks than in the past. Previously, cattle were the backbone of wealth in a Setlharo family. Their youths nowadays have a cosmopolitan lifestyle.

Also, the tendency nowadays for the girl's parents to demand food, such as tea, sugar, bread flour, oil, milk, tobacco, two cases of soft drinks and beer, now tarnishes the image of the original Setlharo customary marriage process. They are seen by the elders as turning the young man's family to be a material source of wealth that milks and drains the young man well before he even commences building his new family.

The civil marriage process came with issues of property ownership between the couples – whether marriage is in or out of community of property, which triggered a sense of material wealth and property ownership. This destabilises some marriages, and causes some couples to take advantage of the loopholes and just marry for financial gains rather than for passion and family creation.

Currently, the young man would have a wife prudently chosen for him by his parents. Their marriage would continue for ages, in most cases, till death separates them. Nowadays, a young man chooses whichever girl he is interested in, falls in love and ultimately gets married, at times without even parental consultation, a point of departure from the original cultural norm. The current marriages struggle to survive, leaving more couples prone to divorce.

An urge amongst the youthful married couples for cosmopolitan lifestyles has divorced them from acquiring the wealth of the culture's marriage life. They find themselves spending a substantial part of their marriage life away from the villages where the culture's lifestyles are a norm. This ultimately results in high rates of divorce cases emanating from the financial challenges that come along with the modalities of urban life.

In the past, it was the chief maternal uncle, paternal aunt and other relatives who would approach the potential bride's family to conduct the preliminary visit process. Currently, it is the parents of the young man who personally conduct the preliminary visit. This emanates from lack of trust amongst close relatives nowadays. It is believed that, unlike in times past, the family delegation is prone to relating misguided information to the potential in-laws, with bid to destruct the marriage process in jealousy against the young man's family.

Inter-marriages on the other hand have diluted or overshadowed the Setlharo culture's marriage process. The original Setlharo marriage culture is becoming a challenge to the current youth who are more conversant with the civil marriage process than their culture's marriage process.

The already disappearing population of Batlharo senior citizens through death leaves the Setlharo culture's marriage and other cultural values susceptible to extinction. This is evidenced from a limited number of Setlharo youth having interest in its future preservation.

## PREVALENT PROBLEMS AND CHALLENGES IN BATLHARO'S TRADITIONAL MARRIAGES TODAY

There is a plethora of problems and challenges faced by traditional marriages currently. They stem from various factors, some of which are below.

Social expectations: traditionally, the newly-married couples had their parents and relatives to assist with the nourishment of their marriage. A father or uncle would contribute some cattle, a ploughing field would be allocated with some ploughing implements, an aunt or seasoned cousin would also render advice here and there on marriage issues. This materially helped the newly-married couple get settled into matrimonial life with a positive momentum. Currently, due to 'civilization', newly-married couples mostly commence their marriage life with accumulated debts arising from the wedding feast – this is where financial expenditure, mostly from the couples' or young man's savings is experienced, in purchasing all that is required to make a modern wedding. After this stage, the newly-married couple has other monthly financial commitments to meet, such as rentals and utility payments, loan repayments, educational and transport costs, and so forth. It is these factors, *inter alia*, that ultimately cause youthful married couples emotional stress and possible early marriage breakdowns.

Competition between traditional and civil marriage laws is yet another factor that impedes on a successful Setlharo traditional marriage. Unlike in the past, where marriage was exclusively through Setlharo processes, its combination with the civil marriage has caused current youth to lose focus on the essence of marriage and to concentrate more on the proprietary and financial aspects of life than on procreation and family building.

The Batlharo elders attribute blame to the current generation of parents, who are said to be relaxed in terms of their children's disciplinary measures. They say the current parental generation acquired the Setlharo traditional rules and norms from their parents, but failed to impart tem to the current youth. Most youth today choose to freely cohabit and bear children outside marriage. This is totally unthinkable in terms of original Setlharo culture. Currently, youth find themselves with cases of infidelity, disrespectfulness, and non-adherence to cultural beliefs.

The system of a son-in-law being adopted by his in-laws, and vice versa is dying out. It is the ever-growing cosmopolitan lifestyle the youths go through that erodes the initial strong relationships between sons-in-laws and their parents-in-law (and vice versa). This has caused a dent in the traditional Setlharo marriage processes, and slowly causing same to lose its intended cultural value.

Parental interference in children's marriages is also identified as a factor that caused some departure from the Setlharo customary marriage. Some parents are seen as administrators of their sons or daughters' marriage lives, making it difficult for the couples to manage their own affairs, ultimately causing the youthful couples to lose faith in traditional marriages and preferring civil ones where parents are less involved.

The disappearance of traditional initiation schools and ceremonies, b*ogwera* for young men and *bojale* for young women, is yet another factor alleged to have contributed to the demotion of Setlharo traditional marriage. These initiation schools were, in the Batlharo tradition, well suited to groom the youth into proper drivers of cultural norms and practices, marriage inclusive. Their disappearance left the current youth almost ignorant on a wealth of Setlharo cultural norms and practices, hence their reluctance to get associated with the same.

## Conclusions and Recommendations

It is evident that the traditional Batlharo marriage processes and procedures have been greatly compromised by various factors, as they pass from generation to generation. Reluctance by the youthful Batlharo to make a clear choice between marrying under customary and civil marriage is evident. Surely, we cannot go back to the drawing board and advocate for a reintroduction of Batlharo customary laws, norms and practices as originally handed down. By virtue of its dynamic nature, society would always go forward with developments and not backward. This entails at least slight, or perhaps vast, departures from the 'normal' way of doing things, at times caused by the civil law's constitutional enforcement. It is such scenarios that Batlharo attribute to the great changes.

The House of Chiefs (*Ntlo Ya Dikgosi*) must strategically seize an opportunity and advocate for a total retention and codification of all the original traditional customary marriage norms and practices. This could be done with necessary changes where the need arises, to fit and suit modern society. At the same time, all the irrational traditional marriage norms and practices must be abolished. This could be for the betterment of the current youth and a dynamic society. At the same time, each ethic group's norms and practices must be documented. This would accord upcoming generations to read and appreciate how their ancestors used to conduct themselves in terms of marriage. Besides, the young generation would still stand an opportunity to embrace traditional marriage norms and practices as a matter of style or pride in their respective cultures. The laws promulgated by the House of Chiefs must further harmonise the traditional norms and practices with the Constitution and the Laws of Botswana generally. This could alleviate the issue of some looking at a marriage as a financial source, putting a monetary price on a girl who earns literally nothing from bride-wealth.

# 12

# BATLOKWA

*Prof. Brankie Nlhekisana & Dr. Pearl Seloma*

**Totem**: *Thakadu* – Antbear/Aardvark

**Clan Poem** (*Leboko la Batlokwa*)

*Ke mafitshwana a go rekwa ka kgomo*
*Mafeta kgomo a fe motho*
*Ba ga Mmanakana-di- Mosima*
*Ba ga Mmanakana-di-ganong*
*Ga ga mosi mmolaya moapei*
*Moapeelwana a sale a lela*
*Ba ga Nkwenyana-a-Nkwe o apereng?*
*Nkwe ke apere tau.*

## BRIEF HISTORICAL BACKGROUND

Tlokweng is a village located to the south-east of Gaborone city and is the headquarters of the Batlokwa ethnic group in Botswana. Batlokwa are one of the Setswana-speaking people of Bantu origin. Batlokwa originated from the Transvaal Province in South Africa, now known as the Northern Province. Records have shown that in around 1856 Batlokwa crossed into Botswana escaping from racial unrest in South Africa. Upon their arrival in Botswana, they settled among the Bakwena ethnic group where they were asked to pay tribute to the Bakwena Paramount Chief but refused to comply, and this later led to the establishment of a separate Batlokwa tribal reserve by the British in 1933. The history of Batlokwa is rife with struggles over land ownership. Batlokwa, who now venerate the ant-bear (*thakadu*), are known in Botswana for the tradition of burying the dead in their yards. Some researchers have viewed this type of burial practice as a subtle communal land protection and safeguarding strategy. Batlokwa are generally proud of their identity hence are still practising most of their rites of passage, with the exception of the initiation rites which do not feature in their traditional life agenda of today.

This chapter focuses mainly on the meaning and importance of *lenyalo* among the Batlokwa of Tlokweng, the steps involved in their traditional marriages, rights and benefits associated with marriage, and the impact of change on traditional marriage rites related activities, among others.

## Understanding Marriage from the Batlokwa's Point of View

With reference to the findings of the field research, conducted in March to April 2017 in Tlokweng, marriage among Batlokwa is a union between two people, which also involves and unites their two families in a cultural context. There are those who believe that marriage was created by God and as such one gets married by the grace from God; others argued that God is the one who created marriage so that the married couple (of a man and a woman) could increase and multiply. For others, marriage is when a man and a woman take a conscious decision to live together so that they raise their children together, and according to what is expected of a husband and a wife culturally. In other words, it is through marriage that the couple is able to build a home and raise their children accordingly. To some marriage is a sign of self-respect and respect for those who are married. This is why in Setlokwa culture, a man who is not married is considered irresponsible and useless and as a result he is referred to as *sekopa* (good for nothing). However, there are those who are of the view that, generally speaking, nowadays people do not respect the institution of marriage as evidenced by the high divorce rate among young couples because some of them were married for financial gains rather than for love and mutual respect.

## Types of Weddings

### Traditional

In terms of the types of *manyalo* (marriages) among Batlokwa, they mainly identify three. The first is the traditional one which they refer to as *lenyalo la Setswana* (Setswana wedding); this is where the couple gets married at the *kgotla* with the *kgosi* (chief) officiating and issuing them with a certificate to verify the union. However, in this type of *lenyalo*, there was no certificate in the past because the presence of the *kgosi* was living proof of wedlock. In this type of marriage, *bogadi* (bride-wealth) is also given to the bride-to-be parents at the *kgotla*. This type of wedding is no longer practised commonly among the Batlokwa of Tlokweng because of the changing lifestyle.

### District Commissioner's wedding

This type of marriage is officiated by the District Commissioner (DC) (*Molaudi*). This is the most common type of *lenyalo* nowadays amongst Batlokwa of Tlokweng.

### Church wedding

The *lenyalo la kwa kerekeng* (the church wedding) is officiated by a priest or religious leader at church. With this type of *lenyalo*, prior to the actual wedding day, the couple usually collects their legal documents from the DC and may sign them at church on another day.

## Some Traditional and Continuing Marriage Rites of Passage

In the past, one could only marry after he or she had gone through the initiation rites to be considered a mature man or woman. This puberty rite culminated between the ages of 16 and 22. Girls who had gone through the initiation rite were considered potential good wives because they would have been taught about their traditional values and gender-specific roles. Insofar as the current research findings are concerned, the ideal age for marriage for men ranged between ages 30 and 35 years, and between 21 and 29 years for women. Others said there was no specific age limit since some girls were married at 18 years old. Most male informants stressed the importance of maturity and the ability to take their responsibilities seriously before one could think of get married.

Consequently, Batlokwa do observe a number of taboos associated with marriage. For example, traditionally, when the wedding day drew nearer, the girl was not supposed to move about in the village (*o ne a sa tsamaye-tsamaye mo motseng*); and she had to safeguard herself against any bad influence (*go ikilela*). This was the time when a traditional doctor would be called to come and fortify the hearth (*go tshwara maiso/go thaya maiso*) where the food for the wedding celebration was going to be cooked, and to protect the marriage against any evil intentions or mishaps. The boy's parents were the ones responsible for engaging their traditional family doctor. This doctor also safeguarded the betrothal clothes (*matsisiwa*). This was done to seal the marriage and ensure that there is no divorce that takes place in the future. It was, and is still, taboo to have extra-marital affairs. Any married person was and is expected to show good moral values (*go itshwara*). *Lenyalo*, on its own, was considered taboo, hence betrothal clothes were brought by the maternal uncle's wife (*mmamalome*) to the bride-to-be's natal home in the evening. Another taboo is that the food cooked for the celebration can only be eaten by any person after the couple has eaten that food first (*ba sena go loma*). Setlokwa marriage follows a number of steps with specific role players.

# THE MARRIAGE PROCESS

## BETROTHAL (*PEELETSO*)

In the past there was a preliminary pseudo-marriage known as *peeletso.* This was when the boy's parents tell the girl's parents that they would like their son to marry their under-age daughter at a later time in life. This practice was common in the past when men used to migrate to South Africa to work in the mines, and very often when returning back home were ready to marry the girl already identified by their parents. This practice has since disappeared, or at leasr is no longer practised, and hence most informants said there is no *peeletso* in the Setlokwa culture. What is commonly practiced nowadays is courtship.

## COURTSHIP

The first step today in the Setlokwa marriage culture is courtship. In the past, however, there was no courtship because it was the responsibility of the boy's parents to find or choose a partner for their son when he had reached marriageable age (*mosimane o ne a batlelwa mosadi*). The parents ensured that they chose a wife for their son from a good and well-mannered family not associated with bad behaviours such as witchcraft (*boloi*) or drunkenness (*botagwa*). However, things have changed because nowadays boys choose their own partners whom they have dated for some time before deciding to marry them. However, to kick-start the marriage process the boy informs his parents through his paternal uncle of his intention to get married. The next step that follows courtship is what the informants refer as *go kokota* or *go itshupa,* which is the preliminary visit of the boy's biological parents to the girl's parents or guardians.

## PRELIMINARY VISIT (*GO KOKOTA*)

After the boy had informed his biological parents that he had found someone he wants to marry, the parents usually ask him who the girl is, where she lives and, more importantly, if he himself is ready in terms of *bogadi*, among other things. On the other hand, the girl would also inform her parents that they should expect a visit from such and such family. After this discussion, the boy's parents visit the girl's parents to inform them of their son's intent. The girl's parents would then tell the boy's parents that they want a certain number of cattle for the bride-wealth (*bogadi*), or, if they want to give it in monetary terms, they would tell them how much each cow would cost. Then the two parties would also discuss the procedures and what is expected of them regarding bride-seeking (*patlo)* and betrothal clothes (*matsisiwa*). This kind of visit by the boy's biological parents is called *go kokota* (knocking at the daughter-in-law to be's parents). After the boy's parents have left, the girl's parents would call their daughter and inform her of the visit officially, and to find out from her if she was in agreement (*a o dumela go nyalwa*). If she says she is in agreement, then the consultation proceedings start (*morero o a simologa*). After the *go kokota* stage, the parents (on both sides) are expected to officially inform the maternal uncle (*malome*), the paternal aunt (*rakgadi*), the mother's younger sister (*mmane*), the father's younger brother (*rangwane*) and their spouses, on each side, about their son's intent or their daughter's willingness to get married. These eight people are called *ditlhogo* (heads) and are the first to know of this secret. Henceforth the *ditlhogo* party now takes over as the go-betweens or spokespersons of the biological parents (*go tswa maoto/ ke bone jaanong ba ba romiwang*). At an agreed time, the boy's maternal uncle and paternal uncle, together with their spouses, go and tell the girl's family that they intend to come and ask for the girl's hand in marriage (*go batla*) and to pay the bride-wealth (*go ntsha bogadi*) at such and such a time. After they have been notified, a meeting is called by the uncles to inform other members of the extended family that their nephew or niece is getting married at such and such a time. Then the last meeting is called where everyone is informed about the upcoming wedding celebration, including distant relatives, friends, neighbours, and the community at large, within that locality. After this step, the bride-seeking preparations follow.

## BRIDE-SEEKING (*PATLO*)

Those who are expected to take the lead in bride-seeking are the *ditlhogo* team, namely maternal uncle, paternal uncle, maternal aunt, paternal aunt and their spouses. However, representatives of other relatives, neighbours and friends may also participate in the process. In the past, *patlo* was held at two different times namely the one for men and another one for women. The men held theirs in the morning at the family *kgotla* led by the maternal and paternal uncles, while the women held theirs late in the afternoon (*maitseboa*) in the compound (*mo lwapeng*) led by the maternal uncle's wife and the paternal aunt.

Nowadays the *patlo* rite takes place around five-thirty or six in the morning. As in the past, men hold *patlo* procedures outside the yard at the family *kgotla* while the women conduct theirs in the compound courtyard. The main participants are still *ditlhogo*, together with other relatives and members of the community. When the men representing the groom arrive at the *kgotla*, they all kneel down and greet the men from the girl's side, who would be seated already on the chairs. After the greetings, the boy's maternal uncle asks that they pray. After prayer, he tells the girl's family team that he has been sent by the groom's parents to come and ask for their daughter's hand in marriage. The girl's uncle would then ask him a few questions such as the name of the girl, the name of her parents and her *kgotla*. After he successfully answers these questions, the boy's paternal uncle may say a few words also. The girl's maternal uncle would then give consent that he gives them the girl's hand in marriage and states the number of cattle he wants for the bride-wealth. The boy's maternal uncle then responds by informing them that they would go and get the bride-wealth, but at this time they are not alone; they are with the women who have also been sent by the boy's parents to ask for the girl's hand in marriage. One of the men would then leave others at the *kgotla* to go and inform the women delegation that they have completed the bride-seeking procedures.

The women from the boy's family would then walk in one straight line in complete silence led by the maternal uncle's wife, followed by the paternal aunt, then the paternal uncle's wife and the boy's mother's young sister; then follow other women who have accompanied them. The belief is that if they talk while in that procession, it means their daughter-in-law to be would also be a talkative wife. While walking in that procession, none of the women should look back because it is believed that if they do the daughter-in-law will go back to her natal home, and not stay long in the marriage. As they enter the compound, they usually find the women from the girl's family already seated on the floor in the same sequence. The wife of the maternal uncle of the boy then greets everybody and asks that they begin with prayer. After the prayer, she would explain to the women that she has been sent by the boy's parents to come and ask for their daughter's hand in marriage. The girl's maternal uncle's wife will then ask for the girl's name, the name of her parents, and that of her *kgotla*. After the answers have been provided, the paternal father's sister, paternal uncle's wife and mother's younger sister also repeat the same words that they have come to ask for the girl's hand in marriage. The girl's maternal uncle's wife would then respond by saying she is giving them the *sego sa metsi* (the water gourd/calabash). The boy's family would respond by ululating and singing to show their joy and happiness.

After this, the boy's maternal uncle's wife would ask that they be allowed to leave for a moment to go and bring the agreed items for the girl. These items are called *matsisiwa*. These are items bought by the boy's family and given to the girl's family on the day of the bride-seeking ritual. They consist of a German print dress, undergarments, shawl, headscarf, night blanket and shoes. These things are bought by the groom for his wife-to-be, but if she already has children, they too will be bought some clothing. *Matsisiwa* symbolise the fact that the man is capable of taking care of his wife (*mosadi gaake a kgase*). *Matsisiwa* are presented or given before *bogadi*. The *ditlhogo* team would then go and get *matsisiwa* clothes from the packed vehicles outside the yard, and when they approach the gate, they ululate to signal to the girl's party that they have come back. The *ditlhogo* from the girl's family would then go and receive the bags from the *ditlhogo* delegates of the boy's family. The clothes are carried on the head, and those who receive them also put them on their heads, and then go straight to the house. The *ditlhogo* from the boy's family would then follow them into the house and open the suitcases to showcase what they have brought for their daughter-in-law to be. The girl's *ditlhogo* team would then inspect the contents of the suitcases to see if they bought what they were asked to buy. If they are happy, they would ululate. After that they all go outside, and the girl's maternal uncle's wife would announces to the women on her side that they have seen the clothes and they are satisfied. The women from the boy's family would then ask to leave so that they go and inform their male counterparts that they have completed the process. Both the men and women from the boy's family would now bring the bride-wealth.

*Patlo* is attended strictly by married men and women. It is mandatory that the men wear long-sleeved jackets of their choice. On the other hand, the women are expected to wear plain royal blue German print skirts, white blouses and shawls, and a headscarf. According to the Batlokwa women, a white shawl represents a good heart that the bride-to-be is expected to have. In the past, Batlokwa used to wear royal blue German print skirt, a black shawl or blanket (*mogagolwane*) and headscarf.

During the bride-seeking procedures there may be some penalties, as in the case when the boy's party fails to keep the time agreed for the *patlo* ritual; the boy's party may be charged a cow. Also, if anyone in the boy's family team violates the bride-seeking traditional rules and regulations, when charged they pay the fine in monetary terms on the spot.

In the case of the groom-to-be and his relatives, at the time of the *patlo* event, they are expected to be humble, respectful and to speak in low tones. They are not supposed to argue, even if they feel aggrieved. The bride-to-be's family on the other hand are expected to be strict, but at the same time respectful. Whatever members of the girl's party tell the groom's team to do, they act on it without questioning anything. However, they are expected also to be hospitable and considerate.

The research findings have shown that changes have taken place in the Setlokwa *patlo* ritual. For example, during the *patlo* event, women used to sit on the floor with outstretched legs and not on chairs. Nowadays, women often sit on chairs. Again, in the past, only the bride-to-be was bought some clothes by her in-laws to be, whereas today even relatives such as the maternal uncle and paternal aunt are bought a jacket and a shawl, respectively. Traditionally, *matsisiwa* clothes consisted of a blanket, unsewn fabric for the girl's dress, and shoes. Currently, other things have been introduced into this package, such as a homemade or store-bought dress and undergarments for the bride-to-be. *Matsisiwa* clothes were also brought into the girl's home in the evening, and were to be seen only by older close female relatives, while today they are presented to the girl's family in broad daylight, and can be seen by everybody. *The patlo* ritual mostly paves way for the bride-wealth event.

## Bride wealth (*Bogadi*)

For Batlokwa, bride-wealth (*bogadi*) is a token of appreciation from the groom's family to the bride's family. They appreciate the fact that they have been given a child who henceforth would be the one running errands (*go rongwa*). *Bogadi* is therefore a sign of love and self-respect (*go itlotla*) hence to marry without giving *bogadi* becomes an awkward case. For instance, that can only happen when the two sets of parents have agreed to the anomaly prior to the *patlo* ritual. Under such circumstances, the *bogadi* may be given at a later time. In the past, it was the boy's parents who gave *bogadi* on behalf of their son. Nowadays, it is the boy who is expected to give the *bogadi* himself.

Among the Batlokwa of Tlokweng, *bogadi* is presented during the *patlo* event. After the boy's family have completed the bride-seeking procedures and have received *matsisiwa* clothes, they often ask to leave to join their male counterparts. Both men and women from the boy's family deliver *bogadi* (in the form of a certain agreed number of cows or in the form of money) to the men from the girl's family at the *kgotla*, outside the compound. The *bogadi* cows are usually transported in a truck. The maternal uncle and groom-to-be would walk side by side in front of the truck pretending to be beating the cows with a stick, whistling and praising them. In the past, the stick that was used to beat the cows was treated by a traditional doctor (*se alafilwe*) to ward off bad luck so that it does not follow the new couple. At this time, the women follow the men, ululating all the way. If *bogadi* is in the form of money, the groom usually holds the money with a stick, and walks side by side with the maternal unclem whistling and praising the imagined cows, while the women ululate all the way to the *kgotla* outside the compound. The boy's maternal uncle would then show the cows to the girl's maternal uncle first and then to everyone around. After the girl's family has received *bogadi*, the girl's maternal uncle goes to the compound to call the women from the girl's family to come and see the *bogadi*. Then the women would ululate for joy and appreciation of the received *bogadi*. Once *bogadi* has been received, the girl is considered married. After this event, the women from the girl's family will invite those from the boy's family to join them in the compound (*kwa lwapeng*), while the men from both families remain in the *kgotla* outside the compound. Thereafter, the boy's maternal uncle (*malome*) would introduce the groom-to-be to his in-laws at the *kgotla* and at the compound. The girl's maternal uncle's wife would also bring the bride-to-be to greet her in-laws, starting with the men at the *kgotla* and then the women at the compound courtyard. If the marriage is going to be officiated by the District Commissioner on the same day, the girl goes back inside the house to get dressed up. While still getting ready to leave for the District Commissioner's office, tea is served to the visitors present.

One thing worth noting is that it is compulsory that the animals given for *bogadi* should all be cows of an even number. Traditionally, two head of cattle were given as *bogadi*, but later the number changed to four cows. Of the four *bogadi* cows, one of them is usually from the boy's maternal uncle, and is the one that walks in front of the other three (*e di etelela pele*). In essence, the boy's maternal uncle gives the girl's maternal uncle *bogadi*. Within the *bogadi* cows, the girl's maternal uncle takes one and gives the remaining three to the girl's biological parents. However, the maternal uncle can only take one of the cows provided he had bought clothes for his niece (*fa a apesitse motlogolo*). Nowadays, *patlo*, *bogadi* and *pholoso* (the day of matrimonial ties) processes are conducted on Thursdays, while the wedding celebration is held on Saturdays. Further, there is another extra cow which the groom has to give to the bride's family known as *tlhagela*, which serves as payment for damages done to the bride by impregnating her before she was officially married. Even if the couple has two or more children, the groom still pays one *tlhagela* cow and not an ox or a bull because to give a male animal would be considered an insult, in Setlokwa culture. It has been observed that there is no difference in procedures discussed above, regardless of whether a Motlokwa woman marries a Motlokwa man or a man from another cultural group.

In the past, however, *bogadi* was given to the girl's parents in secret, while nowadays it is given and received in the presence of everyone present. Nowadays, the *bogadi* cows have increased from two or four to up to eight or ten cows. *Bogadi* also can now be in the form of money rather than cows. The price tag for each *bogadi* cow also varies from family to family, whereas in the past it used to be P1000.00, now it can be as high as P3500.00 each. Also, *bogadi* has nowadays become a commercial commodity rather than a token of appreciation as was the case in the past. Some Batlokwa families charge whatever they want based on their educational, social and economic status, or influenced by the ethnicity of the one paying the bride-wealth. Most of the changes are a result of the fact that Batlokwa now copy cultural practices of other ethnic groups and either abandon or dilute their own. As mentioned earlier, the wedding celebration takes place mostly on Saturdays in Tlokweng.

## Wedding ceremony (*Mokete wa lenyalo*)

In the past, the wedding celebration was held on a Thursday at the bride's home, and on Friday at the groom's home. And at the time, only those who were invited attended the ceremony, whereas nowadays everybody attends, whether invited or not. The bride also used to wear pink or cream white two-piece attire. There were also only two bridesmaids, but nowadays their number is determined by the economic status of the couple. Also, in the past there were no hired tents, because the bride and the groom simply sat under a beautiful *letlhajwa* shelter with a reed (*letlhaka*) canopy. The floor of this shelter would also be beautifully decorated with various cow dung designs (*makgapho*). During the wedding celebration in the past, there were no ushers, because the older daughters-in-law in the compound were the ones responsible for feeding or taking care of the guests.

Over time, the days for the wedding celebration were changed to Saturday and Sunday because most people do not go to work on those days. Saturday was the day when the celebration was held at the bride's home, while on Sunday the wedding was celebrated at the groom's place. Today, the bride wears the white lace gown and a veil, and later on during the ceremony she would wear another set of clothes known as *diaparo tsa tšhentšhi* (literally 'clothes for change'). And after a while the maternal uncle would also ask to take the bride (his niece) to his home to wear the attire that he has bought for her, after which she goes back to her natal home. Later in the day she would be expected to pack her belongings and be escorted to her in-laws' place. Another celebration would then be held there on the Sunday. On Monday morning, her maternal uncle's wife and the paternal aunt would pay the bride a visit at her in-laws to check how she was doing, or if she slept well (*gore o robetse jang?*).

Nowadays, the wedding celebration takes place on two consecutive Saturdays, the first being at the bride's and the second at the groom's place. The celebrations are generally held in a large hired and decorated tent with all its accessories. There is a lot of feasting on this day, cows are slaughtered, and their meat mostly cooked by men, while traditional beer is brewed by women, and different kinds of dishes are prepared by youngsters. All these costs make today's wedding celebrations very expensive, often plunging the newly-wed couple into serious financial problems, debts, quarrels, abuse and divorce.

The bride's maternal uncle is expected to slaughter a cow for his niece, brew traditional beer, buy her some clothes (dress, shoes and a fancy hat), as well as buy milk and tea leaves. This uncle is likewise entitled to be given one of the *bogadi* cows. The groom's maternal uncle's role on the other hand is to seek the girl's hand in marriage. Maternal uncles from both the bride's and the groom's side are also responsible for leading the marriage negotiations (*go tsamaisa morero*). The groom's maternal uncle is expected also to contribute one cow, traditional beer, bread, milk and tea.

The bride's father's younger brother's (*rrangwane*) role is to help the maternal uncle (*malome*) and support or endorse whatever the maternal uncle says during various wedding procedures. The bride's paternal aunt's (*mmane*) responsibility is to ensure that things are done accordingly (*o a laola*); she also gives away her brother's daughter to her in-laws (*o atlhola ngwana kgaitsadie*). If the couple already has children, she is the one who carries the children on her back when their mother is taken to her in-laws, and hands them over to the groom's paternal aunt (*rakgadi*). The paternal aunt, the maternal uncle's wife and the bride or the groom's mother's younger sister are also responsible for dressing the bride in her wedding clothes in the presence of the groom's paternal aunt, maternal uncle's wife and the groom's mother's younger sister. One other responsibility of the bride's maternal uncle's wife is to look after the bride throughout the wedding celebration. Other relatives and neighbours mostly help with all other chores related to the occasion, including general food preparations.

Food is considered especially important at the wedding ceremony, hence a lot of food is usually cooked on the day to cater for everybody present. It is believed that food unites people and is a sign of hospitality. If people are fed well at the wedding ceremony, it is taken as a guarantee that the newly-weds were not going to starve and would likewise emulate the hospitality they were accorded by their families; they would also be caring, loving and giving of what they have to others.

Among the Batlokwa, the groom has to be present at the girl's place when the wedding ritual cow is slaughtered, hence it is taboo to slaughter it in his absence. This cow is believed to have some protective powers (*sepheko*). After the cow is slaughtered, the paternal aunt is given some small pieces of meat to cook, and then give to the bride and groom to eat. The special meat is called *molomo* (literally 'that which you bite'). It is believed to unite the man and the woman forever in marriage. No one is allowed to eat any type of food on the wedding day before the bride and the groom eat this special meat. The couple has to eat this meat together to signify that they are now united as one and should respect each other. In the past, the traditional doctor would secretly treat the wedding ritual cow and the hearth where the food of the wedding celebration will be cooked.

Another important meat portion is called *ngati*. This kind of meat is eaten by married women only. The bride eats this meat for the first time after being given a piece by her mother-in-law. *Ngati* is a meat portion which signals that she must have sexual relations with her husband only, and shun promiscuity.

There is also a meat portion called *motlhana* that is given to the bride's family after escorting the bride to her in-laws' place. This meat portion signals the wish that she should give birth to her own children. This is because it is believed that the fertility seed is found around the woman's waist (*motlhana),* hence expected to give birth to children now that she is officially married.

The groom, on the other hand, is given *lebogo* (one of the front limbs of a cow) as a signal of the fact that he is expected to take care of his family and be helpful to his in-laws. This meat also symbolically encourages him to be generous or open-handed. For example, if he has slaughtered a cow, he should share some of the meat with his in-laws.

Moreover, *masufu* and *mesetlase* meat portions are given to men and women of the village, respectively, the next day after the wedding ceremony. *Diphilo* (kidneys) on the other hand are given to the oldest man in the family, while *sebete* (liver) is eaten by women on the day of the wedding celebration, and it is usually cooked by daughters-in-law. *Tlhogo* (head of the ritual cow) is given to the maternal uncle. It is normally cooked at his place the following day after the wedding ceremony, where he invites close relatives to come and share the meat with him. Lastly, the bride's family usually gives the groom's family a bucket of traditional beer and bread when they leave at the end of the wedding celebration, and the same happens when the bride's family leaves the compound of the groom's family at the end of the wedding celebration.

The informants concur with the fact that today's wedding ceremonies are awfully expensive and costly when compared to the past because of the monies spent on hiring tents and their contents, buying very expensive rings, hiring wedding venues, involving catering services, buying clothes for the bridal team, among other expenses involved.

In the past, during the *patlo* ritual and wedding ceremony, only married women were allowed to serve the bride's family members (*bagwagwadi*) and not ushers who are still not married, as is the norm today. Also, wedding celebrations in the past were held in the natal homes of the bride and the groom, respectively, whereas nowadays some of the wedding celebrations are held at hotels, public halls and or at other wedding venues. Traditionally there is no wedding celebration without pre- or post-marriage counselling.

## Marriage counselling (*Go laya*)

Among the Batlokwa, marriage counselling is a secretive ritual, hence attended only by married people. Counselling of the newly-wed couple is done in the late afternoon in the presence of the bride and the groom. It is done inside the house with doors and windows closed, irrespective of the weather. This is to ensure that people outside do not hear what is being said, so that the wise words of advice from married people should not be overheard by those outside the house. Containing the discussions inside the house also teaches the bride and groom that they should discuss their issues inside the house and not in public. The bride is counselled on the wedding day at her natal home by her male and female relatives, in the presence of her in-laws. This takes place before she is escorted to her in-laws' residence. The bride is counselled while she is seated on a skin mat or kaross (*phate).*

The groom, on the other hand, is counselled while he is seated on a chair at his natal home in the presence of his in-laws. The counselling of the groom is done on the day that his wife is brought to her in-laws' place. The younger brother to the groom's father's is the one responsible for ordering the people to speak one after another. Those who give advice follow this sequence: maternal uncle first, then paternal aunt, the groom/bride's mother's young sister, maternal uncle's wife, mother's elder sister, mother, father and father's younger brother as the last person to speak or to give advice.

During the counselling session, the bride and the groom do not say anything; they simply listen to what the elders are telling them. Generally, the bride and groom are counselled on issues related to marriage life and responsibilities. Since the wedding celebration takes place first at the bride's natal home, there is a need to escort her later to her in-laws place the same day or the following day or week, as arranged and agreed by the couple and their two families.

### TRANSFER OF BRIDE TO HER IN-LAWS (*GO ISA NGWETSI*)

In the past, the bride was taken to her in-laws' place in the late afternoon of the same day that she got married. The bride is taken to her in-laws by the *ditlhogo* team and other family members. Even if her natal home was a distance from that of her in-laws, those responsible always ensured that she did not spend the night at her biological parents' home. Customarily, the bride should not arrive at her in-laws' place at night or after sunset because Bathokwa believe that things will not go well for her. It is also believed that if she arrives after sunset, she will make it a habit of coming home late.

On the day she arrives at her in-laws' home, she enters the compound covered with a blanket so that nobody sees her. Other people are allowed to see her the following day, when she is again wearing her wedding gown. As she enters the compound, sorghum grains are thrown ritualistically on her face to signal the fact that she is expected to plough crops and work in the fields. Thereafter she would be shown her bedroom. Her mother's younger sister would demonstrate to the bride how to make up her bed so as to do the same at all times. She also tells her that her bedroom is a private room for her and her husband only, so friends and her mother-in-law should not sit on her bed at any time. She is also told how to behave when she is with her husband in the bedroom.

On the morning of the following day, she is expected to sweep the yard, prepare warm water for her father-in-law and mother–in-law to bathe with, as well as to make them some tea. Her best lady (*motshwari*) also accompanies her to her in-laws' place and helps her with the household chores upon arrival.

The procedure of taking the bride to her in-laws' place has changed over time. Nowadays the bride is taken to her in-laws a week later. This is because the second and final part of the celebrations is held the following Saturday as dictated by the couple's work schedule. Another obvious change is the fact that the bride is no longer covered with a blanket when escorted and enters her in-laws place for the first time after her marriage. As in some cultures, there is a reverse step – taking the bride back to her natal home.

### BRIDE TAKEN BACK TO HER NATAL HOME

The day after the bride had been escorted to her in-law's home, her new maternal uncle's wife and paternal aunt accompany her back to her biological parents' home so that she can go and pack and take all her belongings. By being escorted back to her natal home gives her the liberty to visit her biological parents whenever she feels like, or when it is necessary as in times of bereavement and to attend wedding celebrations. Marriage among the Batlokwa comes with some rights, privileges and benefits as in many cultures of Africa.

## RIGHTS, PRIVILEGES AND CHALLENGES ASSOCIATED WITH TRADITIONAL MARRIAGE PRACTICES

According to Batlokwa, a married person has the right to participate in the bride-seeking ritual (*patlo*), counselling sessions (*go laya*), and any other negotiation procedure (*morero)* performed by other married people. A married person also gains respect from his/her family and the community at large. Marriage gives him/her dignity. The informants stressed the fact that if a couple had simply signed at the District Commissioner's office (*kwa ga molaodi*) without having gone through the *patlo* process, such a couple is not allowed to take part in the above, until they go through their own *patlo* ritual. According to the informants, marriage is an institution which requires perseverance for one to pass the test.

## Prevalent problems and challenges in traditional marriages today

There are many problems and challenges in marriages today, which may lead to divorce. Some of the problems and challenges expressed by most of the informants include promiscuity, lack of respect for each other, financial problems, insecurity and self-centredness. Some of these problems are a result of luxurious wedding celebrations, social expectations that often clash with individual thoughts or expectations, unreasonable expectations, and existing inequalities between men and women, to name a few. Other problems are associated with mothers-in-law who have not accepted fully their daughters-in-law, or who interfere in the affairs of their son's marriage. However, every ethnic group has its own ways and means of solving some of the problems and challenges referred to above.

Among the Batlokwa when one gets married, he/she is adopted by the parents of the other; which means the bride's new parents are the groom's adoptive parents, and the groom's new parents are now the bride's adoptive parents. Traditionally, if the husband is the source of trouble, the wife was expected to tell her in-laws not her biological parents, and vice versa. The issue would then be discussed and resolved in the home, but if it fails then the maternal uncles were called to come and help with the case. However, very often the couples were encouraged to resolve their own problems first, before involving anybody else.

Quite a number of issues were raised by the informants that they believe to be the root causes of marital problems. Besides the parents who often interfere in their children's marital affairs, there are also issues of individualism, lack of respect for one another, self-centeredness, financial pressures, competition with other couples, living beyond their means, and the tendency to disregard parental guidance and counselling. Most informants, male and female, were of the opinion that nowadays there is no real marriage, but only fake marriages. They also argued that some men and women stay together before they are married, a thing which most informants view as bad behaviour. This means, if such people have already been staying together, by the time they get married, all the love they had for each other would have diminished. Conversely, in the past, the boy would secretly visit the girl's home at night when the parents are asleep and wake up in the early hours of the morning before the parents wake up, if at all he spent the night with his girlfriend. This sneaking in and waking up in the small hours of the morning would ultimately take its toll on him and hw would eventually decide to get married so that he freely visits or stays with his loved one at all times. Nowadays, however, it seems most youngsters who sneak in at night to visit their girlfriends no longer respect or fear parents, hence some get up in broad daylight without any shame. Behavioural change is one of the factors that have greatly impacted traditional marriage rites and activities in Tlokweng, as in locations which are within close proximity to an urban centre.

### Factors of change and their impact on traditional marriage rites and activities

Several factors of change and their impact on traditional marriage have been observed among Batlokwa. Besides the changes pertaining to the increased number of *bogadi* cattle and its equivalent in monetary terms, *bogadi* has become a business rather than a token of appreciation, as already mentioned elsewhere in this chapter. The tendency of copying wedding practices from other cultures has weakened the Setlokwa culture. New business ventures of renting out large tents or wedding venues have affected the familial spirit and other traditional wedding processes that existed in the past. For example, if the wedding celebration is held in a public facility, it becomes difficult to give counselling to the couple in public, moreso that among the Batlokwa counselling is done behind closed doors. Such rented facilities are also very costly, yet other families use them with a competitive attitude in order to display one's abilities or accomplishments.

Another thing that has become common is the issue of combined weddings. This practice affects families in many ways as they feel they are not fully involved in such weddings. Further, the new trend of hiring catering companies instead of cooking celebration food at home, where relatives of the bride and the groom have an equal chance of playing one role or the other with freedom, thus promoting and enhancing communal spirit and a sense of belonging. In the past, also, daughters-in law took care of the bride's or groom's people during the wedding celebration. This was done to show the new in-laws respect and dignity, moreso that the groom's delegation was usually accommodated and fed at another yard and not at the bride's home, as is the case nowadays. It was only after they had eaten at the place where they were accommodated that they would join others in the celebration in singing and dancing to demonstrate the joy of having an additional member in the family.

Several reasons were cited as influences of change, such as modern education, human rights, gender equality, distorted thoughts, economic status, urbanization and globalization. Most informants have expressed the wish to revisit the past and follow the expectations of Setlokwa culture with regard to *lenyalo* in totality. Realising that it will not be easy to stop the clock from ticking, they argue that if any modifications have to be made, they should be minimal as drastic changes distort Batlokwa's cultural identity and pride, among other areas.

## Conclusions and Recommendations

There are evident changes in the Batlokwa marriage processes and procedures. In order for them to maintain their identity and uniqueness, Batlokwa should agree on which changes they can adopt and which ones they should avoid, but with sound justification.

The informants were aware that culture is dynamic, for it changes all the time, hence some of the changes affecting the marriage institution need to be consciously controlled by *dikgosi* and not be allowed to erode people's identity and dignity – as with the issue of the increasing number of *bogadi* cattle and the amount charged per cow. Finally, this case study has given a synoptic view of what has been lost and what is still practised, valued and respected by Batlokwa of Tlokweng today with regard to the traditional marriage institution. Other informants are unhappy about, and disturbed by, the high rate of divorce among young married couples in the village (and Botswana at large), who often treat marriage more or less like a game and not a lifetime contract.

# 13

# Batswapong

*When a man marries a woman, he marries the whole family.*

*Prof. G.T. Tsayang*

## Information Sources and Data Collection

The study adopted a qualitative approach. The data collection methods were in-depth interviews and participant observation. A focus group discussion of two respondents was conducted. This involved much probing to try to get to the bottom of the reasons for a number of marriage actions and processes mentioned. Two individual in-depth interviews were also conducted with one male and one female respondent. Participant observation was also used as a data collection method where the researcher used her inside knowledge and experience to provide data. The researcher belongs to the Batswapong ethic group. She is a married person who also was subjected to the various Chetswapong marriage processes. Therefore, the participant observation data was triangulated with data from the other respondents.

## Brief Statement on Batswapong

Batswapong are an ethnic group found in the eastern part of the Central District of Botswana, along the Tswapong Hills. The culture of Batswapong and language are called Chetswapong.

# MARRIAGE PROCESS

## COURTSHIP (*GO FEREYA*)

In the traditional Batswapong *lenyalo*, marriage was for a family. In other words, there was a general expectation that when one gets married to a woman, they are actually marrying the woman's family. This meant that the woman needed to be chosen from a family which has, in the perception of the prospective groom's family, acceptable values such as being a good family, a family not made of witches, a family that had respect for other people a humane and kind one, as well as being peace loving. It was because of this notion of marriage that marriages were pre-arranged by the adults because they were in a better position than the young woman or the young man to evaluate families that they wanted their children to get married into. With time, the marrying to a particular woman's family was loosened somewhat by allowing the man to do the actual identification of a girl and initiate the courtship. In this respect, the Batswapong *lenyalo* started with the prospective groom courting the prospective bride. This was usually done at the playgrounds when young men and young women would have gone out to play after supper, or when young women would have gone to fetch fire wood or water and the boys meeting them there.

As indicated above, in the olden days, getting a woman to marry started not with the man and woman engaging in courtship, but with the parents from either side, meeting and discussing the possibility of their children getting married. In such cases, the young man's family would identify a family they consider to be a good one, well respected, and not a family known for witchcraft for instance. After the two families met and discussed this possibility, the young man's parents would continuously send him to the young woman's home for this and that. By the same token, the young woman's parents would also continuously send her to the young man's family, also for this and that. This would be an attempt by both families to make their children notice each other and probably become interested in one another. At some point when the young man does not seem to get the cue from the parents, he may be given a clue and be told, this particular family has well behaved young women who could make very good wives, especially woman so and so. With this cue, the young man might start taking notice of the young women, a particular one being, mentioned, and start the courtship. In other cases, the parents would agree to have their children married, to a point where, even if one of them (young man or young woman) does not want the mariage, he or she could be forced into it. The young man's parents would bring gifts to the young woman's parents. The party which is refusing to get involved in the marriage could be summoned by the uncles or aunts as appropriate, under the instruction of the parents so that they show him or her cause why he or she should get married to that particular person in a particular family.

On another front, the courtship could be done face to face or through writing a letter by a young man to the young woman. The young man was always the one who initiated the courtship. It was taboo for a young woman to initiate such, even if she had a liking for the young man. A young woman who would openly show their liking and even approach a young man was regarded as a 'bitch' or as loose. Such a woman would be an embarrassment to the family and the society. Even if a woman liked a man, she would therefore never dare show that, or court him, but rather wait and hope the man would notice her.

This has now changed. Parents rarely choose wives or husbands for their children. A woman and a man, following their courtship, inform the parents once they have agreed to marry. The uncles and aunts are, however, still the first people to be confided in by both the man and woman. This approach of man and woman independently courting has therefore led to situations where parents may show displeasure in their children marrying certain people and their families they do not know, or even those they know but do not have regard for, and therefore disapprove.

This new dispensation has come with modernity, or what can be referred to as democracy, in one's choice of a spouse. This new way of courtship is seen by many as one of the caurses of divorces, because it is viewed as not paying much attention to the type of family one is becoming part of, and such relationships hardly get blessings from parents. In other words, the young man and woman could choose those they love without knowing much about their respective backgrounds.

It can however be argued that the traditional courtship, mainly guided by the parents, also had its own limitations because, well-intentioned as it may have been, did not respect the feelings of the prospective spouses but that of the parents. Even if the two were not in love, it was agreed that love would evolve and develop between them, and as they stay together they would learn to love one another. Traditionally, marriage was a matter for the families of the two spouses, and not just a matter for the spouses as is mainly the case now. The positive aspect of arranged marriages is seen as that the prospective spouses would marry into known families, families whose attitudes, attributes and values would be known, whose cultures would be known and probably appreciated and understood. This perspective is perceived by some Batswapong respondents as providing sustenance for marriages, hence less divorces.

## Process of informing parents or parents informing their son or daughter and family members about the prospective marriage

Once the woman agrees to the courtship and both the young man and woman agree to get married, the man would confide in his uncle, who is usually his father's younger brother (*rangwane*), The young woman on the other hand would go and confide in her aunt, who is usually her mother's younger sister. The uncle and aunt confided in would each go and break the news to the parents. In modern times, however, the Batswapong prospective spouses do not necessarily see themselves owing it to the parents that they must get married. Once they meet, they may or may not inform the parents through the uncles or aunts. They may inform the parents directly and get on with marriage preparations. In some extreme cases, families may be told even after the two have gone to the District Commissioner's office to tie their marriage knots. Many parents would see the young man coming with a wife, both of them already wearing their wedding rings.

There are still some incidents, however, where the prospective spouses would still inform their uncles, who would in turn inform parents. Thereafter, the young man's parents would make an arrangement to visit the young woman's' parents to go and *kokota*, make a preliminary visit.

## THE PRELIMINARY VISIT (*GO KOKOTA*) BY THE YOUNG MAN'S PARENTS

The young man's parents would make a preliminary visit to the young woman's parents to go and see them and make introductions, as well as affirm that indeed the man has interest in marrying their daughter. During the visit, they will be treated to a good meal usually with chicken as relish.

## MEETING OF IMMEDIATE FAMILY MEMBERS

The man's parents will, after their preliminary visit, call a meeting of the immediate family members (*bo rangwane, bomalome, bommangwane, bo rakgadi* and the siblings) from both the mother's and father's side. The family members will be informed of the young man's intention to get married. The gathering would then start interrogating the man to find out if indeed he intends marrying and is ready. The immediate family members would even ask the man about other women-friends (girlfriends) he may be having or has had relationships with, and whether or not he is not just deceiving the family while he may still have such relationships. He would be counselled into abandoning these relationships, because otherwise it would be a mockery of the marriage for him to continue with them. He would be counselled about marriage that, should he continue with such relationships, he would be planning to frustrate the prospective bride and get an early divorce. The family members would then start counselling the man about marriage, and what he should expect by getting into it. One family member after the other would throw in their word of counselling to show the man that he has to know that he is now going to be a man who will be expected to take responsibility for his own family (his wife, and children to be born) and the prospective wife's family.

In the meantime, food will be prepared which will be served after the counselling meeting. After the counselling, singing and ululating will take place and food served as the gathering celebrates the forthcoming marriage.

At the end of this meeting, another day will be set for a bigger meeting with all the relatives (called *babijwa*). The same process of informing them about the forthcoming marriage starts, and interrogations and counselling of the young man take place. Once everyone is satisfied about this then marriage songs are sung and food is served.

The young woman's parents will also call a parallel meeting of the immediate family members, (*bo rangwane, bomalome, bommangwane, bo rakgadi* and the siblings) from both the mother's and father's side. The members will be informed about the young woman's intentions to get married. The gathering would then start interrogating the young woman to find out if indeed she intends marrying and if she understands the implications of such a step in her life. The immediate family members would even ask the young woman about other boyfriends who she could be having or has had; whether or not she has abandoned such relationships, and if not, that she should. She would be asked if she is not just deceiving the family and would probably be continuing with these other relationships, if she has them. She would be advised that if she continues with them, she would be planning to frustrate the prospective groom and even planning for a divorce. The family members would then start counselling the woman about marriage and what she should expect by getting into it. One family member after the other would throw in their word of counselling to let the woman know what the implications of getting married are such as knowing that she is now going to be a wife who will be expected to take responsibility of her own family (husband and children to be born) and the prospective husband's family (the in-laws). Once all is said, food will be served and songs and ululations would ensue. This will be a way of acknowledging the proposed marriage and celebrating it.

The second and bigger meeting will be set for another day where a similar counselling process will take place. This particular meeting is called *wobe.* This means that it is a meeting where all relatives are invited. The same process that would have happened during the meeting of the immediate family takes place. The extended family members will one by one throw in a word of counselling to the young woman.

After all is said to the young woman and the young man by their respective families, each family will identify family members, usually husband and wife who will be the co-ordinators of the marriage processes (*bommaditsele*). These are normally, the uncle and his wife (*rangwane le mmarangwane*), These are the people who will be sent to either side to bring the messages from either family concerning the upcoming marriage.

## Subsequent visits by the man's family go-betweens (*Bommaditsele*)

Once the young man's parents have identified *bommaditsele*, these are sent to the girl's family to break the news of their son having found a woman in their family who he wants to marry. These *bommaditsele* will be communicating with the other set of *bommaditsele* from the young womans' side, where each set will be communicating as go-between and on behalf of their respective families.

## Preliminary and subsequent formal visits by the young man to the young womans' place

Once the two families have agreed to the marriage, the young man is expected to visit the young woman's place accompanied by another man, or best man (*moedane*), on a given day. This is called *go itshupa* by the young man. When the man arrives at the woman's place, she has to kneel on one knee and greet the elders that he will find at the home of the young woman. This, he does from a distance of about 50 metres or so. As a sign of respect, he should not come close to the in-laws. The young men will then be ushered into the young woman's room by the woman's younger sister and will be given chairs to sit on. *Mmaditsele* will then tell the parents that the prospective son-in-law has arrived, whereupon they will come and greet him. They would not get into the room but rather greet him when sitting outside the door, and then leave. Food will be prepared for these two visitors, and this would normally include chicken and *bogobe ja mabele* or *ja lebelebele* (sorghum or milllet porridge). This visit is significant in that it is a gateway for the young man to now come to see the young woman and sleep at her place without hiding or sneaking in at night. On this *go itshupa* visit, however, the young man comes in the morning and leaves in the afternoon. From then on, he comes alone to the young womans' place but should never arrive after sunset. If he did, it was seen as a sign of disrespect and irresponsibility, and his family could be charged a fine for that. This time around when he comes, he is alone and must kneel just after entering the gate to greet the adults before proceeding to the woman's room.

## FORMAL VISIT BY THE YOUNG WOMAN TO THE YOUNG MAN'S' PLACE (*GO YA GO BONA KGORO YA BOGADI*)

'*Go ya go bona kgoro ya bogadi'* literally means 'going to see the entry into the in-laws' place'. Once the two families have agreed to the marriage, and the young man has visited, the young woman is expected to visit the young man's place accompanied by another young woman or her best lady (*moedane*). The young woman's visit lasts for a week. This is called *go ya go bona kgoro ya bogadi* by the young woman. When the two ladies come, they bring with them pounded sorghum as a sign that the bride to be is woman enough to provide food for the family, hence fit to be married. The two ladies will be ushered into the man's room by his younger sister and will be given a mat (*phate*) to sit on. Mmaditsele will then brief the parents that the prospective daughter-in-law has arrived, whereupon they will come and greet her. They would not get into the room but rather greet her from sitting outside the door and then leave. Food will be prepared for these two visitors, and this would normally include chicken and *bogobe ja mabele* or *ja lebelebele*. The woman and her companion will then be given grain (*mabele* or *lebelebele*) to pound to show that indeed she is a strong woman who could fend for her family. She will later be expected to cook the food from the sorghum she had pounded and then serve the in-laws. The *moetsana* will be with her all this time assisting her. This will continue for a whole week. She would also be expected to fetch water and do all that a woman would do in her own home. For instance, she would be expected to wake up in the morning and sweep the yard, make fire and prepare food for the rest of the family, pound sorghum, fetch water and firewood, and so on. After a week she will return to her parents' home. On her return, she is given *nama ya shuba sa nku* to take home. The significance of this part of the meat is that she is a woman who has successfully engaged in conjugal activities with her prospective husband during the week, thereby conveying a message to her parents that she is acceptable. This visit is significant in that it is a gateway for the woman to be recognised as a prospective daughter-in-law (*medji*) who is acceptable to the young man's family, having proved that she is a capable wife to be.

## BRIDE-SEEKING (*PATLO*)

The previous two preliminary visits by the bride and groom are followed by *patlo*. the *bomaditsele* from the man's side will be sent to the other *bommaditsele* to ask where to go when they want to seek the bride. The question asked is, where do we go for seeking (*re batela kae?*). This question is already understood to mean the young man's family is accepting the woman as a bride and will be responded to by the woman's parents by telling them where to go, which is usually the *bommaditsele*'s home. The *patlo* is done by the young man's family which will be comprised of mainly married relatives. The number could be as large as 30 people visiting the woman's *mmaditsele*'s home for at least one full week. Each time they come they are met outside by *bommaditsele*. They will then kneel outside in the sun. Each day they go, they have to say we have been sent by the young woman's family to seek a bride from your family at mister so and so's home. They will be asked if they know the woman, which they will affirm. They will be told 'we hear you' and then will be asked to come the following day until the last day. On the last but one day, they will be given a nod to say yes you can have you bride and can stop coming (*ba emisiwa go bata*). They will be told to come on a given day and date where their request will be granted in a ceremony (*letsatsi la go dumelela mafoko*). They will be told that on that day, they must dress their bride (*apesang medji wa nena dikobo*). This will be understood to mean that they must buy blankets dresses, head scarfs, and so forth. On that last day, *babatli* and other relatives are expected to come with the young woman's clothes (blankets, shawl, dresses and headscarves) for *bommaditsele*, and a dress, shawl and *tukwi* for the young womans' mother, coat and hat (*jase le hutshe*) for the young woman's father, and a blanket for the young woman's uncle (*malome*). The young woman's seekers (*babatli*) will then present these clothes to a gathering of the young woman's people, identifying each item. Once all is done, then ululations will ensue and songs will be sung by the young man's people to show their happiness that they have finally been given a bride. Food will be served, after which singing will continue. Later on, the young man's people will send word to request passage as they have to go back, which request will be granted. The end of this process is called *'o dumelela mafoko'* (acceptance by the woman's people of the request by the man to marry). At this point, marriage has not yet taken place though, even though *patlo* is completed. The indication that marriage has taken place is only when bride-wealth (lobola/*bogadi*) is paid.

In the modern Batswapong marriage culture, the *patlo* is still done but it takes only one day. Once *bommaditsele* have been identified, they play the role of go-betweens. After the two families meet for their respective roles, a letter is written to the man's people making demands for the items they would want to be presented for *patlo* (*dilwana tsa patlo*). Clothes demanded from the man, or the groom, could cover many people such as the woman's parents, the woman's siblings, all the aunts the uncles and the grandparents. These were not as many in olden times. This practice, however, nowadays varies from family to family. The number of items demanded is now dictated by what the young woman's parents may see as the value of their daughter. In other words, *patlo* has now taken a commercial twist where charges are as per the girl's value from the point of view of her parents.

## BORROWING OF THE BRIDE (*GO ADIMA NGWETSI*)

After *patlo*, the young man may want to stay with the bride while preparations are ongoing for the paying of lobola and the wedding ceremony. In that case, *mmaditsele* would be sent to the young woman's family to request or borrow her. Normally the borrowing will be for a particular purpose. If for instance, there may be another function at the young man's family, the bride may be borrowed so that she can come and assist at that function. When the function is over, the bride would be returned to her family to wait for payment of lobola and subsequent marriage procedures and functions. When the young woman is sent back she is taken by *mmaditsele* and will be given *nama ya sehuba sa pudi* or *nku*. This meat signifies to her parents that she is an able woman who can bear children as she was able to sleep with the young man without any complaints.

## PAYING LOBOLA, BRIDE-WEALTH (*GO NTSHA BOGADI* OR *GO JEYA*)

The next step in Batswapong marriage process, after *go dumelela mafoko* is to pay lobola (*go ntsha bogadi* or *ro jeya*). Lobola is paid by the young man or his parents on his behalf to the young woman's people. Lobola in the CheTswapong culture is seen as a cornerstone of marriage. It is seen as a significant token of appreciation to the woman's parents for bringing her up, and also for the young man's people to have her as their son's wife. The appreciation is also due to the fact that the woman will leave her own maternal home, change her surname, and belong to the man's family. She is seen as an asset to the man's family as she will bear them children, look after them and literally become part of them.

Lobola in CheTswapong culture was charged in the form of six head of cattle. In some cases, however, a man could pay less through his parents pleading that they cannot afford the six expected head of cattle. Before the lesser number could be accepted, the woman's parents would grill the man's people for not being able to meet the maximum required and warn them not to play tricks with them and be serious if they really want the bride (*lesang go re tshamekisa le jeye*). This message would be borne by the *bommaditsele* to both families, one requesting a reduced number while the other would be insisting on the correct number. This could go on for some time and could culminate in the man's people being sent back so that they become serious about the marriage. Finally, an agreement could be reached, either by the man's people paying all the cattle or a compromise made if indeed they cannot afford.

In the payment of *bogadi*, the young man's uncle (*malome*) has to pledge a cow to add to those provided by the man's parents (*malome o nyadisa motlogolo*). On the woman's side, which receives *magadi*, the woman's *malome* claims a cow from the *bogadi*. This claiming of a cow is in recognition that if there is trouble, *malome* is the one whom must stand firm and defend the young woman. *Malome*, by taking a cow, says he will stand for any challenges that might affect the niece and the groom (*ke ta di emela tse tsotlhe, malome ga se mosimanyana*).

Nowadays, *bogadi* varies from family to family. Some families charge *bogadi* based on the education that the young woman would have, for instance. For instance, if for argument's sake, the young woman is educated, the parents can charge the *bogadi* up to ten cows with a monetary value of P30,000 or more each in case a man is unable to pay using live cows. The charge in monetary terms could rise up to P50,000.00. The *bogadi* is no longer seen as a sign of appreciation, but rather as a way of payment for having educated a girl child. One can argue that probably it is this idea of apparent commercialization of marriage that could be contributing to poor marriage sustenance. This is because once the man feels as if he is not getting his resources' worth from a woman, he can call it quits. The concept of buying could be seen as overshadowing the concept of appreciation and rendering marriage a business enterprise.

## WEDDING CEREMONY (*KEMO/MOKETE WA LENYALO*)

In the Batswapong South culture, after *bogadi* has been paid, discussions on the day of *mokete wa lenyalo* will be agreed upon by both the young woman's and the young man's people. *Bommaditsele* will still continue being the go betweens. Once the dates are agreed upon, the young man will buy a wedding dress for the wife as well as for the bridesmaid (who was always just one). The dress could be a white wedding gown (*lesire*) or a two-piece suit which was called *costume*. The bridesmaid is the same young woman who would have accompanied the bride to see *kgoro ya bogadi*. The wedding celebrations would always start at the young woman's place and end at the young man's place. where the bride would be left to be with her in-laws, now as a married woman.

A few days before *mokete*, both of the couple's people will prepare to make beer, prepare for cooking the *bogobe* by pounding sorghum or millet. Relatives would pledge a number of food items such as goat meat by donating goats, *bopi ja mabele* or *lebelebele* (pounded sorghum/millet). From the morning of the wedding, both men and women would start cooking. In particular, the sons-in-law from either family will be responsible for slaughtering, preparing and cooking the meat (goats, cattle and sheep). The daughters-in-law on the other hand would be responsible for preparing bogobe by pounding the sorghum/millet and cooking it for the guests. Where there are not enough sons- and daughters-in-law, the sisters and brothers, cousins and other close relatives would come to assist in preparing and cooking food. In this respect, marriage is a collective activity as many other relatives would pledge and bring pounded sorghum, sheep and goats for meat to augment what the immediate family would be providing.

The young man's people would arrive on that same morning, be ushered into the hut or huts, depending on how many they would, be and be offered tea and bread. Each time they have finished eating, to indicate that they are done, they would ululate to communicate that they are done (*ba letse mogolokwane*).

Whilst the cooking of the main meal is ongoing, the process of *go laya banyadi* (marriage counselling) would take place. A table would be set outside with four chairs, two for the bride and groom and the other two for the best man and best lady. The counselling at the woman's place would mainly focus on her. This is done in the open and done by anybody who feels like doing it. People would take turns in counselling the woman in the presence of the guests and in-laws, who would be sitting behind the table for *banyadi*. Marriage counselling would focus on how the bride-to-be should behave as a married woman. Those who do counselling would encourage her not to be an embarrassment to them by bad behaviour, to ensure that she respects the in-laws, take care of them, know that there are disabled people there who she must not be shunned but taken care of, be able to look after her own family by taking care of the farm, not to be lazy, not to engage in extra-marital; affairs, cook for the husband and prepare a bed for him (implying that the man should not be deprived of his conjugal rights), and so forth. All these are said in public for everyone to witness what they, the woman's people are counselling their daughter on.

A similar process would be repeated at the man's place, this time done by the man's people, counselling their son in the presence of everyone else including the man's in-laws. The man would be counselled that he should look after his wife, must buy good blankets for her (implying that he should not deprive her of her conjugal rights), must not have extra-marital affairs, prepare a field for her, and plough and produce food. He must know that he did not only marry to look after his wife, but that he must extend his care to the in-laws as well. Again, all these are said in public and anyone who feels like saying something is allowed to do so. Married or divorced or unmarried, all are allowed. A divorced person for instance, would use his or her experiences leading to such a divorce, to encourage the man or woman not to make similar mistakes that could lead to their divorce.

Each and every person who stands up to counsel either the woman or the man, must pledge some gift such as a cow, a goat, a sheep, a chicken, a bag or bucket of sorghum, pots, axes, plates, cups and spoons. These gifts are given to help the couple to start a home with something. This will be such that when the two start their home together, they would already be having property and therefore do not start from scratch. When counselling happens at either party's place, the parents of both the woman and the man would also counsel their daughter or son respectively. When it is their turn, they would spray sorghum on the faces of the couple, telling them that this is a sign that they must be farmers so that they fend for their families. (Farming was significant as Batswapong mainly depended on it.) The father would normally pledge cattle, while the mothers would pledge goats or sheep as well as bags of sorghum. The parents are the last to do the counselling, and then preparations for *kgoroso* would begin. One of the notable things that would be said during the counselling is that a woman should never ask her husband where he is coming from (*monna ga a botswe*). This means that a woman has no right to demand an explanation of the man's whereabouts. This is not the case with the woman, who would be told to be home all the time (*mosadi o sala mo gae*). These two phrases are still echoed in some Batswapong weddings. However, a number of people are no long subscribing to these phrases as they feel there is injustice towards the young women, especially the *monna ga botswe* concept. They also feel that a woman has a right to demands on the whereabouts of the husband, as he could be involved in some dangerous situations. By asking, she could provide assistace to him.

The current practice of a wedding is slightly different from the past. However, the general preparations at the two families' homes still happen. The public counselling is still maintained, except where such weddings take place in urban areas. When that happens, counselling tends to take the shape of privacy and being conducted by a selected few, with no unmarried or divorced relatives allowed In this respect, some of the Batswapong are adopting cultures of other tribes such as the Bangwaketsi.

In CheTswapong culture, once a woman has been counselled, she cannot be allowed to spend that night there. She was not supposed to arrive after sunset at her in-laws' place either. That is why the counselling had to always start in the morning so that after lunch, the journey to the young man's place begins. She has to be taken to the man's place that same day, arriving before sunset. *Ngwetsi* is not supposed to arrive after sunset as an indication that even during her stay at her matrimonial home, she should not arrive at her home late, or do duties or run errands late. This is symbolic in that by implication, whatever work she does, as a married woman, she must plan properly and complete tasks on time. This practice is no longer observed as the wife could be counselled and then spend a night at her home to be taken to the in-laws' place the following day, even after a week or a month.

It is to be noted that on each of the visits to either the woman's place or the man's place by those entrusted to run the wedding, parents (those of the man and those of the woman) are not allowed to go with these respective teams. They remain at their respective homes as *digopalale*. They are expected to remain lying on their bellies and not to eat anything until the wedding ceremony at either place is completed. It was believed that if they ate anything, they would bring bad luck to their children's marriages. This was an indication that parents needed to be resilient in challenges that could affect their children, and even withstand the loss of their loved children to marriage, by fasting.

On their return, either from the man's or the woman's place, the delegates would have been given a portion of meat called *lebogo* (chuck) which is to be given to the parents (*digopalale*). That is the time they are supposed to eat assured that the wedding processes happened as planned.

## *Kgoroso*

*Kgoroso* is the noun from the verb *go roga* or arrive. It is a marriage process when a woman is taken to the man's place, her matrimonial home. This is the final stage of the wedding processes. Once marriage counselling at the woman's place is completed, food will be served after which preparations will be made for *kgoroso*. The man's people ask for permission to be allowed to return (*ba kopa tsela*) to return to their home taking the now married woman with them. The woman's people also accompany her for *kgoroso.* Those people, who would have been to the woman's place for *mokete*, return to the man's place accompanied by the woman's people, who are bringing her to her matrimonial home. The two groups go together to the man's place.

When they travel from the woman's home to the man's home, each time they cross a road or a stream, the woman must stop and refuse to cross until some money is paid for that by the man's people. When the woman reaches the gate of the man's home, she must also stop until money is paid for her to go in. Therefore as many roads to cross as there are to be crossed, and as many rivers as there are to be crossed, the man's people must be ready to pay, otherwise the woman and her people will not move. This is a way of testing the man's patience and ability to provide and meet the demands of a woman. As these people travel to the man's place, they will be singing wedding songs with ululations (*megolokwane* ) to show that the woman's people are happy that their daughter got married, while the man's' people will be expressing happiness that they received *meji/ngwetsi* or *sego sa metsi*. *Metsi* in Batswapong culture signifies life and *sego sa metsi* signifies one who will fetch water for everybody else. By implication, the *ngwetsi* will provide a good life for the in-laws.

When the woman's people arrive at the man's home, they are ushered into a house or huts and they all sleep there. In the morning, they will be served with water to bathe, and breakfast. After that a table will be prepared for the bride and groom together with the bridesmaid and the best man. This table is placed in the open where the counselling for the man will take place. The same process that would have happened at the woman's place with regards counselling is repeated with a focus on the man. The uncle (*malome*) will always pledge a cow. Again, the parents will be the last to counsel and provide cow/s by the father, and goats, sheep and utensils by the mother of the man. During the counselling, there will be a special emphasis on bearing children, looking after the spouse and children, and taking care of the new family. Counselling emphasis will also be on the fact that the man should now stop any extramarital affairs if he has any, and should not start any new ones, since he now has a wife to look after, He would be told to give water to the wife, implying that he should not deprive her of her conjugal rights. It would be emphasised that he must prepare fields for the in-laws and take good care of them. Again, as would have been the case with the woman's counselling, sorghum grains or millet grains would be splashed over the two as a sign that they must produce food for the family, and as a sign of wealth if they work hard and produce such these grains.

The young woman's people will then prepare to leave after they hand over the bride to the in-laws. This handing over is done by the *mmaditsele*. The bride is set on the mat (*phate*) and the mother in-law puts a headscarf over her head to signify that she is now a married woman who must always cover her head and her ears. The covering of her ears with a headscarf signifies that, as a married woman, she must refrain from listening to petty issues that could destroy her marriage life, and focus on serious issues. Singing and ululations will be the order of the day once the official activities are over. The young woman's people can now return to their home. The young lady will wake up the following morning and prepare food for the family. With time, the couple would be given a yard of their own so that they can now live as husband and wife in their own home outside that of the parents.

## An Alternative Way of Getting Married when a Man Does not Have Enough Resources

CheTswapong culture takes cognisance of the fact that people are not the same in terms of socio-economic status. For instance, in the event that a man cannot afford to have fully-fledged marriage processes, especially with reoect to payment of lobola, he may marry through what is called a *chekomokomo* procedure. This is a situation where a man steals the wife at night. The man and the prospective wife would have agreed on marrying. The families would be notified through the aunt and uncle procedure on either side that the two want to get married. The expectations by the young woman's parents would be the normal processes of *patlo*, lobola payment, *mokete* or wedding and so forth. *Chekomokomo* procedure does not go through these. It happens after the young man has visited for *go itshupa* but before *patlo*. This is because when *patlo* happens, the man would be implying that he has resources that can be used as part of *patlo*. In the event that he has no resources, he will discuss with his parents about stealing the bride (the *chekomkomo* procedure). On the side of the woman, the aunt will be the one informed by the young woman.

The prospective couple and the young man's parents would agree on a day that this would happen. On that day, the young man would visit the girl as usual and at night would take the young woman away when everyone else is asleep. He will leave some money under a mat. In the morning when the woman will be at the man's place, then her mother would wake up, and make sure the son has brought her daughter. Once she establishes this, she will then start singing a song:

*Chekomokomo che ntong,*
*Che khudhute maatho ntong,*
*Chekomokomo che ntong,*
*Che khudhute maatho ntong.*

When the neighbours and relatives hear this song, they automatically know what is happening and would come and join and the song, both men and women. When the song is over, they then sit down and will be briefed about this incident. Then they could all start going to the door to greet the new bride. Once that ceremony is done, the uncle (*rangwane*) will be sent to the young woman's parents to break the news that they should not worry about the whereabouts of their daughter, and know that she is in safe hands with them (the man's people). The *rangwane* will also bring to the young woman's parents a cow called *batelelang kwano* (meaning if you seek for your wife, know that we are with her and come seek from us).

The woman will then be welcomed to the man's home and be shown by the mother-in-law what she has to do as a *ngwetsi*. The stealing process can be an interim measure for a man who does not have resources as yet, but would like to stay with the wife to be, while he is still collecting resources that could be used for *lenyalo*. It can also be the final stage of a marriage if a man cannot afford to raise any resources for *lenyalo*. In the event that he cannot raise any resources for a proper wedding, especially to pay lobola, the in-laws will wait for any daughter of this man to get married, and when lobola is paid, they take it in lieu of the one he should have paid himself. In order not be ashamed, if the man did not pay lobola, immediately one of the daughters reports that she is getting married, the father will immediately arrange to pay lobola even if it is not done through a full wedding process. This stops the daughter's lobola from being claimed by the uncles of his daughter.

The *chekomokomo* procedure still exists but in a slightly modified way. What happens nowadays is that a man who is unable to go through the normal marriage process because of inadequate resources can still get married through what is referred to as co-habitation. This process is different from the traditional one in that the couple does not necessarily involve the parents. They may just decide on their own to move in with each other and then continue with their lives. Children would be born, and life will go on. When lobola gets paid for the first girl child to get married, (unlike in the past where the lobola would be taken by the uncles of the girl or the father's in-laws), the married couple may refuse with the lobola, and keep it for themselves. The claim is that they would have taken the responsibility of bringing up their own children and must reap the fruits of their labour.

## CHARGES

The Batswapong do not have too many charges in a wedding. *Thagela* is about the one charge that is known. It signifies that the man has jumped the fence or has impregnated the woman before marriage (*o thagetse*). Traditionally, in the event that the woman has been impregnated by the man before marriage, the woman's parents will demand a seventh cow called *thagela*. This charge is paid because the man has impregnated the woman (*o chinje mosijana*) before marriage.

# 14

# BAZEZURU

*Ms. Siphiwe Mguni*

## BRIEF HISTORICAL BACKGROUND: AN INTRODUCTION

The Bazezuru of Botswana are from a lineage of the Shona people of Zimbabwe. *ChiZezuru* is one the dialects in the *ChiShona* language. Other dialects are *ChiKaranga*, *Korekore* and *Hwesa*. Research further shows that the Shona are a Bantu group who migrated from the Congo basin at during the 18th century. That migration landed them into present day Zimbabwe where they were notably known for the Mononotapa stone masonry structures.

Colonialization introduced Christianity to people was known as the 'natives' by the colonialists. It was the Portuguese Jesuits who declared that natives practised paganism and therefore converted them to Christianity. The building of missionary schools led to most of the Shona people being converted. There was, however, resistance to conversion to Christianity where some of the people refused to abandon their *Mwari* (God) – an indigenous divine medium spirit. The conflict is documented in the then records of the colonial police. Evidently the indigenous God was experienced directly from above without an intermissary like Jesus. This also included prophetic utterances and exorcisms.

It is from this background that the Bazezuru church was established. They have a shrine in Gandazani village in eastern Zimbabwe where their founder was born and buried. Whereas there are many of the Bazezuru in Botswana who originated from Zimbabwe, as followers of Johane Masowe, there is yet another group of Bazezuru who are followers of Johane Marenge. He too was of the same era in Zimbabwe. He rose to prominence as a healer who is reported to speak in tongues and perform miracles.

Both men preached to Africans as a reaction to white domination and racial discrimination. They too are called Bazezuru in Botswana. Even though they had similar beginnings, the Johane Masowe sect is the subject of this paper because they migrated to Botswana before independence, whilst the Johane Marange sect grew in large numbers in Zimbabwe.

## The Link between the Bazezuru Church and Bazezuru Marriage

Bazezuru marraiges are strongly linked and influenced by the teachings and practices of their church. This started as early as the founding of the church. An influential figure in their regard is Shoniwa Masedza Tandi Moyo a man born to pastoralist parents, Jack and Efie Masedza, in 1914 in Gandazani village. The man is said to have gone through a spiritual transformation over a period of forty days and forty nights eating wild honey and praying in the wilderness of Marimba Hill. According to the interviewed informants, this man, like the biblical Moses, witnessed a burning bush and got instruction to go out and preach to Africans. After returning from the hill, it is said that certain magical healing phenomena and prophesies were also observed, leading to him gaining the name Johane Masowe (John of the Wilderness). His public manner of preaching drew in a lot of converts, and this did not please the colonialists, leading to him being routinely arrested for preaching without documentation (referring to the Christian doctrine). Johane Masowe taught his followers to reject colonial education and medicines. Much is said about his antics in evading the colonial police, like disappearing from locked solitary cells and prophesying. Eventually he and some of his followers took on a pilgrimage to South Africa in the early 1940s, first to Korsten in South Africa. This is well documented in a newspaper article '*Korsten Basketmarkers*'. He forbade his followers to join the mines and work for white monopoly, encouraging craftsmanship and self-reliance amongst themselves. This is still a trademark of Bazezuru: they still do carpentry, tinsmith, ironmongery, basketry, pottery and self-taught auto mechanics. He enforced a strict code of work, whereas the woman hawk their wares on the street, and apprenticeship is key amongst their male youth. As such Bazezuru have been and continue to be champions of *ipelegeng* (self-reliance).

The pilgrimage to South Africa did not last, as after some time the South African apartheid regime repatriated them back to Rhodesia (Zimbabwe). They however later set out from Zimbabwe to other neighbouring countries. They reached as far wide as Zambia, Mozambique, Tanzania and Kenya. Johane Masowe died in Zambia in 1973. The legion of his followers is also known as *Vaspori* (Apostolic). It is well to note that not all people of the Zezuru language are followers of Johane Masowe, or Johane Marenge; only those who converted to this kind of religion are called *Vaspori*.

As the spiritual leader Shoniwa Masedza Tandi Moyo encouraged polygamy, and it is reported that he had three wives. He said that polygamy would ensure that the Africans would prosper and multiply. After the death of the founder Shoniwa Moyo in 1973 in Ndola Zambia, the sect split into two, one led by his first wife and the other by his son.

## Understanding Bazezuru Marriages

Zezuru marriages are largely polygamous, with the man expected to acquire more than three wives. There was no mention of a love relationship by the Bishop interviwed. He said that the fact that the marriages work harmoniously is a reflection of the love that exists between the families. They have a duty to procreate, especially male children. This is key and it may hasten the number of wives that can be acquired. *Maiguru* (the first wife), who may have had the misfortune of not bearing a son, may find herself burdened with a second wife. They say this was encouraged by their founding father Johane Masowe. Nonetheless, Bazezuru polygamy is indistinguishable from other nations, such as the Moslems and the Mormons of the Church of the Latter Day Saints in the United States. In fact the Bishop in Mandunyane cited the practice among the Zulus of Natal in South Africa, as well as the Baherero residing in Botswana. Polygamy is much an African tradition, in most African ethnic groups; even though it was mildly suppressed by Christianity, it was never abolished.

Zezuru marriages are arranged between the parents of both children. The marriage tradition follows a simple process where marriage is only allowed amongst the congregants. Outsiders of the faith are not allowed to marry into the clan. This was the norm in the old days. The practice now is to allow the marriage if an outsider is willing to convent to the faith. Otherwise, whoever marries outside the congregants without converting the spouse is summarily excommunicated: undoubtedly a bone of contention for the youth, who are vehemently opposed to these arranged marriages Furthermore, they argue that their lives are much complicated by modern lifestyles; they want to select their own spouses and they are not keen to marry more than one wife. This is clearly a departure from their long-standing tradition. It does not bode well with the elders, who lament the destruction of their way of life by alcoholism, materialism and education. They say that since their children were required to attend school, much of their behaviour is absurd. Most probably this is the reason why second wives are being brought in from neighbouring countries where education is not enforced.

Bazezuru live in close proximity, such as in communes, in the north-east: a commune is headquartered at Semotswane village, where the Bishop and praying sisters reside. The instance of these sisters is much like catholic nuns. They are celibate and preselected at birth to do this duty for their entire lives. They live a life of prayer, leading the congregants into ecstatic prayer.

The parents of the boy select a wife from amongst eligible young women in the church. It is always the boy's parents who have that choice of a bride. The parents determine when it is ripe for their son to get a first wife. In former times, a girl had no voice in the matter, as this was communicated between the parents. Once the parents had agreed, the marriage was solemnised at church. It is often the boy's family who willingly offer gifts to the girl's parents.

Marriage gifts are clothes, blankets and shoes for both parents. The boy's family prepares a feast to receive the wife, who would most likely meet her husband for the first time on that day.

In relation to polygamy there is a specific role played by *maiguru* as regards the addition of other wives. In many instances, the *maiguru* would suggest a suitable young lady to join the family. In other cases, the husband would identify the young lady and ask for permission from *maiguru* to bring her, most notably her own sisters or cousins. Then the man's uncles and brothers proceed to inform the young lady's family of their intention to marry their daughter.

In the past, marriage unions were largely based on having as many children as possible. Hence the men could simultaneously sire children with as many wives as he was able to, at the same time. The Bishop in Madunyane states that they still prefer larger families in order to help out in their trade.

One aspect of these marriages was the principle that the man must be able to sexually satisfy all his wives equally, even though this of course cannot be measured. The Bishop insisted that if it were not done, the wives would leave. Even though divorce is forbidden, it is now prevalent amongst the younger generation.

Another important factor was that the man must provide equitably for all his wives. Speaking to a certain older *maiguru* in Francistown, she openly declared that she was happily married, along with two of her sisters, to one man, she said that they all stay in the same household and share all their meals.

If the first wife had not borne a son, the husband could ask to marry a younger second wife to bear him a son. Having a son is still the most important aspect of Bazezuru family life. The son is the one who carries the family name.

In other instances, when their daughter is at risk of being old and unmarried, the parents can ask their son-in-law (*mogwe*) to take in that daughter lest she becomes a spinster. It is also a disgrace for the family if their daughters are not married.

In the case of the death of a husband, the brothers or uncles could take over the deceased wives, *kugaranaka*, and inherit the children. According to this custom, it is to protect the family of the deceased. But the Bishop highlighted that this practice was common amongst the Bangwato and Bakalanga ethic groups in earlier years, *seyantlo* and *nkadzana*, respectively.

It is equally interesting to note that in situations where the man is unable to either father a son, or that he is sterile, a secret meeting would be held with his brothers or uncles to enter his brother's wives.

At church, the Bishop blessed the new couple: there are no certificate and no wedding bands. It is the congregation as a whole that witnesses that the wedding has been solemnised. There is no *kgotla* or District Commissioner registration. The Bishop counsels them with the strict code of conduct of the church, that the union is a sacred and holy and must be lived according to the doctrine of the church.

Another point of importance as relates to polygamy is that Bazezuru maintain close relations with their brethren in Zimbabwe, and as such have the practice of annually going for pilgrimage to their shrine in Zimbabwe. These pilgrimages offer the opportunity for some men to acquire more wives and bring them back to Botswana. As stated by one *maiguru*, this practice of getting additional new wives from Zimbabwe is seen by some as another way of retaining the purity of their church, because the 'ladies from Zimbabwe' who mostly would have never gone to school, are generally considered to be loyal.

As regards the age at which one gets married, this varies between males and females. A young man is encouraged to get married as early as the age of 18. This is to allow them to acquire other wives when they are still capable of maintaining and raising children. For females, the average age is often at the illegal ages of 12 to 15 years. Girls are usually booked for marriage through a practice known as *peeletso* in Setswana, where a girl is betrothed to a man much older than her, and is to marry her when she is in her early teens

## Changes and Challenges in Zezuru Marriage

According to the Bishop in Semotswane village, the church now encourages the youth to seek out their marriage partner amongst the congregants and inform the parents of their choice. This is the *ba a jola* way of getting married, the Bishop said. It is only if the parents, after observing the potential partner, recommend that the union be stopped that the parents can intervene once again to find a suitable one. In this instance, a suitable partner is according to the church doctrine, and the girl's social background. Therefore it is still important that the marriage is spearheaded by parents. This new twist came about because of the high rates of divorce in the church.

It is most notable that now, during the week, females wear clothes of different colours instead of the the traditional white. Some women who were interviewed said this was for practical reasons as white clothes easily soil as they walk around selling their wares. On worship day however, the females wear their traditional all white as this what makes them most eligible for marriage consideration.

## Conclusion

In conclusion, Bazezuru as a people are an industrious and self-reliant group who migrated to Botswana in search of a place to worship their *Mwari* in dignity without the interference of white Christianity.

Bazezuru blame Western ways for failing to keep their tradition. Their children attend schools and use modern medicines. They say that the children no longer listen to their advice. It is much like any other tribes in Botswana. One elderly informant reported that they are expecting that their next generation would lead a path very different from theirs, including marriage arrangements. Indeed, at a Moroka village group discussion, the men admitted that they see their old ways of living being eroded by modernity, though they enjoy owning cell phones, sending their children to school and driving *Maufitis* (Honda Vitz vehicles). They lamented on the dying tradition.

On being asked if they were willing to relinquish polygamy, the Bishop in Semotswane village answered in the negative, and cited other nations, in particular the Zulus who are not wearing down on that tradition. This notwithstanding a number of male informants said that the younger wives are difficult to manage as they want to drive cars and do their hair. They also stated that these younger wives now more regularly have a conflict with the *maiguru*, who are older and traditionalist.

# 15

# VEEKUHANE (BASUBIYA)

*Iseso lye Chiikuhane: A Subiya Marriage*

*Dr. Ndana Ndana*

## BRIEF HISTORICAL BACKGROUND

Popularly known as Basubiya, these people refer to themselves as Veekuhane and their language is Chiikuhane. They derive their name from Muniteenge (King) Ikuhane, the second king to succeed his father Iteenge. Muniteenge is a short form of *mwiina itenge* to mean 'owner or ruler of iteenge'. Iteenge, the name of both the Chobe/Zambezi river system and the Subiya kingdom, derives from the name of the first known ruler of the Veekuhane. Iteenge is fondly used by the Veekuhane to refer to the current Chobe District. In Botswana, the largest number of Veekuhane is found in the Chobe District, with reduced numbers in Okavango, Ngamiland and Boteti areas. Outside Botswana, they are found in the Zambezi Region of Namibia, Sesheke of Zambia and Victoria Falls of Zimbabwe. As a riverine people their culture is closely linked to the river ecosystems, as sources of food, building material, entrainment and spirituality.

## BASUBIYA MARRIAGE

The union between a man and a woman among the Basubiya as popularly known in the literature, is an important rite of passage. Among its many functions are: the continuation of the human race through procreation; extension of social relationships. It is also seen as the marking of the transition of an otherwise inexperienced person into adulthood, with added the social responsibilities of not only raising a family, but doing so in the most responsible, mature and dignified manner as to ensure social cohesion, peace and stability. In view of its sensitive functions, it has its own protocols making it more of a process than an event.

The noun *iseso*, and its associated verbs, *kusesa* (to marry) and *kuseswa* (to be married), is the Chiikuhane word for marriage. Depending on the context, it can refer to: the official union between a man and woman as husband and wife, and all the legal and social rights associated with such a union; the actual wedding ceremony; the general institution of matrimony; its associated expectations and all the processes undertaken in uniting a man and woman; a parody for marriage and sometimes as a euphemism or taboo word for sex. The term will therefore be used with these meanings in mind, and in particular, to underscore the fact that *iseso*, is a process beginning with the meeting of either the couple in modern times, or their parents in the olden times of arranged marriages. I also refers to to the dissolution of the marriage, either by divorce, separation or death, and even beyond. Even when the marriage has been officially ended, it tended to leave a permanent mark on the couple and community of Veekuhane

The data for this chapter are gleaned from multiple sources: oral, personal knowledge, observations as a Mwiikuhane (a Veekuhane person), and available literature. This chapter describes marriage among the Veekuhane of Botswana, and Chobe district in particular. It outlines the stages. The description starts with the meeting of the couple through the asking, celebration and beyond. For convenience, I divide marriage into three interconnected broad categories of pre-celebration, celebration and post-celebration, with each phase consisting of several processes. Using this taxonomy, the chapter will also highlight some of the notable changes, themselves not surprising in view of the inherent dynamism in human cultures, coupled with the obvious interaction with other cultures.

## THE MARRIAGE PROCESS

### *KUVEEREZA* (PRE-CELEBRATION PHASE )

This is the phase in which it all begins. As to when it exactly commences depends on the prevailing circumstances. In the context of arranged marriages to which the Basubiya subscribed to a very long time, the parents determined who their child marries. In doing that, the parents aligned their children to a specific family, metaphorically known as *iziko* or *maziko* (singular and plural respectively), for various reasons. *Iziko* is the fireplace in the family dwelling where, from time immemorial, the fire is made, cooking done and a family gather in the evening to eat and relax before retiring to their respective sleeping places. With its permanence, *iziko* symbolises the family's values or vices, which will be known in the community, and therefore to be envied or weary about. Parents therefore endeavoured to avoid certain pitfalls which included the possibility of marrying a close relative, or into a family of questionable reputation, while furthering a particular lineage.

Parents therefore identified their potential sons- or daughters-in-law before they were born, at or after birth. For example, upon seeing an expectant woman, a parent could express his/her desire to have the unborn child as a son or daughter-in-law. Such an expression will similarly be made when the child is already born. In most cases it is the potential bridegroom's parent who will be looking for a prospective daughter-in law. Accepted, directly or tacitly, the prospective mother or father in-law brought *kaluungu* or *kakenge* (a necklace made of beads, or ostrich eggshells) to be worn by the prospective daughter-in law. This will remain in force till they are officially married. This process is called *ku veereza*. A girl with this necklace is said to be *muzike*.

With this necklace, the girl is gradually introduced to her prospective in-laws' family through various means. These include being sent there frequently on certain errands, spending time with them, given presents, generally being welcomed in that family, and even sleeping over. Similarly, the boy will also be made to develop a close relationship with his future in-laws by spending some time with them, undertaking certain chores for them, and getting closer to the girl, although sexual contact will not be allowed as she would still not have come of age. This is designed to allow for a smooth transition when the two actually relocate, especially for the girl, to the in-laws. Both her parents and prospective in-laws have a huge responsibility in keeping a watchful eye on both the girl and the boy so that they stay on the straight and narrow. Should any behave otherwise, they risk embarrassing their parents, who will become society's laughing stock for failing to discharge their parental responsibilities and therefore losing out on the potential benefits such a marriage would have produced. One oral source had it that the girl was made to be fearful of the man and made to run and hide every time he appears.

## *Kafulumani* (puberty)

At puberty (*kafulumani/chimwaalye*), the girl inches closer to the actual wedding. At this stage, known as *kamwalye*, she is isolated for a specific period, sometimes up to two months, under the tutelage of her grandparent and other elderly women who will teach her how to conduct herself as a woman, and future wife, managing her household and satisfying her husband in all respects. During her seclusion she has to keep herself busy by making baskets and mats to avoid sleeping during the day lest she is accused of laziness.

The prospective in-laws are duly updated on this major development, and they would inform their son to ready him for the wedding, which did not take long after the girl has reached puberty. In some cases, the wedding was made to coincide with the ceremony to mark the end of her seclusion. A night prior to the ceremony, there will be a dance to which men are never welcome. What takes place there remains a secret and is known only to those who attend. She will be led to the river where she is bathed in cold water and she must show her strength by not feeling cold. Even if she felt cold, the dance that follows will ensure she is warm in no time. On the next morning, *kamwalye* will be dressed in new clothes and having been away from the public, she would look beautiful and light in complexion. A cup is placed on her head and she is expected to balance it; money will be dropped as gifts on what is her day of admission into adulthood. She is further expected to keep her head bowed and not to maintain an obvious eye contact because she will be betrothed to someone.

## *MAROVORO* (BRIDE-WEALTH)

Bride-wealth was paid before the wedding ceremony took place. Before the advent of money, the price included implements like a hoe which the young man would have produced or secured somehow, cattle, usually one, and working for the in-laws, as in building a house, ploughing, and collecting firewood. In undertaking some of these chores, the boy proved himself as a man who will fend for his new family and not forgetting his in-laws, who he will periodically assist. When both families have agreed on what the price is, it will be delivered by the uncles of the boy to the girl's family where the uncles will receive it. When the exchanges are done, the families will be ready for the ceremony.

## *MUNYEMBU*

Although marriage processes are a serious affair deserving resoluteness, there is room for playing games (and having fun), sometimes to ease tension but also as a means getting the families closer to one another. When the cousins, sisters and brothers escort any of the couple to the house prepared for them, there is ample opportunity to tease them. The jokes largely revolve around sex, gesticulating to either the boy or girl how it should be done on this special day, ensuring that no one disappoints. More important is the practice of *munyembu* where those escorting the girl would refuse to let go or reveal her face to her prospective in laws unless the in-laws paid out some money. Every time they paid, they will continue to hold onto her until they have made sufficient money to share amongst themselves. This game has another function, namely to test the in-laws and the son-in-law's endurance and patience, for it is believed that one who is patient always succeeds.

## *MUKITI WE SESO* (WEDDING CELEBRATION)

The wedding ceremony is an important community event. Depending on the wealth of the families involved, the ceremony could go on for some days, accompanied by singing, dancing and merrymaking. The ceremony took place at the girl's homestead where her in-laws would have arrived a day or two before the big day. As part of the preparations, accommodation for the visiting family, as well as the newly-weds would made available. Both the boy and the girl are now called *vakamwalye*, the plural of. *kamwalye* On the nuptial night, the following order of events take place. First, each one of them, accompanied by either a cousin, brother or uncle, will be made to bath. After bathing, the girl is smeared with oil from cattle so that she smells nice. She will then be led to the room specially prepared for *vakamwalye* where she will find the husband to be waiting. After the first sexual encounter, the man is expected to confirm the virginity of the wife by depositing some money under the pillow. Discovered by the girl's guide the next morning, she will ululate to confirm that indeed the ceremony will take place. If nothing is found, she will wail, thus indicating that the girl is no virgin, and this may mark the end of the planned marriage to the embarrassment and disappointment of the families.

Assured that the ceremony will indeed take place, the couple, led by their guides, will be led from different directions to a central point where the singing and dancing will take place. They will be joined by the hands, as husband and wife. On the woman's head will be a cup which she should not let fall. After all, balancing a pail of water on one's head is an important skill every wife must acquire. The man will be wearing a hat. Both the hat and cup will be the receptacles into which money will be dropped and collected at certain intervals by their guides. This is a crucial part of a Subiya wedding, known as *ku wiisa icherete* or *ayiwe cherete*, never to be missed. One particular song, *ayiwe cherete*, is sung and could last for hours depending on the flow of the gifts, money in particular. The people would dance in front of the couple and then deposit the money in the cup and on top of the hat, singing and sometimes teasing the couple, who should keep their heads down and maintain a serious look.

### *KULAYERERA* (COUNSELLING)

Late in the afternoon, the couple will be led into *irapa* (an enclosure made of reeds surrounding a hut or several of them) where they will be sat on mats surrounded by members of both families for the counselling session. Here, people will take turns, starting with the parents, to counsel the couple, especially the girl, on how to conduct herself at the in-laws', mindful not to disappoint them by behaving badly. This would go on until the parents are satisfied that it has been completed satisfactorily. While this is ongoing, the singing and dancing continues, and to which those participating in the counselling will return. Later in the evening, a group of women will lead the new wife to her husband's house with all her belongings. The ceremony will be over.

### POST-CELEBRATION

With the marriage counselling and wedding ceremony over, the couple is ready to move to their home and face their new life. But before they move to their home, the couple remained at the woman's parents for up to a month, or more. During this time the man will continue to work for his in-laws now as their child, and confirming that indeed he will fend for his wife and the children they are expected to bear. They will then move to their home or the man's parents after which they will return briefly to the woman's family (*ku vooza mateende*), literally, to return her feet, and then return permanently to build their new home (*ku zaaka irapa*). At this stage they can take part in major community affairs as grownups. *Irapa* is the enclosure built around a hut/house. It is made of reeds by women who collect the material from rivers. A well-built *irapa* is attractive and gives the woman status. *Irapa* is also a metaphor for a well-kept and dignified home, whose secrets are kept within the enclosure. How that *irapa* is created and actualised, constitutes the larger part of married life.

## *ICHINCHEH* (CHANGES)

The description above should be appreciated in the context of the continuous change of human culture. So that what informants may recall as the manner in which a Subiya wedding is what they recall to have happened at a particular time and circumstances in a long history of evolution. The above description is premised on the major principle that the Subiya married among themselves, and largely to relatives. In this way you treated your partner not only as a spouse but a relative over whom you had the responsibility to treat well before being a spouse. This they believed made marriages last longer. Marrying within also minimised cultural shocks that come with marrying from outside. For example, the spouses and their parents were not shocked by the bride-wealth, attire and or marriage rites that had to be followed.

While marriage was largely within and to relatives, men of Lozi, Yei and Totela extraction allowed and welcomed marrying Subiya women. These men stayed permanently with the families of their wives for whom they worked throughout their lives. The man was known as *umbwa mulyiziri*, literally, a wandering dog, in search for a place to call home. Such a man is therefore ready and willing to be owned. They attached themselves to wealthy families for whom they worked as *chikombwa* (servant) in exchange for accommodation, sustenance and patronage. Consequently, these men established families by marrying a relative to the host family and even passed for a siblings or member of that family. The industrious ones were even allowed to marry princesses whose children ascended to the Subiya throne on the basis of their mother's royalty.

The interaction with other ethnic groups, especially marrying across cultures, has resulted in some notable changes. For example, the Tswana influence has resulted in the adoption of the *lekana* for the women and the white wedding and associated attire. This in in contrast to the Subiya *mushishi* (multi-layered skirt famously known as 'peacock') and its *mavaanda* (blouse). The changes have also included the holding of two ceremonies, the initial one at the girl's followed by the one at the boy's home. The disappearance of *chimwalye*, considered as a major preparatory stage for marriage, is another notable change. Girls reach puberty away from their parents in educational institutions where they are never taught the cultural significance of that stage. In the age of human rights, some go on to fall pregnant and even marry themselves off, with little or no parental involvement. This has obviously relegated arranged marriages to the backburner, if not to downright irrelevance, as the prospective husband or wife plays a key role in determining who to marry and how the wedding will take place, and even where to settle after they are married. Consequently, the parents have less influence as their children meet in schools, churches and workplaces, only to introduce themselves to prospective in-laws. Those who have adopted the Christian faith differ with their parents on the marriage processes, refusing to follow their culture.

Finally, with modern wedding tents and associated decorations, weddings have not only become expensive, but highly competitive as well. In the tourist area of Chobe, boat cruises and photoshoots in hotels/lodges are a common feature of weddings. By marrying across cultures, people from other parts of Botswana have had the rare privilege of visiting and appreciating a different part of the country, thus opening them up to the diversity of cultures of Botswana. For places like Chobe, which have been known exclusively for the fauna and flora, there has also been appreciation of the diverse people found there. This I believe will contribute in modest ways towards nation building.

# 16

# Hambukushu

*Kandondi Kapweke*

## Brief Historical Background

The traditional account of the origin of the Hambukushu is given in the mythology they have about how Nyambi, the supreme being, created their first ancestors and let them down on a rope from heaven onto the top of the Tsodilo Hills, which they regard as sacred. They point to marks on the rocks in the hills which they venerate as the footprints made by the first people and animals, even though researchers believe these to be no more than ancient San rock art. But the legend may be a symbolic acknowledgement of an embedded San heritage.

Today, however, the Hambukushu in Botswana are part of a large cross-border community also found in Namibia, Angola and Zambia. They traditionally occupied the stretches of land north of the confluence of the Chobe (also called Linyanti and Kwando in other parts of its course), and the Zambezi rivers. According to available records, going back to the 1750s, the Hambukushu, among others, made up the southern part of the agglomeration of ethnic groups that comprised the Luyana Kingdom, as the Barotse Kingdom was then called. Subsequent developments pushed them further southwards along the Zambezi River to the Kwando valley in the Chobe and Caprivi strip area, eventually settling in the villages of Sepopa and Shakawe between 1847 and 1899 (Tlou,1985). The setting up of colonial boundaries in the late 19th century split them among the four countries in which they are found today. More recently the anticolonial wars in Angola and Namibia's Caprivi Strip resulted in further migration of the Hambukushu into the area around Gumare. Following the intensification of these wars, 3,500 refugees came to Botswana and settled around Mohembo and Shakawe on either side of the Okavango River. One source notes that this resulted in obvious overcrowding in the area which the Botswana government dealt with by resettling the new arrivals in the area between Gumare and Sepopa along the Thaoge river in thirteen villages named Etsha 1, Etsha 2, and so on up to Etsha 13.

## Marriage from the Hambukushu Perspective

The term *linyalo* is used in this paper to refer both to the institution of marriage itself and to the cultural practices that are associated with its authentic conduct. As is the case among other communities, among the Hambukushu too, *Linyalo* is a rite of passage into adulthood. Consequently, it is characterised by ritual practices that must be adhered to scrupulously if the process is to be regarded as authentic. Meticulous adherence to these rituals serves two purposes. First, it ensures that at a practical level the events are properly organised and conducted efficiently. Second, the ritual practices are steeped in symbolism, and adherence to their appropriate conduct serves to underscore, especially to the novitiates, the solemnity of the moment of transition into adulthood. Although adherence to traditional authenticity in the conduct of marriages is prized, it nevertheless gives rise to challenges, as the Hambukushu try to adapt to the ever-changing socio-cultural environment in the country. The paper shall also indicate how the marriage process changes as the result of such adaptation. The material for this account was collected from oral interviews with selected informants from the Hambukushu community. Much of the background material on the history and traditions of the Hambukushu was gleaned from secondary sources, notably the ethnographic writings of Thomas J. Larson whose life-long research going back to the early 1950s is a foundational resource on the Hambukushu.

The Hambukushu have a distinctive culture that is now part of the diverse but unified Botswana national culture landscape. What this means is that while they do justifiably take pride in the authenticity of their traditions. They are conscious of the necessity to harmonise these with the traditions of other people with whom they live both in the region, and in the country as a whole. Particularly noteworthy from the point of view of the subject of *linyalo* is that Hambukushu are matrilineal, which means that they trace their line of descent, rank and inheritance through the mother. This contrasts with the Tawana with whom they live in Ngamiland, and most other communities in the country, which are predominantly patrilineal. A further distinctive feature of the Hambukushu is their strong clan-oriented social structure. Unlike other communities in Botswana in which the whole community will share a totem, among the Hambukushu the people belong to different clans and each clan will have its own totem. The clan is crucial because belonging to the same clan, or sharing a totem, does not only mark people as relatives with obligations towards each other, but it also determines who you can and cannot marry since members of the same clan cannot marry or have sexual intercourse.

The clan also signifies ritual powers so that some clans are associated with rainmaking skills, while others have special skills, such as blacksmithing. Even though everyone belongs to a clan by birth, full clan membership is attained only when one marries or when one's parents die. Clans embody the bonds of relationships among the living, and their bond in turn with the community of ancestors or *hatukuru hokarekare* (the forefathers of the olden days) (Larson, 1970:3). Every clan member traces his or her descent through the mother, and through her to the founding ancestress of the clan and ultimately to Nyambi, the supreme being. So, like other communities in Botswana, Hambukushu believe that marriage is instituted by God, Nyambi, for the purpose of procreation and to serve as a rite of passage to the rights, privileges and responsibility of adult life. It is understood that the family is the basic unit of society, and that a properly constituted family, through the correct conduct of the rituals of the marriage process, is the foundation of society. Thus, marriage is a reaffirmation of the bonds both among the living and with 'the ancestral spirits of the supernatural world' (Larson, *op.cit.*).

## TYPES OF MARRIAGE

In the past the Hambukushu practised polygyny, but the practice has virtually disappeared. Marriage as now normally understood is the union of one man and one woman. It is ceremonially solemnised through three types of ceremonies, namely customary, Christian and civil marriage.

Traditionally the Hambukushu marriage began with the choice of marriage partners that led to a formal engagement. Hambukushu practised two forms of choice of marriage partners, namely *kwandekera* and *kushesha* (Larson, 2001). *Kwandekera* as a type of engagement means 'infant betrothal' whereby the families arrange the betrothal of a baby girl or girl to a boy or young man. This type of engagement most often is between cousins, meaning between a boy and his father's sister's daughter or his mother's brother's daughter. This type of engagement is no longer practised. In *kushesha*, when a boy and a girl are courting, either asks the other directly to be his or her future spouse. This initial contact in both types of engagement triggers the elaborate rituals of the engagement process. The process begins when the parents on both sides ceremonially acknowledge the marriage pledges of the couple and ends with a marriage ceremony which normally takes place when the girl is ready for marriage at the completion of her month-long puberty rites.

## THE MARRIAGE PROCESS

### PRELIMINARY VISIT (GO KOKOTA/GO ITSHUPA)

The identification or choice of future marriage partners is followed by the process of informing the parents on both the future wife's and husband's sides and formalising the engagement. It was done through a preliminary visit called either *go kokota* or *go itshupa*. The process was conducted differently under the two kinds of engagement, *kwandekera* and *kushesha*.

#### (a) Under *kwandekera*

Under this type of engagement, the father of the boy or young man was responsible for performing *go kokota/go itshupa*. The preliminary visit to the chosen baby girl's or girl's parents was for the purpose of asking them to consider pledging their daughter in marriage to his son. The father made the visit on behalf of his son and the family because he was the head of the family and knew what is in the best interest of his family, compared to other relatives.

Sometimes, the girl's parents turned down his request for betrothal, in which case he reported back to his family and urged them to look elsewhere. In this form of engagement both the girl's and the boy's consent was not considered; it was the parents from both sides that arranged the match. If the proposed betrothal was acceptable to the girl's parents, they asked the young man's father and his family to give them time to consider the matter with her aunties and uncles. The boy's father reported accordingly to family and awaited a formal reply to his proposition. The reply would come in the form of an invitation to visit the girl's home again, to formally receive the reply.

When the girl's family had approved of the proposed betrothal, the expected invitation to visit again was extended to the boy's family. During the visit the young man's parents were informed by the girl's parents that that their daughter had been released for the betrothal. Then the girl and the young man were introduced to each other. The girl was informed that she was betrothed to the young man, and she had to agree. From then onwards the two were considered engaged, and the young man assumed some responsibility for the welfare of the girl and her family, until both of them were ready to get married.

### (b) Under *kushesha*

This type of traditional engagement is still practiced among some people in the community. Under this type of engagement too *go kokota* is performed by the boy's father. When a young man and a girl are courting, and feel they are ready to marry, it is the responsibility of the young man to inform his parents of their intention. If his parents approve of his match, they approach the girl's family and initiate arrangements for the engagement.

If both sets of parents agree to the proposed future marriage, a payment called *kwala-molomo* (idiomatically, to finalise the discussion) is issued by the young man, through his parents, to the young woman's parents to seal the agreement. In former times an amount of P1.00 to P2.00 was paid for *kwala-molomo*. However, nowadays it has increased to P200.00. The payment marks the formal start of the engagement of the couple. The young woman will be required to spend an agreed period of time at her future husband's home. During the engagement period the couple support each other as prospective husband and wife, and perform required chores at each other's parents' home.

It is noteworthy that both *kwandekera* and *kushesha* types of engagement involve a long period before the actual marriage. This gives the families of both future bride and groom the opportunity to get to know each other and their son- or daughter-in-law.

According to the respondent Mr. Izaiah, nowadays the *kwandekera* form of engagement is no longer practised by the young generation. Young people tend to choose their own partners without their parents' consent, and plan on their own how to inform the parents about their relationships and marriage plans.

# The Marriage Processes of the Hambukushu Today

## Bride-seeking (*Patlo*)

According to the respondents, in olden times *patlo* was not part of the Hambukushu traditional marriage. However, because of influences from other tribes, marriage laws from the *dikgosi tse dikgolo* (paramount chiefs) that the small tribes are under, and cross-tribe marriage, have led to the adoption of the practice in the Hambukushu traditional marriage.

The process is a carefully orchestrated ritual consisting of several stages. During these stages, representatives of the young man's family travel back and forth many times between the homes of the future bride and groom in order to perform the protracted propositioning process. This process is termed 'bride-seeking' or *patlo*. For the purposes of this presentation, it is broken down into seven stages as described below.

## Decision to marry and informing the parents

Since the young man and woman have met and agreed concerning their relationship, they have to find a way to inform their parents on both sides about the future of their relationship. When the father of the young woman has observed and recognised that his daughter is dating a certain man who may even come frequently to their home, he takes a step to ask his daughter about the young man (who he is, what his intention is concerning his daughter, whose son is he, and where is he coming from?). If the young woman says he is her fiancé, her parents make arrangements to inform the young man's parents.

## Formation of *patlo* committees

At first the young man is called by the young woman's parents to their home to be questioned about his plans concerning their daughter. If he says he wants to marry, then he is asked to go and inform his parents. When the young man has informed his parents about his relationship with the young woman and states that he wants to marry her, his parents and relatives meet and set the date for the first visitation to the young woman's place. This is communicated to the young woman's parents through a letter.

A few days (two to three) before the set date, the young woman's parents meet with close relatives (maternal and paternal uncles, maternal and paternal aunties, with the grand-mothers/fathers) and letters are written to invite other married couples around their village to come and help them during the *patlo* process.

At both homes a committee is selected which coordinates the whole bride-seeking process. This committee comprises a selected chairman, uncles, aunts, two male messengers (*barongwa*), two male bride–seekers (*babatli*), married women (*bommaditshale*), married men (*boradibaki*) and other older people.

When the set date approaches, both the young man and woman stay inside the house at their different homes, and everything is provided for them by their assigned helpers. They are not allowed to participate in the first stages of the *patlo* process.

## THE FIRST VISIT

On the set date, early in the morning, at around 5 a.m., the two selected bride-seekers are sent to the young woman's place. When they arrive at the *lolwapa* (compound) door, they cough twice, and then on the third time, the door is opened for them by the committee that awaits them.

The two selected bride-seekers sit down with their legs crossed. No chairs are provided, and no greetings exchanged. Then one of the bride-seekers will start by saying, 'We have been sent to Mr. (stating the name of the young woman's father) to ask for *sego sa metsi* (a water gourd)'.

Then one person from the selected committee from the young woman's side will respond by saying, '*Re lo neetse sego sa metsi*', meaning that your request has been granted. After the words of acceptance, the two bride-seekers go back to the young man's place to inform the committee that their request has been granted.

## *TLHAGELA* PAYMENT

On the same day, in the evening at 5 p.m., the same two bride-seekers from the young man's place return to the young woman's place to further confirm that the water gourd will be given to them. This time around when they arrive, they find the door already opened for them, they enter and sit down, legs crossed, no chairs, and they say the same words that were said in the morning, asking for the *sego sa metsi.*

The selected representative from the committee, upon hearing for the second time about the bride-seekers' request, start by saying, 'yes we have heard you, and we are saying that the *sego sa metsi* will be released, but before that remember your son has been coming to this home (the young woman's place) on his own. He came at night, he saw our nakedness, and it is an insult to us, so he has to pay for that'. The payment is called *tlhagela*, meaning the young man went through the wrong way when he first entered the young woman's home. The payment is in the form of a fit female cow with horns, a heifer (*kgomo ya moroba*). After these words the bride-seekers ask for the way (*ba kopa tsela*) to leave and inform the committee at the young man's parents' home.

Upon arrival, the bride-seekers inform the committee about the request that has been granted and the charge of a heifer. On the second day, early in the morning, the two selected messengers take the cow (*moroba*) to the young woman's place. Upon arrival, the cow is tied up and left at the compound gate. The messengers go inside the compound where the committee is, and inform them that the cow has arrived. Chairs are provided for them to sit on.

The chairperson from the young woman's committee asks the married women (*bommaditshala*) to go and inspect the condition of the cow. If the cow is a healthy *moroba* (a heifer) with horns and no wounds, it is accepted. *Bommaditshala* go back to the committee and inform them that the cow is acceptable. Then one person is selected from the young woman's committee to slaughter the cow and people ululate to show their appreciation. If the cow is not acceptable, they send it back and stop the *patlo* until a healthy one is provided.

The messengers are sent back to the young man's place and told not to come back until they (the bride's family) have finished eating the meat from the heifer. Since the meat is not shared with the young man's people, this usually takes one to two days, depending on the amount of meat. The messenger goes back and informs the committee that the cow was accepted, and they must wait until they are called to go and continue. Two messengers are then sent from the young woman's place to the young man's place to go and inform them that they can continue with the *patlo* the next morning at 5 a.m., or after a day or two.

The next day the bride-seeker again goes to the young woman's place to confirm once more that the *sego sa metsi* will be given to them. Then the committee confirms by saying, yes indeed, the *sego sa metsi* will be given to them. Then the bride's committee confirms by saying that indeed the *sego sa metsi* will be given to them.

### *Diaparo tsa maitumediso* and formal introductions

The bride seeker's party goes back to tell the committee at the young man's place that the bride has been released. Eight *bommaditshale* go to the young woman's place so that they can wipe away the footprints of the bride-seekers, and to confirm again if the *sego sa metsi* will be released. While *bommaditshale* are still seated, the young woman's committee asks them if they know the name of their daughter. If they do not know they are charged an amount of P200.00.

After confirmation, *bommaditshale* go back to the young man's place and inform them that the *sego sa metsi* will be released to them.

On this same day, in the evening, *bommaditshale* are sent to bring some clothes (*diaparo tsa maitumediso*) to the young woman's biological parents. Her mother is given a dress, shoes, two headscarves (*tukwi tse pedi*), a big blanket and P200.00 cash for a half-slip or petticoat. For her father they include a full suit, one pair of shoes and a hat. The young man is the one who is responsible for the purchase of these clothes.

The paternal aunt (*rakgadi*) of the young woman is the one who receives the clothes and gives them to the parents so that they can try them on. If the clothes fit the parents, they inform *bommaditshale*, if not they send them back.

### *Podi ya maitumediso* and formal introductions

Afterwards *bommaditshale* say '*re kopa tsela*' so that they go back to the young man's family to inform them that the clothes are acceptable.

The next morning, the messengers are sent to bring a goat (*podi ya maitumediso*) to the young woman's parents. When they arrive at the gate, one of them goes in and tells them that the goat has arrived. People from the committee come out to inspect the goat. If it is fine, they accept it, and the messengers go back and inform the committee that the goat has been accepted.

In the evening a messenger from the young woman's committee is sent to the young man's place to tell them that they want the young man to visit them so that they can see him, and then he goes back to those who sent him with feedback.

In the morning the whole committee, with the young man, go to the young woman's place. This is the first time the young man comes out since the inception of the *patlo* process. Upon arrival they are given chairs (men) and sitting mats (women) and welcomed.

Then they are asked to greet each other, except for the young man, who is taken by the hand by his paternal uncl and takes him to the young woman's biological parents first to greet them and then to the rest of the relatives. After that he is led to sit down.

The young man's parents, through the committee, then ask to see the young woman. The young woman is led out of the house by her maternal aunt to greet the young man's biological parents, and then his relatives. Then the girl is led back to her mother's side and seated. The young woman's paternal uncle is chosen to introduce the young woman's relatives to the young man's by mentioning their names and how they are related to the young woman.

Afterwards, on the young man's side, the same is done by his paternal uncle. Tea is served to the young man's parents and the committee, after which they ask to be released (*ba kopa tsela ya go tswa*).

## THE BRIDE IS INVITED TO INSPECT HER NEW HOME (*O YA GO BONA MOTSE*)

In the evening the maternal uncle of the young man is sent to the young woman's place to ask if the young woman can visit them. '*Re romilwe go tla go adima sego-sa metsi gore etela, aye go bona motse*', he pronounces. At first, they agree to release their daughter for a month, then she comes back. For her to go and stay with her husband permanently, the young man must pay *bogadi.*

If the young woman is released to go and stay for a month, they send a message two days before that they will bring the young woman. During these two days the young woman is counselled by other married women on how to behave (*jaaka mosadi yo o batilweng*) at her husband's place. On the set date in the morning, the young woman is taken by other married women to the young man's place, and they hand her over to the committee. Once she is welcomed, they go back and inform their people that she has arrived safely, and the in-laws have accepted her.

After the young woman has arrived at her in-law's place, she is free to stay and work with them and help them in all their chores. Since the young woman is released temporarily for a period of a month, after this period she is taken back to her parents' home by the young man's maternal uncles and other relatives.

From this period the young man is free to visit the young woman's place at any time and can even ask the girl to visit him again. But if he wants her to go back for a period of another month, he must pay P500.00.

This concludes the formalities of the process of *patlo*. It is an elaborate ritual which consists of activities which are highly symbolic and are designed to contain important lessons for both the couple and the community.

## PENALTIES

Below is a list of penalties that may be imposed during *patlo*:

(a) Whenever the messengers from the young man's side go to the young woman's place, they must follow each other (*ba ikgata metlhala*). If they stumble or fall, they are charged P100.00. The more they fall, the more they are charged. They are charged because it is said that *ba kgama botsadi* (they dishonour parenthood).

(b) If the clothes that are given to the biological parents of the young woman are not the right size, they are sent back, and the young man's committee are asked to buy new ones.

(c) The young woman is taken to go and stay at her husband's place for a month. If she stays for more than a month, the young man is charged money because this shows disrespect to the family.

### EXPECTATIONS OF THE GROOM-TO-BE

The groom-to-be must be like a son to the young woman's parents, and he must always support them. The bride to be must be treated like a daughter. The parents from both sides are expected to treat each other like relatives.

## CHANGES IN MARRIAGE PRACTICES

### BRIDE WEALTH (*BOGADI*)

*Bogadi* is a gift provided by the young man to the young woman's parents as appreciation for raising and caring for the bride-to be. *Bogadi* can be in the form of cash (P12,000) or cattle (six female cows). It is taken to the young woman's family at a specified time that has been agreed on by the uncles of the young man. This can take place immediately after *patlo* or later, depending on the ability of the young man to pay. *Bogadi* is distributed among close family members of the bride to be.

Among the Hambukushu, if both the woman and man are from the same tribe, *bogadi* can be reduced, but if they are from different tribes the amount may increase. Traditionally *bogadi* belongs to the biological parents, but nowadays a young woman can ask for the whole amount and is the one who distributes it. She can even share it with her husband. Traditionally the young woman could not help her husband pay *bogadi*, however in modern times young ladies partner with their fiancés to raise the money for *bogadi*.

*Kgomo ya serufo*: in Hambukushu called *kgomo ya go gata motlhala* comes after the wedding celebration. *Bogadi* is not part of the broader range of gifting.

### WEDDING CEREMONY (*KEMO/MOKETE WA LENYALO*)

The wedding ceremony can happen immediately after *patlo* or later. It depends on what the partners have agreed, as well as on their resources.

If the partners have agreed to get married, they inform their parents and then they can register at the District Commissioner's office (*go pega maina*). Twenty-one days after registration, the groom and the bride can choose to put on their rings at the District Commissioner's office, or wait until the day of celebration at home.

### ACTIVITIES DURING THE DAY OF THE WEDDING CELEBRATION

When the marriage preparations start, the groom and bride stay at their respective family homes. On the day of the wedding ceremony, very early in the morning, the bride-to-be is dressed by the *mosupi*, her unmarried friend. The selected *bommaditshale* also help the bride put on the wedding dress (*lesire*) and provide her with everything she needs to prepare for the ceremony. The groom also has a companion who dresses him up and assists him.

After all these elaborate preparations everyone goes to the church where all the solemnising and blessings are performed by the priest. The groom, his parents, their relatives and friends arrive first at the church and wait for the bride and her family. The groom is taken by the hand by his paternal uncle and led into the church. When the bride arrives, she is taken by the hand by her paternal uncle, who leads her into the church, where the groom is waiting for her. At this point in time there are ululations. The priest then commences the church service, which includes the exchange of vows and rings by the couple.

After introductions, a prayer is offered to bless the food and then it is served. The best men and bridesmaids first serve the couple and then they feed each other. This symbolises unity, love and that the couple is one and no longer separate. Entertainment is provided, which is usually a healthy mix of traditional and contemporary music.

A cow (*kgomo ya diphiri*) is eaten at night by males, only before the couple goes to the District Commissioner office the next day.

In comparison to the past, today's wedding ceremonies are more expensive, with additional costs covering clothes, venues, photo or video shoots, tent hire, chairs, and entertainment.

## Marriage counselling (*Go laya*)

In the afternoon of the day of the celebration, the groom goes home to change into traditional attire of German print or African attire, returns to the wedding venue for a while, and then goes back to his place in the evening to wait for the bride. While waiting for the bride, the groom is counselled by his uncles, father and mother. The counselling takes place outside the house (*ko patlelong kana ko kgotleng*) because a man is the one who makes decisions that affect the whole compound as head of the family.

Counselling the bride is done after the celebration at her family's house, inside the compound (*lolwapa*) because she is the woman of the house (*ke mosadi wa lolwapa)* who takes care of the household. The counselling is done by *bommaditshale* (married women) including aunties and grandmothers, as they are regarded as having the experience and knowledge to do so.

## Taking the bride to her in-laws (*Go isa monyadi/monyadiwa*)

In the evening of the day of celebration the bride is prepared by *bommaditshale*. The bride puts on specific clothes (*diaparo tsa go bopeletsa*), comprising a long traditional dress, traditional headscarf (*tukwi*) and *tshale* (shawl). After preparation the bride is taken to her husband. She covers her face with a cloth, symbolising the fact that she might not find the way back to her parents' home. At this time, she only takes with her a toiletry bag and a bottle of water.

The bride is taken to her in-laws by *bommaditshale*. When she arrives, she is taken to her husband's side and the husband is asked to uncover her and kiss her. This is followed by ululations. The respondent narrated that all these rituals of *go bopeletsa* were not originally part of the Hambukushu traditional wedding. They are most probably recent borrowings from other tribes in Botswana.

After handing over the bride, *bommaditshale* return home to inform the bride's parents that she arrived well and has been accepted. The bride spends the night with her husband. After the bride takes off the clothes that she wore when she was taken to her in-laws (*diaparo tsa go bopeletsa*), they are given to her mother-in-law.

## Return of the bride to her natal home

Early in the morning the bride is prepared to go back to her natal home. She wears a traditional dress, headscarf (*tukwi*) and tshale (*shawl*).

She is taken back by *bommaditshale* from the groom's side because they have experience with wedding processes. If they are walking, they follow each other (*ba a tlhomagana*) with the bride in the middle, which signifies that she is protected. Upon arrival at her natal home, the bride is taken around the compound by the married women, stopping at each door and being introduced with these words: 'This is the house of so and so and it's not that you are separated from them, they are still your family, but you have been taken to go and join the household of your husband. They are your new family', (*O laela motse*). Here the bride is expected to listen to everything said to her by other married women. After going around the homes, they sit down inside the compound. The groom's committee brings a cow (*kgomo ya kgato motlhala*) which is slaughtered and shared among the bride's family members.

Afterwards, the married women take the bride back to her husband's place, where her family prepares some traditional farming products for her such as grain seeds, pumpkin seeds, a hoe, household utensils, a woven basket (*tlatlana*) and winnowing basket (*leselo*). Married women help her to carry these products which signify that she is a wife and must provide for the family. When she arrives at her husband's place, they welcome her with ululations.

The bride then returns to her natal home with her husband and all her in-laws for final introductions. Just as during the day of celebration, the paternal uncles introduce the family members to each other. If the bride or groom had a child from a past relationship, this is the time to introduce the child to the whole family. Next is the cutting of the cake, which is a task full of symbolism. The bride and groom share a piece of cake before distributing the cake to the guests, to symbolise their union and their promise to forever provide for each other. The bride serves her in-laws, and the groom serves his. This signifies that the bride's in-laws are her parents now, she is part of their household, she is their child. The groom also belongs to the household of his in-laws. The sharing of the cake also signifies unity, one family.

After this the bride bids farewell to her family, packs her belongings and goes with her in-laws. From this time on, the bride is expected to only visit her natal home to see her biological parents, with permission from her husband, as well as during funerals, weddings or family celebrations.

In Hambukushu tradition, the bride had to accept the farming tools and household utensils gifted to her because parents believed that, as a wife, she needed those things to care for her family. However, in this new generation those things are no longer provided because the parents may not have them, or they may no longer be farmers.

Cake eating is a new practice and was not part of the traditional Hambukushu wedding ceremony.

## MARRIAGE RITES AND THE SIGNIFICANCE OF METAPHORICAL LANGUAGE AND SYMBOLIC ACTIONS

### MARRIAGE RITES

Hambukushu weddings announce to the community the union of the individuals marrying, and allow the community to express its approval of, and support for, that union. Wedding rituals throughout the Hambukushu community share several common features. An essential element of nearly all wedding ceremonies is the symbolic expression of the union between the individuals marrying. This union may be signified by the exchange of rings, the change of the bride's surname to her husband's, the signing of the marriage registration form, or simply the joining of hands. Other rituals emphasise the function of the marriage as the foundation of the family. For instance, the bride is provided with some traditional farming utensils to show her that she has to provide for her family. Feasting and dancing at Hambukushu weddings by family and friends signifiy the community's blessing of the marriage.

In the Hambukushu traditional marriage *sego sa metsi* (*mukakuveta meyo*) means 'the one who fetches water'. It is the name given to the young woman while the bride-seeking is in process, before the actual marriage. As the name suggests, she is the one who will be sent by her in-laws to draw water, cook and do household chores in the compound.

### RIGHTS, PRIVILEGES AND BENEFITS ASSOCIATED WITH TRADITIONAL MARRIAGE PRACTICES

Only married men and women are invited to bride-seeking processes and wedding ceremonies. They can attend and make decisions during discussions about weddings. Unmarried men and women do not participate. If a couple is not married, when their child wants to marry, the unmarried parents do not have the right to take part in the marriage processes.

## CHALLENGES IN TRADITIONAL HAMBUKUSHU MARRIAGES TODAY

There are a number of challenges facing Hambukushu marriage, mainly due to modern influences and the influence of oher cultures. These include those below.

(a) Attire /Clothes (*Kapari*)

Traditionally a wife was not allowed to wear trousers when visiting her in-laws, but nowadays she may, due to modern influences, changes in fashion and social status. This change is however not accepted by some sections of Hanbukushu communities.

(b) Lack of support from the couples

Both parents sometimes complain that both the groom and the bride do not work for their in-laws and their lives are centred on themselves. This is influenced by the fact that most of the time the couples live and work far away from their parents and face financial constraints that prevent them from supporting their parents. In the traditional setting if parents felt neglected, they would call their children and inform them about their failure to take care of them.

(c) Polygamy

Traditionally in the Hambukushu culture a husband can decide to take a second wife. There are various reasons why men might want a second wife, such as the desire to have many children or the infertility of the first wife. A wealthy man might also be inclined to take another wife since he has the ability to support more than one family. Polygamy would be a challenge in this era of sexually transmitted diseases as it creates tension between the wife and the husband if the woman is not happy with it. In the traditional setting, problems relating to polygamy were resolved by the parents and sometimes a headman was involved. If the woman was unhappy with the prospect of polygamy, she could complain to both parents and then the headman. Since it was allowed in customary marriage, she was advised to accept their judgement.

(d) Domestic violence

In a traditional marriage a wife is not allowed to go back home when the spouses are in conflict. She must report first to the parents of the groom and wait for their response. She is then faced with the prospect of staying in a toxic and violent marriage. Domestic violence can be caused by adultery, the couple falling out of love, jealousy, insecurity or infertility. In the Hambukushu traditional marriage it was understood that only a woman could be abused by the man and not the other way around. If the woman was abused, she informs the groom's parents, and they call the couple for a meeting. If the abuse continues the headman is consulted and the case reported. The husband may be fined. If he no longer loves his wife, he can send her back to her natal home.

(e) Infertility

When a couple is unable to have children it causes great pain emotionally, physically, and spiritually. The man may get another wife through customary or traditional marriage laws. Infertility can be linked to old age, blocked tubes in the woman, low sperm count in the man or to illness in the man or the woman. Traditionally this was solved by visiting a traditional doctor who was believed to have the medicine to cure infertility. The man could also marry another wife.

# Changes and their Impact on Hambukushu Traditional Marriage Rites

## Bride-seeking (*Patlo*)

*Patlo* was not part of the traditional Hambukushu engagement process. The only process that was used to inform parents of engagements, or to inform sons or daughters about their betrothed, was through *kushesha*, which is still practised by some individuals, especially those who never went to school or those who reside in the village exclusively and want to keep their culture and customs.

## Polygamy

In the past a married man could still take another wife or wives, and he could marry them officially through the traditional process.

## *Kwandekera* (Betrothal)

As a form of engagement *kwandekera* is no longer practised by the Hambukushu community. The people prefer the process of bride-seeking.

## Marriage registration and marriage certificates

The process of marriage registration with the District Commissioner is practised in the Hambukushu community currently. However, in the past in the traditional marriage there was no registration at all. If a man and woman were declared married by their parents and they had followed all the traditional marriage ways, the couple was considered as married by the community at large.

## White wedding celebration

The 'white wedding' was not celebrated in the Hambukushu marriage customs. However, nowadays 'white weddings' are the norm. Couples go to church and the bride wears a white dress with lace and veil, with the groom in white shirt and modern suit.

## *Bogadi* (Bride-wealth)

In the past even two cows could be accepted as *bogadi*. If the husband did not have enough wealth, he gave what he could afford. Nowadays six female cows or P12,000 cash are the standard price. Furthermore, the biological parents were the ones who had control over the bride-wealth and determined how to distribute it, whereas now some brides demand it back from the parents and want to distribute it themselves. This behaviour is obviously not acceptable to the parents and the community as it is seen as disruptive.

## Biological parents' involvement in the marriage practices

In the past the biological parents were part of the major decisions in their children's marriage, even if they were not married themselves. The current practice is that if the parents are not married, they are not allowed to make decisions in their children's marriage.

### Church weddings

Most people among the Hambukushu get married in church rather than in the traditional or customary way.

## Reasons for the Changes in Hambukushu Weddings

### Other peoples' cultures

In the Hambukushu traditional marriage process bride-seeking was not part of the marriage process, but because of the influence of other tribes, especially through inter-marriage, *patlo* became part of the Hambukushu marriage processes. Even the white wedding celebration is a foreign influence from other cultures. Marriage between two people from different cultures also influences the bride-wealth price. If a young Mombukushu woman is married to a young man from a different tribe, the bride-wealth price can be influenced by what is standard or acceptable in that tribe.

### The Christian churches

Christian churches discourage polygamy, and most couples get married in the church as a result. Christianity is the most popular religion in Botswana.

### Education

Traditionally girls were forced into marriages. However, once a child is educated, she or he is no longer influenced by the traditional customs of marriage such as *kushesha* and *kwandekera.*

### The law of the country

Bridewealth, *bogadi*, is standard among the Hambukushu and it is decided by dominant Paramount Chiefs. Local traditional chiefs for the small tribes (*dikgosana*) do not have the power to control the marriage culture of their own tribe. In addition, there is an age limit. Only people who are twenty-one and above are allowed to get married without parental permission.

## Suggestions for Ensuring Stability and Tolerance in Marriage

Interviewees and participants were requested to suggest the different ways that would bring stability in marriages. Suggestions that were made included the following;

(a) **Change the law** – According to one respondent, every tribe and their traditional leaders should be given power to determine their marriage practices. The respondent emphasised that *dikgosana* should be given the power to govern traditional marriages in their societies.

(f) **Base marriage on God** – Faith and religious leaders emphasised that for a marriage to be stable it must be founded on the word of God, as marriage is from God.

(g) **Socio-economic factors** – Respondents said that couples who stay in different places due to work transfers create long distance relationships which affect communication between them. It was suggested that the government should encourage married couples to live and work in the same town or village.

(h) **Bride-wealth reduction** – Other participants said that the bride-wealth must be reduced to at least four cattle, so that it is affordable and does not put a strain on the groom.

(i) **Morality** – Faithfulness, commitment, love, loyalty and honesty we singled out as important values that should prevail in all marriages to ensure stability and tolerance in marriage.

# 17

# KHOISAN (G||ANA PEOPLE OF ZUTSHWA)

*Tshisimogo L. Leepang*

## BACKGROUND INFORMATION OF NEW XADE AND THE G||ANA PEOPLE

New Xade is a settlement that was created in 1997 after the residents of Central Kalahari Game Reserve were relocated by the government in 1997 and 2002. It is home to the G||ana people and other ethnic groups. The ethnic group in question has been influenced by different cultures such as European and Tswana. The G||ana people are believed to have originated from a traditional pit or well (G||ana) but it is not clear where that well was. They refer to themselves as the G||ana-kho, which suggests that they are the people who originate from the well. Some of the G||ana communities intermarried with the other ethnic groups and this had a huge impact on their way of lives as they have lost some of their cultural identities. Most of the children use Setswana names and some of the G||ana prefer to use both English and Setswana names rather than their G||ana names. After intermarriages they started viewing some elements they used to value as barbaric.

## MARRIAGE FROM THE POINT OF VIEW OF THE G||ANA-KHO

There are many perspectives regarding the concept of marriage, and this conceptualization makes different ethnic groups respond to it differently. There are some people who view marriage as a waste of resources as it requires more reserves. Other people feel marriage needs to be reviewed, since some people use it to enrich themselves, while other people believe that marriage plays a positive role in the lives of people. According to the G||ana people, marriage is about building the family and creating a legacy. Traditionally, the G||ana people used to have clans which were regarded as very important in community cohesion. Therefore, marriage was used to strengthen this cohesion. Moreover, G||ana people regarded peace as vital in their day to day lives. The men and women were taught to be responsible partners, parents and in-laws, and this exercise was done through their initiation schools. In addition, marriage was also regarded as an institution that helps the couple achieve their dreams and goals. In every society one of the dreams both boys and girls have is to marry and establish a happy family. The G||ana people perceive marriage as uniting the two families and creating unity between them. There were instances where marriage was between people from the same ethnic group but there were instances where it was between the different ethnic groups, G||ana-kho and the G|ui-kho. Hence it was regarded as something that creates friendship and bond between people and different ethnic groups. When the couples had a conflict, it was regarded as a threat to the friendship and bonds that exist between the two families or ethnic groups. Similarly, the peace that exists between the married couple was seen as vital between the two families. In addition, marriage among the G||ana people was considered a sign of maturity. To encourage this growth when the children were growing up, they were trained in different survival skills to prepare them to be strong, exemplary leaders, responsible parents, and custodians of the culture. Hence marriage was a sign that the married couples were ready to start a new life on their own.

## TYPES OF MARRIAGE AND THEIR SIGNIFICANCE AMONG THE G||ANA PEOPLE OF NEW XADE

In the pre-colonial era the G||ana people would practice their traditional way of life. They would arrange marriages for their children who would accept the choices made by their parents. However, when they got in contact with the Bakgalagari they experienced assimilation and lost most of their values. They stopped practicing their culture and began adopting the Bakgalagari marriage practices because the Bakgalagari would use them as their herd boys and impose the Bakgalagari language and culture on the G||ana people. After independence they experienced another form of assimilation brought about by modernization. Since their culture was regarded as barbaric, they shifted to other so called developed cultures like the Tswana-speaking and European cultures. In modern Botswana the G||ana people started practising the Tswana marriage processes, the Christian marriage procedures and the District Commissioner's marriage practice.

## Traditional G||ana marriage

There are two types of marriages in the G||ana community that can be categorised as arranged and unplanned marriages. First the man who wanted to marry would identify a woman he wished to marry. The man would then inform his cousin, who in turn would to tell his uncle. After the uncle was informed, he would either approve or refuse, based on the behaviour of the family. If the uncle approved, the man would make regular visits until the parents of the woman complain to the parents of the man regarding the man's regular visits. When this happens the parents of the man automatically declare their son's interest in marrying their daughter.

Secondly, marriage was arranged by the parents of the man after realising that he was a mature man who was ready to have his own family. They would identify a woman whom they want their son to marry, and would then inform him about their interest in this woman. At this stage they were not supposed to have any intimacy until a ritual was performed to protect them from diseases. The man waits for the woman to reach puberty. When a girl reaches puberty, she was confined for a certain period. During confinement she was mentored by the older women. She was told that she was now getting into another stage which comes with certain responsibilities. She was taught to take care of herself, to behave well and to be faithful. The man and woman's blood and urine were mixed to protect them from diseases. Furthermore, during confinement the man was invited to come and make fire while facing the opposite direction from the entrance of the house. After confinement the boy would kill a duiker and the skin was treated and the woman wears it. Puberty in girls was called *n|aba*.

After marriage, when one of the couples dies, normally the remaining partner was inherited by the younger sister or brother. This practice was used to protect the legacy. The relationship between the two families would continue due to the fact that the remaining partner was inherited by a sibling. There were instances where the woman would find a second wife for her husband to take care of him especially when she feels she is too old to perform the household duties.

Many things were considered by the boy and his parents when they choose a girl for him. The girl was supposed to be a good woman who can take care of his husband and children. She was supposed to be a woman who can work for her husband, a woman who can gather and prepare food for her husband and her in-laws. On the other hand, the parents of the girl accept the proposal of the boy and his parents when he can provide for his wife and them. They regard him as a good son in-law when he can hunt and have skills such like making animal skin clothing.

Marriage is a private practice between the parents of the girl's and boy's parents and their relatives, but it had great value to not only them but also to the society.

After the G||ana people were relocated from their ancestral land they got in contact with other ethnic groups and adopted some of their cultural practices. Just like other ethnic groups the G||ana people practice Tswana marriage practices – the District Commissioner's and Christian marriage practices. A certain fraction of the population believes that some of these practices are a threat to their cultural practices while a certain fraction embraces them.

The G||ana people believe that their traditional marriage was cheap as it did not require many resources, unlike modern marriages. They believe it was convenient as it was built on mutual understanding, unlike contemporary marriages. In addition, the G||ana people believe that traditional marriages were sustainable as they could last longer, the parents having more power in traditional marriages compared to modern marriages. Moreover, the G||ana people argue that the modern marriages' primary reasons are fame and wealth as compared to traditional marriages whose primary reason was protection, legacy building and bearing children.

## THE G||ANALISED TSWANA MARRIAGE PRACTICES

The G||analised Tswana marriage practices are those Tswana marriages that are partially practiced by the G||ana people. After the G||ana people adopt certain Tswana speaking marriages practices, they partially follow the marriage procedure of the Tswana speaking people. These types of marriages usually occur in intermarriages that occur between the G||ana people and other ethnic groups. First, the woman and the man start dating on their own; their relationship is not arranged. They may have children before marriage but if the parents of both the children are strict, they only have children after marriage. When the man wants to marry, he informs his uncle who informs the woman's parents, and the elders meet and send a message to the woman's parents. After that there is '*go kokota*' in Setswana but the G||ana people referred to this process as *g||aekho kene*. The parents make a visit and declare that their son wishes to marry. During this process the parents of the man are charged a certain number of cattle, based on whether they had children before marriage or not. In most instances they are told to pay eight cattle. As compared to the G||ana people traditional marriages this type of marriage process is not arranged, so the parents have little control over it. The G||ana people believe that this type of marriage is based on creation of wealth unlike the G||ana people traditional marriages. This type of marriage has replaced the G||ana traditional marriage and forced some people who do not have cattle to be reluctant to marry. Moreover, the G||ana people's traditional marriages are not recognised in the contemporary Botswana, which makes most of the men be reluctant to marry. In addition, they believe that this type of marriage does not have any significance as compared to their traditional marriages.

## THE CHRISTIAN MARRIAGE PROCESS AND PRACTICE

Generally speaking, one quarter of the G||ana population is Christian. Since churches play a certain role in societies the members are taught not to have intimacy nor to cohabit before marriage, as prescribed by the Bible. However, some members break this law by having children before marriage, and cohabit.

The church members go through counselling on how to behave as a married couple. Normally they do this after they have gone to the District Commissioner. In most marriages that have taken place, the church members would come and sing during the wedding celebrations, and the pastor gives a word of encouragement. Some of the G||ana communities embrace this type of marriage, whereas a certain proportion of the population does not embrace it because they view some of this marriage as leading to the demise of their traditional marriages. The G||ana people view churches as playing a vital role in the moral development of their society, even though they think it is a threat to the traditional marriage practices.

### The District Commissioner's marriage process

These are the marriages registered at the District Commissioner's office. Registering of the marriage is regarded in Setswana as *go pega nyalo,* which is regarded in G||ana language as *|'on ≠ee.* When the people register their marriage, they are accompanied by few people; two from the man's side and another two from the woman's side. However, on Thursdays the married couples are accompanied by their parents. On Friday they do what is referred to as *go folosa* in Setswana and in G||ana language it is called *|'on ||oaxu.* During this process they take an oath before the District Commissioner and their parents, and declare whether they are marrying in community of property or not. After this they are given a marriage certificate as proof of marriage. The G||ana people whose marriages were celebrated in the past, believe that modern laws do not recognise their marriages on the basis that they were not done before the District Commissioner's office. In addition, when the G||ana people had their marriages, they did not acquire marriage certificates. Some people do not celebrate after this process, while some do.

## Taboos among the G||ana People of New Xade

A taboo is referred to as *ŋaaχo* in the G||ana language. Like other ethnic groups the G||ana people have certain taboos that govern different aspect of their lives namely, food, animal and people's behaviour. There were certain taboos before marriage and those that were supposed to be followed after marriage.

### Taboos before marriage

The boy and the girl were not supposed to have intimacy before marriage because it was believed that they were capable of infecting each other with diseases. Therefore, their blood and urine were mixed to protect them from diseases. The other reason for mixing blood was to unite them and to strengthen them. The girl and the boy would wait for certain traditional rituals before they can have intimacy. After the girl reaches puberty, she was confined and during confinement men were not supposed to come closer to see her, including the man who was chosen for her. Even during the time that he makes fire he was not supposed to face the entrance of the house as he was not allowed to see her.

According to the G||ana people, marriage is sacred and, like other institutions therefore, for it to thrive there must be taboos that govern it. Before the parents of the man meeting the parents of the girl, they make fire and counsel their son. This is done so that the man marrying cannot wake up late when he is at his in-laws (the girl's parents' place). It is believed that the man or the woman should wake up before the sun rises when he/she is at her parents' in-laws' home. The person that wakes up after sun rise was regarded as disrespectful. Therefore, to be regarded as a good in-law you were expected to wake up before sunrise. Women who did not adhere to this taboo were regarded as weak and not exemplary, similarly men who did not were viewed as weak. This relationship between the in-laws is called *n|uik'o*, whereby someone was expected to respect his/her in-laws. The concept of *n|uik'o* was crucial in the creation of a strong friendship and peace between the in-laws. It created an environment whereby the people had to respect their in-laws.

### Taboos during confinement

When the girl was confined there were certain taboos that the old women would tell her, to protect her, the people and the environment. When the girl was confined, she was taken care of by old women, and during this process the grandmother was the one who would lead. The girl would sleep on one side and was not allowed to change her sleeping positions until her grandmother assisted her. In addition, she was not allowed to scratch herself with her hands but would use a stick which was designed for her. It was believed that she would develop wounds on her body if she scratched herself with her hands. The girl was not allowed to make fire until the old women perform a ritual to allow her to do so. Moreover, she was not allowed to gather wild fruits or interact with nature before rituals were performed, allowing her to do so. This was done to protect the environment. When men were in the wild, hunting for animals such as lions and leopards, the girl was not allowed to wake up until they came back.

### Taboos after marriage

The woman was not allowed to speak loudly in the evening. It was believed that the woman who speaks loudly in the evening was capable of exposing her family matters to the other people. Exposing family matters was not condoned because it was regarded as an embarrassment to the family. Any woman who violated this taboo was viewed as an immature woman or wife. In addition, the woman was not allowed to leave the house open; her house should always be closed as this was a symbol of protecting the secrets of her family – as a woman you were expected to protect the secrets of your family. As demonstrated above the G||ana people believed in peace, protection of the families and privacy.

## Bride-wealth (*Bogadi*) among the G||ana People of New Xade

Since the G||ana community did not believe in creation of wealth they did not have a specific number of things that were given to the in-laws as *bogadi*, referred as *kama* in G□ana language. They would provide designed duiker skins to the in-laws as *bogadi*. It was the uncle and his wife, and the paternal uncle and his wife, who would deliver these things to the woman's counterparta. They would hand them to the woman's parents. On one hand the man would continue working for his in-laws in the same way as he used to before the marriage process was carried out. *Bogadi* was more about labour than material things. The G||ana community believed that a man was supposed to be a hard worker and to do that he was expected to work for his in-laws. He was expected to bring food and firewood for them. All the things done for the in-laws were referred to as *kye-‡am*, which means something from the thigh. After their marriage the newly-weds would either stay with the man's parents or they would make their own home.

There were some G||ana communities known as the G||ana-‡ebe. The G||ana-‡ebe are a mixture of the G||ana people and the Bakgalagari. This type of community was formed during intermarriages between the two peoples. This community had goats and they would give their in-laws goats as *bogadi,* depending on their economic status, or on the relationship between the woman's and man's parents.

The G||ana community did not have wedding celebrations other than performing rituals. A dress was designed with animal skins to signify that the woman was married as opposed to nowadays whereby the ring signifies marriage. The dress, shoes and hat were designed by the man marrying the girl. He designs these clothes while she was in confinement, so that she could wear them after confinement.

There was cheating among the G||ana community, but it was not condoned. Those who practised this were regarded as bad examples. This was known as *zaaku* in G□ana. Someone's concubine was called *zaa*. The male one was called *zaa-be* and the female one was referred to as *zaa-se*. This type of relationships caused conflicts and rivalries between the parents of the involved parties. When the woman discovered that her man was cheating, her reaction was based on whether she liked that woman or not. If she loved the woman, she would allow her to continue dating her man. On the other hand, if she hated her, she would not allow her to continue dating her husband. They were instances where the woman would fight this woman or would accept her as the second wife. In addition, when the woman felt that she was too old to do other domestic duties she would find a good second wife that will take a good care of her husband. These women would peacefully share this man.

## Marriage Rights and the Significance of Metaphorical Language and Symbolic Actions among the G||ana People

### Metaphorical language

*Kye ‡am* is used by the G||ana people to refer to work done for the in-laws by their son in-law. In other words, it was labour or gifts from the man to his in-laws. It literally means something from the thigh.

*Zaa-ku*, is a concept consisting of the root *zaa* which refers to tasting, and the suffix *–ku* which refers to doing something to each other. This expression is used to describe people who are cheating their partners. The people who are living together were not described with this term. Another alternative term that was used to describe the cheating partners was *tsa'-ku*. It literally means stealing each other. The terms used to describe this behavior signify that it was not condoned by the G||ana society.

There is another concept that is used to describe the people who are married. *Sie-ku* is a term used by the G||ana people to indicate that the man and woman got married.

The word *sie* means taking something and the suffix *-ku* means doing something to each other as described above. The concept is used to show that the man has taken the wife away from her parents to start a new life with her.

### SYMBOLIC ACTIONS

Confinement was symbolic because it signified maturity. It was a sign that the girl had developed into a woman who was ready to get married and establish her own family. When the man makes fire, he faces away fromthe girl, so that the girl in confinement could not see him. It is believed that they should not see each other when she is confined. This was done because during confinement it was only the older women who were allowed to be there so as to take care of the girl. When they got married the girl and the boy's blood is mixed so as to strengthen them.

## FACTORS OF CHANGE AND THEIR IMPACT ON TRADITIONAL MARRIAGE RITES AND PRACTICES AMONG THE G||ANA COMMUNITY

The G||ana community's marriage practices changed due to contact with other major cultures. The other causes of the changes seen today was the fact that, during this contact, the so-called major tribes did not allow the men from the minority tribes to marry into their tribes. During this process they would impose their cultures on them as they viewed the minority people's cultures as too traditional and undesirable.

The adoption of other cultures, referred to as foreign cultures by the G||ana people, have destroyed some of the fundamental arrangements and values that existed in G||ana communities. When certain traditional marriage practices were weakened, this had a huge impact on the culture of the G||ana people in general. The adoption of foreign cultures brought conflicts between the children and their parents because the parents could no longer arrange marriages for their children. Their children started rejecting arranged marriages, as they believe they have rights to choose for themselves. Nowadays the marriages are not arranged, which makes it difficult for the parents to have much control over their children's choice of partners and marriage. When marriages are not arranged some complications occur in the marriages, leading to divorce.

Modern marriages are based on creation of wealth, which makes it difficult for people without resources to marry. Nowadays there are privileges for the married people. There are some roles and responsibilities for them as compared to what used to happen in the past.

## PREVALENT PROBLEMS AND CHALLENGES IN THE G||ANA PEOPLES' TRADITIONAL MARRIAGES

There are many challenges observed by the G||ana people that threaten their traditions. As the marriages are not arranged, and the elders have little control over them, there are more divorce cases as compared to pre-colonial times when they were still practising their traditional marriages. They believe catastrophic events like passion killing never existed when they were practising their traditional marriages. They argue that some of these things occur because the children never get blessings from their parents. Moreover, the G||ana people believe that modern marriages have many conflicts because so many marriages occur between people who are from different cultures. The G||ana people believe that since the traditional marriages were arranged, and would take place between people who know each other, it was easy to resolve conflicts between the married couple. They strongly believe that most of the changes were brought by assimilation and the idea that the G||ana marriage practices are 'barbaric' and need replacement with 'advanced' practices.

## Conclusion and Recommendations

Marriage in the G||ana community was a private exercise that was done without the involvement of many people, as in contemporary Botswana. The marriages were arranged, but many things were considered before the marriage could be completed or carried out compared to modern marriages that are not arranged by the elders. Some rituals were performed to protect the girl and the boy and also to unite them. In addition, there were some taboos that were followed so as to strengthen the family and create peace between the families. The *bogadi*, *kama* in G||ana, was more about labour than material things. Due to assimilation, the G||ana people started adopting the Tswana, Christian and District Commissioner's marriage processes.

The marriage practices that were performed in the past created cohesion between people, a sense of responsibility, respect between the children the parents and the in-laws, hence there is a need to revive them. This dream can only become a reality if all the community leaders and the G||ana community take action by rethinking and developing the projects that will revive their culture. The G||ana people believe that their traditional dance groups and drama groups should be empowered and supported to display some of these practices during their competitions.

The tribal authorities, as the custodians, should work together with the communities to revive the marriage rites and other important elements of culture. They believe that the marriage practices in G||ana culture need to be documented and taught to the youth so that it cannot die. After creating documentation, sufficient efforts should be made to share with the communities, as this could motivate and encourage them to preserve their culture. A deliberate stance should be taken to recognise some of the cultural practices and the certain arrangements should be made to stop the banning of hunting. Hunting licenses should be reintroduced so that it will be easy for the G||ana communities to practice their marriage practices. The G||ana argue that the G||ana peoples' traditional marriages, just like the Tswana-speaking people's traditional marriages, should be recognised by customary laws and other laws of Botswana.

The G||ana people also argue that the research on their cultural practices should be monitored because they have been exploited by some scholars who never make any sufficient efforts to share their research findings with them. They stated that they should not only be subjects in research but should also be researchers of their cultures.

# 18

# KHOISAN (NARO PEOPLE OF NEW XADE)

*Mr. Isaac Saul*

**Totem**: Steenbok

## INTRODUCTION TO THE NARO PEOPLE AND THEIR TOTEM

The Naro people refer to themselves as the *Ncoakhoe*, literally 'the red people,' or *Dqãe ne*, which means the steenboks or the people of the steenbok. This is because of the skin colour of a steenbok. A steenbok has a light golden-brown or reddish colour, which resembles the skin colour of the Naro people.

Apart from the skin colour of a steenbok, there are several reasons as to why the Naro people identify with the steenbok. Firstly, this animal is gentle and clever. Secondly, it has the tendency to isolate itself from other animals. Thirdly, it grazes within its marked territories. Fourthly, it can survive for longer periods without water, getting moisture from the small plants that it feeds on. Similarly, the first thing one can notice among the Naro people is their gentle, tender, soft-hearted and clever nature.

Secondly, the Naro people just like the steenbok, and have the tendency to isolate themselves from other ethnic groups. Thirdly, the Naro people have their own marked territory, which is the bush where they do most of their activities such as hunting and gathering of wild fruits. No wonder the early ethnographers referred to them as 'the Bushmen' and the early Dutch settlers as '*Boesjemannen*' and the Afrikaners refer to them as '*Boesmans*', which are all derogatory terms (Saul, 2017). Lastly, while in the bush, the

Naro people can survive for long periods without water, feeding on tubers and other small plants for moisture. All these features resemble the features of a steenbok.

The Naro people venerate the steenbok as their totem and meat from a steenbok was prohibited to certain categories or groups of people. An expectant woman or a breast-feeding woman was not supposed to eat steenbok meat. All girls and women were not allowed to eat meat from a steenbok, until they were fully grown up. Traditional healers were not allowed to eat its meat or to even come close to it. Thus, it was believed that all these people were either life-givers or protectors of life, and as such they were not supposed to eat steenbok meat. In the case of an expectant woman, or a breast-feeding mother, it was believed that bad luck could befall the baby. which could die. Similarly, a girl or a young woman was also considered a potential mother to be and was not allowed to eat steenbok meat. If she eats steenbok meat something terrible could happen to her or to the baby that she will give birth to in future. This was seen as a huge threat to the Naro, which could be extinct as a result of eating meat from a steenbok. Likewise, men whose wives were expecting, and men whose wives had young babies, were not allowed to eat steenbok meat, as it was also believed that this could have a bearing on their babies.

Traditional healers were considered to be bringing people back to life or to intercede on behalf of the people to the gods or ancestors. As such they were not allowed to eat steenbok meat or to come into contact with it, as this could affect their patients.

However, other groups of people were allowed to eat steenbok meat, and nothing could happen to them and these included elderly men and women, elderly men and young men whose wives were not expecting or having babies. Apart from the meat of a steenbok, its hides were essential for making such items as clothing for men and women, hunting set carriers for men, and coats for women.

## SENSE OF IDENTITY

The Naro people have praise expressions that they use to identity and distinguish themselves from other ethnic groups. The first of the expressions they have says: *'Dxùu sao gaen x'áè te tite, dxùu saon x'áè te,'* which literally means, 'Will you (women) not make firewood and watch me perform, make firewood and watch me perform.' When properly explained this expression means sing a song and watch me dance to its tunes. In essence, this expression means try me and see what will come out of me. In other words, I have so much to offer, the only thing you need to do is to set me ablaze and watch me. This shows the adventurous nature of the Naro people in exploring nature and their environment. In addition, fire meant a lot to the Naro people as they could gather around the fire in the evenings to tell stories to their children, and they would also sit around the fire at night to perform traditional healing dances.

The second praise expression goes something like, *'Gaxae Nxobe xae, gaxae ziga xae, hààn xae dxãa xoe, hààn xae dxãa xoe, dxãa xoe, dxãa xóé',* literally, 'We are the ciconia birds, we are the cute ones, let us lie in wait, let us lie in wait'. This expression means that, just as these birds can fly around up in the sky in a beautiful circle-like shape to show their beauty, let us relax and show our beauty.

The third praise expression goes something like, '*Cgane sa ko tc'úúa sa cgoa x'oo,* which literally means, 'A guinea fowl dies with its colour.' When properly explained this means the beauty of a guinea fowl never fades away and it dies with it. In the same way, the Naro people believe their beauty never fades away and they will die with it. This expression also includes the beauty of the skin colour of the Naro people, which is their identity as well as the beauty of their character.

The Naro people speak the Naro language, and they belong to the larger group of Khoisan languages found in Botswana. The Naro people are found in the Western part of Botswana in Ghanzi District in the following areas: Ghanzi Township and the surrounding farms and settlements, which include: D'kar, Kuke, Tchabo, East Hanahai, West Hanahai, New Kanagas, Kanagas, Tshobokwane, Grootlaagte, Karakubis, Charleshill and the surrounding farms (Batibo, 2005). Apart from Botswana, Naro speakers are also found in the Eastern part of Namibia along the Namibia–Botswana border in Gobabis, Zelda and the surrounding farms. Naro speakers are estimated to be around 10,000, with roughly 8,000 speakers in Botswana and 2,000 in Namibia, but very little is known regarding the population of Naro speakers in Namibia (Maho, 1998 and Visser, 2015 personal communication). In addition, among the Khoisan ethnic groups extant in Botswana, Naro speakers are considered to be numerically larger than other Khoisan language groups. This language is also used as a lingua franca among speakers of different Khoisan languages found in Ghanzi District (Batibo, 2009, and Hasselbring and Segatlhe, 2000).

The Naro people were originally nomads and would move from one place to the other in search of food. Generally, they are known to be hunter-gatherers. They are identified with their click languages and their golden-brown to reddish skin colour. Their language is related to G//ana, G/ui and Nama Khoisan languages.

## Understanding Marriage from the Naro's Point of View

Traditionally, marriage was perceived as a legal agreement between a man and a woman to become wife and husband. In most African cultures, marriage is regarded as a legal bond between a woman (wife) and her man (husband). This bond can be monogamous – between one wife and husband, or polygamous – between one husband and many wives, depending on the culture of the people. The Naro people regard marriage to be a union between a man and one wife. In other words, the Naro culture recognises only the monogamous type of marriage and does not tolerate polygamy.

In addition, the Naro culture believes that the union between the couple also creates a bond between their respective in-laws. Thus, the Naro people consider marriage to be a union between the husband and his parents, and his wife and her parents.

Furthermore, marriage among the Naro people was patrilocal. Once a girl gets married, she would move out of her father's house to stay with her husband at his father's house. If the girl was not married, she was under the authority of her father, but once she got married, she was under the authority of her husband. Thus, in Naro culture a young couple was to live with the parents of the husband. The parents of the husband were responsible for providing all the necessary support and care to the girl and to mentor and nurture her family. The husband was expected to treat her with love and respect, as this could make him gain favour in the eyes of his in-laws. However, the opposite could create tensions between his family and hers. Therefore, a married couple was expected to be on good terms at all times, so as to bring peace and unity between their respective families (Qhomatca, 2018).

It is worth noting that the Naro people lived as an egalitarian community, and marriages within them were never within the kin, but across clans. Marriages within the kin were forbidden and were considered awkward and shameful. One could not marry a woman bearing his mother's name or his sister's name or even his aunt's name. It was shameful to marry a person bearing your relative's name (Morris, 2018). The reason behind prohibiting marrying a person with the same name as your relative was to avoid marriages within relatives. This also underscores the fact that marriages among the Naro people were based solely on existing ties between the two families and how well they knew each other - and whether they were friends or not.

Cross-cultural marriages were never encouraged among the Naro people. The Naro people believed they would lead to the extinction of their race and bring racial impurity. They are also seen as contributing factors to ethnic conflicts and clashes. Therefore, in efforts to protect their cultural identity and race, the Naro people used only marriages between clans.

To this day, the Naro people have different clans such as the *Q'ao-c'õa nama*, literally the 'Nama with tall legs', who are believed to be Naro of Nama origin and possess Nama-like features, such as having long legs, like their Nama ancestors. There are also the *Xgaoka-dqùri*, literally the ones who struggle with a knife. These people probably owned knives and used them a lot, hence the name *Xgaoka-dqùri*. Another group is the *Suu-tshàa*, which literally means pot water. These people were probably slightly darker in skin-colour, hence the name pot water. Yet another group is known as *Dxòè-nxabo ne*, literally those that wear tortoise shell as their shoe. It is also possible that they wore tortoise shell on their feet to deserve such a name. The last clan was the *Kou-khoe*, which means people from *Kou*. The word *kou* refers to a sandy place. It refers to people of Naro ancestry, who originally came from a place with a lot of soft and fine sand, such as the modern-day East Hanahai and West Hanahai places.

In summary, the Naro people understood marriage to be a legitimate agreement between a man and a woman to become a husband and wife. The primary purpose of such an agreement was to reproduce, to build a home together, to provide for and to protect their parents, children and siblings who were considered a family. A married couple was expected to take care of its parents and children, as well as of that of their siblings. In order to support their family members, a married couple was expected to exercise family planning and to have not more than four children. In a nutshell, family planning was also a common practice among the Naro people. So, we can conclude that marriage among the Naro people was not only a union between a man and his wife and their respective parents, but also had the purpose of preserving their race and culture.

## Types of Marriages and their Significance for the Naro People

Naro culture recognises three types of marriages, which are: (a) arranged marriages, (b) forced marriages and (c) love marriages or cohabitation types of marriages.

Arranged marriages were common among the Naro people and were considered ideal and formal types of marriages among the Naro people. They were considered ideal and formal because children would obtain consent from their parents before getting married. Arranged marriages had two types.

The first type was where the boy would agree with his girl to get married. In this type of marriage, the agreement was solely between the two parties and they would only inform the parents to arrange a wedding for them. The second type was where the parents would arrange a marriage for their boy.

In most cases, the parents of the boy would propose to the parents of a girl on behalf of their boy. When parents choose a girl for their son to marry, they would take into consideration her family background, her family roots and the clan she belongs to. They would also consider the way they relate with her family, as well as her ability to take care of her in-laws and especially her future husband. Arranged marriages were considered to be more legitimate, as they had more support from the parents. In addition, most of the arranged marriages resulted from betrothal or could be made when the girl was fresh from her initiation to womanhood (Tcoma, 2018).

The other type of marriage, which was also not common among the Naro people, but did exist, was the forced type. In this type of marriage, a boy would take a girl by force to be his wife. In most instances, such types of marriages happened when the parents would agree for the two to get married, but the girl could not accept the proposal. In such cases, a boy was allowed to go with his peers to the girl's place and take her by force to his place to be his wife. Even if she refuses to go with him, he would drag her by force to his place. She would eventually give up and go with him, and she would become his wife. This type of marriage was not common among the Naro people and was considered inappropriate (Morris, 2018).

The third type of marriage among the Naro people was the love type. This type resulted from a secret affair between the boy and his girl. In other words, in love marriages a boy would secretly fall in love with a girl, and if he becomes known to her parents and to the rest of the community members, he would then become her lifetime partner. The practice of having a secret affair with each other was known as *ts'ããku*, literally stealing each other. This act was known as having a secret affair, because it was unofficial and was not known to any of the parents nor to any other relative. This secret affair could be equated to cohabitation. A girl who was in such an arangement was not allowed to have another one outside this and the same was true of the boy. Only death would separate such a couple. Thus, a boy who was having a secret affair with a girl and was eventually known to her parents and relatives was given full recognition as her lifetime partner and husband. This practice continues to date, and is the most common type of marriage among the Naro people nowadays.

## Kinship Ties and the Significance of Animal Meat Portions at a Wedding Event

The Naro people preferred eland meat for wedding occasions. The groom, with his father, was expected to hunt down an eland and come back home with its meat. The in-laws were rarely given fresh meat, and were given it dried. However, in case the in-laws wanted fresh meat there were specific portions of meat given to them. The back part of the eland was given to the in-laws, the chest and the skin from the chest was roasted and eaten. It was considered by analogy that the back part is where a child is carried, and the chest is where one is kept for protection. Therefore, the Naro people believed that this was an indication that the parents of the girl took care of their daughter, whom they are now giving over to their in-laws. Thus the care and protection they provided when raising her should be appreciated, and the practice should continue. Likewise, the parents of the girl were expected to do the same to the parents of the boy to show the same kind of appreciation. This practice was known as *kama*, which could be seen as the bride-wealth.

## Traditional Steps of Naro Traditional Marriage and the Role Players in Naro Culture

### Betrothal

Engagement, also known as betrothal, which is a promise of marriage made before the celebration of the wedding was a common practice among the Naro people, especially in arranged marriages where parents were to choose a girl for their son. In Naro culture a girl could only be betrothed to a boy of her age group or her peer. Betrothal happened only to girls who were about to reach puberty stage. It was considered that she was about to become a mature woman, who can make decisions on her own. When a girl has been betrothed, her future in-laws and their son would continue to bring *kama* 'gifts related to bride-wealth to her parents. These gifts came in many forms – anything from food to clothing items and beads. The parents of the girl could also do the same in return. A girl who was betrothed had beads around her neck, wrist and waist to indicate that she was betrothed' (Qhomatca, 2018).

When the girl reaches the puberty stage, and undergoes her first menstruation, she was handed over to the elderly women, who would confine her for two or more weeks. During her confinement she was trained in how to take care of nature, the people around her, and her future husband. The Naro people believed that by isolating the girl they were saving nature from danger. A girl who was undergoing her first menstruation needed ceremonial cleansing before she could mingle with nature and the people surrounding her. She was not allowed to touch hunting tools such as arrows, spears, hunting quivers and so forth with her bare hand without being ceremonially cleansed. If she touches them with her bare hands bad luck would befall them and those that go for hunting would come back empty-handed. In addition, she was not allowed to unplug the first fruits of any fruit tree, even the wild berries. It was believed that once she touches them, they would dry up and wither; and there would be draught.

During her confinement, elderly men were to hunt an eland and bring its meat to the hut where she was being confined. The eland meat would sustain the elderly women taking part in cleansing and the initiation ceremony. This ceremony was performed by elderly women, who would dance without clothes on their bodies (Tcoma, 2018).

Elderly men were only allowed to assist the women taking part in this ceremony – to cut meat into smaller chunks for them, to cook all leftovers was taken care of by the elderly men, while young men were absolutely not allowed to eat from this event, or even come close to the venue of the event.

When the initiation ceremony was over, the girl was taken out of the hut. She would not go out into the bush until she receives her second menstruation, which was now considered a confirmation that she was indeed a real woman. She was to undergo the second menstruation ceremony, known as *cóá sa kabis dis cii sa,* which means 'the ceremony of returning back the girl,' as it was only after this that she was now declared a mature woman, who was free to go out into the bush and meet the real world.

At this stage she would be introduced to some of the household chores, which included going to the bush and gathering wild fruits, collecting firewood, and making fire, as well as digging out of tubers from the ground. In addition, she was taught all the taboos of the bush. The taboos included when to talk, what to say and what not to say. She was not allowed to make any cursing remarks, as it was believed that whatever she curses or confesses could be manifested. She was not allowed to speak out names of wild animals, but rather use euphemisms when referring to such animals. For instance, she would refer to a lion, which is *gàm* as *c'õo-nqare*, which literally means 'a hairy feet creature'. She would refer to snakes and all the other reptiles as *nc'ãa-kg'am tòèse zi*, which literally means 'crawling creatures'. It was believed that once she calls them by their names they would visit at night and would harm the people.

However, once the girl has undergone all these stages, she was now considered a fully grown woman and was eligible for marriage. This also means that she was ready for all the duties of a woman. She was also now free to take part in attending initiation ceremonies for other girls younger than her.

## Courtship

Courtship is a period in a relationship between a boy and a girl that precedes their marriage. In Naro culture, a boy and a girl who were undergoing courtship could not sleep together until they were married. The boy would spend most of his youth days with elderly men learning life skills and hunting tactics, as well as survival tactics in the bush, while the girl spent most of her time with elderly women learning food gathering tactics and other life skills. The two were not allowed to come together until they were mature enough to get married.

As long as the boy and the girl were undergoing courtship, their relationship marked the beginning of the relationship between their parents. Their parents knew that the journey to becoming in-laws and new family friends has just begun. This meant that there should be frequent visits between their parents, and giving of gifts.

### BRIDE-SEEKING

In Naro culture the parents of the boy, together with his grandparents were responsible for seeking a bride for their son. They would go directly to the place where the parents of the girl whom they wanted to be their daughter-in-law, were residing. It was common practice for parents to be accompanied by grandparents, as the elderly were considered wise and knew the family roots. The maternal and paternal uncles had very little roles to play in Naro marriages. The parents would seek a bride immediately after the girl's initiation ceremony, since at that point the girl was considered a mature woman, who was now ready for marriage.

### BRIDE-WEALTH

As already mentioned, there was bride-wealth among the Naro people, which was known as *kama*. The bride-wealth was given by the parents of the boy to the parents of the girl, and the parents of the girl were also expected to give something in return as a token of appreciation for their son in-law. The boy and his father would bring game meat, especially eland meat, while his mother would bring wild fruits such as wild berries, *kg'om*, *cgùì*, *'morama'* and *ntcēe-tcee* fruits. The parents of the girl were expected to do the same. Giving of *kama* was a common practice that was done continuously.

### WEDDING CEREMONY AND MARRIAGE COUNSELLING

The Naro people performed their wedding on one set day. On the set date only the parents and grandparents of the couple were expected to play significant roles. Other relatives were allowed to attend and witness the event, but had no special roles to play.

Although, most of the counselling was done during the initiation ceremony, the bride was given thorough counselling again on the day of her wedding. It was believed that the girl needed more counselling than the boy, since she was soon to be a mother and a housekeeper. The girl's mother and her grandmother, together with the boy's mother and his grandmother, were the ones to give counselling to the girl. On the other side, the boy's father and his grandfather, together with his father-in-law and grandfather-in-law were the ones to provide counselling to him. This was done purposefully, so that women talk to the woman and men to the man.

## MARRIAGE RITES AND THE SIGNIFICANCE OF METAPHORICAL LANGUAGE AND SYMBOLIC OBJECTS AND ACTIONS IN NARO MARRIAGES

On the wedding day, a special ritual was performed by the parents of the groom and bride. A boy's forehead would be pierced with a sharp object to make a cut, and blood would be collected from it. In other instances, the cuts were made on their thighs and the couple's blood mixed and smeared on these cuts. This was a symbol of joining the couple together. It was believed that a couple joined in this manner could only be separated by death. It was at this point when again the couple was given thorough counselling. The symbols of the mixing of blood of the couple, and smearing it on their cuts, was to remind them that they were meant for each other, and could never separate, regardless of the circumstances in life. It was also a sign of unity to show that now they have become one though they are two individuals.

After this ritual the girl was given her own set of tools to start a new life. It was believed that she would use this set of tools to build her home. She was given a blanket made out of gemsbok skin to cover herself and her husband at night. She was also given a small blanket made of duiker skin, to use as a coat to cover her upper part of the body. On top of that, she was given a small blanket made out of antelope skin known as *tcã̱o*, which was to be used to carry wild fruits on her back or side.

She could also use it to carry her child on her back in the event she gives birth to a child, or for carrying anything that she gathers along the way.

She was also given a digging stick known as *ncòè*, which she would use to dig tubers in the bush. In addition, she was given a tortoise shell known as *dxòé tsoro* which was to be used for dishing food and fetching water. She was also given a small tortoise shell known as *dàm̀-tsoro* with special traditional perfumes and charms in it, which she would use to beautify herself and make herself attractive to her husband (Qhomatca, 2018).

On the other hand, the boy was given *dxàes xgào sa*, known as the 'female knife' or a pocketknife, *kg'ao-xgào ba*, a spear, *dtcòò h̀ìi ba*, a spring-hare stick, which was used for hooking spring-hares from their hiding holes and pulling them out. This was to say that you are now a grown-up mature man, so you must go and use these tools to your advantage to bring food to your house and stop depending on your parents.

After this was all done, the couple would go to the husband's place, but without the escort of their parents. During past days, it used to take a couple some time to get used to each other, because it was their first time to meet with someone from the opposite sex. So, their grandparents had to pay them regular visits to teach them how to live and cope with each other. The grandparents would continue to support the couple until the couple settled in.

In Naro culture, there was great respect for the in-laws, and one could not look straight into one's father-in-law's eyes and speak to him. The son-in-law could not speak directly to his mother-in-law, let alone both of his in-laws, but could address them through his own wife. The same was true of the the in-laws – they could ask for his services through their daughter. A request from in-laws could not be declined as it was considered disrespectful and rude to do so. A person who disrespects his in-laws is known as *c'uì-ncoarase*, in Naro, this literally means the one who rides over his in-laws or drags them around. The in-laws were referred to with the use of the second person plural form, which is *asaoè*, for women (you, feminine plural) when referring to the mother in-law, and *axaoè*, for men (you, masculine plural) when referring to his father-in-law. In addition, the son in-law could not speak ill of his in-laws as they were to be taken as his second parents – after his biological parents.

Fire still remains a significant symbol among the Naro people, especially among married couples. A married woman must have fire burning at her home every evening. This concept is known as '*xáéan dxùu-kg'ai sa*', which literally means 'lightening up the face of home' or 'to make fire on the face of home'. The Naro people believed that every home has to have fire burning at night to show that there are people and there is life in that home. It was believed that wild animals could see that there are people and would be scared to come near that home. It was also believed that fire scared off evil spirits and, therefore, to scare off wild animals and evil spirits a married couple was always expected to 'light up' their home at all times.

## Rights, Privileges, and Benefits Associated with Traditional Marriage Practices among the Naro People

In Naro culture there was much respect for a married couple. A married wife had all the rights and privileges and benefits entitled to her in her marriage. This was also true of her husband, he had all the rights, privileges and benefits entitled to him as the husband of the house. If a woman was still married to her husband, she would not have an extra-marital affair, and nor would her husband. She was her husband's companion, and she was also his companion. He would treat her with due respect and not as his property. In case of conflicts, they would ask for the intervention of their parents. This also meant that in case of the death of either of the partners, no family member or relative could come and claim items from the remaining partner (Tcoma, 2018).

A married woman had the right to give her daughter's hand in marriage, or to marry her son off, once her daughter or son was ready for marriage. She was in a position to make decisions, together with her husband, and arrange for her own daughter or son's marriage. She was considered the woman of her home, and no one would make decisions for her in her home not even her in-laws or her parents. She was there to take part in all the activities carried out by women, which included taking part in initiation ceremonies and other community activities. She was there to be consulted for advice in case someone needed it. Likewise, her husband was a mature man who could train his children in the right direction, as he desired. A married man had equal rights with other men in the community and could hunt with them at any time.

Among the Naro people, gender equality was never a problem. A couple could help each other with duties without fighting over responsibilities. There were duties or tasks for women and for men, but a couple knew when to come together to help each other and when to diverge to their respective tasks that equalled their skills and strength. Thus, among the Naro there were no conflicts over responsibilities (Morris, 2018).

## Prevalent Problems and Challenges in Naro Traditional Marriages Today

According to Morris (2018), the biggest problem with modern Naro marriages is that people envy what others do and want to emulate them: people envy other people's wives and their husbands to the extent of having extra-marital affairs with such people. Thus, this is the main problem in most marriages today.

Secondly, due to 'civilization' the Naro people now live among other nations and interact with them through work, schools and the environments we all live in. As a result of social integration there are cross-cultural marriages, which have also resulted in mixed Naro, ranging from Naro mixed ('Coloured') origin to Naro with mixed Bantu. Therefore, the concern to protect the Naro as pure is no longer an issue, which is a problem for the Naro, because pure Naro are becoming extinct (Qhomatca, 2018).

In the olden days, people used to marry among the clans and not among kin, but nowadays Naro young people are not afraid to marry among their kin. So, the practice of not marrying someone with the same name as your relative is not being followed nowadays. Most young people of today consider a name to be just like any other name and do not see anything wrong with it. These young people also believe that these are just common Naro names used by the Naro people, and are not special in any way. These actions, seen as shameful is also a big insult to Naro culture (Morris, 2018).

In modern days, Naro people fall victim to passion killings, divorce cases, and sexually transmitted diseases, such as HIV/ AIDS. The young people of today cheat on their partners and there are issues of mistrust within married couples. Passion killings, divorce cases and sexually transmitted illnesses come through unfaithfulness and carelessness in the way people live. In former times, it was an abomination for a person to claim his or her life, divorce cases were not common, and diseases were there, but not at the alarming rate they are now. Nowadays, divorcing a wife is not a big issue, killing a person and killing yourself is not an issue and being infected with sexually transmitted diseases is not an issue. A person can even live with more than two wives and there is nothing strange about this. However, all these issues are a threat to the identity of the Naro (Qhomatca, 2018).

Traditionally, a girl child was given proper training, so as to prepare her for future. Those days of proper orientation and initiation are gone. Nowadays, girls are not confined and taught life skills.

Formal schools have replaced traditional education. Nowadays, Naro children get formal education in formal schools, not from elders with experience. Our children learn by experimenting. Naro children have lost faith in their cultural beliefs systems and have gained more faith in their modern education, hence the existence of acts, seen as detestable, such as unwanted pregnancies, sexually transmitted illness and many others. Some of these children grew up as orphans, because they have lost their parents to the HIV/ AIDS scourge.

Nowadays, Naro have cases of same-sex marriages, and cases where people get married to people who are not their peers. Sons have lost their fathers and do not have father-like figures to teach them how to treat women with respect, and daughters have lost their mothers and do not have mother-like figures to be role models in their lives to teach them how to live with their husbands. We now live in a dynamic society, where all that we do is centered on us (Qhomatca, 2018).

The efforts by the government to recognise legal marriages and sideline traditional marriages has also created a problem amongst the Naro people. The same can be said of religious marriages, where traditional marriages are not given recognition. Some of the

Naro people feel that the demand for bride-wealth and the need to go to the District Commissioner's office has made them shun away from marrying. In addition, there are many misconception tied to marriages that make Naro people shun marriage nowadays. Some people believe that marriage is for wealthier people, while others feel there is a certain age limit for one to get married. Yet again, some are of the view that when you marry you get yourself into a commitment and you sell your freedom to your spouse, and as such people do not want to commit themselves, let alone sell their freedom to others. So, they want to live a free life. These are just some of the few misconceptions that have trapped so many young people (Qhomatca, 2018).

## Factors of Change and their Impact on Traditional Marriage Rites and Activities

The continent of Africa and especially sub-saharan Africa has been struck hard by the HIV/AIDS scourge. This has made it impossible for some of the marriage rites, such as mixing blood of the couples to take place. Nowadays, it is risky to pierce someone and mix their blood with someone else's blood. There are many diseases that can be transmitted through blood transfusion, and HIV/AIDS is one scourge that has claimed many lives, so the Naro cannot risk mixing blood of the people.

It was believed that once a couple has been joined together only death could separate them; however that is not the case nowadays. Nowadays, people's behahaviour is strongly affected by different life circumstances, and as such they are forced to marry and divorce as they wish, depending on the challenges they face.

The tools that were given to a woman to build her home and to symbolise that she is a woman of her house no longer have value. The blanket made out of gemsbok skin, a small blanket made of duiker skin, a small blanket made out of any antelope skin, a digging stick and a tortoise shell have all lost their significance. The same could be said of the items given to the boy. A pocket knife, a spear, a long spring-hare stick for digging out spring-hares and a digging stick, which were a symbol of manhood have all lost their significance. Modern-day technology has taken the place of all these valuable cultural items of identity.

## Conclusions and Recommendations

The Naro or the *Ncoakhoe*, or *Dqãe ne* have a beautiful culture and should appreciate their culture. The Naro people believed that provision of proper training to a girl child was laying a foundation of good morals for their society. Thus, all the attention was given to training a girl child before it could be diverted to a boy child. Thus, the Naro people strongly believe that if they can go back to those times and give proper training to a girl child all these problems could be solved. Naro need to acknowledge modern 'civilization' and the good and bad things that come with it. Formal schooling should not replace traditional schools, instead formal schooling should complement traditional schooling. The two ways of learning can produce a morally and intellectually competent citizen.

Having a totem and emulating its positive aspects from its attributes, such as gentleness and being clever can be a good starting point in building a peaceful and powerful nation. Thus, the Naro people, with their qualities, should claim their identity and use it as a basis to acknowledge unity in diversity. The Naro people should learn to live in harmony with other nations. Moreover, there are many positive attributes that other nations can learn from the Naro people, and that the Naro can also learn from these other nations.

Culture can be dynamic at times and there can be 'culture shock', but as people living among other people the Naro people ought to acknowledge and appreciate other cultures. Although the Naro people regard marriage as a union between two people – man and wife – we also need to acknowledge that in other cultures there is polygamy. This is not to condone polygamy, but to acknowledge the fact that it does exist and it is real.

The personal values of honesty, compassion, love for all and respect for humanity should always be at the centre of our values. When personal values are properly exercised one can realise that there is need to respect one's culture, marriage, elders and in-laws; and there could even be ways to shun shameful acts such as marriages within the kin and same sex marriages. We live in a world where people have different opinions and rights, we need to acknowledge that, but not to emulate that is not Naro culture.

Finally, we need to understand the primary purpose for marriage. The primary purpose is for a man to have a companion and for them to reproduce and replenish the earth. We also need to understand that a proper home is built through a proper marriage. Proper marriages are a doorway to a happy nation. A properly married and a stable couple can produce a morally upright child who can bring joy to the nation.

## Bibliography

Batibo, H. M. (2005). *Language Decline and Death in Africa: Causes, Consequences and Challenges*. Cleverdon: Multilingual Matters.

Batibo, H. M. (2009). Language Documentation as a Strategy for the Empowerment of the Minority Languages of Africa. In *Selected Proceedings of the 38th Annual Conference on African Linguistics*, ed. Masangu Matondo, Fiona Mc Laughlin, and Eric Potsdam, 193-203. Somerville, MA: Cascadilla Proceedings Project.

Hasselbring S. & Segatlhe (2000). *The State of Khoesan Languages in Botswana*, pp 76-99. Edited by Herman M. Batibo & Joseph Tsonope. Tasalls Publishing and Books for the Basarwa Languages Project, University of Botswana/University of Tromsø Collaborative Basarwa Research Programme. Mogoditshane (Botswana) & Gaborone.

KFO - Kuru Family of Organisations - Letloa Trust. (2012). Naro San Values. Ghanzi, Unpublished Document.

Maho, J.F. (1998). *Few People, Many Tongues: The languages of Namibia*. Gamsberg Macmillan: Windhoek.

Morris, T. James. (2018). (Personal communication, October 8th 2018).

Qhomatca, Xgaiga. (2018). (Personal communication, October 17th 2018).

Saul, I. (2017). The Forms and Functions of Demonstratives in Naro. Master of Arts Degree research project. University of Botswana
Tcoma, Xgara. (2018). (Personal communication, November 12th 2018).
Visser, H. (2014). (Personal communication, December 22nd 2015).

# 19

# OVAHERERO

*Mrs. Esther Vamanuka Kanaimba-Senai*

## BRIEF BACKGROUND HISTORY

The OvaHerero/OvaMbanderu people in Botswana fled into this country from the then German South West Africa (now Namibia) around 1904, following their defeat by German forces. Today, these two communities are found in Ngamiland, Ghanzi, Boteti, Central, Kgatleng, Kweneng and Kgalagadi Districts. These two ethnic groups speak the same language, have similar customs and traditions, save for small variations here and there. The OvaHerero/OvaMbanderu people are Bantu pastoralists who subsist on rearing livestock, mainly cattle. They are said to have migrated from eastern Africa in the 17th and 18th centuries into present day Namibia and parts of southern Angola.

The OvaHerero/OvaMbanderu people trace their lineage through '*Ejanda*' and '*Oruzo*'. When a Herero/Mbanderu male or female person is born, they adopt their mother's '*Ejanda*'. Therefore, a Herero/Mbanderu person identifies themselves in three ways: by their mother's *Ejanda*; then on to the paternal side where one indicates their father's *Ejanda*; followed by their paternal grandfather's *Ejanda*. Thus, a Herero's descent is determined through the mother, father's mother and paternal grandfather's mother. *Oruzo* is much broader and speaks to the norms and dictates of a particular branch of the Herero/Mbanderu, e.g., *Oruzo ro nganda jetu* – which means, 'The way we traditionally do things in our homestead'. This is more aligned to the paternal lineage, but not exclusively so. For example, a person may grow up with his/her maternal uncles and subscribe to the *Oruzo* of an uncle's homestead.

The Herero/Mbanderu people do not have totems in the way Tswana ethnic groups do, e.g., *o bina kgabo/kwena*, and so on. This is possibly because meat is their staple food together with sour milk. However, there are a few branches of the Herero/Mbanderu people who, for example, do not eat a black cow or a yellow cow as part of the *Oruzo* of their homestead. There are also those who do not eat certain parts of an animal, mainly internal organs such as the spleen, again as part of their *Oruzo*. In modern times in Botswana some of these restrictions are no longer strictly adhered to.

According to the 2011 Botswana Population and Housing Census, there were 18,710 people who were identified as using OtjiHerero/OtjiMbanderu as their primary language. However, according to Jabulani Dick of Statistics Botswana, who wrote the chapter titled 'Minority Languages in Botswana: Growth or Decline' in the *2011 Botswana Population and Housing Census Analytical Report*, "The Population and Housing Census question on language is vague, and data collected through the questionnaire cannot be relied upon to determine one's ethnicity".

It can therefore be argued that the population of OvaHerero/OvaMbanderu, as is the case with other minority languages in the country, could be higher if the question of ethnicity had been clearly articulated in the census questionnaire. Jabulani Dick further argues that "the language one uses at home may not necessarily be one's ethnic language. More often than not we speak the language of our spouses and significant others at home than our mother tongue, as a compromise".

For example, some OvaHerero/OvaMbanderu people do not speak the language, such as those from the Kgalagadi District, most of whom speak Sekgothu (known as Damara/Nama in Namibia). In fact, in the *2011 Botswana Population and Housing Census* it is recorded there were only 64 people in Kgalagadi North and 24 in Kgalagadi South who were identified as OtjiHerero/OtjiMbanderu speakers, numbers that are rather low.

Furthermore, some young OvaHerero/OvaMbanderu born out of inter-ethnic marriages more often than not do not speak the language, often defaulting to Setswana or English.

It is worth noting that there was an increase in the number of OtjiHerero/OtjiMbanderu speakers from 10,998 in 2001 to 18,710 in 2011, making 0.7% of the Botswana population.

## SOME CULTURAL ASPECTS

The OvaHerero/OvaMbanderu women are identifiable by their bright-coloured floor length gowns, a throw-back to the Victorian era which they borrowed from 19th century German missionary wives in the then German South West Africa. Germany ruled over this territory during the 'Scramble for Africa' from 1884 until they were defeated in the First World War in 1914, after which the territory was placed under South African administration in 1919.

The floor-length dress known as *ohorokueva* (a derivative from *tokhoes*, the Nama people's word for dress) is generally worn by married and older women daily. In olden times, young women in their late teens were inducted into the wearing of the dress through a ceremony presided over by their father, usually in readiness for marriage. This ceremony, known as *orumbaanda* was often preceded by Bible lessons every Sunday for Christian families, with the final graduation happening in church. In the 1960s in Mahalapye, before the advent of new charismatic/spiritual churches, most OvaHerero/OvaMbanderu in Mahalapye belonged to the Lutheran Church, the church of their former colonial masters, and this ceremony is similar to the modern-day confirmation ceremony at the Lutheran church.

The young women were a sight to behold on their graduation day as they were dressed in all white with a piece of cross-shaped starched fabric hanging at the back of the headgear, *orumbaanda*. Apparently, this was to control the head movement of the young lady. Whenever she had to look back, she had to turn the entire body around instead of just turning her head, which was considered unladylike. The young women were also tutored on how to behave when wearing the dress, including the need to walk slowly and majestically. Although some families still practice this, it has now become fashionable to see young women, including non-Herero/Mbanderu ones, wearing the attire at weddings, funerals and cultural activities. The dress shape and design have evolved over the years to its current style and will most probably continue to evolve over time.

The headgear known as *otjikaiva* (a derivative from *haib*, the Nama word for headgear) accompanies and often matches the dress. In its original form the Herero/Mbanderu headgear was rounded at the top. The old headgear had a knot tied at the forehead and no pins were used to hold it together as is the case today. According to Mrs. Engenie Nguazireko (82), the two-pointed horizontal headgear was introduced in Mahalapye by a lady who had arrived from Namibia (then South West Africa) in around 1954, but it did not become fashionable in Botswana until the late 1960s and early 1970s. To this day, Herero/Mbanderu women in Botswana follow fashion trends as set by their Namibian counterparts.

A Herero Historian in Namibia, Banda Hijangaruu Veseevete, sheds more light on the issue of the Herero/Mbanderu attire. In an interview, Veseevete says in actual fact the current attire has gone through several iterations from the first one copied from the Nama people who had been introduced to fabrics by the Dutch in the mid-1800s, through to the era of German colonization (late 1880s) to the current style that the Herero/Mbanderu women proudly re-designed into the current unique form. According to Veseevete, through the years the headgear has been redesigned to the two-pointed (horizontal) headgear in veneration of cattle, a symbol of pride among the Herero/Mbanderu people. This same point is made in https://en.wikipedia.org/wikiHerero_people.

However, other Namibian historians hold a different view to this version provided by Veseevete. Tracing the origin of Herero/Mbanderu dress to the era of using hides and skins, Namibian Herero historian, Unotjari Bethuel Katjimune, in consultation with other prominent Namibian Herero historians, Jarimbovandu Alexander Kaputu and former Namibian Member of Parliament Katuutire Nathaniel Kaura, says in its original form, Herero/Mbanderu attire was similar to that currently worn by the OvaHimba of Kaokoland. "Originally, Herero/Mbanderu women wore hats/headgear made of skins, with the differentiation being cattle skins for young women and sheep skins for married women. These were in no way shaped like cattle horns", said Katjimune.

These three gentlemen, Katjimune, Kaputu and Kaura, concur on their version of the history of the Herero/Mbanderu headgear. Their version is that the history of the Herero/Mbanderu attire dates back to 1846, when the Reverend Carl Hugo Hahn of the Rhenish Ministry established a church at Otjikango (in central Namibia). He had come with his wife from whom Herero/Mbanderu women copied the long Victorian dresses and the doek (headgear). One Johanna Kazahendeke, an assistant preacher at the mission was the first to put on the floor length dress. She was then joined by Magdalene Maharero and soon many others. At the time, the lady's headgear was similar to that of Mrs. Hahn and other missionary ladies, which was mainly the doek, which the Herero/Mbanderu women tied with a knot in front.

The Herero/Mbanderu women started tying the headgear differently around the 1940s, as they were now copying the German women's hats which were turned-up at the front. The Herero/Mbanderu women even likened this shape to a small hill in Omaruru (central Namibia) called '*Oruue ro ndera*', meaning the bird's stone. In the 1950s, the shape changed again and was somewhat refined and has gone through many iterations since. Therefore, according to the three gentlemen, the Herero/Mbanderu women's headgear was never based on the shape of the cattle horns. It was just an evolving culture with improvements as time went by.

It is important for young people to be informed of the historical shape of the headgear for posterity. This is why the efforts of some Herero/Mbanderu women in Mahalapye, who in recent times, have taken to wearing the 1960s round-shaped headgear at cultural events should be applauded. One Magdeline Vamuina Meroro (61) of Mahalapye, who wore the headgear at the Takarive Herero Festival in February 2018 said, "I wear this headgear to show young Herero people the attire that was worn by their forbearers or great grandparents".

OvaHerero/OvaMbanderu men are often identified by their jackets, hats and walking sticks which are considered standard formal attire especially at cultural events such as weddings and funerals.

## THE OVAHERERO/OVAMBANDERU MARRIAGE CULTURE AND PROCESSES

As is the case with other African ethnic groups, OvaHerero/OvaMbanderu marriages symbolise the coming together of two families. Traditionally, arranged marriages often took place between paternal and maternal cousins. Although this still happens in certain rare instances, today marriages are identified through the falling in love of the couple. Inter-ethnic marriages are also common nowadays.

There is a serious dearth of literature on OvaHerero/OvaMbanderu marriage culture both in Botswana and Namibia where these two ethnic groups originate. It appears this is a topic about which little or nothing has been written to date. Therefore, the information in this paper has been sourced mainly through interviews with informants and the author's own knowledge. The paper will also demonstrate that there are regional variations, albeit minor, in the way OvaHerero/OvaMbanderu conduct marriage ceremonies.

## Courtship (*Okuvareka*)

In the past, marriage processes in the OtjiHerero/OtjiMbanderu culture started in the early teens, when a girl playing house would be spotted by her maternal uncle as a suitable bride for her cousin (the uncle's son).

According to one of the informants to this study, Mr. Henda Joseph Uananisa of Sehithwa, the uncle would then place a 'special bead/small metal ring' (*ohanga*) on the girl's traditional skirt (made of strips of leather known as *otuvanda*, similar to the Setswana *makgabe*). This was corroborated by Mr. Katjirua Kent Kangunde of Mahalapye, Honourable Councillor Jerson Kazombungo of Ombapira, near Nokaneng, and Mr. Patji Maendo of Okotjize near Lentsweletau. This *ohanga* was often placed right on the front of the traditional skirt where the mother of the girl would later easily notice it. The mother would automatically know the significance of that 'bead', and hence only ask the child as to who 'placed it on her'. For his part, Mr. Wilmon Karihindi of Toromoja/Rakops indicated that this could also have been a string of beads which the uncle of the girl could place on her wrist or on her neck.

Today, this has changed significantly. Two people decide they want to get married, the young man tells his parents, the parents tell the uncles and a delegation is assembled to deliver *ohanga* which has now become a monetary issue. Today, *ohanga* now ranges between P100 and P500, which is delivered to the bride-to-be's homestead by a delegation of no more than two uncles. A young man who wants to demonstrate his prowess and desire for the young lady can go as high as possible and even pay P1000 as *ohanga*.

The presentation of *ohanga* is done in dramatic fashion by a two-man delegation that arrives at the bride-to-be's homestead early in the morning just as the sun rises. According to Kangunde, this delegation positions itself on the ground (no chairs) on the right side of the main house. They sit there and try all their tricks to get the attention of the residents of the homestead, including coughing out loud. Once their presence has been noticed, one or two people (usually men) go over to greet them and to hear their story. The delegation indicates their mission by giving the full names of the young lady for which they are paying *ohanga*. Kangunde says there are occasions where the mission of the groom-to-be's delegation can be aborted if they fail to provide the appropriate names of the young lady whose hand in marriage they are seeking. In this case, they return without delivering *ohanga* and have to come back another day with the proper names.

If things have gone well and *ohanga* has been accepted, then the visiting delegation has to request leave to depart. It is worth noting that this whole event takes place while the visiting delegation is sitting on the ground. "The groom's relatives are beggars and must be patient, obedient and very respectful. The bride's parents on the other hand must show that they are reluctant to give the child", says Mr. Jazenga Uezesa who hails from Nakalatswii, near Tsau.

*Ohanga* is usually given to the mother of the bride-to-be who shares it with her siblings and sisters-in-law. The acceptance of *ohanga* marks the beginning of the marriage negotiation process. It is at this stage that parents on both sides would inform relatives about the marriage proposal.

What follows next is a series of meetings beginning with one to follow up on *ohanga* attended by only by men, the same delegation that had brought the *ohanga*. At this meeting, the groom-to-be's delegation is told to bring women along to the next meeting. This is the meeting at which they are told how much the bride-wealth will be (*okurondisiua ko ndeu* – translated as 'to embark on a difficult journey' – that of going to organise the bride-wealth). According to Kangunde, the visiting delegation is not allowed to negotiate the bride-wealth down at this juncture. Rather they would go back and plan a meeting to come and negotiate. This, however, happens very rarely as the Herero/Mbanderu bride-wealth is more or else standard.

Once the groom-to-be's family is ready with the bride-wealth, and are ready to proceed with the wedding, they then return to the bride-to-be's family to declare their readiness (*okuheruka ko ndeu* – literally translated as to get out of the difficult situation). At this meeting, they usually also request dates for the wedding and the formal names of the bride-to-be, to begin the legal process of marriage as per the laws of Botswana.

## Marriage registration

There is regional disparity among the OvaHerero/OvaMbanderu when it comes to the official registration of marriages. According to Uananisa, in Ngamiland this is considered something for the children to do in urban areas: "The older folks at home are only concerned with the traditional ceremony and leave the official registration to be done by the couple". This is usually a no-frills event often featuring the bride- and groom-to-be and their witnesses. Uananisa's sentiments are shared by Mr. Patji Maendo who says marriage registration was never part of the traditional OtjiHerero/OtjiMbanderu marriage culture. Therefore, they always just leave it to the young couple to do. This, notwithstanding, parents do insist that the official registration of marriages happens so as to protect the bride against unscrupulous in-laws who often dispossess the widow (often very young) of her husband's property if he dies.

In Mahalapye, a low-key ceremony is held on the day of marriage registration, the first of many to follow. The groom-to-be's party picks the bride-to-be's party to travel together to the National Registration Office, often accompanied by a few family members.

In the evening, the bride-to-be's family hosts the groom-to-be's family at a meal attended only by very close family. The groom-to-be's family pays P500 or more, depending on how deep their pockets are, to the bride-to-be's family for this event. However, this event seems to be common in the Mahalapye area only, and it is one of the new additions to the marriage processes. Increasingly, young couples from Mahalapye who reside in urban areas do the registration in a no-frills event where they reside, cutting out the evening meal that happens in the village.

As per Botswana law, three weeks after the registration of the marriage, the actual marriage takes place at the District Commissioner's office. On this day, once again the groom-to-be's party picks up the bride-to-be's party to travel together to the District Commissioner's office. For the OvaHerero/OvaMbanderu, this marks the beginning of the pomp and ceremony as their brides and grooms are usually dressed in wedding attire including white gowns and veils, and suits, an influence from Western culture which has added an expense to the wedding ceremony. The bride's face is usually completely covered, while the groom is also usually expected to behave in a subdued manner with sunglasses and a hat pulled over his face. There are contrasting views among women, both young married ones and young unmarried ones, with the latter completely opposed to the covering of their faces during their wedding. The married ladies seem to think covering the bride's face protects her from the stare of people, some of whom she does not know. The official marriage ceremony usually happens on a Thursday, a day before the traditional OtjiHerero/OtjiMbanderu marriage processes begin.

## MARRIAGE CEREMONY

The traditional OvaHerero/OvaMbanderu marriage ceremony takes place over a period of three days, usually from Friday until Sunday. The first day marks the arrival of the groom's party – *E juva ro ngombe o kuhita/ko ngotue onganda* (usually Friday afternoon). This is the day on which the bride-wealth (*ovitunja*) is paid. The day begins with the arrival of the groom's party in the early afternoon. The women would normally cover their mouths with their shawls while the men keep their eyes down, with their hats pulled over their faces. Tradition dictates that they arrive in an orderly manner and wait at the back gate of the bride's homestead. Someone from inside the homestead then meets them there with burning firewood (*sisikalala*) with which he directs them to their camping site behind the bride's homestead. As this man with the burning firewood directs the groom's part to their camping site, he does not utter a word.

In Ngamiland, Boteti and Ghanzi the groom-to-be's delegation would be directed to a spot in the bush, perhaps under a tree, to the eastern side of the bride-to-be's homestead – to set up camp. However, in the more urbanised places, like Mahalapye and Gabane, this has now changed and the groom-to-be's delegation would be accommodated at a homestead selected by the bride's family. The modern choice of a home is meant to facilitate access to ablution facilities and proper housing in case of inclement weather.

Once the groom's party has been ushered to their camping site and have set up camp, they return to the same spot at the back gate. It is worth noting that this is the gate the groom's party will use throughout the three-day ceremony. Another fact worth noting is that throughout these three days there are a number of people who cannot return to their homes until Sunday when they take the bride home, namely, the groom and his chief groomsman and the parents of the groom. This is meant to preserve the sanctity of the marriage process by avoiding too much movement.

This second trip by the groom's party on the first day of the marriage ceremony is for the presentation of the bride-wealth. Traditionally, OvaHerero/OvaMbanderu bride-wealth consisted of only two cattle that are without any sign of blemish whatsoever – a 'clean male ox' which has been well castrated and 'a young clean heifer', which has never mated with a bull. Uananisa says if the ox has not been properly castrated and the heifer has mated with a bull this can be construed as an insult to the bride meaning that the bride may have been met (sexually) by other men before. "This could attract a charge and/or a sending back of the groom's delegation, hence a postponement of the ceremony; depending on the severity of the matter as deemed by the bride's family," he says.

Increasingly the two head of cattle are now being requested as female, perhaps for purposes of rearing, although Mr. Wilmon Karihindi of Toromoja/Rakops says they still insist on a cow and an ox.

According to Honourable Councillor Gabriel Nguahoka of Zootsha/Ghanzi, traditionally, there was a third beast, known as *ozazu* brought by the groom-to-be's family, which used to be slaughtered and consumed at the wedding. According to Nguahoka and Honourable Councillor Jerson Kazombungo of Habu-Nokaneng, this is the ox which has now been turned into a cash component at the wedding as part of the bride-wealth. Asked whether or not there is no opportunity for the OvaHerero/OvaMbanderu people to revert to *ozazu* or its equivalent in cash instead of the exorbitant cash price being paid currently, Kazombungo said only the traditional leadership of the ethnic groups can make a decision on this.

It is now common, especially in Mahalapye for the bride-wealth of two cattle to be accompanied by a hefty sum of money which now ranges between P10,000 and P20,000. The determination of this figure is the bride's family's prerogative, although it is possible to negotiate it down. Most families use this money to pay for the wedding expenses. A group of young Mahalapye unmarried young women who fully supported the idea of bride wealth, were however of the view that this amount should be capped at a maximum of P10,000.

The rest of the evening of this day is spent throughly merrymaking through the singing of OtjiHerero/OtjiMbanderu hymns, mainly translated from the Evangelical Lutheran Church hymn book, a legacy of the German colonisers. The two delegations usually engage in a music competition throughout the night.

The second day is seen as the wedding day (*e juva ro mukandi*, usually a Saturday), and starts off the preparations for the wedding with the slaughtering of beasts and cooking of the food for the meals. A key feature in the OtjiHerero/OtjiMbanderu wedding is the presentation of an ox by the bride's family to the groom's family at their camping site. The bride's family representatives would approach the groom's delegation camping site and as soon as they are close enough, they would release the ox. It is up to the groom's family to be on the look out, and immediately catch the released ox, otherwise if it flees it would be construed that the groom is a weakling who cannot even handle an ox. Furthermore, the groom's party would have no meat to consume and exchange with the bride's family as the two are expected to exchange a well cut out flank from the beasts they would have slaughtered.

In the original and traditional OtjiHerero/OtjiMbanderu culture, both parties prepare and eat their own meals at their two venues on this day. This is still practised in Ngamiland and Ghanzi. However, in Mahalapye, Okotjize, and Gabane, and to a lesser extent in Boteti, this has largely been modified. In addition to the food that they would have cooked at their camping site, the groom's party now participates in the luncheon at the bride's place, at which other modern traits, such as the introduction of family and cutting of the cake, are conducted by some families.

On this day, the bride and groom get adorned in their wedding attire, the white dress and veil for the bride and the suit, hat and walking stick for the groom. Another modern addition is the use of the matron of honour and bridesmaids and groomsmen. In former days the bride had a maximum of two bridesmaids as did the groom's best men. Another modern influence in most places in central and southern Botswana among the OvaHerero/OvaMbanderu people is that the bride is now able to show her face, contrary to what used to happen in the 1970s and 1980s when the bride was completely covered.

It is worth noting that in Ngamiland, GhanzI, and to a lesser extent in Boteti, the covering of the bride is fully complied with. As Uananisa, who hails from Sehithwa, put it, "The bride is not allowed to be seen publicly by anyone during the period of the ceremony, and a few days thereafter, except by the cousins assisting her with dressing up, and her groom in the evening. So, she's normally completely covered under a veil every time she's in the company of the visitors or when she stretches outside the house". This is corroborated by Nguahoka, Karihindi and Kazombungo from Ghanzi, Boteti and Ngamiland districts respectively.

However, it would appear that some elderly people would like to allow their children (brides) to show their faces during weddings while maintaining strict Herero/Mbanderu bride decorum, but are afraid that they will be seen as copying other cultures. They acknowledge that things have changed, and their children have friends who do attend their weddings and often feel very disappointed with the completely covered bride. Some families have even resorted to allowing their children to go for photo shoots on the day they come from the official marriage registration – where they are able to show their faces.

Young unmarried ladies from Mahalapye were adamant that they do not want their faces covered on their wedding day. 'How can I take photos when I am completely covered? How about my friend? They come to see a bride not a white veil … besides this is supposed to be the happiest day of my life, I need to smile," they ask rhetorically. It is clear though that older folks across the board still believe the bride should be covered without offering any justification.

A couple of married young women from Ngamiland support the idea of the covered bride, "…because the bride needs to be protected from the stares of unknown in-laws". When it was put to them that in today's weddings more often than not the couple and the families know each other very well, they admitted that the days of the covered bride are probably coming to an end.

One of the most important activities conducted on the wedding day by the OvaHerero/OvaMbanderu is the symbolic breathing on to the rib (Adam's rib) by the bride and the groom (*o ku suviro rupati*). This is meant to symbolise coming together of the two as stated in the Bible – that the woman comes from man's rib. Kangunde says this is per Genesis 2 verse 18: "It is not good for the man to be alone. I will make a helper suitable for him".

The just married couple blow their breaths onto a cooked rib of the cow that would have been slaughtered for the wedding, and then it is given to the groomsman and the bridesmaid to eat. There have been a few cases of some couples refusing to perform this seemingly innocuous cultural activity, arguing that it clashes with their modern-day Christian doctrine. These few cases have been from young people from the charismatic churches colloquially known as 'fire churches'. But these occurrences are extremely rare, with most OtjiHerero/OtjiMbanderu couples having no issues with this.

However, a young oral historian from Mahalapye, Mr. Muesee Johnny Uaungura was quick to point out that this is actually not a cultural activity but rather a Christian one. What is cultural is the blowing of the breath by the couple on to a piece of cooked meat taken from a cow's mouth. Kazombungo says this symbolises the right of passage by the bride from her father's home to that of her husband. However, this cultural activity is not practiced in most places in central and southern Botswana.

As the wedding day draws to an end, the groom is escorted by his groomsmen to the main house/hut (weddings usually take place at the main hut that usually belongs to the head of the family), where he spends the night with his new bride. However, the groom has to leave very early in the morning and the same groomsmen have to come and escort him out.

As the two lovebirds settle in for the night, the merrymaking by the wedding guests continues with competitive singing between the bride's and groom's delegations, usually until sunrise.

On the third day the bride departs the marital home - *ejuva ro ku toora o mukaendu/ ondjova* (usually a Sunday). Traditionally in Mahalapye, activities for this day begin in the afternoon when the groom's delegation once again arrive through the back gate to come and request to take their bride. However, in situations where the groom comes from a village far away from the bride's village or if the groom's family are planning to have a lunch at their homestead on this day, the activities can be held in the morning. This would have been negotiated with the bride's family prior to the day. In Ngamiland and Boteti this activity normally takes place in the morning.

The groom's family is then ushered into the main house/hut (the one in which the bride and groom spent the night) where the counselling of the bride is conducted. "The new bride is usually counselled on the significance of the new journey she is embarking on and how to behave in her new home", says Uananisa. In some cases, this counselling would be focused on the groom as well.

Once the counselling has been completed and the groom's delegation has requested to take their bride and received the go-ahead, the bride and her belongings, which include a kist, is so taken. In OtjiHerero/OtjiMbanderu culture, the bride is taken by the groom's family and not delivered as happens in Setswana culture. The groom's family provides the vehicle in which the bride, her escorts and belongings will travel.

When the bride arrives at the marital home, a ewe is slaughtered to signify her arrival, and this ceremony is known as *ondjova*. Honourable Councillor Gabriel Nguahoka from Ghanzi says the ewe slaughtered for *ondjova* should have horns, as should the cows for the bride-wealth. This request for livestock with horns is not adhered to in Mahalapye. In OtjiHerero/OtjiMbanderu culture, a bride is considered married only if *ondjova* has been performed for her.

Informants in Ngamiland, Boteti and Ghanzi indicate that *ondjova* is an affair for the groom to display his masculinity and that he is a good and strong provider, at least it used to so be back in the old days. The groom would be required to slaughter the sheep, skin it, cook it and take care of the hide with very little assistance from his age-mates. He would cook the meat, but he would eat none of it. According to Uananisa, this meat cooked by the groom is eaten by his female cousins and his aunts. "Indirectly for the female cousins, it is normally a symbol of appeasing them that he did not choose them for marriage, but rather chose a different cousin. For the aunts, it is normally a 'thank you' for the job well done – that they delivered a wife for him", says Uananisa.

There are some regional variations to the Ngamiland process regarding the cooking of *ondjova* meat. For example, in Gabane, Kgosi Venaune Peter Brown says the sheep is slaughtered and cooked by any available relatives. It is then eaten by married people only. This version is corroborated by Mr. Katjirua Kangunde of Mahalapye.

One of the aspects that is the same across all OtjiHerero/OtjiMbanderu people across Botswana is that the *ondjova* is eaten in one place, and the bones or any other remnants from it buried so that the bride nor the groom could not have any contact with it. It is completely prohibited for the newly-weds to eat the *ondjova* meat, although none of the respondents could provide any reason for this prohibition. The arrival of the bride at the marital home marks the end of the three-day marriage ceremony of the OtjiHerero/OtjiMbanderu culture.

## POST-WEDDING ACTIVITIES

One of the major activities that the bride undertakes upon arrival at the marital home, is the symbolic milking of the cow which happens the following day. In OtjiHerero/OtjiMbanderu culture, it is the women who milk the cows to feed the children sour milk, *omaere*, until modern times the staple food of this pastoral people. It was imperative for the women to do the milking of the cows because, traditionlly, the men would go out to look for cattle that have strayed, a chore that would often take several days, while the women remained holding the fort at the cattle post. Today, the milking of the cow by the new bride is purely symbolism, upholding culture, as most brides do not get to do this except in the very remote and rural areas.

A final activity of the marriage ceremony is the return of the bride and groom to the former's homestead known in OtjiHerero/OtjiMbanderu as *oku jaruro kati*, literally meaning, 'to return the walking stick'. According to Uananisa, the bride is given her father's walking stick when she departs for her marital home on the third day of the marriage ceremony. When she returns for the *oku jaruro kati* activity she goes to her father's kraal, identifies a female cow, and touches it with that stick before handing it back to her father. From that day onwards, that particular cow will become hers, but it will remain under the care of her father, as a sign that she may be gone elsewhere, but would not have been forgotten. Both Uananisa and Karihindi indicate that in Ngamiland and Boteti, this activity takes place in the morning and does not take long. In contrast, in Mahalapye and Gabane the couple spends the night at the bride's homestead, but leaves very early in the morning before anyone wakes up. Kgosi Brown of Gabane says the couple is expected to leave a small amount of money under the pillow, which will be taken by the person who will make up the bed.

In Mahalapye, Gabane and Okotjize many of the cultural aspects, such as the actual carrying of the stick and identifying a cow, are no longer observed, but the returning of the couple to the bride's homestead for one night is upheld.

Like all weddings across Botswana, the OtjiHerero/OtjiMbanderu marriages are full of pomp and revelry. Notwithstanding this, both the bride and groom are expected to behave with utmost decorum and exhibit high levels of shyness.

Nowadays weddings feature theme colours, with the bride's and groom's sides often outperforming each other. For example, at most OtjiHerero/OtjiMbanderu weddings, the attire for Friday would be OtjiHerero/OtjiMbanderu attire made out of German print fabric of a particular colour, and matching shawls for the women, while the men would wear matching suits and hats.

The wedding day attire usually features OtjiHerero/OtjiMbanderu dresses made from bright coloured fabric and shawls, and again, matching suits and hats for the men.

On the day the bride is taken to her new marital home, different attire and suits are also worn. A new trend borrowed from the Namibians, which is fast gaining currency, is the wearing of OtjiHerero/OtjiMbanderu attire made of white fabric by the bride's and groom's closest relatives and friends. The white attire matches the bride's wedding dress, as she normally departs for her marital home in her wedding dress. This is a marked departure from the 1970s and 1980s when the bride would normally wear any other dress except the wedding gown to travel to her marital home.

## CONCLUSION

It is clear from the conversations held with both young and old OvaHerero/OvaMbanderu that they are all extremely proud of their marriage culture and processes as these are quite unique, as is their dress.

The majority of the young OvaHerero/OvaMbanderu women interviewed indicate that they would want to be married according to their culture although some felt that they would like relaxation around the coverage of the bride during her wedding day. Nevertheless, some young women say they would go along with full coverage on their wedding day, just to appease their parents.

Most young women were in full support of bride-wealth, which they said was a sign of appreciation by the groom to the bride's family for having raised the young woman. However, there was concern that there are occasions when the bride-wealth money is shared among people who had never really played a role in raising the bride, just because they are close relatives, while there may be a shortage of foodstuffs and other requirements for the wedding. In Mahalapye, the bride-wealth money is often ploughed back into the wedding ceremony.

There was also concern that in Ngamiland and Ghanzi modern traits like the setting up of a marquee for the wedding are slowly being introduced. However, the bride is not permitted to go to the marquee but remains confined to the hut with an option for the groom to appear at the marquee if he wishes. Effectively, the wedding is celebrated in the absence of the key person, the bride. Viewed differently, this could be construed as gender discrimination against the women.

There is also an opportunity for OvaHerero/OvaMbanderu tribal leaderships to consider reverting to the old cultural tradition of the groom paying *ozazu*, or its equivalent, as part of the bride-wealth instead of the huge amounts of cash being paid currently.

## REFERENCES

Focus Group, young married women, all married in Ngamiland: Leah Uananisa (34), Systems Analyst; Petjiuaje Uananisa (40), Beautician; Ngahupe Marenga, Teacher.

Focus Group, young unmarried women from Mahalapye: Violet Kanaimba (21), unemployed; Talitha Meroro (34), self-employed; Omphile Kambai (33), Accounts Clerk; Neo Kanaimba, Limkokwing University graduate; Lebogang V. Meroro (24), Ba Isago University graduate

Herero People. https://en.wikipedia.org/wiki/Herero_people

Interview: Honourable Gabriel Nguahoka (61), Deputy Chairman, Ghanzi Sub-District Council

Interview: Kgosi Venaune Peter Brown (60), Headman of Arbitration, Herero Ward, Gabane

Interview: Mr. Banda Hijangaruu Veseevete, Historian and Social Commentator (popularly known in Namibia as Dr Banda), Namibia.

Interview: Mr. Henda Joseph Uananisa (44), University Lecturer and Chairperson of the Mbanderu Youth Association of Botswana

Interview: Mr. Jazenga Uezesa (50), Economist, Vice Chairman, Otjiserandu Association, Tsau

Interview: Mr. Katjirua Kent Kangunde (65), Retired Veterinary Officer, Mahalapye

Interview: Mr. Uarotua Daniel Viruua (63), Retired Mechanic, Mahalapye

Interview: Mr. Unotjari Bethuel Katjimune, Herero Historian in Naimbia (he consulted with and agreed his position with prominent Namibian Herero historians, Jarimbovandu Alexander Kaputu and former Namibian member of Parliament Katuutire Nathaniel Kaura)

Interview: Mrs. Engenie Nguazireko (82), Mahalapye

Interview: Ms. Tjingurura Meroro (26) from Charleshill, final year student BSc in Agricultural Economics, Botswana University of Agriculture and Natural Resources

Interview: Ms. Tjiuatjita Uananisa (23) from Sehithwa, 4th year student Public Administration and Political Science, University of Botswana

Kebonang, Boammaaruri Bahumi (1989). The History of the Herero in Mahalapye, Central District: 1922-1984. *Botswana Notes and Records,* Vol. 21 (1989)

Pool, Gerhard (1991). *Samuel Maharero.* Windhoek: Gamsberg Macmillan

Statistics Botswana. (2011). Botswana Population and Housing Census Analytical Report

Vivelo, Frank Roberto (1976). The Entry of the Herero into Botswana. *Botswana Notes and Records,* Vol. 8 (1976)

# 20

# Wayeyi

*Lydia Nyati-Saleshando*

## Information Sources and Data Collection

The data and information used to inform the wriing of this chapter was collected using qualitative methods, specifically interviews with key informants, focus group discussions, and participant observation during a bride-seeking process (*ku shesha/patlo*). The participants were in Maun and Gaborone. Data was analysed employing ecological and critical approaches, in multi-cultural settings.

## Pre-independence Marriage

The division of the periods to separate the past from the present is purely an estimation, with the help of some of my informants. None of them could recall when things started changing since cultural change is normally gradual, subtle and undocumented.

The procedures for Wayeyi weddings were regulated by the Wayeyi's culture, customs and patterns of life. A man would identify a girl child of about five to ten years old. For a girl of this age, the intention would be to follow the *ku patika* process, *go beelela* (engagement). The man would inform his parents that he is interested in this girl. If his parents like the family of the girl, they would allow him to go ahead and start the *ku shesha* process (*patlo*/bride-seeking), unless they decide to wait and marry following *inshembiro* (girl's initiation). It is worth noting that during this period, the Wayeyi married, by and large, among themselves and to relatives. They also intermarried with Basarwa, specifically the Kaakhwe, Bugakhwe and Mekhwe. On very rare occasions did they intermarry with Hambukushu who were endogamous (Tlou, 1985). The distances were not that long, and the expenses were minimum.

The young man would then go to the parents of the girl. They would inform him that we have heard you: however, an uncle lives on the other side of the river, you will need to go and ask him. The young man would go to this uncle. If it is during the ploughing season, he would have to help the uncle for the whole season. The uncle may tell him, but another uncle lives in such and such a village. The young man would go there. If he reaches the place during harvest time, he would have to help with harvesting, as his request is being processed by the uncle, for the whole harvesting season. Eventually one uncle would tell the young man, go to the parents of the girl, please tell them you have seen all of us. This last uncle would then go to the parents and report what they have observed about the young man during the period of stay. The idea of tossing the young man from pillar to post was to test his determination and give the uncles the opportunity to get to know him better. For instance, he would be reported as a good farmer, good at making the dug-out canoe (*uwoto*), fishing, and all the other tasks the young man would have been engaged in during his stay at each uncle would be mentioned. His general conduct was also important, as was how he treated other relatives. The long periods of stay with uncles were to assess whether the young man would be able to provide for the family.

If the uncles did not have a positive view of the young man, they would not approve of the marriage. If approved, then the parents of the girl would ask the young man to bring his parents.

They come very early around 5 a.m. and sit outside the courtyard (*rubaa/lolwapa*) made of reeds, and cough (as a way of indicating that they are the people outside). They would then be allowed in. They would be two men, walking in a line (*ku tungana*). They would come, sit on the ground and say '*Ta ka tumwa ku … ati ti rungire mundiro*' (We have been sent by so and so to come and ask for fire). The Wayeyi regarded a woman as someone who makes fire in the home so that there is no darkness, but light and warmth. The two men would find only the parents of the girl seated in the courtyard. The mother would be at the door of the hut with fire next to her. The father would tell them that he is alone, so they should come again. This would happen for five days. On the fifth day, more relatives would come, and the two men would be told by the maternal uncle that they have been given a wife, and she shall be brought to the young man's home in the near future.

Two maternal uncles would then take the bride-to-be to her husband's home. Upon arriving at home and being received with singing and dancing, they would be seated on a reed mat (*lditjatja/moseme*). She would be integrated into the society with other children of her age and perform similar chores. Her parents would not demand *lditjho, bogadi* (bride token) at the *ku patika* stage. The idea of *ku patika* was also that the two should study each other and see if they can make a family. The parents of the young man should also have the opportunity to study the girl. It was also meant to give the lady the chance to be familiar with the environment. Her mother-in-law would teach her home chores, values and the culture, even though they could be from the same tribe, and even relatives.

At this stage counselling was a secret between the girl and her parents and aunts, before she is taken to her new home. As stated above, there was an option to express interest, and the girl would continue to live with parents until puberty, in which case *inshembiro* (girl's initiation ceremony) would culminate into the wedding. This option became common as *ku patika* and *ku yazima* were fading after the introduction of modern schooling, as discussed below.

The assumption of *ku patika* was that, when reaching puberty, the girl would be brought back to her family for *inshembiro,* during which public counselling would be done over a six-month period of education through singing and dancing. Songs like *Nadia weeke* (Not to eat alone – greed*), Ndji yi mataa ku shemusna* (She gave birth to you, no matter how poor she is, respect her), *Ka qchiwi kani kana zimwe zako* (This house has mosquitoes – not to talk too much – it would create discomfort for your husband), *Shikumbi shanga ka shi patwa ku mubi* (My underwear is not touched by the ugly, essentially meaning only my husband is the handsome man to touch it). It counsels against adultery and prostitution. This was the Wayeyi public education system, counselling girls, and teaching them to dance, and instil societal values.

After reaching puberty and *inshembiro*, then *ldirowuwa* (wedding celebration/*mokete*) would follow, and *lditjho* would be paid. However, in most instances, the couple would start bearing children, and the two families would forget about it for years, even into old age. In other words, while the concepts *of lditjho* and *ldirowuwa* were expected, enforcement was weak. Sometimes when the couple reached old age an uncle in the woman's family may start the conversation on *lditjho* and it would be paid even that late. During those days, *lditjho* would be items like big pots, ploughing implements, honey, a beautiful animal skin blanket or skin trousers and jacket or suit for the uncles. *Ku patika* provided room for people to avoid paying *lditjho* in most instances. The procedure for *ku shesha* (*patlo*) was, however, considered important at the *ku patika* stage.

The other route was *ku yazima* (*go adima*/loan). This would be relevant for a girl who was identified or engaged after reaching puberty, gone through *inshembiro* (girl's initiation), and of childbearing age. In this case counselling would have been done as described above. The process of *ku shesha* (*patlo*) would be followed as described above, and only the father in-law (*shemino*) would take the bride to the new home (*ku tshawura*/*go tsaya*/to take). Still *lditjho* would not be paid at this time. The expectation was that after one year, the girl would be returned, *lditjho* paid and *ldirowura* (the celebration) would be held. As in the case of *ku patika*, after years this may not materialise, and the family would continue to live together for as long as they lived. Some of the marriages that were processed through *ku patika* and *ku yazima*, without *lditjho* and *ldirowura* were revisited after independence, and at least *lditjho* had to be paid.

The second phase within this period eliminated the practice of sending the young man to uncles wherever they lived. But *ku patika*, *ku yazima* and *ku shesha* continued for a while, but later the first two were eliminated as well. This was because during this period, the Batawana arrived in Ngamiland in the 1800s, and introduced the practice of the 'bride token' within the *kgotla* system for both marriage and child adoption. The *lditjho* was two female cows without the option of money or other items. This practice (two cows) continued into the independence period. However, they also had the practice of taking the Wayeyi women (using them for various purposes) and men as slaves without paying anything until 1948, when slavery was abolished.

Due to the elimination of *ku patika* and *ku yazima*, and now that there was direct marriage, the process began with courtship, then *ku shesha/patlo*/bride-seeking. The process was as follows. The young man would identify a young lady he is interested in; sometimes the parents would summon the young man and interest him in a young lady – normally a distant relative. In most cases he would go along with the advice of parents. Then he would approach the parents of the young lady. Her parents would then say, we have heard you, but we need your parents. The young man's parents would make their first appearance. As above, they come very early, around 5 a.m., sit outside the courtyard (*rubaa/lolwapa)* made of reeds, and cough (as a way to show that they are the people outside). The *ku shesha* procedure would be as described above. However, unlike *ku shesha,* which followed *ku patika* and *ku yazima*, this time the two men would find parents and relatives of the girl seated in the courtyard, men on one side and women on the other, with the mother seated next to the door of the hut or house tending fire. The girl would be in another hut, not to be seen. The young man's parents would be told by the younger brother to the father of the girl (*she mupundi/rangwane*/uncle) that we have heard you, but we are not quorate, come tomorrow. On the fifth day, they would be told to bring *lditjho*, two female cows of childbearing age. Once they bring the cows, they were given the wife. It is worth noting that patriarchy had now been introduced to Wayei by the Batawana. The role that was played by the maternal uncles was now played by the paternal brother to the father of the girl.

The following day, the relatives of the young lady would now take her to the husband's home. She would be decorated with beads on her neck, crossing over her back. She would have makeup bought from the ovaHerero or Hambukushu tribes. She would be counselled by married women only, inside the hut – it is only married women who qualify to dress and counsel the bride. She is dressed in *muzhamburo*, *zitshima*, *shikayi shi untamuna (letlalo la namaynane*/calf skin) and *innguwo* (a shawl made of skin). *Muzhamburo* and *innguwo* are made of skin, *zitshima* is beautifully beaded underwear (see picture, left). *Innguwo* was also decorated with beads (see picture of modernised Wayeyi dress, right). The way of dressing would most likely be for a girl who just finished *inshembiro* (girl's initiation). This was the normal age for marriage, emerging from the eliminated traditions of *ku patika* and *ku yazima.*

She was taken by many people this time, men and women all walking in a line slowly, with men at the back. The eldest aunt who carried all the messages would be the very last one in the line. Ladies would be wearing the same attire as the girl, but without beads and makeup. Men would wear beautiful three-quarter length pants and jackets, all made of skin and well decorated.

The property to be taken for the lady would be two beautiful blankets called *zipeeldira* (made of animal skin), and *intjira she shi xe* (*bogobe jwa masinyane*/porridge without relish). It is expected that it would be eaten as is, to demonstrate their acceptance of the girl as she is, and not expect an angel or riches from her. The whole process is complete

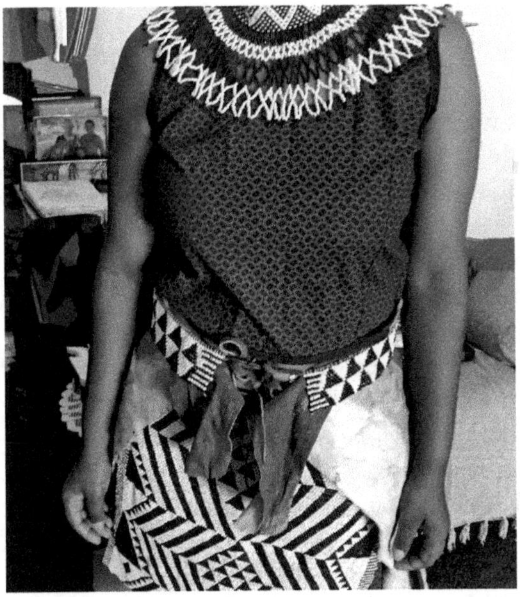

once she is received. The in-laws would receive her with singing and dancing. The songs would be the same as those sung during girl's initiation.

## POST-INDEPENDENCE TO CURRENT PERIOD

### MAIN STEPS

In modern times, men look for the ladies they want to marry. Mostly they meet them in higher education institutions, churches, conferences, funerals and weddings to mention a few. The young man would then inform his parents that he has found someone to marry. These days it could be as far away as across the country. If the Wayeyi man is getting married, they would need to follow the steps of the tribe from which they are seeking the bride.

As stated above, *ku patika* and *ku yazima* are no longer practiced at all among the Wayeyi people. The marriage circle has expanded beyond the family relatives to any corner of the country: the tribes mentioned above were essentially all resident in Ngamiland. As Wayeyi children started getting more educated, moving more down to the south of the country, they began to meet other tribes and interacted with other ethnicities. Despite these interactions, when the Wayeyi are marrying off their daughters, they inform their in-laws to follow the Shiyeyi procedure. This was the case in the *ku shesha* I observed, and as described by my informants in this study.

The participants were a couple: a Muyeyi lady aged 28 and a Lozi young man aged 32. The Lozi had to follow the Wayeyi procedures and processes including the aspects which have become common to most residents of Maun village. Essentially, the procedure above has not changed much, but more aspects have been added, and some aspects have been modified. Some of the additions are adopted from other tribes, when the Wayeyi are the ones who are seeking a bride. What other tribes demanded from Wayeyi, they also in turn began to demand as well.

Most people who were key role players were engaged in formal employment. In the particular procedure that I observed on July 22 and 23, 2019, the procedure of coming early morning to cough at the entrance of the courtyard for five days was reduced to two days. My informants said, in some cases it is even reduced to one day, in which case they come five times within a space of three hours.

On the first day, two men came at 5 a.m., one following in the footsteps of the other, then sat on the floor and said *"Re rumilwe ke . . . go tla go kopa metsi"* (We have been sent by so and so to come ask for water). Note that the Lozi were asking for water, not fire. They were told by the uncle (younger brother to the father of the girl) that we have heard. They were also told to bring a cow (*ye yi ku ndjeena – ya thagela* – for illegal access). This happens even when there had been no child born, or a pregnancy, before this process began. *Ku ndjeena* would mean they have seen this young man around their daughter before he formally asked for marriage. This is an influence of Batawana culture. At about 9 a.m., six men brought the cow, and it was female, of childbearing age. All the close relatives present, and the invited friends and neighbors had to eat this cow. So the meat was cooked and lunch was held at 4 p.m. The aunt to the girl was given the internal parts of the cow.

On the second day (23rd July), the two men came at 5 a.m. in the same manner and relayed the same message as the previous day. The same uncle told them: "Go and tell so and so that the father of the girl has given him the water (*amii/metsi*)". Then at about 9 a.m, the two men brought the bride token (*lditjho*) in the form of money amounting to P12,000.00. This time they were given chairs to sit on.

In a short while, a group of ladies, moving slowly in a line, and a man with a goat at the end, brought the items that were demanded for the maternal uncle of the young lady and the father. The goat is called *makumbirizo* (*maitumedisa*/thanksgiving). This is an external influence from other cultures. Then they requested that they see the young lady. The lady came out with her aunt, and she greeted the family. Then her family asked to see the young man, and he came with the rest of his family. He was introduced, and greetings between the two families were carried out. Breakfast was served to all present, and later the young man and his family left.

Customary Law (Cap 16:01) recognises this process as a legally binding and complete marriage in a traditional sense. However, since the world has become litigious, with the need for certification, and record keeping, most people do not end here. After *ku shesha* (*patlo*/bride-seeking ), the couple can now choose either to go through the customary law or common law process (Cap 29:01). Under Customary Law, the marriage would be solemnised by a *kgosi*. If the couple choose to go through the common law process the marriage would be solemnised by either the District Officer or the Pastor.

For this particular couple, the common law process kicked in, requiring the registration of the banns of marriage, which had to have been announced for three weeks. The marriage was solemnised by the District Officer on the 30th of August, 2019. The wedding celebration was held on 31st of August, 2019 as described below.

## Celebration and final Steps

This section describes what is normally called the wedding day (*ldiroura/mokete*), counselling (*ku kanda/go laya*), transfer of the bride (*ku twara/go isa monyadi*) and the trace-back visit by the bride or taking the bride back to her natal home (*ku ldata muzi/go gata motse*).

## Wedding day

The wedding day is when friends, family and relatives come to share in the joy of the wedding. In Ngamiland, this part seems to be a standardised procedure, and even when the bride is not from the region, her parents would follow these procedures when they come to Ngamiland. Once the legal procedures have been completed, that is, the banns of marriage announced, the couple have declared before the District Officer whether they are marrying out or in community of property, then the couple would have decided whether they will be married by a District Officer or a Pastor. If they are to be married by a District Officer, then the following morning they will join other couples in a large hall where they will take their vows and have their certificates issued. Then *ldiroura* (*mokete*/celebration day) will be the following morning. In this case, they may wish to have a pastoral blessing on the morning of the celebration before they go for picture taking and then lunch with friends and relatives.

Whether the couple's marriage was solemnised by the District Officer, or solemnised by the Pastor, the morning of the wedding would be as follows. At about 5 a.m., the man's aunts will come to dress the bride, and her maids will prepare her for the day, with make-up and hair decorations. The aunts will go back to their home, and take the man to church, where he will wait for the bride (if marriage was solemnised by a District Officer, it will be going to church for blessing and this is optional). As the bride arrives, there is great joy and ululations, with singing and dancing outside church. Then the Pastoral proceedings will begin, and the two will take vows and have their certificate issued (those being married by a Pastor). They will then go for picture taking and then lunch at a designated venue. During lunch there would be introductions of families and speeches, mainly by the couple and their best man/lady.

## Transfer of the bride and counselling

Then the family of the lady will go back home to prepare the lady to be taken to her husband's home in the evening. At about 3 p.m., this process will start with counselling in the house. Then she would be dressed in a long floral dress, duke, and a white cashmere shawl (*tjale*) all bought by her mother. Then she will be taken outside the house into the courtyard where men would be seated on one side and women on the other. She would be seated on a reed mat (*lditjatja/moseme*) with her face down, and counselling would take place. It seems this type of counselling has replaced the public one done through singing and dancing during the six month education program described earlier. This one, done with men and women together, is a new one and could be Batawana culture or something that has evolved through interaction of cultures. Close relatives will give messages to the aunt, as in former times. This time only women would take her to her husband's home, except one man who will be driving a sheep (*serwalo*) at the back of the ladies' line, about five metres distance from them. The sheep is supposed to be slaughtered on arrival, before it passes urine. None of my informants could explain the significance of this since it is a Batawana practice; this is yet another new evolution within the culture. They will be dressed in 'German print' dresses (*mateisi)*, and cashmere shawls (*ditjale*) with different colors – pink, white or yellow. Other colors are being introduced these days. They would walk in a line, with the eldest aunt at the back as the carrier of messages. When they sit in the courtyard where the groom's family would be quietly seated, they would walk in such a manner that the last person would be at the entrance of the court yard. After delivery of the messages, the eldest aunt would request departure and be the first to leave; and they will walk back in a line.

They will carry with them essential bedding and a bottle of water with ash and charcoal in it. The bride is not supposed to eat anything on the night she arrives at her husband's home, but drink only this water. Charcoal removes toxins from the body. In case she had food poisoning from the day's lunch, the ash would help, and any other ailment would be from the husband's home. This is a new concept from Batawana culture. The paternal aunt from the man's side would make the bed for the couple that evening. The groom would then be summoned by elderly men for counselling at the *kgotla*. The following morning, the two families would meet in a place of convenience – the husband or wife's family to read presents and eat the cake.

## THE TRACE BACK (BRIDE IS TAKEN BACK TO HER NATAL HOME).

The bride will spend a day at her in-law's home. She is expected to spend the day with her husband, and her aunt will be cooking and doing everything for them. She is not expected to speak loudly, laugh loudly, but rather be a reserved yet free in spirit. Then on the second day, early in the morning they will take a cow to the natal home of the bride. Also, at about 8 a.m., her aunt and others – they could be other in-laws or relatives, not many – will take the bride to her natal home. She will be seated on a reed mat (*lditjatja/moseme*), and then two of her paternal aunts will take her around the home, into each room of the house. This is to communicate the message that she is free to visit and enter her natal home at any time. If she had forgotten something she could come back later in the day to take it. The party which brought her would be served breakfast, and they then left. The cow which was brought in the morning would be slaughtered and shared among friends and relatives who partook in the entire wedding process on the bride's side.

## REMOVING THE SHAWL

After the trace back session, she is expected to wear her shawl at all times. After a week or so, her in-laws would hold a small ceremony to remove the shawl. It is to be removed by her mother-in-law or her designate. She will be told that now she is free to move around without it, but at weddings she is expected to wear it to indicate her married status.

## Significance of Marriage and Related Language Symbols

The language used to seek a bride in Wayeyi culture symbolised their concept of the role and significance of a woman in the home. *Ku rungira mundiro* (We are asking for fire). *"Wayeyi ware ku tikya mukazi ndji yuu sika mundiro shichuncumu, ka ku mwanana ati muzi wunaa wuna awatu"* (The Wayeyi viewed a woman as the one who makes the fire in a home, to show that there is life in that home), said the 75-year-old lady in Maun. This language is no longer used by Wayeyi even when they are the ones who are seeking a bride. Asked whether this language is still use, the groups in Maun and Gaborone concluded that they do not hear it any more. It therefore seems safe to say it has disappeared. In the wedding process I observed, the Lozi family used *sego sa metsi* (the Tswana equivalent – water gourd). This signifies the influence and socio-cultural domination of the Batawana, and the general use of Setswana across the country. Intermarriage between groups has fostered the use of the national language and culture throughout the country, thus ridding the country of other cultures' ways of thinking in Ngamiland. The Wayeyi did not have practices such as demanding cows for *thagela* (illegal entrance), *nku ya serwalo* (their *serwalo* was porridge), the bride was not taken back to her natal home (no *go gata motse*) or a cow accompanying it. But these changes have been embraced and found to be positive. When asked how these changes are viewed, a 62-year-old said, *"Zinqa – ta ku yisa ingombe yeyi ku ldata muzi ngani pe wii wanii iqaa shisuu"* (These changes are good because, for instance, when the groom's family bring the cow to bring her back, this cow helps us to give thanks to those who helped us during the wedding). When questioned about the bride token, in all four discussion groups, the feeling was that the prices are going up each year. There is need to regulate or even legislate this. *"A Ntlo ya Dikgosi e dire molao"* said one participant in Gaborone. The exorbitant bride token is a new concept to Wayeyi that has swept across the country. Some participants felt that, in the past, it was ignored through the *ku patika* and *ku yazima,* but now it is paid without fail, which is a good thing. *"Pele batho ba ne ba tsewa hela motho abo a go tsohala go sena bogadi' jaanong baa duela, go siame"*, said a 56-year-old in Gaborone.

The significance of marriage as a human institution is seen by Wayeyi as a dictate from God. *"Ldirowura ldi dzwa ku Urezha, tati pakwa ti ku ldi shangana"* (Marriage is from God, we found it when we were born') said the 89-year-old). *"Ku rowurwa, ko ti ka paka wapundi* (You are married so that you can have children", she continued. *"Ldirowura lda ti ku susa, yewe munyana indji ye mugxekwa aywe"* (Marriage brings honor to you the man and to your wife) said the 62-year-old man. All informants agreed on this point. *"Kana ha usa nyalwa o ngwana hela yoo apaa ko dipitseng kwa, ha ote kwano ko lapeng ko morerong"* (You see, when you are not married (reference to a woman), you are like a girl, your role is just to cook, you cannot participate in decision making with adults here in the courtyard), said a 52-year-old lady. *"Se sengwe ke gore bana ba ga go ba na le boswa"* (In addition to that, your children have inheritance). Informants were asked whether they thought marriage will continue or not, given the divorce rate. Those in Gaborone were divided, some felt that it may disappear, and people will just date on the internet and see each other when they wanted to. Others felt that nothing from God can disappear, and in fact more and more girls want to walk down the aisle. *"Aah! le rona re batla go nyalwa"* (We too we want to be married), said a 30-year old-lady in Maun. Those in Maun were unanimous that it will continue to be valued, but some of the practices like *patlo,* and *go gata motse* may disappear since the young people do not understand their significance. *"Basha ba taa ya go ema ko go molaodi kana moruti hela, mme ba dire mokete go e tumedisa ditsala"* (The young generation will just go to the District Officer or Pastor, then have a ceremony to please their friends) stated a 55-year-old man. Others felt that adults will insist on *patlo* since they gain from *bogadi* which has become so expensive and practised across the country. No one would like their girl to be taken for free, they opined.

## CHANGES IN WAYEYI MARRIAGE PRACTICES

As stated under methodology, changes within the Wayeyi culture will be analysed in the context of the three elements within the ecological approach, namely: *it's environment, it's evolutionary nature* and thirdly, *the endangerment aspect* – what has been endangered?

Within the jungle of multiculturalism, Westernization and serfdom, the Wayeyi have lost some of their practices but retained others, which have been adopted within the district. Two of the immediate changes that occurred were the processes of *ku patika* (engagement before puberty) and *ku yazima* (lending after puberty) essentially due to schooling. Children were now going to school at the age of six. This meant that even when *ku patika* occurred (rarely), the girl would not go to live with the husband's parents since she was in school. In this case, the man would take care of her welfare while she was staying with her parents. *Ku yazima* also disappeared as soon as schooling started. The education she would have received about the context in which she was going to get married, the cultural values of that family and expectations on both sides, can no longer be understood and managed. Schooling further disrupted the Wayeyi education system of *inshembiro* (girl's initiation) that provided girls with life skills, the right attitude for marriage, and to be a participant in society. The girl would be confined for six months, and each evening the songs described above would be sung to her, and she would be taught to dance *shincayi* (*modokota*) (now miscategorised by the Department of Culture as *shiperu*). This dance teaches the girl to have a flexible waist so as to perform well in bed. This education system, which taught values, skills and relationships has been wiped out by the new education system. The Wayeyi way of thinking about a woman as the one who lights up the home, keeps it warm, and performs the significant tasks for which human beings need the fire, have been lost, and has evolved to thinking of her as water, a Tswana concept.

The dress code has also changed obviously due to Westernization. One of the participans said that, "Since God dressed Adam and Eve with animal skins during the fall, all human societies evolved from that dress code. Therefore, it is difficult for any society to continue purely with animal skins, due to conservation of animal species, as the human population grows. God has always wanted human beings to partake in his creative power, hence clothing can be made from what God created in the beginning".

The most significant change for Wayeyi within this ecology is the loss of their language under Batawana serfdom (Tlou, 1985). They were not allowed to speak their language, insulted and called *Makoba* (Tlou, 1985). This intimidated them into losing their language and adopting Setswana. In that regard, words like *lditjatja* (*moseme*/reed mat) are rarely used, especially around the Maun area, and yet the item continues to be used. In areas where Shiyeyi is still spoken, like Seronga, Ikoga and so on, one can hear the language being spoken during weddings. The interesting aspect is that, while the word *lditjatja* might not be heard, but rather the Batawana-coined word *moseme,* the object continues to be popular among most tribes in Ngamiland. "Question: *'Warwa imbu ku rasikao lditjatja namushi?'* (Do the Batawana use reed mats in this era? Answer: *'Iii – Warwa ku ldi isikao naqa ngaho, indji waa wamwe koowo'* (Yes, they do, as well as other tribes)", said the 89-year-old lady in Maun. Even in town, the reed mat is still respected and used. *"Ka March re ne re dirisa moseme go amogela mosadi le go mo apola"* (In March we used the reed mat to receive the bride and to remove the shawl) said one informant in Gaborone. Equally, for the Wayeyi staple food *mweende* (water lily root), the Batawana coined a new word '*tswii*' so as not to maintain Shiyeyi language, but adopt the concept and enjoy the food like all tribes in Ngamiland. The word *lditjho* (bride-token) is lost – only one, the 89-year-old lady was able to recall it.

According to UNESCO (2001:13) language is "the means of expression of the intangible cultural heritage of a people, and it remains a reflection of this culture … and when a language disappears, an irreplaceable unit in our knowledge and understanding of human thought and world-view is lost forever". Language loss, therefore, results in the loss of an irreplaceable cultural heritage. Within the multi-cultural eco-system in Ngamiland, the endangerment of the Shiyeyi language has been the greatest loss to the Shiyeyi ways of thinking, acting and preserving their cultural banks. That is, communities act in the manner they think – their world view and accord with their value systems. When their culture and expression (language) is endangered, they lose the way that they think and interpret life, their expression is lost, and they cannot preserve their culture.

An evolutionary change observed is the number of days the young man's family had to come and cough at the entrance of the courtyard. This was only possible for people living within the same locality and not engaged in formal employment. This has been reduced, but still emphasised even in towns and cities with whatever modifications the family may find suitable. Thus, the change is a positive one, accommodating distance travelled by the young man's family who could be from any corner of the country and also employed. The Wayeyi have maintained and even influenced the culture of Ngamiland with regards to moving and walking slowly. The number of additions is evolutionary, resulting from cross-cultural interactions across the country, some possibly from Batawana influencing the socio-political and socio-cultural environments in Ngamiland, as the rulers, subjecting Wayeyi to serfdom. Westernization, such as schooling, and the legal framework contributed to this environment and influenced the processes in Ngamiland. A standard procedure seems to have emerged in Ngamiland. The expensive bride-token seems to be a problem in Ngamiland, which is poverty stricken.

## CONCLUSION

Wayeyi culture has evolved in considerable ways and has experienced endangerment of significant cultural steps such as *inshembiro* which paved way for marriage. The language has been endangered since it is not being passed to younger generations. Other main factors have been serfdom, modernity, nationalist ideologies, and interdependency between tribes. Wayeyi have maintained the practice of entrance into the bride's family with modifications – they have maintained walking in line. Their food *mweende* (water lily root) and the reed mat have been maintained. These practices have been adopted by other tribes in the district. This is essentially due to the numerical strength of the Wayeyi and the beauty of the walk. They have gained from the practice of *lditjho*, which brings revenue to the bride's parents. In the past, while expected, it was never guaranteed due to weak enforcement. Thus, within this ecological system, the Wayeyi have suffered and yet gained. This critical approach provides understanding of the power relationship between the ruling Batawana and other tribes. The practice of serfdom introduced this expensive *lditjho* (*bogadi*/bride token), *serwalo sa nku, kgomo ya go gata motse*, which not only makes the process long but also expensive. While the legal system has had an impact, it is an advantage for record keeping and it is neither expensive nor long.

A convergence of culture seems to have been established, between the Wayeyi culture and other tribes, specifically Batawana (as outlined above), and Western culture of the white wedding dress code. Practices of courtship, bride-seeking, bride token, singing and dancing have been standardised across the district if not the country, creating a new culture. An assimilationist ideology, with very little if any accommodation of diversity of cultures soon will create a unified wedding culture across the country, and dominant cultures will overshadow others if no interventions are made. Studies such as this one are important in recording the past practices for cultural revival.

## REFERENCES

Tlou, T. (1985). *A History of Ngamiland 1750-1906: The formation of an African state.* Gaborone: Macmillan Botswana.

UNESCO (2001). The intangible heritage. Round table discussion. Geneva, Switzerland.

# 21

# SUMMARY & WAY FORWARD

## OBSERVATIONS, CHALLENGES AND REMEDIES OR RECOMMENDATIONS

This book has catalogued a vast array of varying, previous and prevailing practices, as well as processes on the *lenyalo* (marriage) institution in Botswana. These practices and processes, together with their historical evolution, range from varying details of process proceedings, through to marriage practices leading up to, and following wedding ceremonies, such as gifting (*bogadi*/bride-wealth), all the way to inheritance upon death of a spouse, or married partners. The purpose of this book is to inform the reader on marriage in Botswana, its history and changes over time, as well as to spark a national debate and introspection that will hopefully lead to a resolution of marriage-related inconsistency problems, both at policy, legal and practice levels, as well as standardization; through desirable promulgation of relevant legal instruments.

The reader will bear in mind that Botswana has, since independence, experienced dynamic socio-economic changes, rising from one of the world's poorest countries to middle-income country status by global standards. A corollary of this development has been vast population mobility of its otherwise relatively small population, which only recently crossed the two-million humans mark, as recorded in the preliminary results of the 2022 census, at 2,346,179. This population mobility, particularly to urban areas, accelerated intermarriage across otherwise diverse cultural groups through adoption, adaptation, absorption, or downright domination, especially in terms of marriage practices and processes.

As a consequence of increased social, and indeed physical, mobility there has been an exponential increase in inter-community marriage relations, some of which were harmonious, whilst others contradictory. This gave rise to what has been described by some as a scrambled-egg phenomenon, but one whose contents (ingredients) need to be unscrambled, appreciated and at best understood, as well as perhaps standardised for the sake of harmonious marital relations. Indeed myriad arguments surround the marriage institution, all the way from what the correct practice and rituals are, the absence of clear and undisputed remedies for breach, to a hilarious absence of an exit clause.

A significant factor of change to the marriage institution and associated cultural practices discussed in all the chapters of this book is the advent of Christianity. In earlier times, as a patriarchal society, Batswana practised polygamous marriages polygamy (polygyny), and it is still legal, which varied depending on the size of the male's estate. An example is drawn from *Kgosi* Sechele of the Bakwena, who was forced to relinquish his 'harem', except for the first wife, in order for him to be baptised as a Christian. This was not without resistance, as the *kgosi* cited the King Solomon (in the Old Biblical Testament), who had a number of wives. Similarly, in 1892, *Kgosi* Linchwe I of Bakgatla faced vilification from the Christian church forcing him to relinquish some of his wives (concubines as Christians referred to them as), remaining with only one. One could further cite Isaiah 4; verse 1, which reads thus: "When that time comes, seven women will grab hold of one man and say, 'We can feed and clothe ourselves, but please let us say you are our husband, so that we won't have to endure the shame of being unmarried'".

The impact of Christianity on the marriage institution from polygamous (or more precisely polygynous) marriages, which involved men marrying many wives (*lefufa*) (thereby excluding polyandry) to monogamous marriages along paternal lines, is also likely to have worsened the inherited subtle subordination of females. Such female subordination belies evidence that can be adduced from the diverse languages of southern Africa. These cultures depict and attest to vestigial remains of female veneration, if not harking back to a possible era of matriarchy. For example, an African King is not a King without a Queen Mother, ***inkozikazi*** (where the suffix '-kazi' depicts greatness) ,upon whom she wields vast authority over the empire under his oversight. The gender issue continues to pose curious reflection, such as in Setswana, chieftaincy is often venerated and celebrated through feminine labels, such as ***mmabatho*** (the male grand overseer) – note the feminine prefix 'mma-', and *montlepoo* (the **beautiful** bull); *mohumagadi* (the female owner of the wealth – the wife to the male 'Chief') – the suffix '-gadi' depicts greatness; and ***mmadikolo*** (to refer to a highest tertiary institution, such as a university). Throughout Bantu languages, the word suffix ***–gadi*** is used to celebrate feminineness and greatness. Other languages even use the female prefix ***mma-*** to reflect veneration of females attributed to males. Indeed common surnames of Sotho/Tswana peoples and places bear the feminine prefix of ***mma-***, such as ***mmamabolo, mmanthatise, mmasealama, mmankgodi*** (a large eagle), ***mmampodi*** (champion), and ***mmantswitswidi*** (a professional). Hence the assumed/demonstrated patriarchy, may have had matriarchal precedents. The Christian religion and colonialism, as well as the introduction of monetary economy, may well have entrenched patriarchy in a way that further engendered the subservient roles of females to males.

Another practice that was adversely impacted by Christianity was the initiation of mature boys and girls into manhood and womanhood, respectively. The initiation 'schools' typically taught history, moral and family values, as well as numerous life skills. Bakgatla and Balete reintroduced initiation schools in their jurisdictions relatively recently, the Bakgatla in the 1970s, and the Balete, under their first ever female *kgosi*, in the 2000s. These initiation practices formed an important part of traditional pre-marital marriage education, counselling, and a rite of passage.

Given the practices and processes within the *lenyalo* institution catalogued in this book, one observes a wide variation, ranging from traditional pre-arranged marriages – from childhood stage (*peoletlhokwa*) through to marriages fixed at adulthood stage by parents, to, more lately, marriages arranged by the partners themselves. A whole array of behaviours characterise the *lenyalo* events and processes. There is special attention paid to decorum, such as times when activities such as *patlo* can take place, where and when *go laya* can take place, the posture of the bride-seeking party, dress code, marriage verbal address codes (e.g., *dumelang bana* – 'hello, children' – to refer to the groom's male party), the number of times the groom's party can make marriage proposals, and other elaborate processes.

These practices and processes are critically important to the handling and processing of a pivotal aspect of *lenyalo* in Botswana being the practice of giving/paying *bogadi*, otherwise known as lobola, bride-wealth, or dowry. As stated across the chapters of the book, this practice now applies to many communities across the country, whereas it was not as widespread in the past. The San typically do not have the practice of *bogadi*, save for presentation of duiker skins among the G||ana; the reciprocal exchange of eland meat and berries among the Naro; from no *bogadi* to one cow and then a gradual increase in number, among Bakalanga; relatively recent adoption of *bogadi* by Bangwato relatively recently (1980s or thereabouts). Whereas the practice evolved and spread among the southerners in earlier times, ranging from a time where there was no *bogadi* requirement, through to gradual evolution/introduction, entrenchment and engenderment, it has gone all the way to vociferous pre-requisite insistence on the practice of this ritual, in many parts of the country, leading to what some view as commercialization of the *lenyalo* institution, as is commonly the case nowadays.

Further, regarding *bogadi*, the book captures, among others, the onset of *bogadi* expectations, noting for example that Balete used not to expect or require *bogadi* traditionally, and that among Bangwato, an expectation or request for *bogadi* is a relatively recent development, only in the past two decades or so. In other communities, *bogadi* is still treated as voluntary, as opposed to an item of demand. In some communities, one comes across expressions like '*Le tlaa bona gore le itlotla/kgabisa jang*' meaning it is up to the groom's family to determine the amount, if any, of *bogadi* they wish to pledge. As stated earlier, this is in stark contrast to the latter-day, oft outright extortionist demands for *bogadi*, especially conversion of its cash equivalent set at up to four thousand Pula per head of cattle. This practice applies even in areas that are not permitted to export to the European Union, and other countries, because of disease (especially foot and mouth, FMD) – hence the value of cattle being lower. It is not uncommon for residents of such areas to insist on a cash equivalent similar to non-FMD infested areas.

In fact, according to K. Mogapi (1994), originally there was no *bogadi* among Batswana: *"Wa tlholegong ya Setswana, go ne go se na bogadi mo nyalong. … ngwana wa maitibolo o nnela botsetsi kwa ga gabomogolo, bo beilwe ke motsala mmaagwe mosetsana. Go ne gat la gore ba bogwe ba ntshe kgomo – ka bobona – ba e romela kwa bogwagadi, gore e gamelwe motsetsi, ngwana le ene atle a bone mašwi"* (Mogapi, 1994). A primipara would be confined at her mother's place for birth of the first child. The [bride's] in-laws would voluntarily offer a milk-cow for the new mother and the new-born to feed on its milk): *"Ka batho ba rata go gaisana, yo mongwe a ba a ntsha dikgomo di le pedi, a di romela kwa bogwagadi. Tsa nna tsa oketsega jalo, go ya ka go kgona ga batho. Selo se sa fetoga tlwaelo, mme morago sa fetoga mokgwa. Kgabagare ya nna konokono ya thulaganyo ka ga lenyalo"* (*op. cit.*). As people are prone to competition, the number of cows kept increasing (and changing to heifers). This practice turned into a cultural value. It became the quintessence of marriage. In some cultures, such as those of the Bangwaketsi and Barolong, a maximum cap on the number of *bogadi* cows and their cash equivalent has been placed. What is of interest here is that there is no specified minimum, save that the cows should be even in number.

It is possible for wedding rites to take place with *bogadi* deferred, until the male is ready to afford it. But before he does so, he may not receive *bogadi* for any of his daughters. In many cultures of Botswana, the uncle is supposed to contribute at least a beast towards his nephew's *bogadi*, being part of a reciprocal gifting between uncles and nephews. There are well-established protocols regarding how cattle are slaughtered and the distribution of meat in many cultures of Botswana. Refer to *https://d.lib.msu.edu/pula/320* on butchery styles and the processing of cattle carcasses in Botswana, as well as Chapter 3 on Bakgatla: "The distribution of parts of slaughtered ox was strictly done according to well established protocol involving different relatives along with the role they played in the whole marriage process…. *Thupa* was consumed by *banna-ba-lekgotla*, men who spent a lot of time at the *kgotla* attending to cases and generally assisting the *kgosi* in his duties".

Insistence on *bogadi* has not been without frustration to couples resulting in 'shacking up', or informal cohabitation. This has resulted in a number of interventions including the Re A Nyalana project, which is covered in the Bakgatla chapter. What is of interest is that a practice that started out as a voluntary offer of a milk-cow gradually evolved into a formalised key element, gravitas or *raison d'être* of marriage.

Another notable generalization is the expression '*bogwe ga bo bole*' (*bogadi* is never returned – even in the event of divorce, because the strength of marriage inheres in the ties between families in-law); Roberts *et al.*, however, give an account of the circumstances under which *bogadi* was returned among Balete: "*Bogadi* is only returnable on divorce where there are no children to the marriage, and

(a) the wife is divorced on account of her failure to consummate the marriage; or
(b) the husband divorces the wife on account of her misconduct or she insists upon divorcing the husband without reasonable cause."

It is evident that the marriage institution in Botswana has undergone changes in traditional practices including betrothal, ceremonies and formalities, levirate, sororate, and duplicate unions, the evolution of *bogadi*, matrimonial rights duties, settlement of matrimonial disputes, divorce, matrimonial dispute resolution, etc. as well as effects of death upon marriage. According to Roberts *et al*, "…levirate and sororate unions are practised among the Malete; they are both known as *seantlo. The Levirate* – Where a husband dies, his widow may enter a levirate union, provided that the widow's own family agree to this. It is for the senior relations of the deceased to suggest a levir, but the woman may refuse any candidate selected. The levir should preferably be one of the husband's younger brothers, but may be any relative-in-law except the father, elder brother or son of the deceased. Where the proposed levir is already married, negotiations must be conducted with his wife's family before he accepts this office. Children born of this union are regarded as those of the deceased… *The Sororate* – Where a wife dies, the husband may form a sororate union with a younger sister of the deceased provided the sister concerned agrees to this. Where such a union is entered into, any children born are regarded as those of the deceased wife. *Duplicate Marriage (go isa thari)* – Where a wife proves childless, she may take a close relation into her hose to bear children for her. Children born to this woman rank as the children of the wife concerned. Such an agreement has to be made with the husband's consent." In the case of informal unions, in the event of death, the surviving partner was entitled to part of the estate to the surviving party, at the discretion of the courts.

Such were the intricacies of *lenyalo* among Balete, and indeed many communities of Setswana descent, which are no longer common. Such practices are characterised by consultation and consent between families and partners; which, coupled with polygyny, and the practice of adoption of children (*go tsholelwa*) and surrogacy, ensured among others, that eligible women got married, and there were no orphans, or childless adults.

All of these practices have been buffeted by a variety of influences ranging from precolonial, colonial/Christian, migrant labour movements – especially of men going to work in South African mines and farms, modern Western influences blended into traditional practices – those of polygamy (polygyny), non-requirement of *bogadi*, mandatory expectation of such, different standards of *bogadi* and related matrimonial expectations, inheritance problems necessitating serious and concerted national attention.

Yet another change on the marriage radar screen discussed is the perceived increase in divorce cases, and the prevalence of single-headed households, usually with a female head. This may entail adoption of new corrective measures and/or restoration of old values such as *bogadi ga bo sekwe* (*bogadi* is not a matter for litigation, as it is not a charge or levy). Although there are different standards for *bogadi* from one jurisdiction to another, any offer less than the set standard is generally acceptable, provided it is even in number. According to Mogapi, "*Ka Setswana bogadi ga bo ke bo ganwa, go twe bo bonnye, le fa e bile bagwe ba tlhaeletse kgakala le palo e e neng e kopilwe. Go dumelwa gore go gana bogadi ke go tsenya ngwana wa mosetsana sefifi, ka jaana lenyalo ke lesego*" (*op. cit.*). In Setswana culture, lobola is never turned down for reasons of inadequacy. It is believed that to turn down casts bad luck on the marrying daughter, because marriage is a blessed gift.

Roberts *et al.* note that, traditionally among Balete, "…there is no fixed amount of *bogadi* presentable, but the number of beasts must not under normal circumstances be less than four. *Bogadi* must consist of an even number of beasts unless the woman for whom they are presented is already dead, in which case an uneven number is presented. The number of beasts to be presented is decided by the man's family alone, and is not subject to negotiation between the two families. The woman's father or guardian may, nevertheless, request presentation of *bogadi* without specifying the amount."

The practice regarding the number of beasts to be presented without negotiation between the two families has now changed, to a situation where the bride's family stipulates the number of beasts to be presented. This signals a pendulum swing in *lenyalo* power dynamics.

The authors further document the following grounds under which *bogadi* presented for a woman's marriage must be returned, among Balete:

(a) Where she wilfully refuses to consummate the marriage;
(b) Where she is divorced by the husband on account of her fault, or where she divorces the husband without cause, and no children have been born to the marriage.

These observations beg the question, as well as requiring unalloyed and unflinching reflection on, as to what dynamics may have relegated females to dominated/subservient roles; what engendered patriarchy? Did the southern African migrant labour phenomenon, and paid labour uptake by males catapult them into senior social positions of financial sources, thereby relegating women to pariah status subservient to the dictates of males – and through mutual silent collusion, give rise to males being providers, especially due to cash – giving rise to sugar daddies, and subsequently to sugar mummies with cash power? Did the adoption of *bogadi* practice unwittingly entrench the perceived dominant roles of males, giving rise to oft exorbitant monetary expectations on males, interwoven with gender-based violence? With the increased prevalence of single-mother families, why do we experience increasing incidents of gender-based violence and so-called passion killings? Is the boy-child the perpetrator, or the mother, the unwitting instigator, and thereby, equally culpable? Did the ruthless Christian suppression of traditional processes and practice ceremonies that initiated boys and girls into their family roles lead to problems associated with modern families; and has our school curriculum picked up the pieces? These, and many other questions form the focus of this chapter – to evoke and provoke a national reflection as well as introspection on the marriage institution, past, present and future.

Interrogation is needed for the purpose of achieving increased common understanding and greater harmony on matters relating to marriage across the various communities in the country. Accordingly the purpose of the final section of this chapter is structured so as summarise these in terms of observations, remedies and recommendations, but it is in no way intended to be exhaustive. The layout is deliberately intended to provoke further national discourse and narratives arising from the preceding chapters, and other related sources, which would hopefully lead to informed discussions, and reflection that may inform practice, processes, or even legislature on marital law. The major observations and remedies/recommendations are below.

## 1. Ethnic Group Variations

Intra-ethnic group variations abound on the practice of bogadi ranging from: its value perceptions; non-requirement versus pre-requisite, vis-a-vis *patlo;* practices of *bogadi* deferment; inconsistent cattle/cash equivalents, etc.; with all these leading to confusion and conflict in some cases.

### Proposed remedy/recommendation

Legislators to set a uniform standard for bogadi and associated giftings

Over time, there have been, on various public platforms, discussions on standardization of *bogadi* so as to achieve national harmonization and possible curbing of exploitation tendencies. In June 2012 the co-founder of Re A Nyalana, David Morwaagole, made a presentation to *dikgosi* at the Ntlo Ya Dikgosi (House of Traditional Leaders, or literally, House of Chiefs) on the rise in the cohabitation rate and the decline in the rate of marriage. The *dikgosi* agreed unanimously that *bogadi* be regulated and standardised given the very high figures demanded in payment of *bogadi*. Unfortunately there has not been up to now any recorded progress made by the House of Chiefs or any other institution towards bringing this to reality Hopefully some form of legislation would be instituted in order to curb runaway tendencies that are deleterious to the sanctity and stability of the family unit, including the widely acclaimed negative accounts of a nuclear family setting.

Other proposals that have been seen in the public media, with the intent of streamlining and creating greater harmonization across various communities include the below.

- Register *bogadi* with *dikgosi* for verification purposes;
- Make *bogadi* and giftings voluntary/optional; inexpensive gift items like skins of duiker among the G||ana should be deemed acceptable, not the exorbitant *bogadi* and expensive gifts, as well as ostentatious weddings which often cause financial constraint and conflicts between partners.
- Scrap *bogadi* completely, as Kgosi Moremi of Batawana did during his reign, and is a recent adoption/adaptation by others.

## 2. Extramarital Affairs

*Bonyatsi*, extramarital affairs, and infidelity are frequently cited as major sources of marriage breakups, often resulting in prevalence or preference of single parent motherhood:

### Proposed remedy/recommendation

Civil society should pursue strategies to address extramarital affairs. These strategies may possibly include the below.

- Strengthening of pre-marriage and marriage counselling.

- Reduction of social stigma against polygamy as this is a legal marriage arrangement that may hold the promise of avoidance of extramarital affairs.

## 3. Cohabitation

The prevalence of cohabitation, which has been widely reported in Ntlo Ya Dikgosi report and Re A Nyalana initiative, as well as concerns with this.

### Proposed remedy/recommendation

- Civil society and lawmakers to strengthen and enhance common-law rights.
- Lawmakers to study, strengthen and standardise inheritance law.
- Legal instruments to be strengthened so as to support the sanctity of the marriage institution.

## 4. Single Parenthood

Preponderance of single-parent households. As reported by Statistics Botswana: 83.8% of births in 2019 were to single mothers (2019 Vital Statistics Report). Botswana culture in general has a strong preference for children to be raised in a family setting bonded by marriage.

### Proposed remedy/recommendation

- Greater efforts be made by social actors to promote and preserve marriages.
- Efforts to be made by various social actors to reduce the stigma against polygamy (polygyny) and creation of an understanding of the concomitant obligations/responsibilities for those who may choose this type of marriage.

## 5. Passion Killings

Prevalence of passion killings was noted as another growing malady afflicting partnerships (Ntlo ya Dikgosi Report, p.106). Not dissimilar from this observation is the prevalence of gender-based violence, especially female misogyny.

### Proposed remedy/recommendation

Implement strategies for combating toxic masculinity, which is defined in Wikipedia as, "Cultural norms associated with men that are harmful to society and to men themselves". The concept of toxic masculinity is used in academic as well as media discussions of masculinity to refer to certain cultural norms that are associated with harm to society and to men themselves. Traditional stereotypes of men as socially dominant, along with related traits such as misogyny and homophobia, can be considered 'toxic' due in part to their promotion of violence, including sexual assault and domestic violence. The socialization of boys in patriarchal societies often normalises violence, such as in the saying 'boys will be boys' with regard to bullying and aggression.

## 6. Awareness of the Marital Act, its Implications and other Caveats

Many couples could be married out of community of property, albeit against their wishes, because some District Commissioners failed to submit their forms ... in terms of section 7, subsection 4, which mandates that Form A or Form B (in or out of community of property) should be registered by the District Commissioner within ninety days of marriage. Failing this submission, the married couple is assumed to be married out of community of property. Prior to the abolition of marital power, the estate of the couple was registered under the husband – as the head of the household. This practice disadvantaged women in the event of a divorce.

### Proposed remedy/recommendation

Couples should be educated and counselled to understand the implications of creditors, who often would not want a joint estate to be split.

Another caveat that couples ought to be counselled on is the assumption that females should mandatorily adopt the husband's surname, resulting in some adopting double-barreled surnames. The practice of change of surname is a hangover from our colonial past. In a number of southern African societies, the woman retains her name identity, including her totem and veneration poem.

Equally important is the need to harmonise the law in such a way that adjudication of cases of marital infidelity resolution should not be subject to interpretation by the presiding legal officers. There have been cases where financial remedy was granted to an aggrieved spouse, and where it was not granted.

## Epilogue

Compared to many countries, Botswana is in an enviable position not dissimilar to Finland, which has been referred to as a 'nanny state' not in a pejorative sense, but rather a complimentary one. Child-care by the state does kick in through relatively free pre-and postnatal access to public health facilities, but the Finns make an art of state child welfare through a range of metapelot custodial provisions such as, "Every family is entitled to generous parental benefits ... paid parental leave ... until the little one reaches the age of three ... a 'free maternity pack' which is a cardboard cot, full of essential ... baby paraphernalia ... clothes, toiletries, bedding, reusable nappies, toys and the all-important instruction manual of 'how to operate the baby'. Free health clinics look after the next generation's health and inject them with all the possible vaccinations". This 'state-nannyhood' treatment continues throughout schooling, adulthood, and life till retirement. It goes a long way to explain the world-class success story of the Finnish school system and adaptive technologically adept system that saw the dominance of Nokia, and automated public transportation networks.

In a similarly enviable position is the experience of many Batswana who progressed from grade one all the way to well-earned PhD studies through state support or some bilateral assistance arrangement. Support programmes such as the first graduate in the family are but some of the nascent and budding initiatives that can bring the family unit to the centre-stage of development. These modern educational achievements should be blended into dovetailed articulation with traditional education systems and rites of passage.

This book therefore concludes by invoking a national debate on a wide range of interventions aimed at preserving and ensuring viability, as well as stability, of the family unit, and inclusive of, but not limited to a national discourse towards standardising key elements and components of wide-ranging marriage processes and practices. This national discourse should at the very least include: *bogadi*, its evolution and latter-day development, and the way forward with it; the impact of adopted Western culture and religious practices, and their adverse impact on polygamy; a thorough examination of the efficacy of the law to enhance the viability of the family unit; recourse to the gender statistical imbalance; and the sources and causes of toxic masculinity and misogyny and how to remedy resultant passion killings, and other forms of gender-based violence.

## BIBLIOGRAPHY

Mogapi, K. 1994. *Ngwao ya Setswana* (4th edition). Mabopane, South Africa: I.Z. Sikwane Publishers.

Ngugi wa Thiong'o. 1981. *Decolonising the Mind.* Harare: Zimbabwe Publishing House.

Ngwako, Irene Sedibeng. 2019. *Nyalo Ya Setso Mo Botswana.* Gaborone: Printed by Impression House.

Ntlo Ya Dikgosi. 2008. *Report of the Joint Advisory Committee of Ntlo ya Dikgosi and Botswana Council of Churches on Social Values.*

Roberts, S., Campbell, A.C. & Walker, J.M. 1966. *The Malete Law of Family Relations, Land and Succession to Property.* Gaborone: The Government Printers.

Scott, Catriona Tulloch (ed.). 2018. *Xenophobe's Guide to the Finns.* Wiltshire: CPI Antony Rowe.

Willis, P. 2000. *Learning to Labour.* Burlington, Vermont, USA: Ashgate Publishing Company.

# Appendix

**MEMORANDUM OF AGREEMENT**

**ENTERED INTO AND BETWEEN**

**Alumni of the University of Botswana Development Trust (ALUBDEV)**
**(Hereinafter referred to as "First Party")**

AND

________________________________________

(Hereinafter referred to as "Second Party)

**FOR**

**DATA COLLECTION AND COMPILATION ON**
***'LENYALO'***
**MARRIAGE CULTURE AND PROCESSES IN BOTSWANA:**
**PAST AND PRESENT**

**PREAMBLE**

IT IS NOTED THAT

1. That the First Party originates, represented by the Project Manager, Dr. Joseph Tsonope, funds and project manages the research project known as Lenyalo Marriage Culture and Processes in Botswana: Past and Present.
2. That the first party has appointed Consultants from UB to lead and coordinate the conduct of the research.
3. That the Second Party, cognizant of Declaration of Interest and inputs, as well as feedback by the First Party on its project proposal, conduct the research and submit findings to the First Party in line with the agreed deliverables and timelines.

**NOW THEREFORE THE PARTIES AGREE AS FOLLOWS:**

**1. APPOINTMENT**

The first party hereby appoints the second party and the second party hereby accepts to provide the services set out below under SCOPE OF WORKS

## 2. DEFINITIONS

In this Agreement, the following words and expressions shall, except where otherwise stated or inconsistent with the context in which they appear, bear the following meanings and cognate expressions shall bear corresponding meanings:

**Agreement** means the present agreement and its appendices, annexes and schedules as well as all amendments thereto as agreed to between the parties from time-to-time;

**Appendix (ces)** means any document, approved by the First Party and the Second Party, which is, from time-to-time, incorporated in this Agreement in the form of appendices. These documents may be amended in writing, from time-to-time, by mutual agreement between the Parties;

**Client** means First Party as the executing authority;

**Contractor** means Second Party and includes its representatives, successors and permitted assigns;

**Contractor Price** means the total amount of money to be paid by the Client to the Contractor for the performance of the Services as provided for under this Agreement;

**Days** means Monday to Fridays inclusive in each week, except Saturday and Sunday or public holidays, uncles stated otherwise;

## 3. INTEPRETATION

3.1 The headings and numbers used in this Agreement and its Appendices are for convenience only and shall not be construes or interpreted as having a bearing on the contents, context or meaning of its provisions.

3.2 Terms other than those defined in this Agreement shall be given their plain English meaning.

3.3 Any reference to a statutory provision or statute (unless the context clearly indicates otherwise) shall be a reference to a stature of the Republic of Botswana, and shall include any subordinate legislation made from time-to-time under that provision or statutes and shall include that provision or statute as amended or re-enacted from time-to-time.

3.4 Expressions or words defined in this Agreement shall bear the same meanings when used in Appendices, annexes or schedules to this Agreement which do not themselves contain their own definitions.

3.5 Where any term is defined within the context of any particular clause in this Agreement, the term so defined, unless it is specifically in the clause in question that the term so defined has limited application to the relevant clause, shall bear the meaning ascribed to it for all purposes in terms of this Agreement, notwithstanding that the term has not been defined in the Definitions Clause.

4. **PURPOSE OF RESEARCH**

The overall objectives of the research are;

- To understand the meaning and significance of marriage (*lenyalo*) from the perspective of each ethnic group selected in Botswana;
- To identify and examine the various stages (or phases) and processes followed in the different traditional practices of selected cultural groups in Botswana;
- To examine the roles of various actors and those of the different symbols used in the marriage rites of selected cultural groups studied;
- To assess the level of change and its significance in the traditional marriage practices and customs of selected cultural groups in Botswana;
- To find out about the rights and privileges as well as benefits and challenges associated with different types of traditional marriage practices among the various cultural groups studied.

**5, SCOPE OF WORKS**

**General Terms of Reference**

- To assist the ALUBDEV Trust with data gathering on Lenyalo practices and processes in respect of the relevant ethnic group as appears in Appendix 1;
- To deliver the collected data to ALUBDEV for consolidation, harmonisation and write-up by UB researchers;
- To communicate with UB researchers on any requisite follow-ups and queries.

**Specific Terms of Reference**

(i) To identify the steps or stages of the ethnic group marriage process and roles of those who participate at every stage.

a) ***Courtship***
   - Process of informing parents or parents informing their son or daughter

b) ***Preliminary Visit*** (*Go Kokota/Go Itshupa*)
   - Who goes, when and why? Etc.
   - What are the changes? If any.

c) ***Bride Seeking*** (*Patlo*)
   - Who participates, where, when, how (process of bride seeking), when and what is the focus?
   - Are there any penalties? If yes, what kind and why?

- Expectations of the groom-to-be and his relatives/ bride-to-be and her family?
- What are the changes? If any.

d) ***Bride Wealth*** (*Bogadi*)

- Meaning and function of exchanges of material things/bogadi if any?
- What kind? When, who does what, who gets what and why? Etc
- What happens if both man and woman are from same culture?
- What are the changes, if any?
- Among the Bangwaketsi, although *bogadi* is set at eight head of cattle, technically speaking they are six; the seventh would be *kgomo ya motlhakanelwa* to be consumed at the wedding ceremony by both parties; the eighth would be offered to the grooms party to take with and do as a see fit with it upon return from the bride's place. Although there was a set standard number, any even number of cattle was accepted. *Bogadi bo ne bo sa sekwe.*
- How does your culture deal with *kgomo ya serufo, kgomo ya kota,* if at all?
- Is bogadi part of a broader range of gifting practices which could cover the purpose and realms *go ntsha ditlhogo* or *go šoma,* the uncle would *tlhapisa ditlhogo* and *letsema?*
- What are/were the expectations on the part of wedding ceremony attendees in terms gifts?
- Can you tell us about the evolving dress code of LENYALO, e.g. the German print and *paka*

e) ***Wedding Ceremony*** (*Kemo/Mokete wa Lenyalo*)

- When, what happens on the day of the ceremony, Who does what and why? (responsibilities)
- Significance of food at a wedding ceremony
- Meat portions of a ritual animal (e.g. for *kgomo ya metsi or for the mokwele sheep etc*)
- What is the cost of wedding ceremonies like today when compared to the past?
- What are the changes? If any.

f) ***Marriage Counselling*** *(Go Laya)*

- Groom and bride counselling
- When, where, who does what, and why? etc

g) ***Transfer of Bride to her in-Laws*** (*Go Isa Monyadi/monyadiwa?*)

- When, by whom? Etc
- What are the changes? If any.

***h) Bride taken back to her natal home***

- By whom, when, how and why? Etc.
- Is there any welcome ritual or ceremony on the day of her arrival?
- How is the bride expected to behave?
- What kind of reception does the bride receive on that day?
- When is the bride expected or permitted to visit her natal home to see her biological parents?
- What are the changes? If any.

(ii) To outline Marriage Rites and the Significance of Metaphorical Language and Symbolic Actions

- e,g, *sego sa metsi* (water gourd) instead of *ngwetsi (bride)*
- *meaning and significance of such metaphors and symbols*
- *go ja sehuba sa nku ya mokwele* (e,g Barolong) etc

(iii) To outline Rights, Privileges and Benefits Associated with Traditional Marriage Practices

- Those enjoyed by married men and women when compared to the unmarried ones.
- At ritualistic events (e,g, in marriages, funerals and kgotla meetings)

(iv) To outline Prevalent Problems and Challenges in Traditional Marriages Today

- What challenges do some married men and women face in the Ethnic Group's culture
- How are such challenges resolved traditionally?
- What are the causes of some of the challenges mentioned?

(v) To identify Factors of change and their Impact on Traditional Marriage Rites and Activities

- What changes have been observed in the Balete? marriage practices (compared to the past)?
- What could have influenced or brought about such changes?
- What do the people think should be done to ensure stability, tolerance and endurance in today's marriages?

## 6.DATA COLLECTION APPROACHES

- Personal Knowledge and Experience
- Desktop Research
- Interview key informants
- Conduct Focus Group discussions as necessary

## 7. DELIVERABLES

(i) Initial Report which shall be a summary outline covering the Specific Terms of Reference

(ii) Draft Final Report which shall be the proposed complete input submission to the first party

(iii) Final Report which shall be the final submission following incorporation of comments and amendments from the first party

**8. TIMELINES**

(i) Submission of Initial Report which shall be no later than the first day of the 3rd week after signing of contract

(ii) Submission of Draft Final Report shall be no later than the first day of 6th week after acceptance of the Initial Report

(iii) Submission of Draft Final Report shall be no later than the first day of 2nd week after acceptance of the Draft Final Report

**9. PAYMENT**

The contract sum is P15, 000.00 (fifteen thousand Pula).

**10. PAY SCHEDULE**

The pay schedule shall be as follows;
10% on signing of contract
30% acceptance of Initial Draft
40% on acceptance of Draft Final Inputs
20% on acceptance of Final Input

**11. COVERAGE OF COSTS**

As per UB rates and per deum

**Transport Outside Location of Residence**

The second party is to use public, own or arranged transport as agreed with the first party. The cost of transport as approved by the First Party shall be paid in advance as follows:

Return ticket for public transport on each trip;

Own or arranged transport as the UB rate per kilometre for tarred road, gravel and sandy road.

**Focus Group Token of Appreciation**

The Second Party shall be as pre-approved by the First Party be paid in advance or reimbursed the cost of planned tokens of appreciation to Focus Group participants.

**12. RELATIONSHIP BETWEEN THE PARTIES**

Nothing contained herein shall be construed as establishing or creating a relationship of master and servant, employer/employee, principal/agent, partnership or a joint-venture between the Parties. It is agreed that the position of the Contractor and anyone else performing the services on behalf of the Contractor under this Agreement is that of an independent contractor.

**13. COMMENCEMENT AND DURATION OF SERVICE**

This Agreement shall commence on the date of signature.

This Agreement shall remain in force for a period of sixty days, unless earlier terminated by agreement of both Parties, or by either Party in accordance with its terms.

**14. TERMINATION**

14.1 Unless extended in writing in accordance with its terms, or earlier terminated pursuant to its terms, this Agreement shall terminate automatically on the stipulated sixty days completion date.

14.2 The Client may terminate this Agreement at any time by giving the Contractor Fourteen days written notice. In the event of such termination, accrued and unpaid fees and expenses payable to the Contractor at the time of termination shall immediately become due and payable. The Client shall not be liable for any damages arising as a result of such termination.

14.3 The Contractor may terminate this Agreement at any time, if, after giving the Client fourteen days' written notice of a material breach of the Agreement, the Client does not rectify such material breach within ten days of receipt of the notice or such other period as may be agreed.

14.4 In the event the Agreement is terminated on account of the Client's default, accrued and unpaid fees and expenses payable and due to the Contractor for work done shall be paid to its own account.

14.5 The completion, expiration or termination of this Agreement shall not prejudice any rights of either Party, which had arisen on or before the date of completion, expiration or termination.

**15. COPYRIGHT**

15.1 The deliverable reports and other creative work of the Contractor called for by this Agreement, including all written, graphic, audio, visual and any other materials, contributions, applicable work product and production elements contained therein, whether on paper, disk tape, digital file and any other media (the *deliverable work)* is being specially commissioned as work made for hire in accordance with the copyright laws of the Republic of Botswana. The Client is the sole proprietor of the Deliverable Work from the time of its creation and owns all rights, title and interest therein throughout the work including, without limitation, the copyright and all related rights.

15.2 To the extent that it is determined that the Deliverable Work does not qualify as a work made for hire within the meaning of the copyright laws of the Republic of Botswana, then the Contractor hereby irrevocably transfers and assigns to the Client all of its rights, title and interest, thoughout the world in perpetuity, in and to the Deliverable Work, including without limitation all of its rights, title, and interest in copyright and related rights free of any claims by the Contractor or any other person or entity.

**THUS DONE AND EXECUTED IN GABORONE, BOTSWANA**

this…………………………day of ……………………………………………….2018

**FOR AND ON BEHALF OF THE FIRST PARTY**

……………………………………… ……………………………………………

**Name** **Signature**

(being duly authorised in this capacity as

…………………………………………………………………….)

Witnesses: 1……………………………… Name……………………………………

SIGNATURE

2……………………………… Name……………………………………

SIGNATURE

**THUS DONE AND EXECUTED IN ……………………………….., BOTSWANA**

this…………………………day of ……………………………………………….2018

**FOR AND ON BEHALF OF THE SECOND PARTY**

…………………………………… ……………………………………….

**Name** **Signature**

Witnesses: 1………………………….. Name……………………………….
SIGNATURE

2…………………………… Name………………………………
SIGNATURE

CPSIA information can be obtained
at www.ICGtesting.com
Printed in the USA
LVHW062051240922
729203LV00003B/9

9 789991 271637